SPORT PSYCHOLOGY FOR YOUNG ATHLETES

Understanding and applying psychology within youth sport settings is key to maximising young athletes' enjoyment, wellbeing, and sporting performance. Written by a team of leading international researcher-practitioners, this book is the first to offer an evidence-based introduction to the theory and practice of sport psychology for children and young athletes. It provides practical strategies and guidance for those working in or researching youth sport, demonstrating how to integrate sport psychology effectively in a variety of youth sport contexts.

With real-life case studies that demonstrate psychological theory put into practice, it discusses a wide spectrum of issues faced by young athletes and recommends the best approaches to addressing them. Key topics covered include:

- the cognitive, social, and physical development of young athletes
- optimising fun, motivation, and self-confidence
- enhancing young athletes' relationships with coaches, parents, and peers
- managing stress, injuries, and transitions
- effectively developing talent and long-term engagement in sport
- encouraging organisational culture change.

The most up-to-date and authoritative guide to sport psychology for young people, this is essential reading for anyone working in youth sport.

Camilla J. Knight is Associate Professor of Sport Science at Swansea University, UK.

Chris G. Harwood is Professor of Sport Psychology at Loughborough University, UK.

Daniel Gould is Director of the Institute for the Study of Youth Sports and Professor in the Department of Kinesiology at Michigan State University, USA.

SPORT PSYCHOLOGY FOR YOUNG ATHLETES

Edited by Camilla J. Knight, Chris G. Harwood, and Daniel Gould

Routledge
Taylor & Francis Group

LONDON AND NEW YORK

First published 2018
by Routledge
2 Park Square, Milton Park, Abingdon, Oxon OX14 4RN

and by Routledge
711 Third Avenue, New York, NY 10017

Routledge is an imprint of the Taylor & Francis Group, an informa business

British Library Cataloguing-in-Publication Data
A catalogue record for this book is available from the British Library

Library of Congress Cataloging-in-Publication Data
Names: Knight, Camilla J., editor. | Harwood, Chris G., editor. |
Gould, Daniel, editor.
Title: Sport Psychology for Young Athletes / Edited by Camilla J. Knight,
Chris G. Harwood and Daniel Gould.
Description: Abingdon, Oxon ; New York, NY : Routledge, 2018. |
Includes bibliographical references and index.
Identifiers: LCCN 2017020992 | ISBN 9781138682382 (hardback) |
ISBN 9781138682399 (pbk.) | ISBN 9781315545202 (ebook)
Subjects: LCSH: Sports for children–Psychological aspects. |
Child athletes–Training of. | Child athletes–Psychology.
Classification: LCC GV709.2 .S69 2018 | DDC 796.083–dc23
LC record available at https://lccn.loc.gov/2017020992

ISBN: 978-1-138-68238-2 (hbk)
ISBN: 978-1-138-68239-9 (pbk)
ISBN: 978-1-315-54520-2 (ebk)

Typeset in Bembo
by Out of House Publishing
Printed and bound by CPI Group (UK) Ltd, Croydon, CR0 4YY

To mum and dad for always supporting me;
To all the young athletes, parents, and coaches who have given me the
opportunity to support them.
CK

To mum and dad for being role model parents;
To Becs, James, and Millie for the opportunities to be a role model parent.
CH

To all the coaches that made my own youth sport experience a wonderful one;
To the young athletes, sport parents, and coaches who have helped develop my
understanding of how to make youth sport a highly productive and enjoyable
experience for all.
DG

CONTENTS

SECTION II
Key considerations during childhood 55

SECTION III
Key considerations during adolescence 139

SECTION IV
Working with young athletes 229

FIGURES

TABLES

BOXES

EDITORS

Daniel Gould is Director of the Institute for the Study of Youth Sports and Professor in the Department of Kinesiology at Michigan State University, USA. Dan's current research focuses on how coaches teach life skills to young athletes, the psychology of coaching, and developing youth leaders through the sport captaincy experience. Dan has over 200 scholarly publications and over 50 applied sport psychology research dissemination-service publications. Dan has co-authored two books, *Foundations of Sport and Exercise Psychology* (with Bob Weinberg) and *Understanding Psychological Preparation for Sport: Theory and Practice of Elite Performers* (with Lew Hardy and Graham Jones) and he served as one of the founding coeditors of *The Sport Psychologist*. Dan has been invited to speak on sport psychology topics in over 30 countries and has delivered over 200 regional, national, and international scholarly presentations. Dan has also dedicated much of his career to applied sport psychology efforts as a mental skills training consultant, coach educator, and author. Dan is a certified consultant and active fellow in the Association for Applied Sport Psychology (AASP). He was also honored to serve as President of AASP.

Chris G. Harwood is Professor of Sport Psychology at Loughborough University, UK. His research interests lie in the study of psychosocial factors pertaining to athlete development and performance. His work reflects a specific focus on the roles and responsibilities of coaches, parents, and the wider social environment with respect to the performance, health, and wellbeing of young people. He has served as Vice-President of the European Federation of Sport Psychology (FEPSAC), and as Associate Editor for the *Journal of Applied Sport Psychology* before returning to the editorial board. He currently acts as Section Editor in Sport Performance for the *International Journal of Sport & Exercise Psychology* and an editorial board member for *The Sport Psychologist, Psychology of Sport and Exercise, Qualitative Research* *in Sport, Exercise and Health*, and the *Journal of Sport Psychology in Action*. Chris is also an HCPC Registered Practitioner Psychologist and holds dual accreditations with the British Association of Sport and Exercise Sciences (BASES) and British Psychological Society (BPS). He is currently serving a second term as Chair of the Psychology Division for BASES. Chris has held the position of Lead Psychologist within both professional football and in British tennis for the Lawn Tennis Association, with strategic responsibilities for the youth psychological support programmes and development programmes of elite players. He continues to consult with coaches, athletes, and parents, as well as compete as a veteran tennis player for Leicestershire men's team.

Camilla J. Knight is Associate Professor of Sport Science at Swansea University, UK. Her research interests are concerned with understanding and enhancing the psychosocial experiences of children in sport, with a particular focus upon the influence of parents. Camilla is co-author of *Parenting in Youth Sport: From Research to Practice* (Routledge, 2014), as well as 10 book chapters on topics such as youth sport participation, sport psychology, parent–coach relations, and parenting. She has published over 25 articles on similar topics and her work has been presented at more than 60 national and international conferences. Camilla's work has been funded by various organisations including the International Olympic Association, the International Tennis Federation, the Lawn Tennis Association, Sport Wales, and the Erasmus+ programme of the European Union. She is the Youth Sport lead on the Welsh Institute of Performance Science and the lead of the Welsh Research and Evaluation Advisory Group of the NSPCC Child Protection in Sport Unit. Camilla is also a British Association of Sport and Exercise Sciences (BASES) accredited Sport and Exercise Scientist and has had the pleasure of working with numerous young athletes, parents, and coaches to help enhance their experiences and performance within youth sport.

CONTRIBUTORS

Paul R. Appleton is a research fellow in the School of Sport, Exercise, and Rehabilitation Sciences at the University of Birmingham, UK. Paul earned his PhD from the University of Bedfordshire and his research focuses on motivational processes in sport and physical education. In addition, his work concerns the further development and evaluation of the Empowering Coaching™ family of education programmes. His research has been funded by UEFA, the FA, the WRU, Sport Wales, Erasmus+, and the Aspire Academy. He has published 40 book chapters and journal articles, and is on the editorial board of six journals.

Susan H. Backhouse is Professor of Psychology and Behavioural Nutrition and Director of Research in the Institute for Sport, Physical Activity, and Leisure at Leeds Beckett University, UK. Susan and her research team at Leeds Beckett University have established a programme of research investigating doping from multiple stakeholder perspectives. In 2012, she was an invited member of the European Union Ad-hoc Expert Group on Doping in Recreational Sport, producing EU-wide prevention guidelines. Susan is a Chartered Sport and Exercise Psychologist with the British Psychological Society and a Registered Sport and Exercise Psychologist with the Health and Care Professions Council.

Isabel Balaguer is Professor of Social Psychology in the Faculty of Psychology at the University of Valencia, Spain, and Head of the Research Group of Sport Psychology (UIPD) at the same university. Her principal topics of research are optimal development of athletes, particularly from a motivation theory lens, with a focus on both personal and social dimensions of wellbeing. Having published more than 100 articles and book chapters, and authored and edited several books, her research has been presented in several countries around the world. She is associate editor and member of several editorial boards. Isabel has long-term experience working with athletes and coaches as a sport psychology consultant.

Jamie B. Barker is Associate Professor of Applied Sport and Performance Psychology with research interests in psychological resilience, leadership, and psychological techniques to maximise performance. As a consultant he has worked in business and professional sport, including Sony Europe, Sony Mobile, the FA, the England and Wales Cricket Board, Nottinghamshire County Cricket Club, and Great Britain Rowing. Jamie is lead psychologist for the England and Great Britain Cerebral Palsy Football team. Jamie has an international research reputation, with over 50 peer-reviewed research publications and four books. At present, Jamie is Chair for the British Psychological Society's (BPS) Division of Sport and Exercise Psychology.

Erica V. Bennett is a PhD candidate in the School of Kinesiology at the University of British Columbia, Vancouver, Canada. Her research interests are in the areas of aging, body image, self-compassion, and physical activity, with a particular focus on older physically active women's aging body perceptions and management strategies. She has also explored the influence of gendered cultural body norms on women's physical activity-related cognitions and behaviours during pregnancy, as well as on elite women basketball players' body perceptions and experiences in and outside of sport contexts.

Lindsey C. Blom is Associate Professor of Sport and Exercise Psychology and Graduate Program Coordinator at Ball State University, USA. Lindsey is interested in psychosocial aspects of youth sport from the athlete, coach, and parent perspective. For the past decade, she has investigated positive youth development through sport and using sport to promote peace at the individual, community, and international levels. Specifically, her research focuses on maximising the benefits of sport participation through a mastery and cooperative approach fostered by trained coaches and supportive parents, emphasising holistic, long-term athlete development.

Britton W. Brewer is Professor of Psychology at Springfield College in Springfield, Massachusetts, USA, where he teaches undergraduate and graduate psychology courses and conducts research on psychological aspects of sport injury and self-identity in sport. He is a Certified Consultant, Association for Applied Sport Psychology, and is a Fellow of both the American Psychological Association and the Association for Applied Sport Psychology.

Melissa A. Chase is Professor in Sport Leadership at Miami University, in Oxford, Ohio, USA. Her research focuses on understanding behaviour in sport within the conceptual framework of self-efficacy theory. Her work in the development of self-efficacy in children and coaching efficacy in coaches aims to improve sport experiences for athletes and coaches. Dr Chase recently co-authored the text-book *Best Practice for Youth Sport*. She is the founding editor for the *Journal of Sport Psychology in Action*, a Fellow and Certified Consultant of the Association of Applied Sport Psychology, and a research fellow of the Research Consortium.

Dave Collins holds a PhD from the University of Surrey and is Professor of Coaching and Performance at the University of Central Lancashire, UK, and director of Grey Matters Performance. He is also fellow of the British Association of Sport and Exercise Sciences, an associate fellow of the British Psychological Society, and an ex-Royal Marine. From an applied perspective, he has worked with over 60 world or Olympic medallists as well as professional sports teams, performers, and business executives. His research interests include performer and coach development, cognitive expertise, and the promotion of peak performance across different challenge environments.

Robin Cooley is a graduate student at Miami University in Ohio, USA, working towards a Masters degree in Sport Leadership and Management with a focus on sport psychology. She completed a Bachelors degree in Psychology from Skidmore College (NY). She is a current member of the Psi Chi and Phi Beta Kappa honor societies. Her research interests include gender in sport, social psychology of sport, and group cohesion in sport.

Sam J. Cooley is a research fellow in Sport and Exercise Psychology at the University of Birmingham, UK. His expertise lies within the fields of life skills, positive youth development and outdoor adventure education. As a researcher and practitioner, Sam adopts a pragmatic and strengths-based approach when facilitating and evaluating programmes aimed to develop social and emotional skills. He co-developed Mental Skills Training for Life (MST4Life™). MST4Life™ draws on approaches typically used in sport psychology and applies them to the challenges faced by homeless young people, to support them in their development of resilience, self-worth, and life satisfaction.

Peter R. E. Crocker is a professor in the School of Kinesiology at the University of British Columbia, Canada. He completed an undergraduate degree in Psychology and a Masters degree in Kinesiology at Simon Fraser University. His PhD at the University of Alberta focused on sport psychology and skill learning. His research focuses on stress and adaptation, with a particular interest in understanding sport, exercise, and health-related behaviour. Ongoing research includes investigating stress, emotion, and coping in athletes, self-compassion, body image, and coping with the aging body. He has published over 140 refereed research articles and book chapters.

Brendan Cropley is Professor in Sport Coaching at the University of South Wales. Brendan has been a BASES Accredited Sport and Exercise Scientist (Psychology) since 2007 and a Chartered Scientist since 2014. He has provided a range of consultancy services to athletes, coaches, and NGBs as well as having an emerging research profile that has helped to shape training and development programmes in the sport sciences and sport coaching. This contribution has been recognised by the British Association of Sport and Exercise Science (BASES), which awarded Brendan Fellowship status in 2014.

Jennifer Cumming is Senior Lecturer in Sport and Exercise Psychology at the University of Birmingham, UK, and is a Chartered Psychologist and Associate Fellow of the British Psychological Society. Her current research focuses on community-based approaches to developing practical and culturally tailored interventions for athletes and, more recently, individuals who are traditionally considered 'harder to reach'. She is interested in how individuals learn to effectively regulate their thoughts, feelings, and behaviours with mental skills training, and determine the impact of self-regulation (or dysregulation) on performance, health, and wellbeing.

Anthony G. Delli Paoli is a PhD candidate in the Department of Kinesiology at Michigan State University, USA. He is interested in social and cognitive dimensions of sport and exercise, specifically studying the links among higher-order cognitive processes, feeling states, peer social interactions, and physical activity. His current research examines how physical activity may benefit those who experience social challenges, such as being ignored, left out, or rejected. This work focuses on young adults, typically developing children and children with ADHD. His research appears in the *Journal of Sport & Exercise Psychology* and *Journal of Clinical Child and Adolescent Psychology*.

Travis E. Dorsch is Assistant Professor in the Department of Family, Consumer, and Human Development with an adjunct appointment in the Department of Kinesiology and Health Science at Utah State University, USA. He is also Founding Director of the Utah State University Families in Sport Lab. His research programme targets the role of children's sport participation – in youth through intercollegiate sport contexts – on family relationships and children's developmental outcomes. Dr Dorsch's evidence-based programming is used by sport leagues, administrators, and parents to construct more developmentally appropriate sport contexts and to evaluate the role of parent involvement in organised sport.

Joan L. Duda is a professor at the University of Birmingham, UK, and is internationally known for her expertise in motivational processes and determinants of adherence and optimal functioning within physical and performance-related activities such as sport, exercise, and dance. Developer of the *Empowering Coaching*™ family of training programmes, she also has an extensive applied and research background in the promotion of psychological skills in sport and other performance domains. One of the leaders of her profession, Joan is currently President-Elect of the European College of Sport Sciences, President of Division 12 of the International Association of Applied Psychology, and a Past President of the Association of Applied Sport Psychology.

Kelsey Erickson is a research fellow in the Institute for Sport, Physical Activity and Leisure (ISPAL) at Leeds Beckett University (UK). Her expertise is in the psychology of drugs in sport and she is particularly interested in developing an understanding of the psychosocial factors that influence performance-enhancing drug use. Given her cross-cultural background (former US and UK student-athlete), exploring potential cultural and contextual differences associated with doping behaviour is also a principal interest. Kelsey's research to date has been supported by the International Athletics Foundation, the International Olympic Committee, and the World Anti-Doping Agency.

Brandonn S. Harris is Program Director and Associate Professor of Sport and Exercise Psychology at Georgia Southern University, USA. He is a certified consultant with the Association for Applied Sport Psychology, and is listed on the USOC's Mental Training Registry. He completed his Bachelors degree in Exercise Science at Truman State University. His Masters degrees in Sport and Exercise Psychology and Community Counseling, as well as his PhD, were completed at West Virginia University. Dr Harris teaches undergraduate and graduate courses in sport and exercise psychology, and also conducts research in youth sport, ethical issues in sport psychology, and burnout.

Kristoffer Henriksen is Associate Professor at the Institute of Sport Science and Clinical Biomechanics at the University of Southern Denmark. His research in sport psychology takes a holistic approach and looks at social relations and their influence on athlete development and performance with an emphasis on successful talent development environments. His employment includes a specialised function as a sport psychology practitioner in Team Denmark. In this function he focuses on developing mentally strong athletes and coaches and high-performance cultures in national teams, and supporting athletes at World Championships and the Olympic Games.

Denise M. Hill is Senior Lecturer in Sport and Exercise Psychology at the University of Portsmouth, UK. While she has published widely on the subject of choking under pressure, she has a broad range of academic interests within performance psychology. As a BPS Chartered Psychologist and a BASES Accredited Sport and Exercise Scientist, Denise also offers mental skills training to numerous elite athletes across sports, particularly in golf, where she supports several professional golfers on the Ladies European Golf Tour.

Mark J. G. Holland is Senior Lecturer in Sport and Exercise Psychology at Newman University, Birmingham, UK. Mark's research interests span elite performance and youth development through sport – specifically, how applied mental skills training, or other support programmes, can be implemented to support the individual's motivation, wellbeing, and performance. While focused on youth populations, Mark's applied work has ranged from elite athletes to underserved groups, including young people who are homeless.

Andreas Ivarsson is Assistant Professor in Sport and Exercise Psychology at Halmstad University in Sweden. His research interests include psychological aspects related to sport injuries, statistical and methodological issues within psychological research, and mindfulness. Andreas is currently a board member of Hallands soccer district association. He is also currently working as a sport psychology consultant with athletes from different team sports.

Urban Johnson is Professor in Sport and Exercise Psychology at Halmstad University, Sweden. After gaining an elite trainer certificate, Dr Johnson worked for several years as a professional trainer in handball. His main research focus is on psychological aspects of sports injury, prevention, rehabilitation, and intervention. Dr Johnson has vast applied sport psychology experience, especially with team sport athletes. He has been a member of the Medical Committee of the Swedish Football Federation since 2001 and a member of the FEPSAC managing council between 2003 and 2011. Currently Dr Johnson is a member of the Swedish National Centre for Research in Sports scientific committee.

Ciera Jones is a multi-sport athlete, having played softball in college and field hockey abroad, and continues to play club field hockey as a graduate student at The George Washington University, USA. In addition to her studies and graduate assistant responsibilities teaching undergraduate exercise physiology and kinesiology labs, she also coaches several high-school team sports. Her research involves studying approaches to alleviate relative age effect in organised youth sport.

Richard J. Keegan is Assistant Professor in Sport and Exercise Psychology at the University of Canberra, Australia. He completed his MSc and PhD at Loughborough University, and before that, a degree in Psychology at the University of Bristol. His research focuses on four areas: motivational processes in sport and exercise; physical literacy; applied sport psychology practice; and psychological resilience. He is currently working on a project with the Australian Sports Commission to define and develop support products for physical literacy. Richard is a qualified sport and exercise psychologist, and his book *Being a Sport Psychologist* focuses on understanding the role of practising sport psychologists.

Gretchen Kerr is currently a professor in the Faculty of Kinesiology and Physical Education at the University of Toronto, Canada. Her research focuses broadly on athlete maltreatment, with a specific interest on emotional abuse within the coach–athlete relationship. Gretchen also conducts studies of coach education, with a focus on advancing developmentally appropriate methods of enhancing the psychosocial health of young people in sport.

Lindsay E. Kipp is an assistant professor at Texas State University in the Department of Health and Human Performance. Her research area is in positive youth development through sport and physical activity, specifically how coaches and peers can promote psychosocial and physical benefits for youth, such as positive self-perceptions, self-determined motivation, sportspersonship, and enjoyment. Her research studies have taken a developmental approach by examining change or stability of outcomes over time, comparing results across age groups, or controlling for developmental markers such as physical maturity.

Carsten H. Larsen is an assistant professor at the Institute of Sport Science and Clinical Biomechanics at the University of Southern Denmark and sport psychology practitioner at Team Denmark. His research in sport psychology looks at talent development environments, psychosocial skills, and applied sport psychology. His employment at Team Denmark includes support at European, World Championships, and the Olympic Games, with a focus on culture, peak performance, and developing resilient athletes and coaches.

E. Earlynn Lauer is a doctoral student and graduate teaching associate in the Sport Psychology/Motor Behaviour programme in the Department of Kinesiology, Recreation, and Sport Studies at The University of Tennessee, USA. Her research interests are in the area of applied youth sport psychology, and she focuses on working with youth sport psychology professionals and coaches to develop effective relationships with young athletes and integrate mental skills training in youth sports to promote optimal performance and personal development.

Larry Lauer is a USTA Player Development mental skills specialist, and leads mental training for American junior and professional tennis players and the national coaching staff. Larry has a PhD in Exercise and Sport Science, specialising in Sport Psychology from the University of North Carolina Greensboro. Formerly, as Director of Coaching Education and Development in the Institute for the Study of Youth Sports (ISYS) at Michigan State University, Larry researched tennis parents, coaching, coach education, hockey aggression, and youth life skills development. In Detroit, Larry led training for Detroit police officers and coaches to mentor youth athletes for the Detroit PAL.

Áine MacNamara obtained her PhD from the University of Central Lancashire, where she is currently Reader in Elite Performance. Her research, framed by a 'pracademic' perspective, is focused on talent development with a particular interest in the role of psychological characteristics as facilitative of development and the design of talent development systems. Her work involves collaborations with national governing bodies of sport in the UK and Ireland as well as research collaborations across a number of institutions. Her work has been published in peer-reviewed journals in sport, music, and education as well as in over ten book chapters.

Ellen MacPherson is a PhD candidate in Sport Psychology in the Faculty of Kinesiology and Physical Education at the University of Toronto, Canada. Ellen's research interests centre on relationships in the sport context, including the influence of peers on psychosocial development, athletes' experiences of peer-to-peer bullying, and fan–athlete relationships on social media. Ellen has shared her research at several conferences within Canada and abroad and currently holds a Social Sciences and Humanities Research Council of Canada Doctoral Scholarship.

Devon Mann is studying Cognitive Science with minors in both Linguistics and Spanish at Occidental College, USA. He has been a sports enthusiast for as long as he can remember, with a particular love for soccer, having played, coached, and officiated the sport for many years. A Washington, DC native, Devon had the pleasure of working as a summer intern with Dr Amanda J. Visek and her research team at The George Washington University, gaining valuable research and writing experience combining his love of cognition and psychology with sport science.

Heather Mannix earned her masters degree in Exercise Science from The George Washington University, where she was the recipient of the Excellence in Research Award for her thesis work using self-determination theory as a framework for understanding causality orientations with respect to individuals' exercise modality preferences. As a research associate, she co-authored the conceptualisation paper of the fun integration theory with Dr Amanda J. Visek, whom she continues to work closely with, writing papers and presenting applied workshops domestically and internationally.

Paul J. McCarthy is Director of the Practitioner Doctorate in Sport and Exercise Psychology at Glasgow Caledonian University. His research explores two main themes: applied sport psychology and positive psychological interventions in sport and exercise settings, especially attention and emotion in sport performers. He has written and co-authored several books in sport and exercise psychology. He was appointed the first ever sport psychologist at the Old Course in St Andrews, supporting coaches and golfers on the European Tour and Ladies European Tour. He also supports athletes and teams from his private practice clinic in Glasgow.

Rich Neil is Reader in Sport and Exercise Psychology at the Cardiff Metropolitan University, UK, and the University's Portfolio Manager for Professional Doctorates. Rich's research interests include resiliency, stress, wellbeing, and performance (e.g. projects with the DVLA and FAW), life skill development (e.g. projects with Carmarthen Golf Club and the Golf Union of Wales), and leadership (e.g. projects with the DVLA). Rich is currently the Lead Sport Psychologist for the Golf Union of Wales and the Welsh Rugby Union U20s.

Rachael A. Newport is a PhD researcher in Sport Psychology at Swansea University, UK. In addition, Rachael is a trainee Sport and Exercise psychologist, currently completing her British Psychological Society Qualification in Sport and Exercise Psychology. Rachael has spent eight years studying sport psychology, achieving a Bachelors degree with Honours from the University of Central Lancashire and a Masters degree with Merit from Brunel University. Over the last three years, Rachael has provided sport psychology and performance lifestyle support to elite athletes supported by Sport Wales. Rachael has consulted within athletics, swimming, equestrian, badminton, bobsleigh, and football.

Albert J. Petitpas is a fellow and certified consultant of the Association of Applied Sport Psychology and a fellow of the American Psychological Association's Division 47. He has served on the planning and programme development teams for several youth-oriented initiatives, including the NCAA Youth Education through Sports (YES) Program, The First Tee, Pop Warner Football Coach Education Seminars, the NFL/NFF Coaching Academy, Play It Smart, Academics in Motion, and CNN Adopt-an-Alouette. His research interests include the counsellor/client relationship, identifying transferable skills, and youth development through sport. He currently directs the Springfield College Center for Youth Development and Research.

Scott Pierce is an assistant professor in the School of Kinesiology and Recreation at Illinois State University, USA. He is from New Zealand and he completed his PhD at Michigan State University in Sport Psychology. His research interests focus on the development of psychological skills for sport performance and the development and transfer of life skills from sport. Scott has experience as a sport psychology consultant at the youth and collegiate level and is involved in the development and implementation of education programmes in youth sport that aim to communicate scientific knowledge in a practical way to coaches and athletes.

Alan L. Smith is Professor and Chairperson in the Department of Kinesiology at Michigan State University, USA. He studies physical activity and psychosocial functioning in young people, with emphasis on peer relationships, motivation, and behavioural disorders such as ADHD. Smith has served on the editorial boards of *Child Development*, *International Journal of Sport Psychology*, *Journal of Applied Sport Psychology*, *Journal of Sport & Exercise Psychology*, *Kinesiology Review*, and *Sport, Exercise, and Performance Psychology*. He is a former president of the North American Society for the Psychology of Sport and Physical Activity and a fellow of the (US) National Academy of Kinesiology.

Juliette Stebbings is a researcher in the School of Sport, Exercise, and Rehabilitation Sciences at the University of Birmingham, UK, and has expertise in the areas of coach behaviour, coach and athlete motivation and psychological health, coaching practices, and coach education. Juliette's most recent role involved managing a collaborative research project between the University of

Birmingham and the UK StreetGames charity. The focus of this project was to customise and evaluate the *Empowering Coaching*™ education programme within StreetGames Doorstep Sport settings, to ascertain the effects on the motivation, psychological health, and life skills of young people growing up in disadvantaged communities.

Karl Steptoe is an HCPC registered, BPS chartered Sport and Exercise Psychologist and Senior Lecturer in Psychology at the University of Greenwich. He is the lead Sport and Exercise Psychologist at Leicester City Football Academy, works with players on both the men's and ladies' European Golf Tour, and provides consultancy services to wheelchair athletes on Paralympic performance programmes. As an applied practitioner, Karl provides sport and exercise psychology services in line with the core cognitive, cognitive-behavioural, and humanistic principles that guide his consultancy. Karl's research focuses on human cognition, attention processes, accelerated expertise, and skill breakdown under stress.

Ashley Stirling is currently Assistant Professor, Teaching Stream in the Faculty of Kinesiology and Physical Education at the University of Toronto, Canada. She has conducted several research projects on athletes' experiences of maltreatment in sport and strategies for athlete protection. In 2012, Ashley co-wrote a coach education module for the Coaching Association of Canada on creating positive and healthy sport experiences. She has presented at numerous international conferences and has several publications in the areas of athlete welfare, athlete emotional abuse, and positive and developmentally appropriate athlete development.

Louise K. Storm is an assistant professor at the Department of Sport Science and Clinical Biomechanics at the University of Southern Denmark. Her research looks at how culture influences talent development, particularly the athletes' social learning, relationships, developmental pathways, and their developmental environments. Her research has a strong applied focus. In the context of Danish elite sport, national elite sport institutions and sport federations have used her research as a foundation for designing guidelines and developing programmes on important fields such as coach education.

Lauren Szczygiel is a doctoral student specialising in the psychosocial aspects of sport in the Department of Kinesiology at Michigan State University, USA. Her research interests include under-represented minorities and at-risk populations' experiences in sport and exercise. Lauren has also worked as a youth sport psychology consultant for both individual and team sports. She proudly represented her native country, The Bahamas, as a personal coach and mental skills trainer at the 2015 Track and Field World Championships in Beijing, China.

Katherine A. Tamminen is an assistant professor in the Faculty of Kinesiology and Physical Education at the University of Toronto, Canada. Her research and teaching in sport psychology focus on two main areas: stress, coping, and emotion in sport; and young athletes' experiences in sport. She has been awarded funding for her research through multiple grants from the Social Sciences and Humanities Research Council of Canada (SSHRC), the Canadian Foundation for Innovation (John R. Evans Leaders Fund), the Province of Ontario Ministry of Research and Innovation (Early Researcher Award), and the University of Toronto (Connaught New Researcher Award).

Richard C. Thelwell is Head of the Department of Sport and Exercise Science at the University of Portsmouth, UK. Richard's research interests are within the area of coach psychology, psychological skills and behaviour change, and practitioner development. He serves as Associate Editor for *Case Studies in Sport and Exercise Psychology*, and on the editorial board for *International Review of Sport and Exercise Psychology* and *International Journal of Sport Psychology*. Richard has extensive applied-practitioner experience and is a Registered Practitioner Psychologist with the HCPC, a Chartered Psychologist of the BPS, and an Accredited Sport and Exercise Scientist with BASES.

Martin J. Turner is a senior lecturer, researcher, published author, and consultant psychologist based at Staffordshire University, UK. Martin specialises in human performance under pressure and adversity. He is the lead author of *Tipping the Balance: The Mental Skills Handbook for Athletes*. He is known mostly for his work examining the use of Rational Emotive Behaviour Therapy (REBT) within performance settings. Martin works with elite sporting and blue-chip business organisations, helping people to 'think smarter', become more resilient to adversity, and take control of their reactions to pressure. Martin is currently Lead Psychologist with FA England Futsal.

Judy L. Van Raalte is Professor of Psychology at Springfield College, USA, Certified Consultant, Association for Applied Sport Psychology, and listed in the United States Olympic Committee Sport Psychology Registry. Dr Van Raalte has presented at conferences in 18 countries, published over 100 articles in peer-reviewed journals, and produced more than 20 sport psychology videos. She served as President of the APA Division of Exercise and Sport Psychology and as the Vice President of the International Society of Sport Psychology. She is a fellow of the American Psychological Association and the Association for Applied Sport Psychology.

Robin S. Vealey is Professor in the Department of Kinesiology and Health at Miami University in Ohio, USA. She teaches courses in sport psychology, coaching effectiveness, and youth sport. Dr Vealey's research has focused on self-confidence, burnout, mental skills training, and coaching effectiveness. She has authored three books, *Best Practice for Youth Sport*, *Coaching for the Inner Edge*, and *Competitive Anxiety in Sport*. Dr Vealey is a Fellow, Certified Consultant, and Past President of the Association of Applied Sport Psychology and former Editor of *The Sport Psychologist*. She is also a Fellow of the National Academy of Kinesiology.

Amanda J. Visek is an associate professor and scientist-practitioner at The George Washington University, Milken Institute School of Public Health, in the Department of Exercise and Nutrition Sciences, in Washington, DC, USA. She has authored over 25 peer-reviewed papers, 7 book chapters, and given more than 122 refereed and invited talks. Her applied youth sport research has garnered global attention from grassroots to national sport organisations. Committed to leveraging fun in children's early, positive sport experiences, she is the recipient of early career achievement awards from the Association for Applied Sport Psychology and the American Psychological Association's Division 47.

Lisa Whitaker is a researcher working as part of the Centre for Sports Performance in the Institute for Sport, Physical Activity, and Leisure (ISPAL) at Leeds Beckett University (UK). Her main research interest lies within the anti-doping domain. Specifically, she is interested in developing an understanding of the psychosocial factors influencing doping and nutritional supplement use in sport. Lisa is a member of the British Association of Sport and Exercise Sciences (BASES) Clean Sport Interest group and the International Network of Doping Research (INDR).

Andrew G. Wood is a lecturer in Sport and Exercise Psychology and is completing a PhD investigating the effects of Rational Emotive Behaviour Therapy as an intervention to enhance performance within the context of elite sport. As a consultant Andrew has worked with a wide variety of athletes, teams, and coaches, providing psychological support to develop sporting excellence and personal well-being. Andrew is coming towards the end of his training as a Sport and Exercise Psychologist with the British Psychological Society and is currently the Lead Psychologist for the England Blind Football Team.

Paul Wylleman is full-Professor at the Vrije Universiteit Brussel. His research and publications focus on athletic transitions, (dual) career management, and sport psychology support services. He coordinated the European Erasmus Sport projects 'Gold in Education and Elite Sport (GEES)' and 'Be a Winner in Elite Sport and Employment before and after athletic Retirement (B-Wiser)'. Paul is head of the university department Topsport and Study, and the research group Sport Psychology and Mental Support. Finally, Paul is the High Performance Manager of Performance Behaviour with the Netherlands Olympic Committee NOC★NSF and was the team psychologist to the Dutch Olympic team TeamNL at the 2016 Rio Olympic Games.

Rebecca A. Zakrajsek serves as Assistant Professor of Sport Psychology in the Department of Kinesiology, Recreation, and Sport Studies at The University of Tennessee, USA. She is a certified consultant through the Association for Applied

Sport Psychology. Dr Zakrajsek's research focus is on sport psychology service provision and coach education. More specifically, she is interested in ways sport psychology consultants can build relationships and work effectively *with* and *through* coaches and athletic department support staff (athletic trainers, strength and conditioning coaches, etc.) to contribute to optimal performance and development.

1

AN INTRODUCTION TO SPORT PSYCHOLOGY FOR YOUNG ATHLETES

Camilla J. Knight, Chris G. Harwood, and Daniel Gould

Throughout our careers, we have all had the pleasure of working with and learning from numerous children, athletes, parents, coaches, and practitioners. Through such work we have developed a passion for gaining a greater understanding of youth sport. Particularly, we have devoted our energies to identifying and developing strategies to enhance the experiences of all individuals involved. We have committed to learning about psychological characteristics and skills used by young performers at all levels, explored the psychosocial experiences of young athletes, sought insights into the experiences and involvement of parents in sport, and examined the engagement and knowledge of youth sport coaches. From such research and work, we have come to the belief that the highest quality youth sport environments are ones that facilitate intentional psychosocial growth, and take this mandate very seriously as a means not only to healthier, happier athletes but also to better performing athletes in the long-term.

Such a focus is, at least in our opinion, particularly important given the cultural changes that have occurred in youth sport over the last decade or so, particularly in relation to 'talented' or 'elite' young athletes. Isolated 'young phenom' success stories have been mirrored by the spectrum of negative chapters that emerge in the annals of youth sport – from deselection, dejection, and dropout to cases of athlete abuse and maltreatment, identity foreclosure, depression, and life skill deficits. The ongoing trend of well-publicised mental health challenges disclosed by elite adult athletes and the ever-snowballing 'cheating narrative' that is beleaguering several medal-fixated sport governing bodies have created a societal sense that something wrong is going on; our moral compass is off, relevant education and support is missing, and this is not good for the next generation. Indeed, in light of the concerns highlighted above, the most recent Sport Duty of Care Review launched by the Department for Culture, Media and Sport in the United Kingdom aims to develop a comprehensive plan for how government and the whole sporting system can more effectively look after people who take part in grassroots sport and people who perform at the elite level, including those on a talent pathway (DCMS, 2016).

Fortunately, sport psychology researchers and practitioners are well placed to draw upon a breadth of scientific and applied knowledge from outstanding scholars and practitioners from around the world to support the psychological health and wellbeing of young athletes. However, despite access to such excellent work, as practitioners we have each encountered times when we struggled to understand how best to apply such knowledge in practice or appreciate what it is really like to work in different youth sport contexts and with different audiences. In the highly emotional, complicated, and dynamic world of youth sport, we have realised that more often than not we are 'learning on the job'; working out how to adapt to different situations, expectations, and needs, while spontaneously developing 'creative' ways in which to engage young athletes and communicate complex ideas. Despite such challenges, we believe that working in youth sport and having the opportunity to positively impact upon the lives of young athletes, as well as their parents and coaches, is incredibly rewarding and one that we would recommend to all researchers and practitioners.

Given such a belief, as well as an awareness of the issues we have encountered when working in youth sport, we felt that a book examining both sportpsychology research and practice related to young athletes was important and necessary. Specifically, we wanted to bring together some of the world's best research practitioners to share their scientific understanding of different psychological constructs and considerations as they apply to children and adolescents. Further, we sought to draw on these individuals' extensive applied experiences to help shed light on how exactly practitioners could or should go about working on these topics with young athletes, parents, and coaches. By producing this book, which combines literature overviews with case studies, scenarios, practical suggestions, and lessons learnt, we hope that we have produced a valuable resource for future and current practitioners, as well as coaches and sports organisations, with an interest in the psychosocial elements of youth sport.

To address our initial aims for this book, we have brought together 60 researchers and practitioners who have shared insights regarding sport psychology for young athletes across 26 chapters. These chapters are split into four sections: Section I – Setting the scene; Section II – Key considerations during childhood; Section III – Key considerations during adolescence; and Section IV – Working with young athletes. Within each section we have sought to provide examples of pertinent and timely topics that we have found to be critical in our own work with young athletes at different ages.

Section I comprises four chapters designed to provide a broad overview of key ideas that should be considered throughout all subsequent chapters. Larry Lauer, Rebecca Zakrajsek, and Earlynn Layer start by illustrating the importance of sport psychology in youth sport, particularly highlighting the valuable role of psychological skills training with young athletes. Next, Rich Neil and Brendan Cropley provide personal insights into the challenges that can be encountered when working within a variety of youth sport contexts. Strategies to overcome these challenges based on Rich and Brendan's extensive applied experiences are also provided. The final two chapters in this section, by Lindsay Kipp and Mark Holland, Sam Cooley, and Jen Cumming respectively, highlight important developmental considerations that must be accounted for when working with children and adolescents. First, Lindsay examines the cognitive, social, physical, and environmental changes that occur throughout childhood and adolescence, and provides examples of how to account for such changes when working with young athletes. Next, Mark and colleagues examine neurological changes that occur during adolescence and present a range of strategies for identifying the psychological needs of young athletes.

Having set the scene and introduced important developmental considerations, Section II focuses on a small selection of key considerations during childhood. Broadly considered as the first decade of life (Slater, Hocking, & Loose, 2003), childhood is an important time in which to introduce children to sports and facilitate the development of a range of physical skills in a fun and enjoyable environment (Côté & Hay, 2002). Parents are the main source of influence during this time (Holt & Knight, 2014), and children are starting to establish their perceptions of physical competence and self-confidence that can influence both their long-term positive development through sport and their chances of fulfilling their potential (see Holt 2016 and Baker, Cobley, Schorer, & Wattie, 2017 for extensive discussions).

Drawing on the aforementioned ideas, the first chapter in this section, by Richard Keegan and Camilla Knight, seeks to illustrate the importance of developing physical literacy and intrinsic motivation to encourage lifelong participation in sport and physical activity for all children. Next, Amanda Visek and colleagues explore the vital role of fun in youth sport while providing extensive, evidence-based strategies for enhancing children's fun in sport. Joan Duda, Juliette Stebbings, Paul Appleton, and Isabel Balaguer then extend many ideas presented in the preceeding two chapters by examining strategies to optimise children's motivation in sport. Drawing on a number of large-scale interventions, this chapter provides practitioners with clear, practical strategies for working on motivation in youth sport. In the next chapter, Robin Vealey, Melissa Chase, and Robin Cooley illuminate the complexity of children's self-confidence in youth sport. Underpinned by self-efficacy and self-confidence theories, this chapter guides practitioners through seven scenarios commonly encountered when working with young athletes.

Recognising the vital role of parents during childhood, the next chapter by Travis Dorsch critically evaluates approaches to optimising family involvement in youth sport, with a particular emphasis on two parent education programmes from the UK and the USA. Section II then concludes with two chapters by Áine MacNamara and Dave Collins, and Scott Pierce, respectively, which explore specific approaches to developing young athletes. Áine and Dave present an approach to talent development underpinned by the systematic development of Psychological Characteristics of Developing Excellence, while Scott reviews and evaluates knowledge of strategies to promote positive youth development in and through sport.

Proceeding from Section II, we move into Section III, which comprises eight chapters focused upon some of the key considerations for adolescent athletes. Adolescence is a period of substantial change (Arnett, 1999); young athletes experience an increase in training and competition demands, work within larger and more complex support networks, and must negotiate numerous physical and psychological changes (Côté & Hay, 2002; Wylleman & Lavallee, 2004). As such, aligned with the movement from childhood to adolescence, we start Section III with a chapter from Paul Wylleman examining the transitions young athletes can encounter throughout their lifetime. Based on a holistic approach to understanding transitions, Paul explores the intricate and important role sport psychologists can play in supporting athletes during both normative and non-normative transitions.

The next four chapters then focus upon individual topics that, in our experience, are increasingly pertinent in the current youth sport climate. First, Britton Brewer, Albert Petitpas, and Judy Van Raalte discuss the critical issues of self-identity, paying particular attention to the challenges associated with identity foreclosure and athletic identity. Second, Peter Crocker, Katherine Tamminen, and Erica Bennett draw on theory and research examining adolescent athletes' experiences of stress, emotion, and coping in sport. Particularly, through the use of detailed, practical examples, the authors highlight numerous strategies practitioners can employ to help athletes manage the often challenging world of youth sport. Third, Urban Johnson and Andreas Ivarsson explore strategies to facilitate the prevention of injuries among adolescent athletes, as well as rehabilitation and re-introduction to sport. Fourth, Susan Backhouse, Kelsey Erickson, and Lisa Whitaker discuss the extremely complicated topic of doping in sport. Drawing on the latest research in this area, as well as extensive applied experiences, this chapter examines the role of sport psychology practitioners in educating and supporting parents, coaches, and athletes to prevent doping in sport.

Next, in the second part of this section, three chapters examine social and environmental factors influencing adolescents' experiences. Alan Smith and Anthony Delli Paoli first provide a comprehensive review of peers and friendship in sport. Based on decades of research, Alan and Anthony detail a range of strategies to enhance friendships and peer relationships and manage conflict within teams. Denise Hill and Richard Thelwell then examine the key components of successful athlete–coach relationships and the influence of coaches in the lives of adolescent athletes. Drawing on a case study of a cricket coach, Denise and Richard describe how practitioners can work with coaches to improve their communication and engagement with adolescent athletes. Finally, Kristoffer Henriksen, Louise Storm, and Carsten Larsen discuss the impact of organisational culture on coach behaviours and athlete outcomes. Based on an ecological approach to talent development, this chapter encourages practitioners to utilise strategies aimed at facilitating a supportive organisational culture to enhance athlete development.

In concluding this text, Section IV draws together many of the preceding ideas and focuses specifically upon working with young athletes. Recognising the various approaches to working with athletes, as well as accounting for the important developmental considerations associated with young athletes, this section includes insights across seven areas. Brandonn Harris, Lindsay Blom, and Amanda Visek start by reviewing considerations practitioners need to be aware of when working with young athletes. For instance, this chapter examines ethical considerations, the role of technologies in consulting, as well as specific strategies for engaging and maintaining young people's involvement. Gretchen Kerr, Ashley Stirling, and Ellen MacPherson then examine the important role of practitioners in protecting the physical, emotional, and psychological health of young athletes. Particularly, in this chapter Gretchen and colleagues propose the value of consultants adopting an ethic of care approach when working with young athletes.

Next, Paul McCarthy and Andrew Wood and colleagues present two differing approaches to working with young athletes: Paul reflects upon his work with young athletes using a cognitive behavioural approach, while Andrew Wood, Jamie Barker, and Martin Turner examine the utility of adopting rational emotive behaviour therapy to enhance young athletes' resilience. This section then concludes with three chapters examining specific examples of sport psychology delivery. Dan Gould and Lauren Szczygiel first consider the effective delivery of group presentations, highlighting key factors to consider, ranging from purpose and content to strategies to maintain athletes' interest. Chris Harwood and Karl Steptoe then describe and illustrate the principles of integrated service provision in sport psychology, and focus on four examples of work with athletes and coaches that showcase the delivery of prominent psychosocial themes in youth sport. Finally, Camilla Knight and Rachael Newport examine the importance of understanding and working with parents, and share lessons they have learnt through their experiences of working with individual parents as well as delivering group workshops and programmes.

Through the research, theory, and real-life experiences presented in this book, we think we have covered many of the important sport psychology topics and considerations as they relate to young athletes. However, decisions regarding the topics to include and how best to focus ideas across different sections were incredibly difficult. As is abundantly clear throughout this text, youth sport is a nuanced, sometimes challenging, but always exciting environment in which to work. Further, the psychological considerations pertaining to young athletes are extensive. As such, we could have included three to four times as many topics as we have and considered them across more specific age ranges, cultures, and settings. Further, we could have easily doubled the number of case studies, examples, and practitioner suggestions. Unfortunately, however, we had to limit what was included, but we hope we have provided a range of interesting insights and experiences that will stimulate discussion and reflection about sport psychology for young athletes. Most importantly, we hope that the information shared throughout this book will enable all of us to work more efficiently and effectively with young athletes and help us to support young people to enjoy their sporting experiences and reach their individual potential.

References

Arnett, J. J. (1999). Adolescent storm and stress, reconsidered. *American Psychologist, 54,* 317–326.

Baker, J., Cobley, S. Schorer, J. & Wattie, N. (Eds.). (2017). *Routledge Handbook of Talent Identification and Development in Sport.* Abingdon, UK: Routledge.

Côté, J. & Hay, J. (2002). Children's involvement in sport: A developmental perspective. In J. M. Silva & D. E. Stevens (Eds.), *Psychological Foundations of Sport* (pp. 484–502). Boston, MA: Allyn & Bacon.

DCMS (2016). *Sport Duty of Care Review: Call for evidence.* Retrieved from www.gov.uk/government/consultations/sport-duty-of-care-review-call-for-evidence.

Holt, N. L. (Ed.). (2016). *Positive Youth Development through Sport.* Abingdon, UK: Routledge.

Holt, N. L. & Knight, C. J. (2014). *Parenting in Youth Sport: From Research to Practice.* Abingdon, UK: Routledge.

Slater, A., Hocking, I. & Loose, J. J. (2003). Theories and issues in child development. In A. Slater & G. Bremner (Eds.), *An Introduction to Developmental Psychology* (pp. 34–63). Oxford, UK: Blackwell.

Wylleman, P. & Lavallee, P. (2004). A developmental perspective on transitions faced by athletes. In M. Weiss (Ed.), *Developmental Sport and Exercise Psychology: A Lifespan Perspective* (pp. 503–524). Morgantown, WV: FIT.

SECTION I
Setting the scene

2

THE ROLE OF SPORT PSYCHOLOGY FOR YOUNG ATHLETES

Larry Lauer, Rebecca A. Zakrajsek, and E. Earlynn Lauer

A male 18-year-old tennis player is about to start competing in the qualification draw of a large professional tournament for the first time. In the preceding week he has been struggling with his strings and racquets, missing shots he does not normally miss in the dry desert air. He is frustrated as he approaches one of the biggest tournaments and opportunities of his tennis life. His coach is pushing him hard to find accuracy in his groundstrokes because the coach sees the opportunity to qualify for the main draw. The player's confidence is waning. His talk during practice is becoming more negative, and his body language is suffering; definitely not the preparation the player and coach were looking for prior to the tournament.

Rewind to when this player is 15 years of age and one of the best junior tennis players in the country. Winning is an expectation; in over 90 per cent of the matches he plays he is the favourite. Even on his bad days he can win easily against the majority of his competitors. In these circumstances it is hard not to have a fixed mindset; he is better than others without fully preparing for the match and does not need to look for new ways to push himself physically, mentally, or emotionally in practice. Playing in professional events in two years with the likes of Djokovic, Federer, or Nadal is not unrealistic; juniors play on the same courts as these players and sometimes practice with top tour players. However, competing at such a level is far enough away that it still seems like a dream, it is not yet truly tangible. Thus, it is hard for this player to be inspired in training every day for professional tennis. However, every practice, every match, prepares this young player for professional tournaments. The times when he is fully engaged, as well as those when he is not, create a total sum of his adult game. What he learns about himself during these times, how he responds to stress, and how he copes with challenges will become the habits that, for good or bad, underpin how he will compete in the early part of his professional career.

Back to present time, this player is now competing in the first round of the qualification draw. As one might expect, he is struggling with a slow start, not feeling confident, missing more than he can accept, but he digs deep and keeps fighting. His goal is to compete on every single point, especially when the previous point was not a good one. On this day it is more important to be tough and resilient than it is to play 'clean tennis'. To his fortune, his opponent flinches, plays a poor service game, and loses the first set. He starts to feel a little better, but frustration with his performance can be seen in his eyes. Nonetheless, and as he has been trained to do, he starts to bounce on his toes to energise his feet and begins to explore ways to stay in the lead. As he begins to focus more on the process of how to play his opponent and less on how poorly he is striking the ball, his performance level raises. With a little more confidence and much better self-talk and body language, he is able to win the second set and move on to the final round of qualifying.

Although the big moments such as qualifying at a professional tournament are exciting, it is the work done at the earlier ages that prepares players for these moments. The goal of early training is to create a foundation of performance perspectives, skills, and strategies that are supported over time to create more refined, mature approaches to performance (e.g. creating more in-depth and customised preparation routines that lead to optimal performance states). And, when young athletes are not performing to their usual levels, how they have learned to master their thinking, manage their feelings, and respond in an effective manner will determine if they make a huge step in their sport careers.

Sport psychology training with young athletes

Psychological skills training (PST) programmes have primarily targeted elite athletes. It has been argued that elite athletes' physical skills are well developed and differences in abilities become smaller as they continue to excel (Weinberg & Williams, 2015). Therefore, fine-tuning performance through psychological skills often dictates who wins and who loses. In other words, at the elite level, strong psychological skills often distinguish the best from the rest. In addition, working with the 'elite' often generates much excitement in the minds of both emerging and practicing sport psychology consultants. However, we argue that young athletes are primary consumers that have been overlooked in PST and professional practice research (Vealey, 1988). Although the effectiveness of PST with elite athletes is well documented and working with these performers is quite exciting, it can be argued that PST is even more important for younger athletes (Burton, 1991). Young athletes are developing physically; most of their training is traditionally focused on nurturing fundamental sport skills, as it is 'easier to develop proper physical technique in a beginner than it is to modify poor technique in a more experienced athlete' (Weinberg & Williams, 2015, p. 332). With this same principle in mind, young athletes are also developing psychologically and are more ripe for PST intervention than older athletes who have already internalised dysfunctional responses to competition. Thus, PST with younger athletes can be especially effective and rewarding as a means of helping youngsters develop appropriate psychological skills for sport competition.

(Vealey, 1988, p. 323)

Providing a foundation of mental and coping skills that will give young athletes the best chance to perform (and excel) in any moment, regardless of the competition, is a great reason for conducting mental training. If young athletes have one, two, five, or ten years of PST they will, in most cases, have a great advantage over their opponent. However, young players who do not have the skills or a plan on how to manage stress, emotion, doubts, fears, and poor performances will likely be in for a rude awakening as they progress in sport. There is also the very important benefit of developing the character attributes and skills that can make young players better people. Below we highlight four major reasons why all people involved in youth sport settings should care about integrating PST with young athletes.

Reason 1: Pressure is an inherent part of organised youth sport

McCarthy and colleagues (McCarthy, Jones, Harwood, & Olivier, 2010) argued that young athletes are rapidly becoming an important group for PST programmes, especially when considering the growth of organised youth sport as well as sport-specific centres of excellence around the world. Regardless of whether these young athletes are considered elite or non-elite, they compete in organised sport and are exposed to pressure and a variety of stressful situations. Therefore, coaches, applied practitioners, and sport organisations have a responsibility to make sure young athletes learn psychological skills and strategies to cope with pressure and enhance their physical, social, and psychological development (Orlick, 1982; Weiss, 1991). Integrating PST into the competitive sport environment can help young athletes reach their full potential, promote positive self-esteem, perceive competition as challenging instead of threatening, develop resilience, enjoy their sport experience, stay involved in sport, and nurture personal growth in other aspects of life (e.g. school; Burton, 1991; Tremayne & Newbery, 2005).

In addition, Sinclair and Sinclair (1994) argued that effective psychological skills and strategies are crucial for proficient performance and an inseparable part of the learning process. Those working with youth athletes must therefore value psychological skills and strategies as highly as they value the physical skills required for performance. Rather than viewing PST as a component that can be added on when needed, it is imperative that those working with young athletes integrate the physical, emotional, and psychological aspects of performance directly into practice (Foster, Maynard, Butt, & Hays, 2015; Sinclair & Sinclair, 1994). This integrated approach allows young athletes to develop the coping strategies needed to effectively manage the inevitable performance pressures that are a part of competitive sport.

Reason 2: Young athletes are capable of using psychological skills and strategies

Applied sport psychology professionals have strongly advocated for the use of PST with young athletes. For instance, Orlick and McCaffrey (1991) stated that doing PST with young athletes has demonstrated to them that children 'are highly capable of learning and applying a variety of important mind/body skills (e.g. imagery, goal setting, relaxation, focusing, and refocusing)' in a number of settings (e.g. sport, school, performing arts, recovering from illness) (p. 324). Burton (1991) also reported that the young athletes (ages 8–17 years) he worked with successfully developed and implemented a variety of psychological skills and strategies (e.g. imagery, arousal control, relaxation, self-talk, and goal-setting), while Chase (2010) argued that children have a stronger ability than adults to engage their senses and image a variety of situations (both real and pretend).

Research in applied sport psychology has yet to demonstrate at what age or developmental stage young athletes can effectively learn and engage in specific psychological skills and strategies (Chase, 2010; Foster et al., 2015). In a recent study, young athletes aged 13–16 years reported a greater understanding of goal-setting, imagery, self-talk, and relaxation compared to those who were 7–12 years of age (McCarthy et al., 2010). To our knowledge, this is the only empirical investigation that has illustrated such developmental differences in young athletes' implicit understanding of abstract sport psychology concepts. Although it may be difficult for young athletes aged 7–12 to think abstractly (especially for those who are still in the concrete operational stage of development; see Chapter 4 for further information), this does not mean they are incapable of learning and using PST methods effectively. In fact, empirical and anecdotal evidence is growing and clearly supports the use of PST with young athletes (both children and adolescents): imagery and arousal regulation strategies have been found to enhance free-throw percentage with 10–12-year-old boys (Wrisberg & Anshel, 1989); relaxation, video observation, and imagery training was found to significantly improve performance with 7–10-year-old table tennis athletes (Zhang, Ma, Orlick, & Zitzelsberger, 1992), and; more recently, Haddad and Tremayne (2009) found that the use of a centring breath with 10–11-year-old basketball players improved their free-throw percentage.

Overall, the same approaches used with elite performers have been found to be relevant to young athletes, as long as these approaches are adapted and simplified to be developmentally appropriate (Burton, 1991; Orlick & McCaffrey, 1991). Not only are young athletes capable of learning psychological skills and strategies, they are also playful, imaginative, and open (Orlick & McCaffrey, 1991). These qualities make PST fun and rewarding for those who have the pleasure of working with young athletes.

Reason 3: PST builds a foundation for immediate and long-term development

It is an important responsibility for those working with young athletes to make sure they develop a solid base of psychological skills and strategies to facilitate future development (Foster et al., 2015). When young athletes learn physical sport skills they must learn foundational skills before being able to move onto more complex ones. It would make sense that children and adolescents need a similar approach to learning psychological skills and strategies. As such, a solid foundation of psychological skills is an essential component of young athletes' future progress with psychological development (Foster et al., 2015). Thus, in line with Sinclair and Sinclair's (1994) model of introducing foundational psychological skills to athletes, we suggest that simple versions of psychological skills should be introduced, taught, and expanded upon incrementally as children grow and mature. Delivering a developmentally driven psychological programme to young athletes will provide them with the tools for immediately dealing with stressful sport situations. Perhaps even more importantly, developing a strong base of psychological skills and strategies can help athletes cope with the changing demands and pressures they will experience as they continue their sport careers, thus enhancing long-term development and future success.

Reason 4: PST can have parallel benefits for life skills and character development

Although one of the goals of PST with young athletes is performance enhancement, what might be even more exciting about working with this population is the relevancy of personal development as an outcome of PST (see Chapter 12 for more information about the purposeful development of life skills through sport). Importantly, PST for performance enhancement and PST for life skills and character development do not have to be mutually exclusive. A PST framework geared towards performance enhancement can easily include elements of life skills (e.g. coping with conflict and adversity), which will help to maximise the benefits associated with sport participation among all children.

Using sport psychology with young athletes

Having highlighted the important role of sport psychology in youth sport, the following section explores a specific PST programme led by Dr Larry Lauer for the United States Tennis Association Player Development programme. This programme is underpinned by the four reasons outlined above for conducting PST with young athletes and provides great insight into how PST can be used to support the development of elite young athletes as resilient, confident competitors. Although the following example focuses upon elite youth athletes, it is important to remember that these same principles could be applied with athletes across all abilities.

USTA Player Development's (USTA PD) Target 22: Developing resilient, confident competitors

The USTA PD mission is to develop Top 100 professional tennis players that perform well in Grand Slams and major events. To reach this mission Larry Lauer

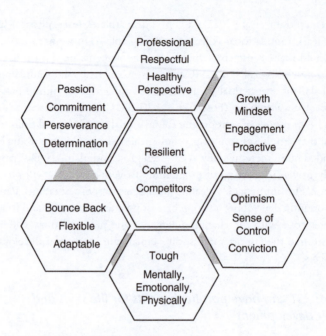

FIGURE 2.1 USTA Player Development Target 22

and the national coaches and performance staff at USTA Player Development must develop young players' psychological skills so they are equipped to become great performers with great character by the age of 22 (training begins as early as age 8 at camps). This age is seen as the time when a player needs to be highly adaptable and ready to compete against the best players in the world. Hence, Target 22 (see Figure 2.1) provides a national direction for the development of psychological characteristics and life skills in our junior players. The hope is to provide these players with an array of strengths that are associated with high levels of success in sport and life. The Target 22 mission keeps us mindful of the process of developing players systematically over time, understanding that psychological and emotional maturation and growth will occur at different rates, and a player's success on a particular skill or characteristic will be dependent on timing. For instance, during transitions to higher levels of competition, it is not unusual for players to struggle in particular areas (e.g. confidence) until they become more experienced at the level, get used to the competition, face a number of challenges and adversity, and potentially rework their mental game.

What is a resilient, confident competitor?

Resilient players bounce back from, adapt to, and become stronger because of adversity. When faced with difficult situations, they embrace the opportunity to grow, handle their own and others' doubts, find a way to succeed, and focus on problem-solving. Confident players believe in their ability in all game situations.

They are not afraid to play anyone, are very clear on the strengths they possess, and trust in how they are going to play. Competitors are ready to play each point with full focus on what matters in that moment, with positive energy, and with a belief in their plan for the point.

Why focus on resilient, confident competitors?

Best practices with players and coaches – including the Playing Tough and Clean Hockey Programme (Lauer & Paiement, 2009) and recent research (Sarkar & Fletcher, 2014) – has revealed that the highest achievers experienced adversity and developed resilience as a quality and as a skill. Typically in tennis, successful players make a large number of unforced errors. Being alone on the court and watched by others makes every unforced error that much more meaningful and difficult to manage emotionally. There is no diffusion of responsibility in tennis; players are solely accountable for what happens (sometimes being too hard on themselves). Furthermore, only one player wins a tournament, while the rest finish with a loss (unless there is a back draw). Therefore, players must be able to bounce back from adversity and continue to learn, grow, and thrive from mistakes and losing.

How to develop resilient confident competitors

How do we develop competitors that are prepared to play every point, have an aura of confidence, never give up, and are always looking for a way to win? We do it with PST that is systematic, integrated, and defines different areas of training and development necessary to achieve optimal performance. Target 22 asserts an intended 'target' or major goal for development, but five areas provide the methods for achieving the target.

Area 1: Player's personality and history

This includes an understanding of the players as people, how they have been socialised and parented – including how they compete and interact with others – and how that intersects with the tennis environment. For a sport psychology practitioner this basic understanding of players is needed, even though some aspects may not be able to change. Therefore, a practitioner must spend time getting to know players using questioning and listening skills.

Area 2: Awareness

The development of resilient, confident competitors begins through players becoming aware and understanding their tendencies and habits, how they see themselves, and how they view achievement. A greater understanding of self as a person and a competitor allows players to make the necessary changes needed to develop as well as anticipate and understand why they respond as they do to stress. Self-awareness is enhanced via reflective journaling, learning to communicate effectively with coaches, and doing assessments to profile psychological skill use and effectiveness. Gaining self-awareness then promotes goal-setting, action planning, and monitoring of performance. Journaling and goal-setting help create a mindful player who anticipates issues, adapts as needed, and trusts core strengths and game style.

Area 3: Learning to commit and prepare

The purpose of training is to create a commitment to *doing the right things* consistently. The coaching staff (including the mental coach) educate the players on the habits necessary for performance, including how to optimally prepare for practices and matches (e.g. nutrition and eating habits, sleep, recovery, stretching, strength and fitness workouts, mental preparation and training). Many of the characteristics of Target 22 are demonstrated in these habits, such as optimism, growth mindset, and being proactive in talking with coaches about their game. Creating such habits helps develop consistent performers who can achieve optimal performance states more often.

To develop habits, players must first make the choice to change by creating a value statement: 'I am resilient or I will be resilient by …'. Simultaneously, the staff and the player must define the target behaviour and then break the behaviour down into chunks/gradients. For example, if a player wants to accelerate on her shots and is only doing it 25 per cent of the time in practice, we define what accelerate means and then set a realistic goal, such as accelerating 30–40 per cent of the time. The coach then orchestrates a progression through different drills and intensities to bring the player to the target behaviour. To be accountable, the athlete is asked to reflect on their habit after drills and after practice with the coach. The mental coach assists in helping the player commit and stay with habit development as well as cope with the variance in performance. The final progressions are to bring the habit in to practice matches and eventually matches, again starting realistically and progressively advancing the performance.

The three areas described above are the foundation of a resilient, confident competitor. However, alone they are insufficient; a player must also discipline the mind and train under stress, which leads to our final two areas of focus.

Area 4: Developing a disciplined mind

Once players have committed to good habits and preparation, they will likely feel more confident. However, how players view what happens during a match will largely determine their level of resilience, confidence, and competitiveness. Thus, players must discipline the mind by managing self-talk, which includes learning to reframe, counter, and use performance cues. In addition, players learn about the kinds of thoughts that are unhelpful for performance and how to restructure them. For example, players who are perfectionistic believe things *should* go just the way they expect. Helping perfectionistic players accept that they can make mistakes, that mistakes are normal, and that the only abnormal expectation is to be perfect helps players create relevant counter thoughts. Furthermore, players are taught to use imagery and visualisation to create a comprehensive approach to preparing for matches as well as performing in the moment. Imagery and visualisation aid the players not only in creating readiness to enact their game plan, but also in enhancing feelings of confidence, motivation, and composure. Many players will visualise stressful situations (either rehearsing upcoming matches or reflecting on previous matches) and then visualise deploying their mental game plan to compete with confidence and resilience. This creates a stress inoculation effect off-court.

Area 5: Pressure training

Psychological skills learned must be used under progressively greater degrees of pressure and adversity. Players are taught to use simple and memorable routines that help them integrate psychological skills and strategies into performance. Every player is taught a between-point routine to ready them to play the next point. Using Ravizza and Hanson's approach in *Heads-Up Baseball* (1995) adapted to tennis (Lauer, Gould, Lubbers, & Kovacs, 2010), this is the 'green light routine', which includes the following stages:

1) Response – the immediate response to the last point where players are asked to minimise negative responses and maintain positive body language.
2) Recovery – players review the last point and use deep breathing to reduce the heart rate and slow breathing.
3) Refocus – players move on from the last point and refocus by planning the next point.
4) Ready – players quiet the mind and trust the plan that was created with an external focus. This stage involves rituals where the players bounce the ball a certain number of times or sway back and forth as they prepare to return serve.

The player's age and developmental stage determine the complexity of the routines. At younger ages we ask players to use one or two steps in the four-stage 'green light routine' first, typically maintaining positive body language and having a simple plan for the point. As players master these fundamentals, they add more stages and more depth is added to each stage. For example, players begin to control the speed of play between points, taking time to regulate their breathing and identify errors or areas for improvement in the previous point. This four-stage 'green light routine' provides opportunities to use deep breathing and other relaxation techniques, visualisation or imagery, performance cues, and other self-talk strategies. Effective use of this routine allows players to be consistently ready, positively energised, and focused on and believing in their plan with a simple, quiet mind.

Once players start to develop their 'green light routines', the coaches create situations and pressures that will challenge players use of these routines, as well as other psychological skills and strategies. For instance, to help players work on focusing in distracting situations coaches will have players play points while making noises and talking to the players during the point. The coach can also prompt negative thoughts that players may be thinking in a given situation. The sport psychology practitioner is there to encourage players to follow their routines and use psychological strategies. Practice matches with rewards attached to achieving certain markers (e.g. 60 per cent on first serve, winner has dinner paid for by opponent) create stress and an opportunity to work on routines and skills. For more on drills to create pressure see the *USTA Mental Skills and Drills Handbook* (Lauer et al., 2010).

When the green light routine is not preparing the player for the next point we ask players to use a 'yellow light routine' (Ravizza & Hanson, 1995) and take more time to prepare. Children and adolescents' greatest sport stressors are usually playing poorly and making mistakes. It is essential that players deal effectively with mistakes, continue to give effort, to listen, and to learn. Being resilient is crucial to continuing to grow and develop. Therefore, in our programmes with players aged 8–12 years we teach them the 'Breathe and Believe' technique. That is, when distracted, nervous, frustrated, or when emotions are blocking young players from being ready to play the point, they are taught to take extra time at the towel, where they take deep breaths and think of one simple idea that their coach would tell them to make the situation better.

Teaching 'Breathe and Believe' is aided by players' understanding the role of stress, emotion, cognitions, and the environment on performance. Then, the fundamentals of diaphragmatic breathing are taught, and players are able to experience the effect it has on heart rate, breathing, and overall level of comfort and ability to think clearly. Teaching 'Breathe and Believe' to a young (e.g. 10-year-old) player takes time, patience, and creativity. The mental coach will introduce the skills in several ways: on-court and how it can be used as part of a routine, and off-court breaking the skills down into fun and educational experiences. For instance, off-court players experience breathing exercises while doing fitness or even when doing a challenging exercise or game to improve performance. Concurrently, players are taught the correct breathing techniques, why it works, and what is happening.

After a few weeks of training breathing on- and off-court, players are taught how thinking influences emotions and performance and how to restructure thoughts. For example, we tell the players to say one thing to themselves that their coach would say to help them. This routine is then used on-court and supported by the coaching staff including during point play and using drills to emphasise the importance of using Breathe and Believe (e.g. a challenging drill where the players will make mistakes and giving them time to use Breathe and Believe). Identifying situations that create negative trigger responses (e.g. missing several forehands on break points leading to a thought of 'my forehand is awful') and then creating new self-talk responses that are positive and productive (e.g. 'I missed two forehands, I will make the next one by getting in position') adds the second step of the routine. Again, players use this on-court and the coaches are involved in encouraging and holding the player accountable. Finally, after several weeks of training, breathing and believing are combined into one routine and practised on- and off-court.

Developing psychological skills and effectively creating a resilient, confident, competitive mindset is not possible without the support of parents and coaches. Hence, integrated educational programming and on-court training are essential in creating systematic, effective approaches to PST. A sport psychology practitioner's best work may come in the form of helping parents manage emotions and responses to their child's tennis performance (see Chapters 10 and 27) or helping coaches to create an inviting, mastery-climate in practice (see Chapters 8 and 26). Parents and coaches should be informed of the PST that players are receiving so they can support, not conflict with or undermine, its effects. Furthermore, coaches must learn how to creatively and effectively engage players in PST in an exciting, relevant way, that is motivating (see Chapter 25).

Conclusion

A main goal of sport psychology with young athletes is to provide them with the skills to perform optimally in sport and life (including being resilient, confident competitors). If the player described at the beginning of the chapter has been engaged in systematic, integrated PST for a number of years, he will have a much better chance of succeeding in an adverse situation in the future. This foundational training can, and should, start from a young age and be part of the practice environment. Not only is it effective, but we are doing our children and adolescents a disservice if we are placing them in stressful sporting environments without helping them develop appropriate psychological skills and strategies.

References

Burton, D. (1991, Winter). Issues and answers: Psychological skills in youth sport. *Association for the Advancement of Applied Sport Psychology Newsletter*, p. 10.

Chase, M. A. (2010). Children. In S. Hanrahan & M. Andersen (Eds.), *Handbook of Applied Sport Psychology* (pp. 377–387). Abingdon, UK: Routledge.

Foster, D., Maynard, I., Butt, J., & Hays, K. (2015). Delivery of psychological skills training to youngsters. *Journal of Applied Sport Psychology*, 1, 1–16.

Haddad, K., & Tremayne, P. (2009). The effects of centering on the free-throw shooting performance of young athletes. *The Sport Psychologist*, 23, 118–136.

Lauer, L., Gould, D., Lubbers, P., & Kovacs, M. (2010). *USTA Mental Skills and Drills Handbook*. Monterey, CA: Coaches Choice.

Lauer, L., & Paiement, C. (2009). The playing tough and clean hockey program. *The Sport Psychologist*, 23, 543–561.

McCarthy, P. J., Jones, M. V., Harwood, C. G., & Olivier, S. (2010). What do young athletes implicitly understand about psychological skills? *Journal of Clinical Sport Psychology*, 4, 158–172.

Orlick, T. (1982). Beyond excellence. In T. Orlick, J. T. Partington, & J. H. Salmela (Eds.), *Mental Training for Coaches and Athletes* (pp. 1–7). Ottawa: Coaching Association of Canada.

Orlick, T., & McCaffrey, N. (1991). Mental training with children for sport and life. *The Sport Psychologist*, 5, 322–334.

Ravizza, K., & Hanson, T. (1995). *Heads-Up Baseball: Playing the Game One Pitch at a Time.* Chicago, IL: McGraw-Hill.

Sarkar, M., & Fletcher, D. (2014). Ordinary magic, extraordinary performance: Psychological resilience and thriving in high achievers. *Sport, Exercise, and Performance Psychology, 3,* 46–60.

Sinclair, G. D., & Sinclair, D. A. (1994). Developing reflective performers by integrating mental management skills with the learning process. *The Sport Psychologist, 8,* 13–27.

Tremayne, P., & Newbery, G. (2005). Mental skill training program for children. In D. Hackfort, R. Lidor, & J. Duda (Eds.), *Handbook of Research in Applied Sport Psychology* (pp. 93–106). Morgantown, WV: Fitness Information Technology.

Vealey, R. S. (1988). Future directions in psychological skills training. *The Sport Psychologist, 2,* 318–336.

Weinberg, R. S., & Williams, J. M. (2015). Integrating and implementing a psychological skills training program. In J. M. Williams & V. Krane (Eds.), *Applied Sport Psychology: Personal Growth to Peak Performance* (pp. 329–358). New York, NY: McGraw-Hill.

Weiss, M. (1991). Psychological skill development in children and adolescents. *The Sport Psychologist, 5,* 335–354.

Wrisberg, C. A., & Anshel, M. H. (1989). The effect of cognitive strategies on the free throw shooting performance of young athletes. *The Sport Psychologist, 3,* 95–104.

Zhang, L., Ma, P., Orlick, T., & Zitzelsberger, L. (1992). The effect of mental-imagery training on performance enhancement with 7–10-year-old children. *The Sport Psychologist, 6,* 230–241.

3

DELIVERING SPORT PSYCHOLOGY ACROSS YOUTH SPORT CONTEXTS

Rich Neil and Brendan Cropley

Over the past ten years we have had the privilege of working with a number of sporting organisations across a range of sports including golf, rugby union, association football, and netball. Our work has been with elite national teams, professional and amateur developmental squads, and university teams, with much of the effort focused on developing the psychological competencies of youth sport performers, aged 12 to 21 years. We have been fortunate that the organisations we have worked with have generally been open to our proposals on how to support the development of their performers, and we have often been afforded the opportunity to shape the provision of the youth performance structures. Specifically, we have advocated the need to develop the person alongside the performer, facilitating the competence of the person across all aspects of his or her life by focusing on the nurturing of psychosocial skills that could be used to help the individual be successful within and beyond sport.

Nevertheless, we have been faced with a number of challenges when delivering sport psychology services aligned to the agendas of the organisations – challenges that, we argue, were a result of: (1) our naivety when starting out with certain organisations; (2) flaws in our planning and promotion of sport psychology services; and (3) our attempt to balance our consultancy with our academic commitments. Within this chapter we highlight some of these challenges in relation to the extant literature. We then offer insight into what we did to navigate these challenges, maintain effective relationships with sporting organisations, and improve our provision of support within these youth contexts.

Challenges faced when delivering sport psychology services across youth sporting contexts

Within the academic literature, sport psychologists have referred to the challenges faced when attempting to implement interventions with young people (e.g. Gould

& Carson, 2008; Henriksen, Larsen, Storm, & Ryom, 2014). Within this section we aim to discuss some of the challenges that we have encountered that originate from the organisations we have worked with *and* some of the personal challenges that impacted the delivery of our sport psychology provision.

Management of different expectations

A critical challenge for both of us has been the management of different expectations within the sporting cultures in which we have worked. For example, within one sport we are often working in a professional environment with amateur youth performers who only frequent this 'professional' stage. Specifically, the performers are not yet being paid to compete in sport, they live with their parents, and still attend school – yet when they attend our developmental camps they are expected to conduct themselves as sporting professionals. This will include wearing the right kit/uniform, adopting a structured protocol the night before and morning of camp, practising purposefully in their designated 'own' practice time, setting goals, and demonstrating appropriate 'organisational citizenship behaviour'. Consequently, the organisation often has higher expectations of the performers than the performers have for themselves. Some performers struggle to adapt to these expectations and rarely 'live' them, while others may adapt only temporarily, reverting to their previous normative behaviours as soon as they leave.

In another context, we have a mixture of professionally contracted and amateur youth sport performers who come together within camp set-ups. Although the expectations of the organisation and coaches are often met, those who are from amateur backgrounds sometimes struggle with simple expectations such as knowing their roles, getting ready for each session, and arriving at sessions on time. In a third context, the youth performers are on full-time schedules with the organisation and, alongside the standard professional expectations identified above, they are also expected to partake only in that sport. Work with their parents has highlighted a worry that the wellbeing of these young people may suffer if they are released by the professional club – as they would not have another identity outside of that sporting organisation. The parents, therefore, expect the organisations/us as support staff to prepare performers for this transition.

In sum, the expectations of organisations can differ across sports, but in essence they are all focused on developing professional winning behaviours. Potentially due to funding affecting the time spent with the performers, the objective of helping athletes meet these expectations can be challenging. In addition, balancing expectations of organisations, coaches, parents, and athletes themselves increases the complexity of supporting the athletes.

(Lack of) funding affecting frequency of contact

A further cultural challenge when working with sporting organisations in the UK is that some are Government funded, which means they are accountable for achieving key performance indicators (Fletcher & Wagstaff, 2009). In addition, the funding is sometimes limited to the extent that the coach–athlete contact time is infrequent across the year, which means we (applied mental performance consultants) also have minimal contact with athletes but are expected to have a significant impact on performance. Realistically, it is up to the governing body of the sport to put in place systems that help nurture performers towards success which, in turn, will help increase the funding. Consequently, this provides us with a challenge to develop a progressive system of psychological support and development within a restricted time frame that can be measured against the identified key performance indicators.

Within one particular environment where there is limited funding we have attempted to overcome these issues by providing work-based learning and supervisory opportunities for postgraduate students who are training towards becoming chartered/accredited practitioners through the British Psychological Society (BPS) or British Association of Sport and Exercise Sciences (BASES) pathways. This is a beneficial system for the neophyte practitioners-in-training as it exposes them to a variety of different experiences that help them tailor their practice philosophy and skills (McEwan & Tod, 2015). The challenge for us, however, has been to design a systematic programme that aims to help young people succeed in performance settings by guiding the development of their psychosocial competencies within a youth structure (i.e. from 12 to 21 years of age), with limited contact, while supervising postgraduate students with differing levels of experience and ability.

Building multiple relationships

In some of the environments in which we work, funding for support services is considerably larger. This brings about different challenges, such as having to build relationships within a large support network. In one case, this network included 16 additional support staff (i.e. performance director, team manager, coaches, doctor, physiotherapists, nutritionist, performance analysts, strength and conditioning coaches, and interns) in an organisation that has never employed a sport psychologist within the senior elite set-up, let alone within the youth context. McDougall, Nesti, and Richardson (2015) found that building and developing multiple relationships across different levels of an organisation was a challenge for experienced sport psychologists, while Winter and Collins (2015) showed that integrating with the coaching team was vital for effective consultancy. In this context we were 'thrown in the deep end', being asked to immediately drive cultural change within the youth context. Although this was enjoyable, the need to become familiar with the dynamics of the management group and players was fast tracked. To do this through infrequent contact (one to two sessions per week) tested our planning and communication skills. We were afforded more time, but the competing responsibilities of being academic-practitioners resulted in us having to restrict our availability – consequently, it proved challenging to achieve our objectives of familiarity and culture change.

Negative subcultures

With regards to the culture within youth sporting contexts, our view is that culture represents the behaviours a team/club demonstrates within an environment on a daily basis directed towards a common goal. For example, in our experience individuals have used the term 'vibrant culture' to describe a group of individuals being enthusiastic, energetic, and generally positive in a training context. In comparison, individuals have used the term 'festerous culture' to describe a group of individuals that work in 'cliques', are not honest with each other, and work to disrupt the training context. When we were recruited to work within two particular youth contexts to address the training/performance cultures we did notice a number of 'cliques' that negatively influenced the functioning of the group. We are by no means saying the culture was festerous, but there was a challenge to bring these negative subcultures together – a challenge documented in the academic literature (see McDougall et al., 2015). Given that we propose culture is a representation of behaviours, we aimed to help guide the athletes to identify the accepted high-performance behaviours that they would 'sign up' to adhere to throughout that performance year. We discuss the development of this culture through behaviours later in the chapter. Once we had identified these accepted behaviours (or expectations of each other), we then had the challenge of monitoring how well each athlete 'lived' these behaviours. The difficulty, once more, was that in both these youth performance settings the players only frequented the 'professional' environment, and we were not always on site at the camps to monitor the accepted behaviours in action.

Governing body requirements: What's desired versus what's needed

Even though we were afforded freedom to develop support programmes for each of the sporting organisations we are discussing in this chapter, there were times when the politics of the organisation challenged the work we were conducting with the young athletes. For example, at different points of the preparation and playing season the performers can have 'pinch' points that can have an effect on their wellbeing and, subsequently, performance. Within the age grade squads with which we work, exam periods can cause high stress for the athletes throughout the year. Across the sports we do attempt to tailor our work to include education and guidance on planning, preparation, and managing nerves prior to these critical periods; work that evolved due to our increasing awareness of these demands. However, during these times athletic performance can suffer as a result of training taking a back seat.

It is at these points that the organisation's desired 'outcomes versus what is required' becomes a challenge. In one example, coaches and other members of the organisation voiced concerns about the performances of their academy players during these periods – citing such things as the lack of ability to manage high-pressurised environments and lack of confidence as the potential causes. Consequently, the typical 'quick fix' was suggested by these individuals – requesting us to adapt our approaches to manage that current 'perceived' issue. The 'quick fix' has been well documented as a frustration for practitioners (e.g. Martin et al., 2001), and is often identified as the right approach instead of supporting the performers on the underpinning issues, which we were attempting to do. We evidently needed to work better with our colleagues at the organisation to reduce their expectations during these periods, as competing responsibilities result in the athletes changing their priorities during these times.

Maintaining a work–life balance and self-preservation

The maintenance of a work–life balance has been identified as a key determinant of wellbeing in many sport professions (Wagstaff & Lerner, 2015), and has been reported recently as a key demand for sport psychology practitioners (Cropley et al., 2016). Within our recent experiences in providing support across different sports, ensuring a work–life balance has been challenging due to our competing responsibilities as academic-practitioners. However, we feel as though we have managed these commitments well through self-monitoring, reflection, and peer support (discussed later in this chapter).

What has been more challenging is the promotion of work–life balance to the coaches and support staff with whom we have worked, with the necessity to assist 'self-preservation' (Haberl & Peterson, 2006). With regards to self-preservation within the work–life context, Haberl and Peterson refer to such factors as the appropriate amount and quality of sleep, regular exercise, suitable nutrition, and regular contact with family at home. In many of the contexts in which we have worked, it is apparent that the coaches and support staff often work long days – visibly between 8am and 10pm (after which they go to their rooms to continue to work), and rarely make time for rest, days off, or family time. The gradual result of this intense work ethic is a noticeable increase in fatigue as well as a decrease in patience and concentration – all of which can affect wellbeing, the relationship between the staff and the athletes, and the working environment.

Having sufficient sporting knowledge

During the early parts of our careers, we experienced first-hand the importance of having sufficient knowledge of the sports in which we work. For instance, we both encountered athletes and professionals who initially acted indifferently about our work when learning that we had not competed in their specific sport at a high level. This importance of 'knowing' the sport has been identified consistently within the professional practice literature, to limit potential negative consequences such as psychology support not being taken seriously or practitioners being ostracised by athletes, coaches, or support staff (e.g. Lubker, Visek, Watson II, & Singpurwalla, 2012; MacIntyre, Campbell, & Turner, 2014; Winter & Collins, 2015). Although it is important for us to be familiar with the sports in which we work (in order to gain entry and maintain the interest of the young people with whom we are working), it has proved a challenge with the neophyte practitioners-in-training that we have supervised in these performance environments. We advocate the need to be accustomed with the culture and language of each sport, yet there are occasions when coaches have highlighted the need for our practitioners-in-training to further increase their knowledge as they *may* not be relating to the young performers as well as they could be. Some of the solutions that were identified to overcome this issue include: (1) shadow performers and coaches within that sport to understand better the language and other complexities of the sport; (2) consult in the actual environment (Henriksen et al., 2014), as delivery will be more effective within this context and practitioners become more familiar with that sporting organisation; and (3) completing basic coaching courses or reading coach education materials.

Managing challenges for the benefit of the young athletes

Within this section we offer insight into some of the strategies we have put into place to manage or eliminate the challenges we have identified above and ensure that we are able to best support the psychosocial development of the young people we work with.

Reflection and peer support

To navigate through the challenges, or to eliminate them before they surface, we aim to work proactively as an individual or through our support network. Individually we regularly talk to our colleagues and write about our experiences to enable us to reflect on our practice. This allows us to identify ways to maintain good performance and improve our work (Cropley & Hanton, 2011) and also facilitate a constant learning experience (Stambulova & Johnson, 2010). The role of a practitioner and an academic can be an arduous one in that our work is variable and voluminous and we are 'consulting' daily with clients, students, and other staff. Therefore, ignoring our own need to 'talk to people' can be detrimental to our own wellbeing and, as a result, negatively affect our consultancy effectiveness. The creation and use of a peer/mentor support network can address this issue (Cogan, Flowers, Haberl, McCann, & Borlabi, 2012; McCormick & Meijen, 2015), and also help to proactively deal with situations and identify demands that may occur.

This need for a peer/mentor support network is the main reason why, in 2013, we set up a monthly sport psychology support group meeting for the neophyte practitioners-in-training who work with us within various sports organisations. With over 20 members of this group, we address different themes (e.g. changing culture, self-awareness, goal setting, working with parents) each month through a variety of formats (e.g. practical and discussion sessions) that help prepare the practitioners for consultancy and assist them in developing a comprehensive network of peers to discuss future experiences with, while also providing us with the opportunity for purposeful reflection on our own practice based on the experiences of those within the group (Cropley & Neil, 2016).

Management of different expectations and negative subcultures

Within each youth sporting context, we have aimed to develop a healthy work-ing culture through engaging with the young athletes to identify their own high-performance expectations. These expectations are, in essence, behaviours that the group identify are essential for them to be successful as individuals and as a group within their home, training, and performance environments. Once they have iden-tified their list of behaviours, categorised under key headings (e.g. 'do your role-related homework' and 'everyone turn up on time' could be categorised under 'discipline'), we would then challenge the group on a regular basis about how they are 'living' the expectations. Aside from using this approach to help ensure expec-tations are adhered to, it can also be used to help build bridges across the group due to the personal-disclosure and mutual sharing about what is important to the individual or how he or she has seen someone else in the group lead by example (Evans, Slater, Turner, & Barker, 2013). In addition, reflecting on expectations helps to build confidence and communication skills within the group as the athletes are supported to talk within their group environment.

This process of developing and reflecting upon expectations is loosely informed by Self-Determination Theory (Deci & Ryan, 1985) in that first we are attempting to develop a level of *autonomy* within the youth contexts as the players identify, live, and then police their accepted behaviours – in our experience the players engage well when they drive this process, but only if regularly challenged! Second, we are aiming to build *relationships* through the development and monitoring of the expectations conducted within groups, with each individual supported to provide an opinion. Third, we guide the youth to reinforce what they have done well spe-cifically in relation to their expectations – consequently helping to build a percep-tion of *competency* within the individuals and group.

Planning and engaging neophyte practitioners-in-training

Some of the key challenges we identified earlier included the lack of funding and competing responsibilities arising from being a practitioner and academic, both of which limit the amount of time that can be spent in sporting contexts. In order to navigate these challenges, we attempt to improve our planning of content as well as our delivery of support. With regards to planning, we have worked with the coaches and support staff across each sport to identify what psychosocial attributes 'elite' athletes need when they reach the senior level to help them succeed in that sport and everyday life. We then work backwards and identify which attributes should be introduced at each specified age within that sport (e.g. which attributes are important and should be introduced for athletes aged 12 and 13 years compared to athletes aged 14, 15, or 16) and how the development of these attributes could be facilitated from that point onwards. In other words, we may introduce a key attribute at a certain age, but we will aim to continue to nurture this throughout the following age grades.

As previously explained, to further overcome funding and time challenges, we have also engaged with a number of postgraduate students (neophyte practitioners-in-training) who work with us. Within one particular context, the practitioners-in-training will work in pairs with a specific age grade squad of players to deliver practical workshops followed by one-to-one on the field support. Our rationale for pairing up the practitioners-in-training is that some will be delivering for the first time, so working with a more experienced practitioner can aid development and confidence. This work is supported by the monthly meetings we described earlier, where those who work across each context can share experiences and ideas, and engage in bespoke role play sessions where we work through 'what-if' scenarios (e.g. what if an athlete does not buy into sport psychology or what if there is conflict among support staff) to help prepare the practitioners for multiple experiences (Cropley & Neil, 2016).

Building multiple relationships

Whenever we are asked to work with a sporting organisation, whether within the youth or senior framework, we always adopt the principles that: (a) we will need to first understand the culture and language of the organisation before we provide a proposed plan of support; and, (b) any proposed work will be conducted with and through the coaches (see Chapter 26 for examples). This, in our opinion, helps to build initial relations with the performance directors and coaches as it can instill confidence in the organisation that we will be thorough in justifying our approach and that we will work with them as team players. This approach also results in us acting as sounding boards for coaches, due to us working with them as opposed to working in isolation.

During our reconnaissance of the sporting organisation, and then when we begin working within the youth context, we aim to gradually build and strengthen relationships with the coaches and support staff by being in the environment as often as we can and observing their work on a regular basis. By 'being in the background' (Arnold & Sarkar, 2015), we find that the coaches and support staff become more familiar with us and start to engage in discussions with us about their sessions. We also invite feedback about our sessions, which again helps to encourage conversations that help build the professional relationships that are needed to be trusted and work effectively within youth contexts.

With regards to our specific sessions with the young athletes, whenever we conduct workshops we always aim to make them practical, fun, and engaging (Sharp, Woodcock, Holland, Cumming, & Duda, 2013), and we often invite the coaches and support staff to be involved. For example, at the start of any workshop we will conduct a 'mindset warm-up', which involves different cognitive activities to encourage such qualities as working as a group, effective communication, and leadership; the activities are also used to help the young athletes get focused for the main work that will follow. These types of activities help us to build relationships with the coaches and support staff as they are often enjoying themselves, which leads to a more relaxed and congenial environment post-workshop – a period where they engage with us to chat about ideas they may have to do something similar within their sessions or about what they have done in the past to help develop similar qualities.

Over time, the building of these relationships has helped us manage the issue of the governing body requirements, as our views have been better received during the pinch points for the youth within each context. Admittedly, we have also needed to get better at explaining to the organisation why we were doing what we were doing at each stage of the year. As a result of improved relations as time has passed, we have worked with the organisations to accept an increase in the provision of work that focuses on planning for the youth, along with the concept of 'off periods' that are scheduled at these pinch points. This work has also supported the relationships with the youth, as they feel they have been listened to and are supported by the organisation during critical personal periods.

Work–life balance/self-preservation

A lack of self-management and self-preservation can have negative effects on a coach's wellbeing, which in turn can have a debilitating effect on his or her work within the youth context. To elaborate, if the coach works long hours, does not eat well, sleeps poorly, and does not spend much time with family members then there is a chance that the coach's life satisfaction and sense of fulfilment may decrease. Alongside being generally fatigued, the decrease in psychological wellbeing may result in poorer functioning within performance settings (Neil, McFarlance, & Smith, 2016). Within our work, we attempt to guide young athletes, coaches, and support staff to identify their ideal 'performance mindset' and how they consistently achieve it. That is, when they are working at their best, what does that experience feel like? What are they thinking? Once these questions have been answered, we challenge the individuals about whether they know how they get to that ideal performance mindset. Here, we challenge them to think about the specific details over the week leading up to performance, including: when they spend time with family, when they eat, what time they put electronic equipment away, when they exercise, when they rest (and what that looks like), and so on. This helps them to create a structured time line across the week that they can be guided to stick to and constantly review to improve. We have explored and adopted this strategy ourselves – and seen the benefits in our mood and functioning. Similarly, we have observed the improvements in the mood and behaviour of the young performers and coaches when they have worked through this very simple process.

Conclusion

Within this chapter we have attempted to identify for the reader some of the challenges we have faced when working across numerous youth sporting contexts. There are so many more examples we could offer, challenges that we constantly reflect upon and aim to learn from so that we are able to manage the challenges better in the future and, as a result, provide a better experience for the young performers. As a closing comment, working with youth sporting organisations is extremely rewarding, but also often frustrating, so it is vital for any practitioner to develop coping strategies to work successfully within these contexts (Cropley et al., 2016). This, we have found, is best supported by a functioning peer support network which can provide both the emotional and the practical support needed when working as a sport psychologist.

References

Arnold, R., & Sarkar, M. (2015). Preparing athletes and teams for the Olympic Games: Experiences and lessons learned from the world's best sport psychologists. *International Journal of Sport and Exercise Psychology, 13*, 4–20.

Cogan, K. D., Flowers, R., Haberl, P., McCann, S., & Borlabi, W. (2012). Putting the team in sport psychology consulting: Five sport psychology consultants collaborating service for athletes at the USOC. *Journal of Sport Psychology in Action, 3*, 77–87.

Cropley, B., Baldock, L., Mellalieu, S. D., Neil, R., Wagstaff, C. R. D., & Wadey, R. (2016). Coping with the demands of professional practice: Sport psychology consultants' perspectives. *The Sport Psychologist, 30*, 290–302.

Cropley, B., & Hanton, S. (2011). The role of reflective practice in applied sport psychology: Contemporary issues for professional practice. In S. Hanton & S. D. Mellalieu (Eds.), *Professional Practice in Sport Psychology: A Review* (pp. 307–336). Abingdon, UK: Routledge.

Cropley, B. C., & Neil, R. (2016). Supervising from the swampy lowlands: A case study of collaborative approaches to supervision. In L. Tashman & G. Cremades (Eds.), *Global Practices and Training in Applied, Sport, Exercise, and Performance Psychology: A Case Study Approach*. Abingdon, UK: Routledge.

Deci, E. L., & Ryan, R. M. (1985). *Intrinsic Motivation and Self-Determination in Human Behaviour*. New York, NY: Plenum.

Evans, A. L., Slater, M. J., Turner, M. J., & Barker, J. B. (2013). Using personal-disclosure mutual-sharing to enhance group functioning in a professional soccer academy. *The Sport Psychologist, 27*, 233–243.

Fletcher, D., & Wagstaff, C. R. D. (2009). Organisational psychology in elite sport: Its emergence, application and future. *Psychology of Sport and Exercise, 10*, 427–434.

Gould, D., & Carson, S. (2008). Life skills development through sport: Current status and future directions. *Sport and Exercise Psychology Review, 2*, 10–18.

Haberl, P., & Peterson, K. (2006). Olympic-size ethical dilemmas: Issues and challenges for sport psychology consultants on the road and at the Olympic Games. *Ethics & Behavior, 16*, 25–40.

Henriksen, K., Larsen, C. H., Storm, L., & Ryom, K. (2014). Sport psychology interventions with your athletes: The perspective of the sport psychology practitioner. *Journal of Clinical Sport Psychology, 8*, 245–260.

Lubker, J. R., Visek, A. J., Watson II, J. C., & Singpurwalla, D. (2012). Athletes' preferred characteristics and qualifications of sport psychology practitioners: A consumer market analysis. *Journal of Applied Sport Psychology, 24*, 465–480.

MacIntyre, T., Campbell, M., & Turner, M. (2014). It's good to talk … From baptism to immersion: How wet should we get in consulting? *Sport & Exercise Psychology Review, 10*, 65–74.

Martin, S. B., Akers, A., Jackson, A. W., Wrisberg, C. A., Nelson, L., Leslire, P. J., & Leidig, L. (2001). Male and female athletes' and non-athletes' expectations about sport psychology consulting. *Journal of Applied Sport Psychology, 13*, 18–39.

McCormick, A., & Meijen, C. (2015). A lesson learned in time: Advice shared by experienced sport psychologists. *Sport & Exercise Psychology Review, 11*, 43–54.

McDougall, M., Nesti, M., & Richardson, D. (2015). The challenges of sport psychology delivery in elite and professional sport: Reflections from experienced sport psychologists. *The Sport Psychologists, 29*, 265–277.

McEwan, H. E., & Tod, D. (2015). Learning experiences contributing to service-delivery competence in applied psychologists: Lessons for sport psychologists. *Journal of Applied Sport Psychology, 27*, 79–93.

Neil, R., McFarlane, H., & Smith, A. (2016). Positive wellbeing in sport organisations. In C. Wagstaff (Ed.), *The Organisational Psychology of Sport: Key Issues and Practical Applications* (pp. 101–19). Abingdon, UK: Routledge.

Sharp, L., Woodcock, C., Holland, M. J. G., Cumming, J., & Duda, J. L. (2013). A qualitative evaluation of the effectiveness of a mental skills training program for youth athletes. *The Sport Psychologist, 27*, 219–232.

Stambulova, N., & Johnson, U. (2010). Novice consultants' experiences: Lessons learned by applied sport psychology students. *Psychology of Sport and Exercise, 11*, 295–303.

Wagstaff, C. R. D., & Lerner, R. J. (2015). Organisational psychology in sport: Recent developments and a research agenda. In S. D. Mellalieu & S. Hanton (Eds.), *Contemporary Advances in Sport Psychology: A Review* (pp. 91–119). Abingdon, UK: Routledge.

Winter, S., & Collins, D. (2015). Why do we do, what we do? *Journal of Applied Sport Psychology, 27*, 35–51.

4

DEVELOPMENTAL CONSIDERATIONS FOR WORKING WITH YOUNG ATHLETES

Lindsay E. Kipp

As youth sport professionals help athletes learn and perfect their sport skills, they should also be mindful of the cognitive, social, physical, and environmental changes that young people navigate from early childhood to late adolescence. For example, abstract thinking develops over time and physical maturation affects self-perceptions and motivated behaviours. Physical skills, mental skills, and sport strategies must be taught in developmentally appropriate ways, so practitioners must be knowledgeable about and consider their athletes' developmental stage to effectively bring about the benefits sport has to offer (Weiss, 1991). Developmental stages and corresponding approximate ages include: early childhood (3–6 years), middle childhood (7–9 years), late childhood (10–12 years), early adolescence (12–14 years), middle adolescence (15–17 years), and late adolescence (18–21 years) (e.g. Harter, 1999; Piaget, 1952). The ages listed should be interpreted as guidelines, as some athletes experience developmental changes earlier and others later than average.

The purpose of this chapter is to describe the developmental changes that children and adolescents experience so practitioners can be purposeful in teaching developmentally appropriate skills. In the next four sections, theoretical perspectives are used to describe developmental processes with supporting research from the sport domain. Then, practical recommendations are provided for delivering youth sport programmes while accounting for developmental issues. Youth sport professionals equipped with this information can ultimately maximise young athletes' enjoyment, skill learning, and performance in sport.

Cognitive development

Key cognitive developments during childhood and adolescence include transition from concrete to abstract thinking, expansion in the self-perception system, and change in conceptions of effort and ability (see Horn, 2004a, 2004b; Smith, Dorsch,

& Monsma, 2012; Weiss & Williams, 2004 for reviews). Piaget's (1952) stages of cognitive development signify a process whereby cognition becomes more sophisticated as children assimilate new experiences with what they know and reorganise cognitive structures to adapt new information. During early childhood the pre-operational stage is characterised by egocentric, concrete thought. For example, a team of 5-year-old soccer players follow the ball around the field instead of holding their positions because kicking the ball is a concrete task compared to the abstract idea of defending the goal. From 6 to 12 years old, concrete operational reasoning progresses and children learn to reason logically, but abstract thought is restricted to what they have experienced (e.g. reflecting on yesterday's practice) and hypothetical thinking is not yet developed (e.g. creating new sport strategies). Formal operational reasoning emerges during adolescence and is defined by the presence of abstract reasoning and monitoring thought processes (Horn, 2004b; Smith et al., 2012). In sport, abstract and hypothetical reasoning are important for creating long-term goals, visualising sport strategies in terms of 'what if' scenarios, and self-regulation of thoughts and emotions.

Harter (1999) explains developmental changes in the content, structure, and accuracy of the self-perception system throughout childhood and adolescence. Young people in early-to-middle childhood conceive of themselves in terms of concrete, observable skills and characteristics (e.g. I can run fast, I have a lot of friends), and they cannot yet integrate those abilities into an overall self-worth. Around 8 years old, children learn to differentiate their ability in various domains and determine which domains are important to them (e.g. physical, academic, social), which helps articulate a global self-evaluation (e.g. I like how my life is going). Although young children cannot verbalise a global self-worth, they may still exhibit behaviours characteristic of high self-esteem (e.g. curiosity) or low self-esteem (e.g. lack of initiative). Throughout adolescence, additional competence domains reflect the various roles and social contexts adolescents are exposed to and signify the start of recognising one's own complexity. Middle adolescents endure a period of confusion about this complexity while trying to figure out 'the real me'. For example, a high-school volleyball player who feels competent in her sport but incompetent in academic tasks may have difficulty accepting opposing views of herself. In late adolescence, however, these different 'selves' across contexts are accepted and even preferred (Horn, 2004a).

Nicholls' (1989) Achievement Goal Theory (AGT) considers change in conceptions of effort and ability with age. Adolescents understand that if Jen exerts less effort than Sam and performs just as well, Jen has greater ability than Sam. Children, however, cannot differentiate ability from effort (Smith et al., 2012; Weiss & Williams, 2004). For example, children aged 5 to 6 years display an undifferentiated view of ability where they believe greater effort indicates greater ability. During middle and late childhood (7 to 11 years old), young people develop a partially differentiated view of ability; they realise that differences in ability can explain unequal performances, but they still believe that more effort leads to higher ability. Around 12 years of age, or possibly not until 13–14, according to research in the physical domain (Fry & Duda, 1997), adolescents progress to a mature view of ability where they know that differing ability levels may limit the effect of effort on performance outcome. Thus, they are fully able to use norm-referenced cues to determine success and may readily adopt an ego goal orientation in which they define success by winning and outperforming others, as opposed to a task goal orientation in which success is defined by effort, learning, and improvement (see Chapter 8 for further information). It is possible for children with a partially differentiated view of ability to adopt an ego goal orientation, especially in competitive environments where social comparison and winning are emphasised. Young children with an undifferentiated view of ability may watch their peers, but their reason for watching others is to better master the task at hand rather than compare ability. An ego goal orientation is associated with maladaptive outcomes such as reductions in effort, perceived competence, and intrinsic motivation (Weiss & Williams, 2004). Thus, sport professionals must reinforce effort, improvement, and learning as keys to success to foster the motivational benefits of a task orientation throughout childhood and adolescence.

Social development

Important social changes include the increasing importance of peer acceptance and close friendships (see also Chapter 18), learning to take others' perspectives and express empathy, and using different social agents to inform ability beliefs (see Crocker, Hoar, McDonough, Kowalski, & Niefer, 2004; Horn, 2004a; Weiss & Stuntz, 2004 for reviews). Research on social development in sport has been informed by Sullivan's (1953) interpersonal theory, which explains the importance of peer relationships throughout childhood and adolescence. During early childhood, peer interactions simply include shared activities. Throughout middle-to-late childhood, children desire acceptance by a peer group to fulfil the need for belonging. Peer acceptance or social status continues to be important during adolescence, but close dyadic friendships become more important as a source of self-worth, security, and wellbeing. Close friendships help facilitate social development and may buffer the negative effects of any undesirable social experiences (Smith et al., 2012; Weiss & Stuntz, 2004). Greater feelings of peer acceptance and close friendship in youth sport are associated with positive self-perceptions, enjoyment, and persistence (e.g. Kipp & Weiss, 2013).

Piaget's (1952) work also addresses social development in the form of perspective-taking. As young people learn to think abstractly, they can imagine what it is like to be 'in someone else's shoes' and empathise. Peers are seen as an integral part of this process. For example, when peers disagree, discuss, and resolve conflicts, they are provided opportunities to learn others' points of view and problem-solve to find an agreeable solution (Weiss & Stuntz, 2004). Social development also impacts how athletes experience emotions (Crocker et al., 2004). For example, children can describe how they are feeling and observe the emotions of others in concrete terms, but they cannot yet anticipate how their actions affect others. As young people move through adolescence, the development of perspective-taking allows them to empathise with teammates and share emotional experiences, which is important for developing close, supportive friendships. They gain a better understanding of how their sport behaviours may affect others' emotions; for example, skipping practice may cause resentment from teammates.

According to Harter (1999) and subsequent work in the physical domain (Horn, 2004a; Horn & Amorose, 1998), changes in the structure of the self-system are accompanied by changes in sources of competence information (see also Chapter 9). Social development and cognitive development account for these changes, so they are both addressed here. During early childhood, children focus on concrete sources to determine their ability in sport, including simple task accomplishment (e.g. kicking a ball) and personal effort (e.g. 'I worked hard at practice so I know I'm good!'). Another source of competence information during early childhood is evaluative feedback from significant adults. Young children are not yet able to accurately self-evaluate their ability, so they take adult feedback at face value, which is most often enthusiastically positive. These sources of information lead to an overinflated view of sport ability at this stage. During middle-to-late childhood, young people integrate more sources of information; peers and coaches become important while parents become less important sources of feedback.

By the end of late childhood, children can compare feedback from significant adults to other sources of information, including peer comparison, performance outcome, and skill improvement. This allows children to become more accurate in their perceptions of sporting ability. During adolescence, several additional sources of information are added, including achievement of self-set goals, pre- and post-game feelings, and the ability to differentiate social sources from each other, including parents, spectators, coaches, and peers. The ability to integrate multiple social and self-evaluative sources of competence information leads to fairly accurate perceptions of ability during adolescence and is associated with higher levels of perceived and actual competence (Weiss & Amorose, 2005). It is important for practitioners to be aware of these changing reference points because the types of sources used affect the level and accuracy of young people's competence beliefs.

Physical development

The progression from childhood to adolescence is marked with numerous physical changes (including neurological changes, see Chapter 5) for boys and girls that may affect their psychosocial experiences and their behaviours (Malina, 2008). Puberty typically occurs between the ages of 9 and 14 years in girls and 11 and 16 years in boys. Pubertal status is associated with self-perceptions and other wellbeing outcomes. For example, physical self-perceptions increase for boys throughout the maturation process (e.g. Smith, 1999), but girls show decreased sport-specific and global self-perceptions and lower physical activity levels after puberty (e.g. Cumming, Shearer, Gammon, Standage, & Malina, 2012; Kipp & Weiss, 2013).

Pubertal timing relative to peers also makes a difference in young people's sporting experiences. For boys, early maturation (growth spurt before age 13) is linked with successful sport performance and heightened social status among peers. These boys are generally taller, heavier, stronger, and perform better on speed and power tasks than later-maturing boys (growth spurt after age 15). These strength and performance differences disappear by late adolescence. For girls, early maturation (menarche before 12 years old) is linked with decreased physical self-perceptions, lower self-esteem, and sport dropout (Horn, 2004a). Late-maturing girls (menarche at age 14 or later) tend to experience sport success and persist through adolescence. Scholars have suggested that the tendency for early-maturing girls to drop out of sport may be partially due to social influences (Horn, 2004a; Malina, 2008). For example, an early-maturing girl may experience a decline in sport-related support from coaches if they assume she is not good at sport because she 'looks unathletic' (i.e. looks too feminine).

Research comparing early- and late-maturers accentuates the effects of physical maturation on self-perceptions and sport experiences, but most young people fall between the extremes (e.g. are in the average or 'on time' category for pubertal development). Psychosocial and behavioural outcomes for 'average' youth fall in between the extremes and show considerable variability. To promote positive self-perceptions and subsequent motivated behaviours, sport psychologists, coaches, and parents should provide sport-related support to girls and boys throughout childhood and adolescence while being cognisant of the various messages that early-, average-, and late-maturing adolescents might be receiving regarding their 'athletic' status or ability.

Environmental changes

As young athletes transition to higher sport levels, the changing environment can affect their self-perceptions, motivation, and moral development (see Weiss, Smith, & Stuntz, 2008; Weiss & Williams, 2004 for reviews). At higher competition levels, the sport environment evokes increasing social comparison cues, such as making or not making the team, winning games, and being the best. The increased focus on norm-referenced criteria for success puts young athletes at risk for lower levels of perceived competence and in turn lower intrinsic motivation (Weiss & Williams, 2004). In many sports, social comparison is an unavoidable part of the social context, but when the context also includes significant others who emphasize effort and self-referenced criteria for success, athletes report higher self-perceptions and motivated behaviours (e.g. Kipp & Weiss, 2015).

The changing sport environment also plays a role in athletes' sportspersonship behaviours. Youth in higher competition levels report greater unsporting behaviour, likely due to (a) greater emphasis on winning, (b) the perception that coaches, parents, and peers condone unsporting behaviours, (c) positive reinforcement for using unsporting behaviours, and (d) observing role models using these behaviours (Weiss et al., 2008). For example, Smith's (1979) research has shown that youth athletes' perceptions of parents', peers', and coaches' approval of unsporting behaviour as well as the athletes' own unsporting behaviour increased with competitive level.

Theoretical perspectives related to moral development can also help explain changes in sportspersonship. Kohlberg's (1981) model of moral development outlines six stages that fall into three broader categories. Young people in early-to-middle childhood reason at the preconventional level where they look to possible consequences to determine whether an action is right or wrong. For example, a young hockey player may decide not to trip an opponent because she knows she will get penalised by the referee. Around 9 years of age through adolescence, athletes move into the conventional stage, which is characterised by rules and social norms. For example, a soccer player dribbling the ball toward the goal notices that an opponent is down, so he kicks the ball out of bounds. This behaviour is in line with a social norm that allows the injured player some time to get out of harm's way and get help if needed. Some adults reach the postconventional stage where moral decisions are made based on adherence to moral principles, not just rules and norms. Although adolescents can reason at conventional levels, some will regress to preconventional levels, shown by cheating or breaking rules if they believe they will not get caught. If significant others in the youth sport environment emphasise a win-at-all-cost mentality, young athletes are less likely to reason through dilemmas at the conventional level. Instead, they make decisions based on the consequences (e.g. Will I get caught? Will I win?). When coaches discuss potential moral dilemmas with athletes and emphasise fair play, youth athletes are more likely to reason at higher levels and behave in sportspersonlike ways (e.g. Weiss et al., 2008).

Bandura's (1986) social cognitive theory addresses the importance of social-contextual factors in influencing moral behaviour. Specifically, reinforcement, punishment, and modelling by significant others allow young people to internalise societal standards and norms. Youth sport research has shown that the influence of parents, coaches, and peers changes over time, in line with social developmental changes described above (Weiss et al., 2008). For example, Stuart and Ebbeck (1995) found that young people's perceptions that mothers', fathers', coaches', and teammates' disapproval of antisocial behaviours were related to players' disapproving themselves. All social sources emerged as important correlates of legitimacy beliefs, but the strongest source for younger players (ages 9–11) was mother disapproval and for older players (ages 12–13) was teammate disapproval. Weiss, Kipp, and Goodman (2015) found that early-to-middle adolescents' perception of teammate approval of an unsporting act was the strongest predictor of their own unsporting attitude, compared with coach and parent approval. Results reinforce the importance of peer influence during adolescence. Thus, the changing sport environment and athletes' cognitive and social development can affect their sporting behaviours.

Practical recommendations

Theory and research have allowed us to draw conclusions about developmental changes that occur through childhood and adolescence. It is therefore important that sport psychologists and other youth sport practitioners are cognisant of these progressions as they design programs and interact with athletes to ultimately provide developmentally appropriate activities. The following sections are organised by developmental stage and include a summary of key issues children and adolescents undergo with recommendations aimed at maximizing self-perceptions, motivation, enjoyment, sportspersonship, and overall success.

Early-to-middle childhood (5–10 years old)

Children learn best with concise, concrete cues and goals for mental and physical skills. For example, tell a gymnast to kiss her knees to learn a 'pike jump', and tell a soccer player to imagine the smell of the grass and see the goal fixture while visualising. Later in this stage children start to develop logical thought, but abstractions are restricted to what they have already experienced, for instance reflecting on an earlier performance. Young children cannot comprehend hypotheticals, such as new sport strategies or situations. Accordingly, practitioners' expectations should be consistent with athletes' developmental abilities (see Chapter 24 for further examples).

During the first half of this stage, children have very high perceived sport competence because they rely on simple task accomplishment, effort, and parents' feedback as evidence of their ability. Thus, practitioners should provide plenty of opportunities for participation, skill learning, and having fun. These optimistic youngsters are not concerned with who is better than whom; they just want to play, showing high intrinsic motivation. During the second half of this stage, peer and coach feedback become important sources of competence information, along with peer comparison and performance outcome. Therefore, perceived competence may decrease to a more realistic level, and in turn, intrinsic motivation may decrease. To optimise motivation, sport psychologists can help these children set short-term goals to promote small successes and enjoyment, and coaches can provide individualised feedback so children focus less on peer comparison. Further suggestions for enhancing motivation and competence are provided in Chapters 6, 8, and 9.

Halfway through this stage, children start to distinguish multiple domains of ability (physical competence, academic competence, social competence, physical appearance, behavioural conduct) and develop an overall sense of self-worth based on those five domains. Thus, young athletes' sport competence beliefs help to inform their overall self-esteem. This may be a critical period for practitioners to reinforce to athletes what they are good at and provide opportunities for success to increase young people's perceived sport competence and ultimately self-esteem. Sport-related encouragement and instructional feedback is especially important for 9–10-year-old girls showing signs of early physical maturation.

Late childhood to early adolescence (11–14 years old)

During this stage, youth athletes develop a fully differentiated view of effort and ability, further allowing them to compare their abilities to others as a source of competence information. Social comparison is inherent in many competitive sport settings (e.g. Who will win? Who will get the best score?), which may lead athletes to focus solely on winning to feel successful. Sport psychologists and other significant adults can remind young athletes that there are multiple ways to demonstrate success, such as achieving a personal best or giving 100 per cent effort. Pointing out multiple sources of competence information should help youth progress in their ability to integrate multiple sources of feedback moving into adolescence.

Given the importance of peer relationships, practitioners should provide opportunities for youth athletes to get to know their teammates and develop friendships through activities like partner drills, team outings, and positive peer reinforcement. Peer conflict is to be expected during this stage and can actually aid cognitive development by providing opportunities for perspective-taking, problem-solving, and conflict resolution. For example, a basketball player takes a game-winning shot and misses and his teammate accuses him of being a ball hog. Practitioners can step in to facilitate a discussion; each player shares his view about how the situation should have been handled, and they figure out a future plan of action. Thus, conflict can provide opportunities for youth athletes to understand differing viewpoints and work together to resolve issues.

Puberty is underway for most during this stage, which typically leads to increased self-perceptions for boys and decreased self-perceptions for girls. Early-maturing girls are at risk for low self-esteem and sport dropout; practitioners can play a critical role by providing encouragement and helping with goal-setting to promote persistence. Exceptional athletes may get 'moved up' during this time period to compete with youth athletes of similar physical size and ability, but practitioners must be careful because early adolescents may not be cognitively, socially, or emotionally ready to take on these challenges. In addition, players who dominate their peers in sport early on should be reminded that adolescents develop at different rates. Friends and teammates may catch up and even surpass their ability. If this happens, it is important that early sport stars know they have not lost ability, but that others are simply developing later and catching up. Sport psychologists should also keep in mind that performance slumps may well be due to physical maturation. For example, pubertal changes may cause a decrease in ability to execute a skill (e.g. a boy who had a fast growth spurt) or a decrease in motivation and effort (e.g. an early-maturing girl who is self-conscious about her body) (Weiss, 1991).

Middle-to-late adolescence (14–18 years old)

As competition level increases, coaches are pressured to win and may in turn convey that pressure to athletes. Pressure to win may lead adolescents to internalise unsporting behaviours from observation of coaches, teammates, and higher-level players. Sport psychologists can work with coaches, organisations, and athletes to structure the sport environment to promote moral development. For example, practitioners should reinforce the importance of fair play and praise athletes for good sporting behaviour to promote internalization of social norms and rules.

Environmental changes during adolescence should also be accompanied by an emphasis on learning, improvement, and effort (i.e. mastery motivational climate) to optimise self-perceptions, motivation, persistence, and performance. Sport psychologists can encourage athletes to set self-referenced goals and remind coaches to reinforce effort and improvement.

Cognitive development leads to a more complex view of the self at this stage. Perceptions of ability may differ from physical to academic to social domains, and this can be stressful as middle adolescents try to figure out who they are. Practitioners can remind athletes about their strengths and unique role on the team to reinforce their sense of self. Close friendships become an important source of self-esteem and motivation during adolescence. Opportunities for teammate bonding can enhance commitment and enjoyment in sport. Practitioners can facilitate ice-breaker activities, plan team meals, and urge teammates to congratulate each other.

Adolescents can think abstractly and integrate various sources of competence information. Youth sport professionals can encourage this group to self-evaluate their ability based on various cues, which can ultimately promote self-regulation to monitor and improve physical and mental skills on their own. Adolescents can create long-term goals, visualise sport strategies in terms of 'what if' scenarios, and reason through moral dilemmas. Youth sport practitioners can use opportunities for teachable moments in practices and games to help adolescents develop skills for success, such as goal-setting, problem-solving, and prosocial behaviours, which can be used as life skills in the future.

Conclusion

Cognitive, social, physical, and environmental changes from early childhood to late adolescence can influence young athletes' sport experiences. For example, abstract thought is developed, peers become a dominant social influence, physical maturation affects self-perceptions, and significant others often condone unsporting behaviour in the transition to higher competition levels. Being cognizant of these changes will allow practitioners to understand how an athlete's cognitive, social, or physical stage of development may be influencing their physical performance, comprehension of sport strategies, interactions with teammates, and self-regulation of thoughts and feelings. Ultimately, knowledgeable youth sport professionals can purposefully engage in best practices specific to the developmental stage they are working with to maximise youths' enjoyment, motivation, and success.

References

Bandura, A. (1986). *Social Foundations of Thought and Action: A Social Cognitive Theory*. Englewood Cliffs, NJ: Prentice-Hall.

Crocker, P. R. E., Hoar, S. D., McDonough, M. H., Kowalski, K. C., & Niefer, C. B. (2004). Emotional experience in youth sport. In M. R. Weiss (Ed.), *Developmental Sport and Exercise Psychology: A Lifespan Perspective* (pp. 197–221). Morgantown, WV: Fitness Information Technology.

Cumming, S. P., Sherar, L. B., Gammon, C., Standage, M., & Malina, R. M. (2012). Physical activity and physical self-concept in adolescence: A comparison of girls at the extremes of the biological maturation continuum. *Journal of Research on Adolescence, 22,* 746–757.

Fry, M. D., & Duda, J. L. (1997). A developmental examination of children's understanding of effort and ability in the physical and academic domains. *Research Quarterly for Exercise and Sport, 68,* 331–344.

Harter, S. (1999). *The Construction of the Self: A Developmental Perspective.* New York, NY: The Guilford Press.

Horn, T. S. (2004a). Developmental perspectives on self-perceptions in children and adolescents. In M. R. Weiss (Ed.), *Developmental Sport and Exercise Psychology: A Lifespan Perspective* (pp. 101–143). Morgantown, WV: Fitness Information Technology.

Horn, T. S. (2004b). Lifespan development in sport and exercise psychology: Theoretical perspectives. In M. R. Weiss (Ed.), *Developmental Sport and Exercise Psychology: A Lifespan Perspective* (pp. 27–71). Morgantown, WV: Fitness Information Technology.

Horn, T. S., & Amorose, A. J. (1998). Sources of competence information. In J. L. Duda (Ed.), *Advances in Sport and Exercise Psychology Measurement* (pp. 49–64). Morgantown, WV: Fitness Information Technology.

Kipp, L. E., & Weiss, M. R. (2013). Social influences, psychological need satisfaction, and well-being among female adolescent gymnasts. *Sport, Exercise, and Performance Psychology, 2,* 62–75.

Kipp, L. E., & Weiss, M. R. (2015). Social predictors of psychological need satisfaction and well-being among female adolescent gymnasts: A longitudinal analysis. *Sport, Exercise, and Performance Psychology, 4,* 153–169.

Kohlberg, L. (1981). *The Philosophy of Moral Development: Moral Stages and the Idea of Justice.* San Francisco, CA: Harper & Row.

Malina, R. M. (2008). Biocultural factors in developing physical activity levels. In S. J. H. Biddle & A. L. Smith (Eds.), *Youth Physical Activity and Sedentary Behaviour: Challenges and Solutions* (pp. 141–166). Champaign, IL: Human Kinetics.

Nicholls, J. G. (1989). *The Competitive Ethos and Democratic Education.* Cambridge, MA: Harvard University Press.

Piaget, J. (1952). *The Origins of Intelligence in Children.* New York, NY: International University Press.

Smith, A. L. (1999). Perceptions of peer relationships and physical activity participation in early adolescence. *Journal of Sport & Exercise Psychology, 21,* 329–350.

Smith, A. L., Dorsch, T. E., & Monsma, E. V. (2012). Developmentally informed measurement in sport and exercise psychology research. In G. Tenenbaum, R. C. Eklund, & A. Kamata (Eds.), *Measurement in Sport and Exercise Psychology* (pp. 131–141). Champaign, IL: Human Kinetics.

Smith, M. D. (1979). Towards an explanation of hockey violence: A reference-other approach. *Canadian Journal of Sociology, 4,* 105–124.

Stuart, M. E., & Ebbeck, V. (1995). The influence of perceived social approval on moral development in youth sport. *Pediatric Exercise Science, 7,* 270–280.

Sullivan, H. S. (1953). *The Interpersonal Theory of Psychiatry.* New York, NY: Norton.

Weiss, M. R. (1991). Psychological skill development in children and adolescents. *The Sport Psychologist, 5,* 335–354.

Weiss, M. R., & Amorose, A. J. (2005). Children's self-perceptions in the physical domain: Between- and within-age variability in level, accuracy, and sources of perceived competence. *Journal of Sport & Exercise Psychology, 27,* 226–244.

Weiss, M. R., Kipp, L. E., & Goodman, D. (2015). Unsportsmanlike play in youth ice hockey: Gender and age differences in attitudes and perceived social approval. *International Journal of Sport Psychology, 46,* 1–17.

Weiss, M. R., Smith, A. L., & Stuntz, C. P. (2008). Moral development in sport and physical activity: Theory, research, and intervention. In T. S. Horn (Ed.), *Advances in Sport Psychology* (3rd ed., pp. 187–210). Champaign, IL: Human Kinetics.

Weiss, M. R., & Stuntz, C. P. (2004). A little friendly competition: Peer relationships and psychosocial development in youth sport and physical contexts. In M. R. Weiss (Ed.), *Developmental Sport and Exercise Psychology: A Lifespan Perspective* (pp. 165–196). Morgantown, WV: Fitness Information Technology.

Weiss, M. R., & Williams, L. (2004). The *why* of youth sport involvement: A developmental perspective on motivational processes. In M. R. Weiss (Ed.), *Developmental Sport and Exercise Psychology: A Lifespan Perspective* (pp. 223–268). Morgantown, WV: Fitness Information Technology.

5

UNDERSTANDING AND ASSESSING YOUNG ATHLETES' PSYCHOLOGICAL NEEDS

Mark J. G. Holland, Sam J. Cooley, and Jennifer Cumming

Mental skills training (MST) is commonly considered the foundation of sport psychology for many athletes. It is often the first mode of psychological support introduced to athletes and the basis of many practitioners' work (see Chapters 2 and 25). Thus, the methods and processes of MST have received extensive attention from researchers. Although past MST research has predominantly focused on adult athletes, younger populations are receiving greater consideration. Nonetheless, there is limited literature addressing the nature of youth MST. Recognising the limitations in the currently available literature, and drawing on our applied experiences, in this chapter we present a conceptual model of MST for young athletes. Further, we address developmental considerations relevant to MST in youth populations, and discuss the process of undertaking a needs analysis to identify the areas to target within a training programme.

Mental skills training

Vealey (2007) defined MST as 'the learning and implementation of mental techniques that assist individuals in the development of mental skills to achieve performance success and well-being' (p. 288). This definition highlights the distinction between the mental skills (i.e. the capacity to regulate one's own cognitive, affective, and behavioural state) and mental techniques (i.e. the methods used to regulate one's mental state such as imagery, self-talk, goal-setting, routines, etc.) within the process of MST. Holland and colleagues (2010) also acknowledged the importance of considering mental qualities, that is, the desired mental state achieved through mental skills (e.g. high robust confidence, high-quality motivation, etc.).

These distinct components interact to provide the central mechanism underpinning MST; that is, using techniques to develop skills that in turn achieve desired mental qualities. For example, a desired mental quality for young athletes is a high and robust confidence. This quality requires the athlete to display the skill of developing and maintaining his or her own confidence, which is a form of self-regulation, a deliberate and effortful process to alter thoughts, feelings, and behaviours in the pursuit of desired outcomes (Baumeister, Heatherton, & Tice, 1994). To achieve such self-regulation of confidence in this example, techniques such as imagery or self-talk may be employed.

These three components (i.e. techniques, skills, and qualities) of the MST process have been the subject of extensive research among adult athletes (e.g. Gould, Dieffenbach, & Moffet, 2002; Hampson & Harwood, 2016; Williams & Cumming, 2015). Consequently, sport psychologists are aware of the broad set of mental techniques, skills, and qualities required by adult athletes to achieve and maintain elite performance. In contrast, more limited attention has been paid to understanding these aspects of MST among younger athletes. This is despite recognition that findings from adult athletes cannot be generalised to younger populations due to their stage of development and associated biological, psychological, and social differences (see Chapter 4). Therefore, providing youth with a traditional programme of MST based on research with adult athletes is clearly inappropriate. Within an applied context, sports psychologists need to consider the nature of the young athlete(s) and their environment as well as the desired outcomes of the intervention (see Figure 5.1).

Vealey (2007) noted that outcomes of MST in adult athletes include athletic performance and wellbeing. However, a broader range of outcomes may be appropriate for younger populations compared to adult populations. For instance, in a study of youth rugby players, Holland and colleagues (2010) found that athletes required a set of mental qualities distinct from those of adult athletes, including adaptability to various coaching and adult influences, the capacity to be a self-aware learner,

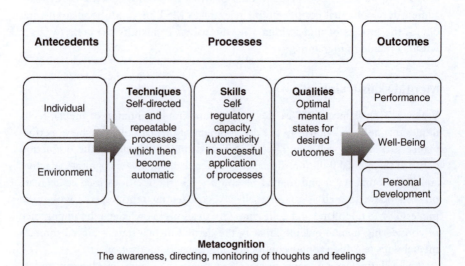

FIGURE 5.1 A conceptual process model of youth mental skills training

and the ability to take increasing responsibility for their own training and development. Although such qualities are undoubtedly important for adult athletes, their meaning and importance may not be equal due to differences in biological, psychological, and social demands on the development of the athlete. Additionally, both MST and broader positive youth development literature have argued that personal development is a valuable goal for youth MST (see Chapter 12; Lerner, Brentano, Dowling, & Anderson, 2002), and this again will likely differ from that required for adult athletes. Features of personal development that might be addressed include self-esteem, resilience, and group-work skills. Again, these qualities are fundamental to adult populations, but the nature of adolescence as a period of transition and development necessitates that these skills require greater consideration among young athletes.

To tailor the MST process to target specific outcomes we must understand the nature of the individual or group with whom we are working. In doing this, we must account for both individual and environmental factors. For instance, Duda, Cumming, and Balaguer (2005) highlighted the role of both individual and environmental factors when examining the development of MST and self-regulation. They identified environmental factors such as the social support network and motivational climate, which not only influence an athlete's use of mental techniques and skills but also their engagement in developmental programmes. Similarly, physical, cognitive, emotional, and social characteristics also influence young athletes' capabilities to effectively engage with, and understand, different elements of MST (see also Chapters 4 and 21). We also argue that to more fully understand how, and why, such characteristics influence young athletes' engagement with MST, consideration of the neurological processes of development that young athletes are experiencing is also needed.

Neurological processes of development

Adolescence (10 to 19 years old; Sawyer et al., 2012) is a transitional period from dependent child to independent adult that includes large neurological changes (Ahmed, Bittencourt-Hewitt, & Sebastian, 2015). Neuroimaging studies show structural and functional brain developments occur well into a person's twenties, and these changes contribute to many of the typical adolescent behaviours such as increased emotional reactivity and greater risk-taking (for a review, see Blakemore & Choudhury, 2006). For sport psychologists to more fully address the needs of young athletes, a greater understanding of these changes is needed so that interventions are developmentally appropriate (McCarthy, Jones, Harwood, & Olivier, 2010).

In brief, fine-tuning of the neural networks occurs over several years following puberty through synaptogenesis, an experience-dependent process whereby frequently used synaptic connections are strengthened and those used infrequently are pruned. The remaining circuits are more specialised and efficient, reducing the overall synaptic density of the brain to reach adult levels. Areas of the frontal lobe involved in higher-level cognitive activities, in particular executive function and social cognitive processing, are among the last to mature (Blakemore & Choudhury, 2006).

Executive function is our general capacity to control and coordinate thoughts, feelings, and behaviours, which includes goal-setting, problem-solving, holding a plan in mind, filtering out unimportant information, and other psychological skills fundamental to success in both sport and life. These processes are heavily related to those of self-regulation needed for mental skills. Executive function and self-regulation depend on three interrelated brain functions: working memory (i.e. keeping information in an active, quickly retrievable state and shielding this information from distraction), task-shifting (i.e. the mental flexibility to shift back and forth between multiple tasks or mental sets), and self-control (i.e. inhibition of dominant, automatic, or strong impulses) (Hofmann, Schmeichel, & Baddeley, 2012).

Working memory, task-shifting, and self-control improve throughout adolescence but coaches, parents, and other significant adults can help to promote this development through direct teaching and indirectly by acting as positive role models and by providing opportunities for young athletes to practise self-regulation (e.g. training and competition, overcoming adversity) (Gould et al., 2002). Indeed, the plasticity of adolescent brains can be viewed as a window of opportunity for the learning and development of self-regulation strategies (e.g. reappraisal of emotions, support-seeking) in youth athletes. As this age group is particularly vulnerable to emotional dysregulation and anxiety and stress-related disorders, any adaptive psychological skill development that occurs in sport may also help facilitate positive and long-term consequences for mental health and future regulatory capabilities (Ahmed et al., 2015; Wekerle, Wacchter, Leung, & Leonard, 2007).

Social cognition processes are important for effective interpersonal functioning and include skills related to successful communication such as emotion processing (e.g. deciphering my teammates' facial expressions after I make mistake) and the ability to take someone else's perspective (e.g. how my coach would feel if I did not turn up to practice) (Vetter, Leipold, Kliegel, Philips, & Altgassen, 2012). These skills enable us to understand and predict other people's behaviours and to adjust our behaviours accordingly (e.g. imaging the actions of an opposing player in response to my move).

Social cues also become much more salient during adolescence, which may explain why youth athletes become more strongly influenced by their peers, and are highly motivated by social rewards (Choudhury, Blakemore, & Charman, 2006). They may also be increasingly susceptible to social anxiety due to their heightened self-consciousness and preoccupation with other people's concerns about their thoughts, actions, and appearance. Surprisingly, however, little is known about the development of social cognitive processes in adolescence, and despite the implications for team cohesion and coach–athlete relationships, sport psychology interventions have mostly overlooked this developmental consideration.

Overall, due to the large neurological changes that occur during adolescence and early adulthood, this may be a key time during which we can maximise the benefits of MST. However, for such benefits to be realised it is critical that these changes are understood and accounted for by practitioners. Particularly, given the dynamic nature of adolescence and the importance of athletes' physical and social environment, a robust needs analysis with relevant stakeholders is warranted before developing any MST intervention

Understanding youth athlete needs

Models of applied sport psychology practice all recognise the importance of a needs analysis process for identifying both the individual and the environmental characteristics and needs of the target group (e.g. Visek, Harris, & Blom, 2009). Based on the aforementioned neurological process, the following sections address how sport psychologists might conduct a robust needs analysis.

Understand the purpose of a needs analysis

It is important to recognise that a needs analysis is often the first introduction to an MST programme. It should therefore support positive attitudes and future engagement towards a subsequent intervention. Too often the needs are assessed (or at least perceived to be assessed) in terms of weaknesses and inadequacies. In fact, the very label of 'needs analysis' may imply the hunt for deficiencies within the individual or group that need to be remedied. A positive psychology approach (see Seligman & Csikszentmihalyi, 2000) uses existing and desired strengths as a starting point rather than one's deficits. This encourages practitioners to empower stakeholders through a collaborative consultation to identify strengths, resources, and opportunities. The result, when compared to a deficit approach, is greater future buy-in and engagement, particularly in those who are initially more reluctant.

While adopting a strength-based approach, a needs analysis has a number of important purposes:

1) To build a supportive relationship and shared commitment between those involved.
2) To understand the goals of MST in terms of mental qualities and outcomes as well as how they relate to the athletes' stage of development.
3) To learn about the organisational and performance demands (psychological and physical) of the athletes.
4) To assess the social environment and support network around the athletes.
5) To consider the effective means of integrating MST into any existing athletic programme.

Account for athletes' experiences and knowledge across stages

Young adolescent athletes are progressing through different macro-stages of talent development over a relatively short period of time (Abbott & Collins, 2004;

Chapter 13). According to Côté's developmental model of sport participation (DMSP; Côté & Hay, 2002), those who decide to commit to sport will face their first significant career transition when moving from the initial sampling years (age 5–12 years), characterised by purposeful play and enjoyment, to the specialising years (age 13–16 years), during which deliberate practice and competition are increasingly emphasised. By the end of the specialising stage, young athletes will face the difficult decision of whether to increase their commitment to the pursuit of sporting excellence (i.e. transition to the investment years), focus on more recreational pursuits, or withdraw from sport altogether. Further, athletes will have encountered micro- and meso-stages throughout their development such as injury, selection processes, and changing coaches or clubs (Abbott & Collins, 2004). Although these transitions will be constrained to some extent by motor and physical factors as well as resources (Abbott & Collins, 2004), the underlying neurological changes described above will also contribute to young athletes' decisions to commit to, or withdraw from, sport, as well as their ability to cope with the stressors involved. Moreover, these transitions represent a major life event for the young athlete and occur at a point of great biological, social, emotional, and psychological change (see Chapters 4 and 13 for further details).

Sport psychologists need to be mindful that as the training and performance focus changes between and within developmental stages, so too will the psychological support needs of the athletes change (Abbott & Collins, 2004). Due to the idiosyncratic nature of how athletes progress, the needs analysis process is a necessary first step in helping the practitioner to achieve a better understanding of the psychological demands of a particular sport within a developmental stage for a particular athlete or groups of athletes. For example, in a study with elite 14–15-year-old rugby union players, Holland et al. (2010) identified 11 perceived qualities necessary for success in their sport. Some qualities, such as an appropriate attentional focus, confidence, and mental toughness, were similar to those acknowledged by adult counterparts (e.g. Gould et al., 2002). However, certain qualities were specific to the specialising stage, including the ability to adapt to new environments, becoming a self-aware learner, and taking responsibility for one's athletic development. Interestingly, these qualities are also reflective of the aforementioned development of executive function and self-regulation.

A related consideration is the possession of psychosocial skills and metacognitive strategies that facilitate successful navigation of a stage as well as the transition to the next one. The needs analysis process should therefore include some assessment of the young athlete's knowledge, skills, and attitudes (KSAs) towards the psychological aspects of their sport as well as different techniques. It is likely that cognitive development will impact upon a young athlete's ability to understand and implement different psychological techniques such as goal-setting, mental imagery, relaxation, and self-talk (Holland et al., 2010; McCarthy et al., 2010).

Taking mental imagery as an example, improvements in adolescents' ability to mentally perform a motor task coincide with known maturational changes in areas of the brain involved with the generation of internal models (i.e. parietal cortex) and cognitive control (i.e. prefrontal cortex) (Choudhury, Charman, Bird, & Blakemore, 2007). Moreover, young athletes have a less sophisticated understanding of how imagery can aid learning and performance compared to adults. For instance, McCarthy et al. (2010) found that athletes aged 10–15 years only identified three out of the five functions of imagery (i.e. cognitive general, motivational-specific, and motivational general-mastery) typically identified by older athletes. Such findings suggest the need for interventions to include an education component that helps young athletes to understand the where, when, what, why, and how to use the different techniques.

Integrate stakeholders' views

Another implication for the developmental differences in self-awareness and implicit knowledge of psychological skills is related to the depth and quality of data collected as part of the needs analysis process. When using psychometric assessments, such as the Test of Performance Strategies (TOPS; Thomas, Murphy, & Hardy, 1999), Woodcock and colleagues warned that scores may be influenced by misinterpretation or miscomprehension of the items resulting in problems such as ceiling effects (Woodcock, Duda, Cumming, Sharp, & Holland, 2012). They suggested providing athletes with simplified explanations of terms with the potential to cause confusion as well as to ensure that questionnaire administrators are available to provide clarification and guidance as needed.

To overcome such issues with psychometric tests and young athletes' awareness, it is also important to gather the views of other key stakeholders in the young athletes' development who can confirm as well as elaborate on areas of psychological strengths and weaknesses. Woodcock, Holland, Duda, & Cumming (2011) interviewed coaches, parents, and sport administrators connected to the rugby union players in Holland et al.'s (2010) study. The adults discussed the majority of psychological qualities identified by the players but also highlighted further ideas that helped to clarify the qualities necessary for rugby success. For example, under the theme of Game Sense, coaches added that players need to be problem solvers who are able to adapt and overcome challenges faced in game situations, and parents contributed to the Mental Toughness sub-theme by emphasising the need for players to deal with the psychological demands of injury.

However, highlighting the potential for conflicting views between stakeholders, parents also emphasised the need for players to maintain a balanced lifestyle and pursue multiple activities in addition to rugby, which was not identified by other stakeholders. By including more than one perspective in the needs analysis process, sport psychologists can identify the potential for mixed messages being received by the young athletes and better understand the social environment in which they participate. Furthermore, the inclusion of stakeholders encourages their commitment and support of the programme by demonstrating their role and value.

Adopt various approaches to identify athletes' needs

A robust needs analysis with young athletes and their stakeholders will likely require a range of approaches to gain insight from each party. Being flexible in these approaches enables the athlete and stakeholders to provide information in a way that is most accessible and comfortable to them, aligned with their developmental stage, and gives a voice to those who may not have engaged if only one particular approach was used.

Dialogue

A common method of gathering information is via formal and informal meetings between the parties involved. Dialogues are able to address all the aims of the needs analysis. When formal, such a meeting should be facilitated in a way where all parties contribute on an equal footing. It is important that all parties recognise it as an opportunity to gain knowledge from each other, rather than for the sport psychologist or coach to impart their knowledge. Allowing the athlete to contribute freely without concern of evaluation from coach or parents is crucial for it to be effective and ethical. It is important to recognise the value of such interactions not only to gain an understanding of the athletes but also for stakeholders to learn about, and build effective working relationships with, the sport psychologist.

When discussing the goals and content of MST, the facilitator may benefit from strategies such as motivational interviewing (Miller & Rollnick, 1991). Rather than the practitioner explaining to the athlete(s) why and how they are going to develop their mental skills, motivational interviewing involves asking questions in a way that helps the athlete to think differently about their mental skills and consider what is important to them. This increases the likelihood of the athlete adopting an intrinsically motivated view of the resulting intervention. In our experience, this approach is likely to be particularly beneficial when stakeholders have no experience of MST, hold biases towards psychological support, or feel MST is being done to them rather than with them.

Questionnaires

Questionnaires can be an efficient way to gain understanding of the athletes, particularly when delivering MST to large numbers. Alongside gathering important demographic information (e.g. age, experience, exposure to sport psychology), multiple scales can be used to measure the athletes' preferred styles for receiving information, socio-environmental factors, and existing mental skills and qualities. However, as previously mentioned, young athletes may have a limited capacity to complete questionnaires. This is due to the process of completing questionnaires, which involves understanding the language used, correctly interpreting the meaning of sentences, retrieving information from memory, and responding appropriately (Tourangeau, Rips, & Rasinki, 2000). Younger athletes with limited comprehension or metacognitive capacity are unlikely to be able to complete the questionnaires as accurately as more developed athletes.

In some cases these concerns may result in questionnaires being an inappropriate tool. However, certain strategies may enable practitioners to overcome these issues without serious reduction in the validity or reliability of the measures. For example:

- Reading questionnaire items aloud to facilitate athletes' understanding.
- Providing explanations for particular words or phrases.
- Offering brief education to support athletes' understanding of certain concepts (e.g. when assessing mental technique use, clarifying a process of effective goal-setting might prevent over-estimation of one's current practices).
- Recalling specific and concrete scenarios upon which athletes can draw (perhaps with video analysis to support recall if available).
- Providing graphical and/or absolute values for response criteria (including pictures or videos of what a particular response may look like).

In addition, presenting measures in ways that will engage young athletes is crucial and likely to include evolving technologies.

Performance profiles

Performance profiling is an autonomy-supportive technique encouraging athletes and stakeholders to identify the mental skills and qualities that are meaningful to their desired outcomes (see Weston, Greenlees, & Thelwell, 2013). Once a list has been established, each skill/quality is defined by the athletes in order to facilitate a shared understanding of the concepts. Typically, an athlete may then rate their current and desired standards for each concept. These scores combined with the importance of quality can provide a discrepancy score. A larger discrepancy score indicates a quality in which improvement may bring about the most meaningful change.

Performance profiling enables athletes to identify their areas of strength and weakness, which can inform their personal goals during MST. Similar to the effects of motivational interviewing, it is the athlete who identifies their own goals and is therefore more intrinsically motivated to achieve them. Performance profiling is very adaptable and the precise process should suit the target audience. For example, younger athletes may benefit from a simplified version in which only their current standard (if they are able to appraise it) is measured. Also, gaining parents' perspective on the mental qualities is likely to provide a broader view of the young athlete within home, school, and social contexts. Within performance profiles, parents may identify psychological qualities but are unlikely to be required to provide any scoring.

Indirect methods

Less formal methods of establishing athletes' needs are also useful, particularly if an athlete or stakeholder is difficult to engage (possibly due to age, ability, or commitment). Informal approaches typically use an activity that is fun as a vehicle to starting a dialogue. For example, one activity we have found to be particularly effective with young athletes is the Future Selves Poster. This activity involves providing athletes with a diverse selection of magazines and asking them to create a poster using drawings or cut outs to reflect how they would like to see themselves in the future (i.e. their 'Good Lives'; see Ward, 2002). This process can be used to prompt discussions about future goals and the mental skills required to reach them.

Immersion

Immersion is a fundamental approach for all parties involved in planning MST. The sport psychologist should spend time immersing themself in the environment of the athlete and/or stakeholder. Likewise, the athlete and stakeholder(s) may immerse themselves in MST, either by observing an MST programme taking place in another context or by experiencing an MST 'taster'. This process enables parties to gain first-hand experience of the systems and cultures one another operates in, providing vital information on which to build a new MST programme. For example, through immersion within the athletes' athletic context the sport psychologist may become aware of specific opportunities or previously unknown barriers (e.g. resources, athlete preferences, etc.). This shared understanding will also help to build trust and rapport, a central component of a successful MST programme.

Reflection

Facilitated reflection is another technique that can be used by all parties involved in the needs analysis. The athlete and/or stakeholders could be guided to reflect on their past experiences of MST or their intuitive use of mental techniques with their sport. Similarly, sport psychologists might reflect on previous MST experience with the athletes to gain a greater understanding of the intervention process and enable meaningful adaptations. The objectives of this reflection should be to improve our understanding of strengths and weaknesses, areas for improvement, and underlying values (Park & Son, 2011), which may inform the design and delivery of MST.

Conclusion

For a sport psychology programme to be meaningful and engaging for youth athletes, we posit that a thorough analysis of athletes' needs, including appropriate stakeholders, is required. Establishing meaningful goals and intervention strategies requires a suitable understanding of the specific individual or group. In seeking to gain this understanding, practitioners must ensure that their analysis of athletes' needs accounts for the neurological, physical, and social changes that young athletes are experiencing. In accounting for these factors, practitioners should also understand that as the athlete and their surrounding develops (athletically and personally), assessment of athlete needs should be revised and changes incorporated within the ongoing programme of work. By ensuring that a needs analysis is broad in its audience and flexible in its methods, we believe practitioners will be best positioned to tailor a programme to the needs of the target population.

References

Abbott, A., & Collins, D. (2004). Eliminating the dichotomy between theory and practice in talent identification and development: Considering the role of psychology. *Journal of Sports Sciences, 22*, 395–408.

Ahmed, S. P., Bittencourt-Hewitt, A., & Sebastian, C. L. (2015). Neurocognitive bases of emotion regulation development in adolescence. *Developmental Cognitive Neurosicence, 15*, 11–25.

Baumeister, R. F., Heatherton, T. F., & Tice, D. M. (1994). *Losing Control: How and Why People Fail at Self-Regulation*. San Diego, CA: Academic.

Blakemore, S., & Choudhury, S. (2006). Development of the adolescent brain: Implications for executive function and social cognition. *Journal of Child Psychology and Psychiatry, 47*, 296–312.

Choudhury, S., Charman, T., Bird, V., & Blakemore, S. J. (2007). Development of action representation during adolescence. *Neuropsychologia, 45*, 255–262.

Choudhury, S., Blakemore, S. J., & Charman, T. (2006). Social cognitive development during adolescence. *Social Cognitive and Affective Neuroscience, 1*, 165–174.

Côté, J., & Hay, J. (2002). Children's involvement in sport: A developmental perspective. In J. M. Silva & D. Stevens (Eds.), *Psychological Foundations of Sport* (pp. 484–502). Boston, MA: Merrill.

Duda, J. L., Cumming, J., & Balaguer, I. (2005). Enhancing athletes' self regulation, task involvement and self determination via psychological skills training. In D. Hackfort, J. Duda, & R. Lidor (Eds.), *Handbook of Research in Applied Sport and Exercise Psychology: International Perspectives* (pp. 143–165). Morgantown, WV: FIT.

Gould, D., Dieffenbach, K., & Moffett, A. (2002). Psychological characteristics and their development in Olympic champions. *Journal of Applied Sport Psychology, 14*, 172–204.

Hampson, R., & Harwood, C. (2016). Case Study 2: Employing a group goal setting intervention within an elite sport setting. *Sport & Exercise Psychology Review, 12*, 22–31.

Hofmann, W., Schmeichel, B. J., & Baddeley, A. D. (2012). Executive functions and self-regulation. *Trends in Cognitive Science, 16*, 174–180.

Holland, M. J. G., Woodcock, C., Cumming, J., & Duda, J. L. (2010). Mental qualities and employed mental techniques of young elite team sport athletes. *Journal of Clinical Sport Psychology, 4*, 19–38.

Lerner, R. M., Brentano, C., Dowling, E. M., & Anderson, P. M. (2002). Positive youth development: Thriving as the basis of personhood and civil society. *New Directions for Youth Development, 95*, 11–33.

McCarthy, P. J., Jones, M. V., Harwood, C. G., & Olivier, S. (2010). What do young athletes implicitly understand about psychological skills? *Journal of Clinical Sport Psychology, 4*, 158–172.

Miller, W. R., & Rollnick, S. (1991) *Motivational Interviewing: Preparing People to Change Addictive Behavior*. New York, NY: Guilford Press.

Park, J. Y., & Son, J. (2011). Expression and connection: The integration of the reflective learning process and the writing process into social network sites. *Journal of Online Learning and Teaching, 7*, 170–178.

Sawyer, S. M., Afifi, R. A., Bearinger, L. H., Blakemore, S., Dick, B., Ezeh, A. C., & Patton, G. C. (2012). Adolescence: A foundation for future health. *The Lancet, 379*, 1630–1640.

Seligman, M. E. P., & Csikszentmihalyi, M. (2000). Positive psychology: An introduction. *American Psychologist, 55*, 5–14.

Thomas, P. R., Murphy, S. M., & Hardy, L. (1999). Test of performance strategies: Development and preliminary validation of a comprehensive measure of athletes' psychological skills. *Journal of Sports Sciences, 17*, 697–711.

Tourangeau, R., Rips, L. J., & Rasinski, K. (2000). *The Psychology of Survey Response.* Cambridge, UK: Cambridge University Press.

Vealey, R. (2007). Mental skills training in sport. In G. Tenenbaum & R. Eklund (Eds.), *Handbook of Sport Psychology* (3rd ed., pp. 287–309). Chichester, UK: John Wiley and Sons.

Vetter, N. C., Leipold, K., Kliegel, M., Philips, L. H., & Altgassen, M. (2012). Ongoing development of social cognition in adolescence. *Child Neuropsychology, 19*, 615–629.

Visek, A. J., Harris, B. S., & Blom, L. C. (2009). Doing sport psychology: A youth sport consulting model for practitioners. *The Sport Psychologist, 23*, 271–291.

Ward, T. (2002). Good lives and the rehabilitation of offenders: Promises and problems. *Aggression and Violent Behavior, 7*(5), 513–528.

Wekerle, C., Waechter, R. L., Leung, E., & Leonard, M. (2007). Adolescence: A window of opportunity for positive change in mental health. *First Peoples Child Family Review, 3*, 8–16.

Weston, N., Greenlees, I., & Thelwell, R. (2013). A review of Butler and Hardy's (1992) performance profiling procedure within sport. *International Review of Sport and Exercise Psychology, 6*, 1–21.

Williams, S. E., & Cumming, J. (2015). Athlete imagery ability: A predictor of confidence and anxiety intensity and direction. *International Journal of Sport & Exercise Psychology, 14*, 268–280.

Woodcock, C., Duda, J. L., Cumming, J., Sharp, L. A., & Holland, M. J. (2012). Assessing mental skill and technique use in applied interventions: Recognizing and minimizing threats to the psychometric properties of the TOPS. *The Sport Psychologist, 26*, 1–15.

Woodcock, C., Holland, M. J. G., Duda, J. L., & Cumming, J. (2011). Psychological qualities of adolescent rugby players: Parent, coaches, and sport administration staff perceptions and supporting roles. *The Sport Psychologist, 25*, 411–443.

SECTION II

Key considerations during childhood

6

INITIATING INVOLVEMENT AND BUILDING FOUNDATIONS FOR THE FUTURE

Sampling, physical literacy, and intrinsic motivation

Richard J. Keegan and Camilla J. Knight

Clare is the mother of two young active children, Daniel aged six and Bryony aged eight. Clare is keen for her children to have enjoyable sporting experiences and perhaps reach a high level, if they have the ability and interest. However, as she starts to investigate options for her children, she is overwhelmed by the different programmes on offer, and becomes increasingly confused by the conflicting messages she is confronted with regarding the best way in which to introduce Daniel and Bryony to sport. Based on her own experiences, Clare thinks it might be best to introduce her children to lots of different sports so they can learn as many skills as possible and then choose one sport they like the best. However, lots of Clare's friends have registered their children for only one or two sports. Coaches have told her friends that if they want their children to be chosen for representative teams, selected for elite academies, or eventually reach an elite level in sport, they need to demonstrate their commitment to a select programme and focus all their efforts on one sport. They argue that children who commit early to one sport will develop the sport-specific skills needed to excel and children involved in multiple sports will lag behind and miss out on team selections. Clare does not want to disadvantage her children so, despite her initial intentions, she decides to choose one sport for each of her children to focus on – tennis for Bryony and football for Daniel. However, after a year or so, Daniel starts to lose interest in football and does not want to start any other sports because he does not think he'll be good enough. Clare is worried she made the wrong decision.

Although Clare's story is fictitious, we both frequently find ourselves engaged in conversations with parents, coaches, and sports organisations regarding the best ways to introduce children to sport and encourage both long-term participation and elite performance. For many, there is a perception that, from an early age, a distinction needs to be made between children who are going to commit to reaching an elite level in sport and those who are 'just' going to participate for long-term fun and enjoyment (see Chapter 7 and 11 for further discussion). However, based on available literature, in this chapter we will examine why all children, whether they are seeking to become active, adult exercisers or Olympians, can benefit from opportunities to sample a range of sports and develop their physical literacy.

The chapter will first introduce the importance of rethinking sport specialisation. From this basis, we explore the concepts of physical literacy and intrinsic motivation, both of which are closely aligned to the aims of the sampling career stage. We then begin to explore the ways that parents and coaches can support the development of these two attributes in children as they experience the sampling stage, and the likely role of a sport psychologist in this process. Practical tips are offered to help psychologists assist parents and coaches in creating the optimal experience – whether it be in creating a future champion or a lifelong love of active living.

Developmental stages of sport participation

There are several models depicting athletic career progression, each of which describes expected stages and implications for the experiences and demands on young athletes (see Chapter 13). In particular, the models developed by Bloom (1985), Côté and Hay (2002), and Wylleman and Lavallee (2004) are widely supported by research with elite athletes. In each of these models, the early years of a child's sporting involvement should be characterised by engagement in numerous sports and physical activities. In this initial stage, the emphasis should be on children having fun, developing their physical competencies, and learning specific sport skills through purposeful play activities (Côté & Hay, 2002; Wylleman & Lavallee, 2004). From this base, children's pathways may diverge; some children may decide that they want to continue playing lots of different sports, while others might decide that they want to specialise in one or two sports (Côté, Baker, & Abernethy, 2007).

However, as illustrated in Clare's case, in our experience, some parents are being encouraged to skip this sampling phase and instead encourage their children to specialise in one or two sports from the outset. Such early specialisation is not supported by scientific evidence and in fact may lead to fragility with regard to sport participation (e.g. Baker, Cobley, & Fraser-Thomas, 2009; Committee on Sports Medicine and Fitness, 2000; Malina, 2010). For example, if an athlete only trains at one sport and does not 'make it', then they may not feel suited to any other sports. Further, early specialisation has been linked to increased injury risk, as children may not have experienced movements outside the normal range for that sport, as well as increased psychological stress, burnout, and earlier dropout from sport (cf. Jayanthi, Pinkham, Dugas, Patrick, & LaBella, 2013).

Given the issues associated with early specialisation, this chapter argues that an important role of sport psychology and sport science practitioners is to help parents, coaches, and sports organisations understand why such an approach may not be the most appropriate. Moreover, specifically, we (and many others; see for example Chapter 11) propose that practitioners can play an important role in helping others to understand the benefits associated with sampling numerous sports and, more specifically, the value of developing physical literacy.

Physical literacy

The concept of physical literacy, which has made appearances in the literature for over 100 years, was more recently advocated by Margaret Whitehead in 2001, and has since spawned a large number of practical interventions and programmes (see Keegan, Keegan, Daley, Ordway, & Edward, 2013). Central to Whitehead's work was the idea that moving and interacting with the environment is a critical challenge faced by humans across history: a fundamental and existential problem that defines human experience.

Frequently defined as the motivation, confidence, physical competence, understanding, and knowledge to maintain physical activity at an individually appropriate level, throughout life, the core attributes of physical literacy (Whitehead, 2001, 2010) are as follows:

- In a wide range of physically challenging situations (dance, sport, music, art and crafts, self-expression, day-to-day travel), the physically literate person will move with poise and grace, with economy of movement, and with confidence.
- In physically challenging situations, the physically literate person will be able to read the situation, predict, and/or anticipate what is likely to happen next as the situation unfolds, and then be able to react through movement in an appropriate manner.
- The physically literate person has the knowledge, skills, attitude, and motivation to fully use their capacity and potential for movement.
- The skills developed by a physically literate person will be appropriate to their local culture, and be based on the limits to their movement potential or their ability or physical disability.
- The physically literate person will have a well-established sense of their physical self: that they feel 'at home' in their body, and comfortable with their physicality (see also Chapter 9).
- The physically literate person will have a high level of self-confidence and self-esteem that comes from confidence in their body and its abilities.

Recent work by the Australian Sports Commission (ASC, 2017) has further defined physical literacy through four defining statements:

1) *Core* – Physical literacy is lifelong holistic learning acquired and applied in movement and physical activity contexts.
2) *Components* – Physical literacy reflects ongoing changes integrating physical, affective, cognitive, and social capabilities.
3) *Importance* – Physical literacy is vital in helping us lead healthy and fulfilling lives through movement and physical activity.

4) *Aim/aspiration* – A physically literate person is able to draw on their integrated physical, affective, cognitive, and social capacities to support health-promoting and fulfilling movement and physical activity – relative to their situation and context – throughout their lifespan.

This approach distinguishes between the inherent potential that every person has to develop physical literacy and the aspirational level we seek to promote; wherein individuals are sufficiently empowered and enabled to manage, develop, and benefit from physical activity and movement throughout life.

Drawing on the above definitions, it is apparent that if all children are encouraged to become 'physically literate' – empowered to manage and drive their own unique journeys through physical activity and to learn about the world through physical means – more children and subsequently more adults will be capable and better adapted to negotiate the physical, emotional, social, and mental challenges that are encountered in life. Moreover, children (and adults) will have the opportunity to gain the range of physical and mental health benefits associated with engagement in frequent and plentiful physical activity (e.g. Eime, Young, Harvey, Charity, & Payne, 2013; Janssen & LeBlanc, 2010). In contrast, if we focus on early sport specialisation rather than physical literacy, children's physical skill development may be restricted to specific sports (see also Chapter 11), their identity development may be limited (see Chapter 14 for further information), and they may burn out (Jayanthi et al., 2013; Malina, 2010). Consequently, if these children 'fail' (e.g. do not reach an elite level in their sport), which the vast majority will, we may have condemned them to a lifetime of sedentariness or the absence of fulfilment through movement pursuits (Baker et al., 2009; Malina, 2010).

However, for children and adults to obtain the positive outcomes associated with physical literacy, it is important to ensure that physical literacy is understood and developed in its entirety. Physical literacy comprises integration across four domains: physical, affective, cognitive, and social (ASC, 2017). Much of the existing work on physical literacy appears to have overlooked this integration, seeming to focus almost exclusively on physical skills and fitness. Although these physical skills are undeniably important, the concept of physical literacy was originally offered with a view to positioning physical development as inseparably entwined with affective, cognitive, and social development. Remaining mindful of this consideration has important implications for how sport psychology practitioners might support the development of physical literacy. Particularly, understanding the relationship between physical literacy and motivation is likely to be beneficial for practitioners.

Physical literacy and motivation

In private conversations and conference presentations, some key protagonists in this area recognise that physical literacy depends heavily on the motivation to choose and persist with physically meaningful pursuits throughout one's life. In popular parlance, motivation is often characterised as simply desire, effort, energy, and determination, which has led some to argue that motivation can be inferred from behavioural indices (e.g. attention, effort, and behaviour choice) (e.g. Atkinson & Birch, 1970). Deci and Ryan (1985), however, posited that motivation should concern the 'why' question in behaviour. In this interpretation, motivation refers to the reasons behind behaviour (or absence of a behaviour). For instance, are behaviours intrinsically or externally motivated? When considering physical literacy, the ideas of intrinsic motivation depicted within Deci and Ryan's Self-Determination Theory are thought to be particularly important.

Self-Determination Theory

Deci and Ryan's (1985; 2000) Self-Determination Theory (SDT) has been a dominant approach to studying motivation for over 30 years, making several important contributions to the study of motivation. A thorough review of SDT is beyond the scope of this chapter, with further details provided in Chapter 8. However, there are a few important considerations with regards to the links with physical literacy.

Firstly, SDT provides researchers with a conceptualisation of 'good', 'bad', and 'non-existent' motivation – in the forms of intrinsic regulation, extrinsic regulation, and amotivation, respectively. SDT also posits several levels in between (Ryan & Deci, 2000) and these aspects of SDT are explicitly derived from Organismic Integration Theory (OIT – Deci & Ryan, 1985). Within Organismic Integration Theory, intrinsic motivation can be defined as the impetus to perform an activity for its own sake – for the pleasure and satisfaction inherent in participating in a task (Deci & Ryan, 1985). That is, an activity is performed when no external inducement is required (or perceived). On the other hand, extrinsic motivation (or more specifically, external regulation) refers to engaging in an activity as a means to an end and not for its own sake (Ryan & Deci, 2007). Behaviours that are more intrinsically motivated will continue even after the 'ends' associated with them are achieved (e.g. children continuing to be 'physically active' even after training sessions have finished). Intrinsically motivated behaviours will also produce experiential rewards such as enjoyment and pleasure (Deci & Ryan, 1985), resulting in improved longer-term outcomes. Given such outcomes, fostering children's intrinsic motivation to be physically active seems to be a core component of successfully developing physically literacy.

Secondly, SDT offers a mechanism/model of the ways in which motivation can be influenced. To increase the likelihood of individuals being intrinsically motivated to participate in activities, SDT posits that the three needs of competence, relatedness, and autonomy need to be fulfilled. Competence represents 'a need to feel effective in dealing with and mastering one's environment' (Markland & Vansteenkiste, 2008; p. 91). Relatedness refers to 'a concern about connections with others and the quality of our interpersonal relationships' (Allen & Hodge, 2006, p. 268), while autonomy refers to the degree to which athletes 'engage in the activity for their own valued reasons and feel that they have freely chosen to be involved'

(Allen & Hodge, 2006, p. 267). When children find themselves in social contexts that provide opportunities to satisfy these three basic needs, their motivation, performance, and development are likely to be maximised (Deci, Vallerand, Pelletier, & Ryan, 1991). As such, attending to these needs to enhance children's intrinsic motivation may be a key strategy for supporting the development of physical literacy.

Encouraging sport sampling and developing physical literacy in practice

Drawing on the four domains of physical literacy, and particularly the central role of motivation in physical literacy, the following section comprises a range of practical recommendations to help practitioners work to encourage parents, coaches, and organisations to focus on the development of physical literacy in the sampling years of a child's life.

Promoting the whole child

Firstly and most simply, every interaction with coaches, parents, and organisations should be promoting a message of developing the whole child, rather than focusing solely on physical development to achieve an elite level in sport. Evidence indicates that coaches who have explicitly sought to develop better people, not just winners, are often the same coaches that get the best results in competition (e.g. Gould, Collins, Lauer, & Chung, 2007; Chapter 12). Such findings could be taken to reinforce the physical literacy notion that if you want to reach a high peak of the mountain of your physical skills, you need to have a solid foundation of emotional, mental, and social skills too. For example, how many times do coaches assert that under-performance is not caused by lack of skill or fitness, but some other lapse such as anger, fear, loss of concentration, poor communication, etc.? By developing the 'whole child' through a focus on physical literacy, coaches can ensure that such cognitive and affective elements are also addressed.

As an example of promoting integrated 'whole child' learning, the ASC (2017) physical literacy resources use a 'building blocks' metaphor, inspired by chemistry's periodic table. The model allows the practitioner, parent, coach, teacher, or child to build representations of task requirements and/or the child's current capabilities (and then compare them), drawing on all four domains: physical, affective, cognitive, and social. Even seemingly simply tasks such as learning to pass in an invasion game can draw from all four areas. Physical skills might include locomotion and object manipulation, whereas fitness elements may pertain to cardiovascular fitness. Affective elements might include expression – to communicate more effectively – the management of fatigue, and (hopefully) enjoyment. Cognitive elements might include strategy (planning and problem-solving), tactics (implementation and execution), and following rules. From the social domain, there are many considerations around how we interact with others, manage risks, and respond to ethical issues such as cheating and foul play.

Fostering autonomy in physical activity settings

There are numerous well-established and well-researched ways of promoting intrinsic motivation, and the internalisation of motivation for tasks (reviewed by Keegan, Spray, Harwood, & Lavallee, 2011). For example – perhaps predictably – offering choices has been shown to promote feelings of autonomy. However, the nature of the choices is also important, such that if the choice is between two highly undesirable tasks, no real autonomy is being offered or experienced (cf. Moller, Deci, & Ryan, 2006). Providing explanations and rationales, rather than requiring unquestioning compliance, has also been shown to support autonomy, even when no actual choices are offered (e.g. Deci, Eghrari, Patrick, & Leone, 1994). Recognising the importance of providing rationales and choice, in a recent study in Melbourne (Australia), coaches and teachers were encouraged to connect activities to the intended whole child learning outcomes (rationale), and seek the children's opinions regarding which activities to undertake and which sports to learn (choice) (Keegan, Telford, Olive, Keegan, & Telford, 2017). However, in doing this, it became apparent that there were occasions when children did not realise they had such a choice of sports and physical activities. As such, practitioners can play an important role in facilitating feelings of autonomy by taking time to create awareness of different activities and foster links to local clubs and organisations where even quite unconventional activities could be learned and practised (cf. Keegan et al., 2017).

In a similar vein, attempting to use informational language, as opposed to controlling language, is also linked to facilitating perceptions of autonomy (e.g. Assor, Roth, & Deci, 2004). Even acknowledging and accepting a child's negative emotions when they do not like a task or activity (as opposed to ignoring or punishing them) has been suggested to enhance autonomy (Reeve & Jang, 2006). Wherever possible, of course, the aim of promoting autonomy is to nurture the child's inner motivational resources – rather than seeking compliance – so that they become increasingly capable of self-motivating towards sport, movement challenges, and recreational physical activity.

Developing perceptions of physical competence

Developing a child's competence, and perceptions of competence, has also been well researched and readily aligned to concepts in physical literacy. For example, offering tasks that provide optimal challenge – wherein the level of task is 'optimal' as opposed to too difficult or too easy – is one of the core predictors of enjoyment, engagement, and feelings of competence (Csikszentmihalyi, Rathunde, & Whalen, 1993). Providing positive and constructive feedback regarding competence is also beneficial, whereas negative feedback usually undermines feelings of competence (Vallerand & Reid, 1984). Likewise, offering tasks that have clear goals and structure, as well as support in pursuing those goals, is also important (Taylor & Ntoumanis, 2007).

Hence, in the study described above by Keegan and colleagues (2017), teachers and children were encouraged to adopt multiple and very varied indicators of success, which were personalised and sometimes even chosen by the individual, and to engage frequently in diverse activities. This had the effect of ensuring there was never one child who was 'always the best', as the tasks changed frequently, and around the ages of 8 to 10 very few children had become adept at multiple activities, so they reported that they were 'always learning', which supported perceptions of competence. Likewise, of course, while not everybody can win each activity, the adoption of multiple criteria enabled each child to feel they had achieved something, and improved, even if they lost the game. Repeating games and frequently rebalancing/mixing teams ensured that the same children never won or lost too often, but instead had to learn to work with new teammates (promoting the learning of social skills and problem-solving).

Finally, environments that are explicitly tolerant of mistakes and failure and do not punish them have been linked to improved feelings of competence in children (Clifford, 1990). Games can be designed to gloss over mistakes and allow time for multiple games, and de-emphasising scoring can also ensure that mistakes are less of a punishment and simply part of the experience. One teacher in the above-described study (Keegan et al., 2017) reported adapting scoring systems to reinforce different attributes, such as positive communication, inclusion (e.g. of weaker players), or even just fairly arbitrarily resetting the scores at the flip of a coin. In these cases, fun and learning were emphasised over the score and the fear of mistakes or losing. This latter consideration is, perhaps, much easier to incorporate when simply pursuing a broad notion of physical literacy as opposed to high-stakes competition, which is often inherent to early specialisation in sport.

Facilitating a sense of relatedness across contexts

Finally, while there are many potential approaches to promoting relatedness, it is important to define whom the relatedness is between. Is it between child and parent, child and coach, child and peer/colleague, or child and a particular group/team, wherein belonging would become a consideration? For the main part, wherever a child perceives a strong social bond – beyond mere involvement, such that the 'other' knows and accepts 'the real me', then perceptions of relatedness should be increased (Deci & Ryan, 1995). One teacher in Keegan and colleagues' (2017) study reported unexpected benefits of running the physical activity sessions required by the experiment. Children initially tried to stick with their close friends, who they sit with all the time, and she felt this was undermining both classroom teaching and physical education classes. During the physical activity sessions she began requiring children to mix with new peers, and to interact with a more diverse range of classmates in solving problems together through physical games and sport. Unexpectedly, when they returned to the classroom they were also more likely to mix – unprompted – and speak to new friends during maths and literacy sessions. This enabled her to arrange groups that were better matched to challenge each other (and less likely to distract each other!). The opportunities provided by physical activity and sport for frequent mixing, social interaction, and group membership are often undervalued – but to a large extent we simply need to permit them to happen and not be constrained by the strict forming of enduring teams, 'houses', or ability groups.

Conclusion

This chapter set out to provide answers to the question: how can emphasising physical literacy complement, amplify, and enhance the positive outcomes associated with optimal motivation in sport, physical activity, and movement challenges? First, physical literacy emphasises developing the whole person to become a happy, healthy, and well-adjusted adult, by building a person's capability across physical, affective, cognitive, and social domains. Every single person exists with a physical body, so can accumulate some kind of physical literacy. However, when someone reaches the stage where they are empowered to adapt to almost any life challenge and yet still engage in health-promoting and fulfilling physical activity, we might call them physically literate. To reach such a level, children must have been able to engage in a wide variety of physical pursuits – which might be called 'late specialisation' or even 'multi-specialisation' – developing peaks of capability and expertise across several contexts and tasks. To encourage such development, children should have been able to engage in these pursuits in ways that promote their own learning, motivation, and development, so that they are empowered and neither obliged nor addicted to participating in sport/physical activity. By drawing on the strategies identified above, it is hoped that sport psychology practitioners, coaches, and parents can work together to create environments in which physical literacy is encouraged and facilitated in all children.

References

Allen, J. B., & Hodge, K. (2006). Fostering a learning environment: Coaches and the motivational climate. *International Journal of Sport Science and Coaching, 1*, 260–277.

ASC (2017). *Physical Literacy: What Does It Mean for Me?* (1st ed.). Canberra, Australia: Australian Sports Commission.

Assor, A., Roth, G., & Deci, E. L. (2004). The emotional cost of parents' conditional regard: A self-determination theory analysis. *Journal of Personality, 72*, 47–88.

Atkinson, J., & Birch, D. (1970). *The Dynamics of Action*. Chichester, UK: John Wiley & Sons.

Baker, J., Cobley, S., & Fraser-Thomas, J. (2009). What do we know about early sport specialization? Not much! *High Ability Studies, 20*, 77–89.

Bloom, B. S. (1985). *Developing Talent in Young People*. New York, NY: Ballantine.

Clifford, M. M. (1990). Students need challenge, not easy success. *Educational Leadership, 48*, 22–26.

Committee on Sports Medicine and Fitness (2000). Intensive training and sports specialization in young athletes. *Pediatrics, 106*, 154–157.

Côté, J., Baker, J., & Abernethy, B. (2007). Practice and play in the development of sport expertise. In G. Tenenbaum & R. C. Eklund (Eds.), *Handbook of Sport Psychology* (pp. 184–202). Hoboken, NJ: Wiley.

Côté, J., & Hay, J. (2002). Children's involvement in sport: A developmental perspective. In J. M. Silva & D. E. Stevens (Eds.), *Psychological Foundations of Sport* (pp. 484–502). Boston, MA: Allyn & Bacon.

Csikszentmihalyi, M., Rathunde, K., & Whalen, S. (1993). *Talented Teenagers: The Roots of Success and Failure*. New York, NY: Cambridge University Press.

Deci, E. L., Eghrari, H., Patrick, B. C., & Leone, D. R. (1994). Facilitating internalization: The self-determination theory perspective. *Journal of Personality*, *62*, 119–142.

Deci, E. L., & Ryan, R. M. (1985). *Intrinsic Motivation and Self-determination in Human Behavior*. New York, NY: Plenum.

Deci, E. L., & Ryan, R. M. (1995). Human autonomy: The basis for true self-esteem. In M. Kernos (Ed.), *Efficacy, Agency and Self-Esteem* (pp. 31–49). New York, NY: Plenum.

Deci, E. L., & Ryan, R. M. (2000). The 'what' and 'why' of goal pursuits: Human needs and the self-determination of behavior. *Psychological Enquiry*, *11*, 227–268.

Deci, E. L., Vallerand, R. J., Pelletier, L. G., & Ryan, R. M. (1991). Motivation and education: The self-determination perspective. *The Educational Psychologist*, *26*, 325–346.

Eime, R. M., Young, J. A., Harvey, J. T., Charity, M. J., & Payne, W. R. (2013). A systematic review of the psychological and social benefits of participation in sport for children and adolescents: Informing development of a conceptual model of health through sport. *International Journal of Behavioral Nutrition and Physical Activity*, *10*, 98–129.

Gould, D., Collins, K., Lauer, L., & Chung, Y. (2007). Coaching life skills through football: A study of award winning high school coaches. *Journal of Applied Sport Psychology*, *19*, 16–37.

Janssen, I., & LeBlanc, A. G. (2010). Systematic review of the health benefits of physical activity and fitness in school-aged children and youth. *International Journal of Behavioral Nutrition and Physical Activity*, *7*, 40–56.

Jayanthi, N., Pinkham, C., Dugas, L., Patrick, B., & LaBella, C. (2013). Sports specialization in young athletes: Evidence-based recommendations. *Sports Health: A Multidisciplinary Approach*, *5*, 251–257.

Keegan, R. J., Keegan, S. L., Daley, S., Ordway, C., & Edwards, A. (2013). *Getting Australia Moving: Establishing a Physically Literate & Active Nation (GAME PLAN)*. Canberra, Australia: University of Canberra Press.

Keegan, R., Spray, C., Harwood, C., & Lavallee, D. (2011). From 'motivational climate' to 'motivational atmosphere': A review of research examining the social and environmental influences on athlete motivation in sport. In B. D. Geranto (Ed.), *Sport Psychology* (pp. 1–52). Hauppauge, NY: Nova Science.

Keegan, R. J., Telford, R. M., Olive, L., Keegan, S. L., & Telford, R. D. (2017). A qualitative process evaluation of a Physical Literacy Facilitator Program in urban-metropolitan primary school settings. Manuscript submitted for publication.

Malina, R. M. (2010). Early sport specialization: Roots, effectiveness, risks. *Current Sports Medicine Reports*, *9*, 364–371.

Markland, D., & Vansteenkiste, M. (2008). Self-determination theory and motivational interviewing in exercise. In M. S. Hagger & N. L. D. Chatzisarantis (Eds.), *Intrinsic Motivation and Self-Determination in Exercise and Sport* (pp. 87–100). Champaign, IL: Human Kinetics.

Moller, A. C., Deci, E. L., & Ryan, R. M. (2006). Choice and ego-depletion: The moderating role of autonomy. *Personality and Social Psychology Bulletin*, *32*, 1024–1036.

Reeve, J., & Jang, H. (2006). What teachers say and do to support students' autonomy during learning activities. *Journal of Educational Psychology*, *98*, 209–218.

Ryan, R. M., & Deci, E. L. (2000). Self-determination theory and the facilitation of intrinsic motivation, social development, and well-being. *American Psychologist*, *55*, 68–78.

Ryan, R. M., & Deci, E. L. (2007). Active human nature: Self-determination theory and the promotion and maintenance of sport, exercise, and health. In M. S. Hagger & N. L. D. Chatzisarantis (Eds.), *Intrinsic Motivation and Self-Determination in Exercise and Sport* (pp. 1–19). Champaign, IL: Human Kinetics.

Taylor, I., & Ntoumanis, N. (2007). Teacher motivational strategies and student self-determination in physical education. *Journal of Educational Psychology*, *99*, 747–760.

Vallerand, R. J., & Reid, G. (1984). On the causal effects of perceived competence on intrinsic motivation: A test of cognitive evaluation theory. *Journal of Sport Psychology*, *6*, 94–102.

Whitehead, M. (2001). The concept of physical literacy. *European Journal of Physical Education*, 6, 127–138.

Whitehead, M. (2010). *Physical Literacy: Throughout the Lifecourse*. Abingdon, UK: Routledge.

Wylleman, P., & Lavallee D. (2004). A developmental perspective on transitions faced by athletes. In M. Weiss (Ed.), *Developmental Sport and Exercise Psychology: A Lifespan Perspective* (pp. 507–527). Morgantown, WV: Fitness Information Technology.

7

INTEGRATING FUN IN YOUNG ATHLETES' SPORT EXPERIENCES

Amanda J. Visek, Heather Mannix, Devon Mann, and Ciera Jones

A mass of research literature clearly establishes early positive sport experiences as the foundation to ensure continued sport participation, whereas negative and uninspiring experiences push children to drop out (e.g. Bailey, Hillman, Arent, & Petitpas, 2013). Over the years, many factors have been the focus of children's participation retention and attrition. The Sport Commitment Model (Scanlan, Carpenter, Schmidt, Simons, & Keeler, 1993), however, was the first to identify sport enjoyment, among other factors including involvement opportunities, personal investments, social constraints, and involvement alternatives as determinants of whether children choose to continue playing sport or drop out. Of the five determinants, sport enjoyment was and continues to be the strongest predictor of sport commitment (Chairat, Naruepon, Li, & Harmer, 2009; Iñigo, Podlog, & Hall, 2015; Scanlan et al., 1993). This means that if young athletes enjoy playing, they are more likely to be intrinsically motivated (see Chapters 6 and 8) to continue their involvement in sport.

Interestingly, 'enjoyment' has been the dominant term in the sport science literature used to describe children's positive experiences. However, children more commonly use the colloquial word 'fun' when recounting and describing their experiences (Bengoechea, Strean, & Williams, 2004). For instance, when children are asked why they continue playing, fun is the number one cited reason (Eitzen & Sage, 2009; Petlichkoff, 1992; Scanlan et al., 1993). Alternatively, when asked why they dropped out, it is because it was not fun anymore. Scanlan and Simons (1992) maintain that enjoyment is a broader and more inclusive term that encompasses fun. Still, according to dictionaries, fun is synonymous with enjoyment and both terms are used interchangeably. Therefore, more contemporary scientific efforts have focused on incorporating the child's voice and thus use the word fun.

The need for evidence-based applications of fun at every level of children's athletics has never been greater than now. For example, according to Sports and Fitness

Industry Association (2013) data (as cited by Aspen Institute Sports & Society, 2015), there is a significant decline among 6–12 year olds' overall sport participation and attrition from team sports is higher than ever. For these reasons, the purpose of this chapter is to bridge established theoretical frameworks and science with recommended applied practices for promoting the most fun possible within sport. First, we provide the scientific basis for what fun is in youth sports today. Second, using a global sport framework we illustrate how immediate fun experiences, amassed over time, are essential to children's sport performance, personal development, and enduring sport participation. Third, we offer practical suggestions for purposefully incorporating fun that are appropriate for every level of youth sport.

Towards an understanding of fun

Fun is largely considered a self-described, emotively driven experience. We know when we are having fun and we certainly know when we are not. But, what makes sport participation fun for children? A recent study engaged hundreds of young athletes, parents, and coaches to identify the relative importance of all things that make playing sports fun for children ages 8–19 years. This resulted in what are known as the FUN MAPS, a series of 360-degree data-driven blueprints, conceptualised entirely by youth sport stakeholders. The FUN MAPS are the basis of the fun integration theory (Visek et al., 2015a).

Fun integration theory

According to the fun integration theory (Visek et al., 2015a; 2017), fun is the accumulation of immediate experiences derived from contextual, internal, social, and external sources of fun-determinants. Fun-determinants are specific, actionable behaviours for fostering fun, of which the fun integration theory identifies 81, organised within 11 interrelated fun-factors (see Table 7.1).

Contextually, within physical activity settings, there are specific determinants of *Games* and *Practices* that contribute to children's fun. Examples of the fun-determinants within these two fun-factors include, but are not limited to, *getting playing time* and *well-organised practices*. Internal sources of fun, however, are derived from *Trying Hard*, *Learning and Improving*, and *Mental Bonuses*, which are fostered from determinants such as *trying your best*, *being challenged to improve*, and *keeping a positive attitude*. Socially, fun is derived from *Positive Team Dynamics*, *Team Friendships*, and *Team Rituals* that include fun-determinants such as *supporting and getting along with teammates* and *high-fiving*. External sources of fun include *Positive Coaching*, *Game Time Support*, and *Swag*. *Positive Coaching* includes, but is not limited to, *being a positive role model* that gives *clear, consistent communication*. *Encouraging behaviour* by parents and spectators, along with *consistent calls by referees* are some of the fun-determinants of *Game Time Support*. More superfluous things, such as *sports equipment*, are an example of *Swag*.

The fun-determinants encapsulate major concepts and specific constructs of well-established models and theories used to understand children's participation motives,

TABLE 7.1 Fun-determinants

One thing that makes playing sports fun for players is…

Trying Hard
- Trying your best
- Working hard
- Exercising and being active
- Getting/staying in shape
- Playing well during a game
- Being strong and confident
- Competing
- Making a good play (scoring, big save, etc.)
- Setting and achieving goals
- Playing hard

Positive Team Dynamics
- Playing well together as a team
- Supporting my teammates
- When players show good sportspersonship
- Being supported by my teammates
- Getting help from teammates
- Warming up and stretching as a team

Learning and Improving
- Being challenged to improve/get better
- Learning from mistakes
- Improving athletic skills to play at the next level
- Ball touches (dribbling, passing, shooting, etc.)
- Learning new skills
- Using a skill learned in practice during a game
- Playing different positions
- Going to sports camp
- Copying moves and tricks of pro athletes

Games
- Getting playing time
- Playing your favourite position
- Playing against an evenly matched team
- Being known by others for your sport skills
- Playing on a nice field
- Playing in tournaments

Mental Bonuses
- Keeping a positive attitude
- Winning
- It relieves stress
- Ignoring the score

Game Time Support
- A ref who makes consistent calls
- Parents showing good sportspersonship (encouraging)
- Being congratulated for playing well
- Having people cheer at the game
- Having your parent(s) watch your games
- Getting complimented by other parents

Team Rituals
- Showing team spirit with gear, ribbons, signs, etc.
- High-fiving, fist-bumping, hugging
- End-of-season/team parties

Positive Coaching
- When a coach treats players with respect
- A coach who knows a lot about the sport
- Having a coach who is a positive role model
- When a coach encourages the team
- Clear, consistent communication from coach
- A coach who listens and considers players' opinions
- A coach who allows mistakes, while staying positive
- A coach who you can talk to easily
- A nice, friendly coach
- Getting compliments from coaches
- When a coach participates during practice
- When a coach jokes around

Practice
- Having well-organised practices
- Taking water breaks during practice
- Having the freedom to play creatively
- Doing lots of different drills/activities in practice
- Scrimmaging during practice
- Partner and small group drills
- Practicing with specialty trainers/coaches

Team Friendships
- Getting along with your teammates
- Being around your friends
- Having a group of friends outside of school
- Hanging with teammates outside practice, games
- Being part of the same team year after year
- Meeting new people
- Talking and goofing off with teammates

- Going out to eat as a team
- Doing team rituals
- Carpooling with teammates to practices/games
- Doing a cool team cheer

Swag
- Having nice sports gear and equipment
- Earning medals or trophies
- Travelling to new places to play
- Wearing a special, cool uniform
- Eating snacks/treats after the game
- Staying in hotels for games/tournaments
- Getting pictures taken

Note: The 11 fun-factors (bolded) and the 81 fun-determinants (bulleted) beneath each fun-factor are listed in order of importance from highest to lowest.
Source: Adapted from Visek et al., 2015b.

predict their sport behaviour, and cultivate positive, healthy sport experiences (Visek et al., 2015). For example, 24 of the 81 fun-determinants relate to achievement goal theory (e.g. Nicholls, 1989; see Chapter 8) and 32 fun-determinants link with competence motivation theory (e.g. Harter, 1978; see Chapter 9). Likewise, as many as 68 of the 81 fun-determinants promote autonomy, competence, and social relatedness, which underpin the self-determination theory of motivation (e.g. Deci & Ryan, 1985; see Chapter 6). To provide for children's fun needs, the determinants can be applied to practice and game plans, set standards for sideline behaviour, inform coach education, as well as establish league policies (Visek et al., 2015a).

Debunking myths about fun

The fun integration theory categorically discredits commonly held ideas about fun that warrant addressing. For example, having fun is frequently thought of loosely as simply laughing about and goofing around, and thus often seen as incompatible with high-level sport. However, the notion that fun is just a casual good time minimises the significance it plays in the experiences of young athletes. In fact, data from US Olympic athletes underscores the significance of fun in sustaining young athletes' early sport participation and also sporting excellence. Specifically, when asked to rate the importance of 12 potential motives for their early sport participation, fun was ranked fourth by Olympians from the 2000–2012 Games and second among those from the 1984–1998 Games (Snyder, 2014). When asked to rate the level of influence these same factors had on their motivation to pursue excellence in their sport, fun again ranked near the top. For these Olympians, fun sport experiences early in their young athletic careers significantly influenced their desire to play and solidified their commitment to strive for distinction at sport's highest level. Thus, fun is clearly not a mutually exclusive experience apart from athletic development.

Remarkably, when we conduct educational workshops teaching parents and coaches ways to integrate fun into sport, they grasp the multivariable nature of fun when presented with the fun integration theory and the FUN MAPS. However, as soon as the FUN MAPS (see Visek et al., 2015a) and the associated inventory of fun-factors and determinants (Table 7.1; Visek et al., 2015b) are no longer displayed in front of them, both parents and coaches often revert to their original, default concept of fun as a one-dimensional, vaguely defined emotive experience. Consequently, transforming adults' schema for fun is an unusually challenging process requiring thoughtful and intentional effort at many different levels within organised sport.

One way that has helped us to do this is to associate strong action verbs and nouns of the fun-determinants with the word 'fun' in very explicit ways. For instance, fun is synonymous with *learning, effort, knowledge, improving,* and so on. Statements like 'Our players value knowledgeable coaches that help them have fun by learning and improving' underscore the value of knowledgeable coaching when engaging volunteer coaches to attend coaching education. Similarly, reminding teammates that the game is more fun when they do things *together* by *helping each other* is an informative and encouraging way to use positive team dynamics to promote fun for young athletes among one another. Interestingly, it is common for organisations to purport that they provide sport programmes that are fun, or maintain that fun is the foundation on which their programmes are built. However, no systematic approach is used to ensure that children are having fun. In these cases, we recommend that youth sport organisations shape the overall sport culture by using the fun integration theory to establish and reinforce positive sport norms and create developmentally appropriate programmes for young athletes.

To more fully integrate fun within a sport culture, it is important to address long-held perceptions of fun. For example, fun is commonly believed to be a function of gender, in which social determinants of fun are thought to be of upmost importance to girls, whereas for boys task- and mastery-focused determinants are considered more important. What young athletes consider fun is also thought to change over time, implying their fun needs are a function of age and maturation. Additionally, recreational programmes are often touted as where children go to 'have fun' and competitive, select 'elite' programmes are where they go to improve, perhaps even at the expense of having fun. However, a recent study (Visek et al., 2015b; 2017) assessing group differences among young athletes found that, regardless of a young athlete's age (younger vs. older), gender (girls vs. boys), or sports programme (recreational vs. travel), *Trying Hard*, *Positive Team Dynamics*, and *Positive Coaching* were reported as the fun-factors of chief importance (see Table 7.2 for a list of the 11 fun-factors that athletes collectively rank, from most to least important).

This is not to say that group differences do not exist or that fostering the fun-determinants requires the same approach for every team or individual athlete. Generally speaking, though, Visek and colleagues' (2015b, 2017) findings illustrate that what one athlete considers the most fun is also the most fun for another. Future studies are needed to further assess group differences among young athletes related

TABLE 7.2 Fun-factors ranked by importance

Primary Importance
　　1. Trying Hard
　　2. Positive Team Dynamics
　　3. Positive Coaching
Secondary Importance
　　4. Learning and Improving
　　5. Games
　　6. Practices
　　7. Team Friendships
　　8. Mental Bonuses
　　9. Game Time Support
Tertiary Importance
　　10. Team Rituals
　　11. Swag

Source: Visek et al., 2015b.

to their prioritisation of the fun-factors. However, based on the evidence to date, providing developmentally appropriate opportunities to promote the determinants of the fun-factors identified as of primary importance in Table 7.2 is likely the most efficient and constructive means to foster fun for any young athlete.

Physical literacy the key to fun

Successful sport programmes of any kind ensure two key components for children: (a) they are having fun, and (b) their physical activity programming is grounded in fundamental movement principles (e.g. agility, balance, coordination) fostering physical literacy (Garcia, Garcia, Floyd, & Lawson, 2002; see Chapter 6). At the core of physical literacy is the development of a child's movement vocabulary and physical movement competence, as well as the confidence and pleasure derived from participation (Cairney, Bedard, Dudley, & Kriellaars, 2016; see Chapter 6). Although physical competence and confidence are said to be the gateway to active participation, high-quality, immediate fun experiences act as the bridge to sustaining athletes' participation over time. Whether they choose an inclusive recreational sport route or a selective elite pathway (Visek et al., 2017), the cultivation of physical competencies and overall physical literacy are key to fun (e.g. see the fun-determinants of *Trying Hard*, *Learning and Improving*, and *Positive Coaching* in Table 7.1; Visek et al., 2015b).

In fact, physical competence and confidence, built on a fun and challenging pathway, equip children for failures and successes. For example, young athletes have identified fun-determinants such as *being challenged to improve at my sport* and *learning from mistakes* amongst others as highly important. However, to build children's confidence, determinants such as *a coach who allows mistakes while staying positive*, *being supported*, and *supporting my teammates* highlight the importance of creating a safe and encouraging environment. Therefore, providing children of all abilities with learning opportunities in an environment that is psychologically safe is critical to athletic development (see Chapter 22 for details). This type of sport culture promotes fun as a result of being challenged, while removing the fear of making mistakes. Providing opportunities to fully develop young athletes' competence, across a variety of movement skills, in a healthy, fun environment builds confidence and leads to an increased desire to continue playing.

A personal assets approach to fun

Adapted from the positive youth development (PYD) literature, the Personal Assets Framework (PAF) of sport (Côté, Turnnidge, & Vierimaa, 2016) proposes a global approach for cultivating improved *performance*, sustained *participation*, and *personal development* (the 3P's). Known as the long-term developmental benefits of participation, the 3P's are contingent upon structuring programmes around the development of children's personal assets known as the 4C's: *competence*, *confidence*, *connection*, and *character* (see Chapter 12 for further information). In other words, when there is commitment to the promotion of a young athlete's physical competence and confidence, within a social setting that provides opportunities to develop close connections

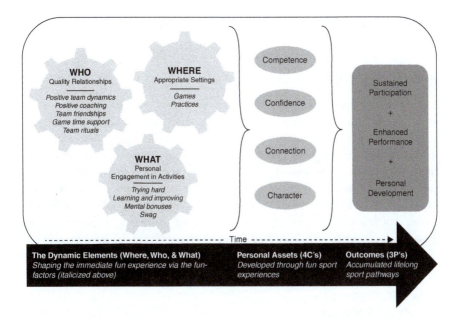

FIGURE 7.1 An integrative applied approach to the PAF for sport, towards the development of personal assets and positive outcomes via fun
Source: Adapted from Côté et al., 2016.

between peers and adults, while also creating situations that build character, there are resulting improvements in the 3P's (Côté & Hancock, 2014). Therefore, the promotion of a young athlete's 4C's is dependent on consistent accumulation of independent, positive, fun exposures via practices, games, and team gatherings that provide opportunities to create *quality relationships*, during activities that are *personally engaging* within *appropriate settings* (i.e. the PAF's dynamic elements).

Figure 7.1 illustrates an adapted, temporal approach that utilises the fun integration theory as a 'how to' catalyst for integrating the PAF for sport's dynamic elements, thereby translating science into practice. Specifically, the fun integration theory complements the PAF for sport's global framework by using the fun-factors and associated determinants to identify the 'who', 'what', and 'where' required to create sport environments that foster personal engagement (e.g. *Trying Hard, Learning and Improving*), quality relationships (e.g. *Positive Team Dynamics, Positive Coaching*), and appropriate settings (e.g. *Practices, Games*). Subsequently, repeated exposure to fun enhances the development of a young athlete's 4C's, in turn positively influencing the 3P's (Côté et al., 2016).

Fostering the dynamic elements of fun

Fun can be cultivated in many different and creative ways, as evidenced by the robustness of the fun integration theory. In this section, we first briefly describe the significance of the dynamic elements towards fostering fun and conclude with specific applied practices that can be used to establish fun youth sport norms for young athletes.

Personal engagement in activities

During early sport participation (sampling years; ages 6–12) children are encouraged to participate in diverse physical activities rather than specialise in one activity (Côté et al., 2016; see Chapters 6 and 11). During this time, play is more impactful than deliberate practice, especially if practice comprises drills in which children spend considerable time waiting in line for their turn. Instead, by 'thinking small' we can involve young athletes simultaneously to make practice more personally engaging and fun for everyone. For example, *well-organised practices* that provide young athletes with learning opportunities through a variety of *partner and small group activities*, particularly those mimicking cooperative and competitive play, keep children active and get them a greater number of *touches on the ball*, a critical component of personal engagement in practice and play activities.

Quality relationships

Quality relationships act as a significant driving force socially for fun (Visek et al., 2015). Coaches (Santi, Brunton, Pietrantoni, & Mellalieu, 2014; see Chapter 19), along with parents (Fredricks & Eccles, 2004; see Chapter 10), siblings, peers (see Chapter 18), and friends are social influencers uniquely positioned to impact a child's experience. As such, these individuals have an obligation to create positive experiences where they can (Bailey et al., 2013). This is achievable via fun-factors such as *Positive Coaching, Game Time Support, Positive Team Dynamics, Team Rituals*, and *Team Friendships*. When children trust, respect, and value the relationships fostered with their coaches, teammates, and parents, they can have fun while taking risks, being creative and innovative, and succeeding and failing, especially in psychologically safe settings that challenge them to improve, yet embrace their mistakes as opportunities to learn and grow.

Appropriate settings

The fun integration theory identifies specific determinants of practice and game settings that facilitate fun (e.g. *well-organised practices, partner and small group drills, playing a well-matched team*). Of note, practice and games settings are ultimately the by-product of adult planning and preparation. Therefore, parents and coaches must focus efforts towards creating fun, child-centred, physical and social environments that foster quality relationships and promote personal engagement for every child.

Tables 7.3 and 7.4 include a collection of successful suggestions for fostering fun social and physical environments based on our applied experiences, as well as those shared with us during parent- and coach-education workshops. These tips and activities target specific fun-factors and determinants for encouraging a young

TABLE 7.3 Select suggestions for fostering a fun social environment

Peer Relationships	Coach–Athlete	Parent–Athlete	Individual
Positive Team Dynamics	**Positive Coaching**	**Game Time Support**	**Positive Team Dynamics**
Team Rituals	**Learning and Improving**		**Team Friendships**
• Tip: Incorporate team-building activities at the beginning of the season to establish social relationships and create team cohesion built on respect.	• Tip: During small-sided games, pull an athlete aside that is having difficulty performing a specific skill for quick individualised instruction while the others continue to play. After a few tips and practice repetitions, encourage the athlete to join the play again. Avoid stopping everyone to address one athlete. If several of them are making the same mistake, briefly stop the activity, demonstrate the incorrect and correct way of performing the skill, then allow play to resume.	• Tip: Require that spectating behaviour at youth sporting events mimics that of other types of youth performances or shows (e.g. positive cheering). This includes refraining from yelling at athletes, coaches, or referees. Keep things in perspective by remembering the difficulty involved in performing well in front of an audience, especially one that is not kind and supportive.	• Activity: Create a 'family-like' atmosphere among teammates to foster a sense of belonging by placing them in small groups to warm up, stretch, and do practice activities together. Switch up the groups every few weeks. Emphasise the importance of encouraging and supporting family members. Praise these behaviours often.
• Activity: At the first practice, have athletes say two things they enjoy doing outside of the sport they are playing. This team-building exercise gives athletes the chance to discover common interests among one another.			
Team Friendships	**Mental Bonuses**	**Mental Bonuses**	**Trying Hard**
			Learning and Improving
• Tip: Declare the playing surface a 'Positive Play Zone' where acceptance of all abilities and cooperative behaviours boosting confidence and motivation are the norm; negative behaviours (e.g. teasing, ridiculing) are not permitted in the zone.	• Activity: A 'Mistake Ritual' helps to 'reset' after making an error. Two fingers swept across the brow can signal 'no sweat'. This can help the athlete leave the mistake in the past and focus again on the immediate play.	• Tip: Set up a conversation between coaches and parents early in the season. Establish clear objectives that maintain a child-centred focus on skill development by having fun.	• Tip: Create an inclusive social atmosphere that will allow children to give their full effort during the physical aspects of the game without fear of being singled out or embarrassed for mistakes that are part of the learning process. This reduces the fear of making mistakes.

TABLE 7.4 Select suggestions for fostering a fun physical environment

Peer Relationships	Coach–Athlete	Parent–Athlete	Individual
Trying Hard **Learning and Improving** • <u>Activity</u>: 'Success squad' includes forming partners or small groups and asking each athlete to write out a goal for the week. Partners/ groups support and push each other toward achieving their goals each week. Switch partners weekly until each athlete has been paired with everyone.	**Practices** • <u>Tip</u>: Use unconventional games in practices with crossover skills. Many fundamental movement skills are transferable between sports. For example, a flag football station fosters technical development of running, dodging, throwing, and catching. This can be a fun, engaging way to improve overall skill development.	**Mental Bonuses** **Team Rituals** • <u>Tip</u>: Keep conversations to and from the sport arena supportive and light; focus conversations before practices/ games on what the athlete is looking forward to most; focus post-play discussion on what they did well and what was the most fun.	**Learning and Improving** • <u>Tip</u>: Use the 'PCE (pronounced peace) approach', which includes providing *positive* feedback, followed by *constructive correction*, and ending with *encouragement* when coaching. This fosters motivation to continue trying hard to improve rather than dwelling on mistakes.
Positive Team Dynamics • <u>Activity</u>: 'I got your back' includes having athletes writing their name on a sheet of paper followed by the word 'Strengths' and taping it to their back. Then have them walk around and write down a strength they see in each one of their teammates. Have them read their list to the team, hang on lockers, or place inside a luggage tag so they can attach it on their sport bag. Encourage them to keep it somewhere everyone will see it.	**Games** • <u>Tip</u>: When a team has diverse skill levels, to ensure playing time for all, play less developed athletes early in games rather than at the end. This reduces putting less experienced athletes in high-pressure situations.	**Game Time Support** • <u>Activity</u>: Using a 'fun badge', designate a parent each week to act as the team fun liaison (TFL). The TFL leads by example, reminds parents of allowable sideline behaviours, and curbs behaviours impeding athletes' fun as it occurs. This ensures sideline behaviour is respectful towards the athletes, coaches, and referees.	**Practices and Games** • <u>Tip</u>: Allow athletes opportunities to try each position in a game. As the season continues, ask which position they like best and why. If they like certain ones because they lack skills and confidence to play others, focus on developing the skills of those positions prior to selecting which position to play.

athlete's personal engagement in activities according to the quality relationship she or he has with peers, the coach(es), parent(s), and within her or himself. These suggestions are by no means exhaustive; instead, they are launching points for promoting further innovative ideas towards systematic efforts to intentionally integrate fun for young athletes.

Conclusion

The knowledge provided in this chapter can and should be shared to educate and alleviate common misconceptions of fun, particularly among adults responsible for structuring young athletes' sport experiences. In fact, awareness of these fun fallacies is a critical first step towards shaping more accurate schemas for fun. Consequently, greater accuracy in our understanding of fun will facilitate purposeful, systematic efforts to integrate and establish fun as a youth sport standard.

References

Aspen Institute Sports & Society. (2015). *Sport for all, play for life: A playbook to get every kid in the game.* Retrieved from http://youthreport.projectplay.us/.

Bailey, R., Hillman, C., Arent, S., & Petitpas, A. (2013). Physical activity: An underestimated investment in human capital? *Journal of Physical Activity & Health, 9,* 1053–1055.

Bengoechea, E. G., Strean, W., & Williams, D. J. (2004). Understanding and promoting fun in youth sport: Coaches' perspectives. *Physical Education and Sport Pedagogy, 9,* 197–214.

Cairney, J., Bedard, C., Dudley, D., & Kriellaars, D. (2016). Towards a physical literacy framework to guide the design, implementation and evaluation of early childhood movement-based interventions targeting cognitive development. *Annals of Sports Medicine and Research, 3,* 1073.

Chairat, C., Naruepon, V., Li, F., & Harmer, P. (2009). The sport commitment model: An investigation of structural relationships with Thai youth athlete populations. *Measurement in Physical Education and Exercise Science, 13,* 123–139.

Côté, J., & Hancock, D. J. (2014). Evidence-based policies for youth sport programmes. *International Journal of Sport Policy and Politics, 8,* 1–15.

Côté, J., Turnnidge, J., & Vierimaa, M. (2016). A personal assets approach to youth sport. In K. Green (Ed.), *Routledge Handbook of Youth Sport* (pp. 243–55). Abingdon, UK: Routledge.

Deci, E. L., & Ryan, R. M. (1985). *Intrinsic Motivation and Self-Determination in Human Behavior.* New York, NY: Plenum.

Eitzen, D. S., & Sage, G. H. (2009). *Sociology of North American Sport* (8th ed.). Boulder, CO: Paradigm.

Fredricks, J. A., & Eccles, J. S. (2004). Parental influences on youth sport involvement in sports. In M. R. Weiss (Ed.), *Developmental Sport and Exercise Psychology: A Lifespan Perspective* (pp. 145–164). Morgantown, WV: Fitness Information Technology.

Garcia C., Garcia L., Floyd J., & Lawson J. (2002). Improving public health through early childhood movement programs. *Journal of Physical Education, Recreation & Dance, 73,* 27–31.

Harter, S. (1978). Effectance motivation reconsidered. *Human Development, 21,* 34–64.

Iñigo, M. M., Podlog, L., & Hall, M. S. (2015). Why do athletes remain committed to sport after severe injury? An examination of the sport commitment model. *The Sport Psychologist, 29,* 143–155.

Nicholls, J. G. (1989). *The Competitive Ethos and Democratic Education*. Cambridge, MA: Harvard University Press.

Petlichkoff, L. (1992). Youth sport participation and withdrawal: Is it simply a matter of FUN? *Pediatric Exercise Science*, *4*, 105–110.

Santi, G., Bruton, A., Pietrantoni, L., & Mellalieu, S. (2014). Sport commitment and participation in masters swimmers: The influence of coach and teammates. *European Journal of Sport Science*, *14*, 852–860.

Scanlan, T. K., Carpenter, P. J., Schmidt, G. W., Simons, J. P., & Keeler, B. (1993). An introduction to the sport commitment model. *Journal of Sport & Exercise Psychology*, *15*, 1–15.

Scanlan, T. K., & Simons, J. P. (1992). The construct of sport enjoyment. In G. C. Roberts (Ed.), *Motivation in Sport and Exercise* (pp. 199–215). Champaign, IL: Human Kinetics.

Snyder, C. (2014). The path to excellence: A view on the athletic development of U.S. Olympians who competed from 2000–2012. Initial Report of the Talent Identification and Development Questionnaire to U.S. Olympians (S. Riewald, Ed.), USOC Sport Performance and Coaching Education Divisions.

Visek, A. J., Achrati, S. M., Mannix, H. M., McDonnell, K., Harris, B. S., & DiPietro, L. (2015a). The fun integration theory: Toward sustaining children and adolescents' sport participation. *Journal of Physical Activity and Health*, *12*, 424–433.

Visek, A. J., Mannix, H., Chandran, A., Achrati, S., Beckley, L., McDonnell, K., & DiPietro, L. (2015b). *The FUN MAPS pattern-matched across sex, age, and competition level: Gender and developmental assumptions debunked*. Presentation at the Association for Applied Sport Psychology Annual Conference, Indianapolis, IN.

Visek, A. J., Mannix, H., Chandran, A., Cleary, S. D., McDonnell, K., & DiPietro, L. (2017). *Towards further understanding in youth sport: A test of the gender differences and similarities hypothesis*. Manuscript submitted for publication.

8

TOWARDS MORE EMPOWERING AND LESS DISEMPOWERING ENVIRONMENTS IN YOUTH SPORT

Theory to evidenced-based practice

Joan L. Duda, Paul R. Appleton, Juliette Stebbings, and Isabel Balaguer

Sport psychology research over many decades has focused on the implications of coach behaviours on the emotions (e.g. enjoyment, anxiety), thoughts (self-confidence, concerns about failure) and behaviours (e.g. continuing, dropping out) of young people who participate in sport. Overall, this extensive body of literature indicates that coaches can influence athletes' motivation, enhance the quality of young people's sport engagement, and play a role in facilitating sustained partici-pation in sport (Bangsbo et al., 2016; Duda & Balaguer, 2007). However, we also know from past research that there can be other, more maladaptive coach influences (Bartholomew, Ntoumanis, & Thorgersen-Ntoumani, 2010). That is, coaches can act in a way that leads to young people 'losing' or 'ruining' their motivation, feeling worse about themselves and harbouring negative thoughts about their sport.

In seeking to optimise the impact of coaches on young athletes' motivation, it is important to appreciate and take into account: (a) the important characteristics of coach behaviours and the 'climate' they create, (b) the processes by which differ-ent motivational climates can lead to the positive as well as negative outcomes we observe in youth sport, and (c) how we, as sport psychology practitioners, can best intervene to optimise the behaviours of coaches. To address such questions, we advo-cate pulling from contemporary theories of motivation and findings from research conducted based on these theories and focused on the context of youth sport.

In this chapter, we first briefly review the theoretical underpinnings of our applied work that centres on influencing the 'what' and 'how' of coach impact on motivation within youth sport. Next, we briefly show how this theoretical ground-ing guided the development of a training programme that aims to promote more positive coaching behaviours and more autonomous motivation in young sport participants (i.e. *Empowering Coaching*™). We then provide suggestions on what the sport psychology consultant might assess to inform and evaluate their intervention efforts to promote more adaptive coaching practices. We conclude by suggesting some strategies that coaches might be encouraged to understand and endorse to facilitate a more positive 'climate change' when working with young athletes.

Coach-created environments in youth sport and their implications for motivation

Achievement goal theory

When considering what aspects of coach behaviours hold relevance for young athletes' motivation, two contemporary theories provide clear direction to sport psychology consultants. One of those frameworks is achievement goal theory (AGT; Ames, 1992; Nicholls, 1989). AGT draws attention to the motivational and achievement-related implications of differences in how individuals *define* or *judge* their competence and, as a result, on what bases they feel successful. That is, it is assumed in AGT that young athletes experience personal success in sport when they demonstrate high levels of ability but the emphasis in this theory is on *how* young athletes decide whether they demonstrated a high level of competence or not.

Two ways of judging one's competence are delineated in AGT:

1) The use of task-involving criteria (or what is referred to as adopting a *task goal perspective*). When a young athlete is primarily task-involved, they experience feelings of success and competence through exerting effort, learning, task mastery, gaining insight, and/or witnessing a personal best.
2) The use of ego-involving criteria (or adopting an *ego goal perspective*). If a young athlete is primarily ego-involved, the emphasis is on showing that they are better than others and possess superior levels of competence.

It is important to note that being ego-involved is not always overtly problematic; for example, a pronounced ego goal perspective can correspond to high performance and persistence when the young athlete is very confident and capable, sport engagement is going very well, and/or the emphasis placed on task goals is robust (Roberts, 2012). However, particularly in competitive sport, there is vulnerability inherent in a strong and prevailing ego goal perspective because it is difficult, if not impossible, to always demonstrate superiority. A large and compelling literature, however, points to the advantages for all athletes, particularly youth sport participants, of adopting and maintaining a strong task goal orientation (Roberts, 2012).

Importantly and relevant to our focus here, AGT speaks to the impact of the social environment on achievement goal (task and ego) adoption (Ames, 1992; Duda & Balaguer, 2007). From the standpoint of AGT, the social environment operating in sport is referred to as the *motivational climate*. The coach-created motivational climate is comprised of what coaches do and say. That is, the motivational climate is created by how coaches interact with their athletes, provide feedback, evaluate, respond to desired performances, and react to performances that are deemed lacking:

- A more *task-involving* coach recognises and emphasises exerted effort and cooperation, indicates that mistakes are part of learning, and conveys to his or her players that everyone has a contribution to make to a team, regardless of ability level. Task-involving coach behaviours are likely to fuel an orientation towards task goals in young athletes and have them be prone to focusing on working hard, ways they can improve, and whether or not they are getting better at their sport-related skills.

- *Ego-involving* coach behaviours include providing greater recognition for and giving more attention to the more talented athletes, punitive responses to mistakes, and reinforcing that young athlete's need to outdo each other, even if on the same team. A strongly ego-involving motivational climate makes it more likely for young athletes to orient themselves toward ego goals and subsequently concern themselves with how good they are compared to others and dread the possibility of failing.

Previous AGT-based research indicates the many beneficial outcomes accrued by young athletes when they play sport under a motivational climate that is strongly task-involving (Álvarez, Balaguer, Castillo, & Duda, 2012; Reinboth & Duda, 2006). Past studies also point to the negative implications of markedly ego-involving coach behaviours on youth sport participants (Duda & Balaguer, 2007; Ntoumanis, Taylor, & Thogersen-Ntoumani, 2012).

Self-Determination Theory

The other contemporary theory that can be used to understand and optimise coach influence on children's motivation is Self-Determination Theory (SDT; Deci & Ryan, 1985; Ryan & Deci, 2017). As applied to the context of youth sport, SDT points to the determinants and implications of young athletes feeling competent (they perceive they can meet the demands of the activity) but also having a sense of personal autonomy (they feel they have a voice and choice when it comes to their sport participation) and connection with their coach and others on their team (they experience a positive relationship with the coach and/or teammates and feel they belong and are cared for in this setting). According to SDT, young athletes' feelings of competence, autonomy, and relatedness are 'basic' and necessary *needs* that are important to nourish in youth sport. If these needs are satisfied, young athletes are more likely to experience wellbeing (e.g. feelings of vitality, positive emotions, positive feelings of self-worth) in and via sport (e.g. Balaguer et al., 2012; González, Tomás, Castillo, Duda, & Balaguer, 2016). Children are also more likely to be autonomously motivated (i.e. they play because they love the sport, personally value what sport adds to their life, and engage out of their own volition) (Balaguer, Castillo, & Duda, 2008). Autonomous reasons for sport participation are considered to be high-quality and beneficial motives for actively playing and continuing with sport (e.g. Fenton, Duda, Quested, & Barrett, 2014).

If the needs for feeling competence, autonomy, and relatedness are not met, or even actively frustrated by the coach, young athletes are prone to experiencing ill-being (e.g. anxiety, burnout, diminished self-esteem) with regard to their youth sport participation (Balaguer et al., 2012). Moreover, under these conditions, young athletes are more likely to report they engage in sport for controlled reasons, i.e. sport engagement is underpinned by internal contingencies (such as feeling guilty if one didn't participate) or external factors (such as significant others' demands or potential extrinsic rewards to be gained). Subsequently, over time, it is assumed that young athletes in this position can eventually become amotivated (that is, they feel that they no longer have any viable reason for continuing their participation). According to SDT and past research in the youth sport setting, controlled motivation for sport participation is considered to be low-quality motivation, as it is likely to lead to compromised youth sport participation. Amotivation within the youth sport setting has been found to correspond to negative outcomes and, unless forced to engage, it is doubtful that any young person who is amotivated will continue with their sport.

In seeking to understand children and adolescents' motivation for, responses to, and likelihood of remaining in sport, SDT (Ryan & Deci, 2017) also implicates the social environment created by significant others (such as the coach). From an SDT perspective, three important dimensions of the motivational climate are the degree to which the coach is autonomy supportive, controlling, and socially supportive:

- *Autonomy supportive* coaches solicit input from their athletes and involve them in decision-making (Conroy & Coatsworth, 2007). When and where possible in training and competitions, they provide meaningful choices and try to shine more light on the intrinsic reasons for playing sport. They also tend to consider their athletes' perspectives and provide a rationale when making requests or recommendations. Research conducted in the youth sport setting has supported the assumed desirable motivational processes and outcomes associated with more autonomy supportive coach behaviours (Duda & Balaguer, 2007).
- *Controlling coaches* tend to dictate and legislate what happens in training and competitions and can be intimidating when conveying such demands or perceiving that their young athletes are not doing as they are told (Bartholomew et al., 2010). They are more likely to use extrinsic reinforcements to get their young athletes to do what they want, and show they are pleased with their young athletes when they behave according to the coach's wishes. Past studies have demonstrated the negative costs of controlling coach behaviours on youth sport participants, and it is suggested that controlling coaching will promote more controlled motivation for engagement (Hodge & Lonsdale, 2011).
- From a SDT perspective, *socially supportive* coaches (also referred to as *involvement* in the SDT literature) take an interest in athlete welfare, are there to help, can be trusted, and care for the athlete as a young person above and beyond the level of the sport performance exhibited. A socially supportive coach respects his or her athletes and does not demand respect in return. Rather, respect

for the coach is a valued recognition that is earned as a function of how the young athletes are treated. Previous research in youth sport setting supports the presumed positive consequences of socially supportive coach behaviours (Sheridan, Coffee, & Lavallee, 2014).

An integrated model of empowering and disempowering motivational climates

Not surprisingly, there are interdependencies between the various features of the motivational climate that are highlighted by AGT and SDT. For example, when a coach is more autonomy supportive, it is likely that his or her athletes also perceive the coach-created climate as more socially supportive. There are also similar consequences of coach behaviours accounted for in the different theories. For instance, when studied individually, task-involving, autonomy supportive, and socially supportive coaching behaviours are linked to a similar array of more positive consequences for young sport participants, while ego-involved coach behaviours and controlling coach actions can lead to similarly detrimental outcomes.

Given the associations between the environmental dimensions and patterns of findings across SDT and AGT, Duda (2013; Duda & Appleton, 2016) proposed a conceptualisation that unites key features of the coach-created motivational climate from the perspective of both AGT and SDT. As can be seen in Figure 8.1, the label *Empowering Climate* was used to describe an overarching coach-created climate that tends to be marked by task-involving, autonomy supportive, and socially supportive features. A *Disempowering Climate* is one in which the coach tends to be highly ego-involving and controlling (and within that intimidating, uncaring) in his or her actions, expressed attitudes, and demeanour.

In terms of how an empowering or disempowering motivational climate might impact athlete motivation and their responses, Duda's (2013) model considers the role of the three psychological needs (i.e. competence, autonomy, and relatedness) from SDT as well as the AGT-proposed features of the motivational climate. Namely, the model suggests that how task- and ego-involving the coach tends to be is relevant to satisfaction (or, retrospectively, frustration) of young athletes' psychological needs and motivation. Research has supported the expected positive relationship between a perceived task-involving climate and young athletes' feelings of competence, autonomy, and relatedness (Reinboth & Duda, 2006). Perceptions of a task-involving environment also have been found to positively relate to players' intrinsic motivation, while perceptions of an ego-involving motivational climate have been found to be predictive of less self-determined/more controlled reasons for participating in sport (Duda & Balaguer, 2007).

Duda's (2013) conceptualisation also recognises that the features of an empowering climate will have implications for how an athlete is likely to judge their level of competence. That is, we would expect an empowering climate to be predictive of young athletes' tendency to adopt a task goal perspective when defining their competence. When the coach-created climate is more disempowering, young

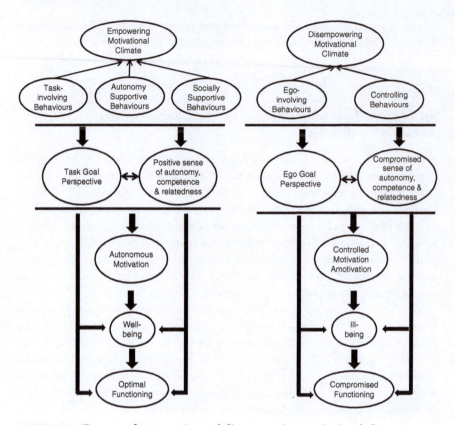

FIGURE 8.1 Features of empowering and disempowering motivational climates

athletes' orientations toward ego goals are likely to be exacerbated and we would expect a propensity toward using ego-involved criteria when they judge how competent they are in their sport. It is also assumed that if a young athlete is strongly focused on a task goal perspective in contrast to an ego goal perspective, there are (positively and negatively, respectively) implications for his or her feelings of competence, autonomy, and relatedness.

Finally, as shown in Figure 8.1, the model makes differential predictions in terms of conditions under which we are more likely to see optimal engagement (e.g. enjoyment, wellbeing, embracing the challenge) in young sport participants. Specifically, it is suggested that a positive and adaptive experience of and response to youth sport is more likely to be evident when children participate in an empowering climate, are more autonomously motivated, and have a strong orientation to task goals. When the coach-created climate is more disempowering, and the young people involved have more controlled motivation and predominantly emphasise ego goals, engagement in sport is likely to be compromised. The predictions embedded in this model are aligned with a recent consensus statement on the optimal determinants and benefits of young people's engagement in physical activities (such as organised sport) in their leisure time (Bangsbo et al., 2016).

From theory to practice: Principles of *Empowering Coaching*™

A theoretical understanding of the coach-created climate (and related motivational processes) is important as this can and should guide the development and delivery of sport psychology interventions in youth sport. As an example, the *Empowering Coaching*™ training for coaches/leaders (www.empoweringcoaching.co.uk) has evolved over years of advancements in theory (such as AGT and SDT) and related research findings. In particular, this training programme is grounded in Duda's (2013; Duda & Appleton, 2016; Figure 8.1) conceptualisation of the motivational climate and the processes by which coach behaviours can impact on athletes, both young and older. One key component of the workshop revolves around what constitutes and contributes to players feeling competent and a sense of autonomy and belonging, and why these are desired perceptions in young athletes.

Different versions of the *Empowering Coaching*™ workshop exist, but generally, as applied to the youth sport setting, they include a workbook, PowerPoint presentation, interactive and practical learning games, discussion of video clips showing youth sport coaches being more or less empowering and disempowering, self-reflection on current and future coaching practice, and guided small group discussions. The workshop outlines to coaches what more empowering coach behaviours are (and leads them to be more aware of what behaviours may be disempowering and *why*). Workshop content and activities also aim to convey how the empowering principles provide insight into and can promote young peoples' autonomous motivation, emotional welfare and feelings of self-worth, and continued involvement in sport. Coaches are encouraged to apply these principles when considering *how* they can be more empowering (and less disempowering) in training and competition, and consider likely barriers to doing so.

In sum, the pedagogy of and philosophy behind *Empowering Coaching*™ training is to work with coaches so that they can: (a) better understand the importance of creating a sport environment which is more empowering and less disempowering for the young people they coach, and (b) realise what they currently do and what they can do in the future to be more empowering and less disempowering. The workshop activities are also designed to facilitate coaches' commitment to and confidence in creating a more adaptive motivational climate when interacting with their young players.

Working with a youth sport team: What can be assessed to determine the motivation and motivational climate operating?

Based on existing theoretical frameworks and previous research, there is good justification for intervening in youth sport to help make this setting more motivationally constructive. This literature also provides helpful guidance on how the sport psychology practitioner might do just that. In order to intervene in an informed manner, though, it is essential that the sport psychology practitioner determine the current status of the motivational climate operating in the targeted youth sport setting and the quality of motivation that the young athletes exhibit. In light of recent advancements in the assessment of the motivational climate and participants' motivation, the applied practitioner has a number of valid and reliable, self-reported and objective empirically tested options to assess the coach-created motivational climate operating and the individual motivations of the young athletes with whom the coach or coaches in question work.

With regards to the determination of young athletes' motivational regulations, measures such as the Behaviour Regulation in Sport Questionnaire (BRSQ; Lonsdale, Hodge & Rose, 2008) are available to use if practitioners are conducting an intervention in the youth sport setting and evaluating their efforts. Comprising five subscales, the BRSQ captures sport participants' levels of autonomous motivation, controlled motivation, and amotivation. Based specifically on Duda's aforementioned conceptual model, the 34-item Empowering and Disempowering Motivational Climate Questionnaire (EDMCQ; Appleton, Ntoumanis, Quested, Viladrich, & Duda, 2016) was developed, and offers applied practitioners a means of assessing athletes' perceptions of the overarching empowering and disempowering features of the coach-created motivational climate. Complementing the EDMCQ, a Multidimensional Motivational Climate Objective System (MMCOS; Smith et al., 2015) has been validated which enables the sport psychology practitioner the possibility to observe, code, and differentiate the extent to which the coach-created climate is empowering and disempowering. In contrast to coach behaviour rating systems that count the frequency of what a coach says or does, the MMCOS adopts a potency rating that reflects the motivational quality of a coach's behaviours and how pervasive the environment is in terms of its motivational 'meaning' (Smith et al., 2015).

Such validated measures might prove useful for the practitioner to assess and compare athletes' and coaches' self-reported perceptions of the motivational climate (Smith et al., 2016). Are they 'on the same page'? If there is a discrepancy, why is that? What is one party picking up that the other is not aware of or seeing quite differently? Triangulating individuals' assessments (see Chapter 5) could also yield discrepancies between the different individuals' views (e.g. athlete versus athlete, or coach versus athlete, the objectively assessed versus perceived motivational climate), thus highlighting the need for interventions particularly targeted at, for example, coach communication, coach–athlete relationship development, the enhancement of self-reflection skills for coaches, or team (cohesion) building.

As an alternative option to administering established questionnaires to young athletes (and perhaps their coach), the practitioner may wish to consider utilising exemplar questions tapping the targeted constructs as a basis for interviews. This may be beneficial in numerous ways. For example, it might give structure to consultations, and/or may be a less formal approach for individuals who may be reluctant or unable to complete formal questionnaires. Further, interview techniques will likely yield additional and more in-depth information on perceptions and understandings of motivation and the motivational climate, and such discussion may also help to build rapport between the practitioner and the coaches and young people with whom they are working.

Young people's motivation for engagement in youth sport

To start the conversation regarding players' motivation, the practitioner may pose some general questions such as:

- Why do you play your sport?
- What is it that made you get involved in your sport?
- What are the reasons you still play/train/compete now?
- What do you like/dislike about your sport involvement?

Pulling from our contemporary understanding of motivation, however (in particular, what is assumed in SDT), motivation is multi-dimensional and it is important to take stock of the quality of that motivation. Thus, we recommend that the queries posed become more focused, with the aim of discerning the extent to which the youth sport participant engaged in the conversation is autonomously motivated, controlled in his or her motivation, and/or amotivated. Example questions that could guide such a conversation are presented in Table 8.1.

TABLE 8.1 Questions to pose to youth sport participants to discern the quality of their motivation for engagement

Autonomous Motivation	• Do you find playing your sport fun? Do you get a sense of enjoyment out of it? Do you love playing your sport? • Do you think there are other benefits to being involved in your sport? What are the benefits that matter to you most? • Why is playing your sport important to you?
Controlled Motivation	• Do you play your sport because other people (e.g. friends, coach, parents) say you should? • Do you worry that you will let yourself or other people down if you quit? • How important are trophies (and other rewards associated with winning/doing well in sport) as reasons why you play your sport?
Amotivation	• Do you sometimes wonder why you bother coming to training? • Do you ever feel like there is no point practising or competing? • Do you think that playing your sport is a waste of time and that you could be doing other things?

How empowering and disempowering is the coach-created climate?

Addressing young sport participants' views on the coach-created climate, we can again commence the discussion with more general queries:

- Tell me a bit about your coach.
- What are some examples of things he/she does or says?
- What is he/she like during training/matches/competitions?
- What are your interactions with your coach like?

Being true to our understanding of the motivational climate to be a multi-dimensional concept, though, the questions then need to become more targeted. In particular, we would want to address the particular features or types of coach behaviours that constitute overarching empowering and disempowering climates. Examples of such questions are provided in Table 8.2.

TABLE 8.2 Questions to pose to young sport participants to ascertain whether the coach-created climate is marked by more empowering and/or disempowering characteristics

Autonomy Support	• Does your coach give you meaningful choices and options for you to decide on during training and competition? • When your coach asks you to do something, does he/she explain *why* this would be good to do?
Task-Involving	• Does your coach say or do something which makes you feel good when you try your best or get better? • Does your coach ensure everyone has an important role on the team and encourage everyone to work together and learn together?
Social Support	• Do you feel you can count on your coach to care and provide help no matter what? • Does your coach see past what you are able to do in your sport and help you grow/get better as a person, 'not just an athlete'?
Controlling	• Does your coach become less friendly with you, or become less supportive, if you are not training and/or playing well? • Does your coach shout at you or threaten to punish you in order to make you do certain things? • Does your coach try to interfere in your life outside of sport?
Ego-Involving	• Does your coach yell at you (or somehow punish you) when you make a mistake/perform poorly? • Does your coach praise only the players who perform the best, and give them the most attention?

Strategies for promoting more empowering and less disempowering climates in youth sport settings

The opportunity to work with a coach (or club coaches) to facilitate the creation of a more positive and health promotive youth sport environment may come by request and/or be informed by assessment of players' motivational regulations and/or determinations of the prevailing motivational climate within the team or club. Table 8.3 outlines a variety of examples of empowering strategies that can be discussed with coaches with the aim of fostering basic psychological need satisfaction (autonomy, belonging, and competence), and, in turn, more autonomous motivation (and likely task goal focus too!) in youth sport participants. Also presented are potential disempowering strategies that sport psychology consultants can assist coaches in recognising and realising why they are not adaptive or desirable, particularly in the long run.

TABLE 8.3 Examples of empowering and disempowering coach behaviours and strategies

	Empowering Strategies	*Disempowering Strategies*
Autonomy	• Everyone on the team is encouraged to share ideas and make decisions within the session, and the coach considers these • Players are encouraged to focus on having fun, being healthy, enjoying the tasks and understanding the relevance and benefits of *why* they are doing such activities • Participants are provided with meaningful and attractive choices about how the training is run, and feel they have input into competition strategy	• Coach communication is 'one-way traffic', with little input from players • Only certain individuals (e.g. best players/more outgoing players) are listened to and asked for input • Rewards and reinforcements (e.g. praise, treats) are used to 'motivate' players so such rewards become the reason players engage in the task or behaviour • Coaches intimidate players if they do not do what they ask
Belonging	• Participants are encouraged to work together. They share ideas and work towards group/team goals • All players feel that they have an important role to play in the group/team, and everyone understands they each contribute to the success of the team • Coaches take an interest in players as people by asking about their lives outside of sport (school, home etc.)	• Coaches ignore players' feelings and perspectives and coach the way they want to • Coaches demand respect from players and act cold and uncaring, especially when players underperform or there is a loss • Coaches show they care or are happy when the player or team does what they expect
Competence	• Individual-based learning and improvement are continually discussed and emphasised after successes *and* failures • Coaches emphasise that mistakes are essential to the learning process and allow players to feel comfortable in making errors • Where possible, games and activities are designed to challenge each person at their individual level	• Coaches' feedback is primarily tied to outcomes such as winning and being better than others • Coaches make it clear (via the attention and rewards given) that they value players based on sporting ability • Coaches make comparisons between players, emphasise differences in ability, and create within-team competition for roles and positions • Coaches tend to respond in a punitive manner when players make mistakes

Final note

The world of youth sport holds much potential and promise in regard to impacting young people's motivation, emotional wellbeing, psychosocial growth, and perspectives on sport in potent and enduring ways. But to create a youth sport experience that is more empowering for all children, it is important to consider the bigger picture. We would suggest that the empowering principles presented above should not only underpin work conducted with and by coaches, but should also facilitate and be embraced by any of the other key social agents in a youth sport context (e.g. club managers, parents). The sport psychology consultant can work with any or all of these individuals as necessary to develop and embed a culture of empowerment within the team or club. This is healthy and optimal for youth sport participants themselves but also for all of the adults involved in the day to day happenings of youth sport.

References

Álvarez, M. S., Balaguer, I., Castillo, I. & Duda, J. L. (2012). The coach-created motivational climate, young athletes' well-being and intentions to continue participation. *Journal of Clinical Sport Psychology, 6*, 166–179.

Ames, C. (1992). Achievement goals, motivational climate, and motivational processes. In G. C. Roberts (Ed.), *Motivation in Sport and Exercise* (pp. 161–176). Champaign, IL: Human Kinetics.

Appleton, P., Ntoumanis, N., Quested, E., Viladrich, C. & Duda, J. L. (2016). Initial validation of the coach-created Empowering and Disempowering Motivational Climate Questionnaire (EDMCQ-C). *Psychology of Sport and Exercise, 22*, 53–65.

Balaguer, I., Castillo, I. & Duda, J. L. (2008). Apoyo a la autonomía, satisfacción de las necesidades, motivación y bienestar en deportistas de competición: Un análisis de la Teoría de la Autodeterminación. *Revista de Psicología del Deporte, 17*, 123–139.

Balaguer, I., González, L., Fabra, P., Castillo, I., Mercé, J., & Duda, J. L. (2012). Coaches' interpersonal style, basic psychological needs and the well- and ill-being of young soccer players: A longitudinal analysis. *Journal of Sports Sciences, 30*, 1619–1629.

Bangsbo, J., Krustrup, P., Duda, J., Hillman, C., Andersen, L. B., Weiss, M., ... Elbe, A. M. (2016). The Copenhagen Consensus Conference 2016: Children, youth, and physical activity in schools and during leisure time. *British Journal of Sports Medicine, 50*, 1177–1178.

Bartholomew, K. J., Ntoumanis, N., & Thorgersen-Ntoumani, C. (2010). The controlling interpersonal style in a coaching context: Development and initial validation of a psychometric scale. *Journal of Sport & Exercise Psychology, 32*, 193–216.

Conroy, D. E., & Coatsworth, J. D. (2007). Assessing autonomy-supportive coaching strategies in youth sport. *Psychology of Sport and Exercise, 8*, 671–684.

Deci, E. L., & Ryan, R. M. (1985). *Intrinsic Motivation and Self-Determination in Human Behavior*. New York, NY: Plenum.

Duda, J. L. (2013). The conceptual and empirical foundations of Empowering Coaching™: Setting the stage for the PAPA project. *International Journal of Sport & Exercise Psychology, 11*, 311–318.

Duda, J. L., & Appleton, P. R. (2016). Empowering and disempowering coaching behaviour: Conceptualization, measurement considerations, and intervention implications. In M.

Raab, P. Wylleman, R. Seiler, A.-M. Elbe & A. Hatzigeorgiadis (Eds.), *Sport and Exercise Psychology Research: From Theory to Practice* (pp. 374–390). London, UK: Elsevier.

Duda, J. L., & Balaguer, I. (2007). The coach-created motivational climate. In D. Lavallee & S. Jowett (Eds.), *Social Psychology of Sport* (pp. 117–130). Champaign, IL: Human Kinetics.

Fenton, S. A. M., Duda, J. L., Quested, E., & Barrett, T. (2014). Coach autonomy support predicts autonomous motivation and daily moderate-to-vigorous physical activity and sedentary time in youth sport participants. *Psychology of Sport and Exercise, 15*, 453–463.

González, L., Tomás, I., Castillo, I., Duda, J. L., & Balaguer, I. (2016). A test of basic psychological needs theory in young soccer players: Time-lagged design at the individual and team levels. *Scandinavian Journal of Medicine & Science in Sport*.

Hodge, K., & Lonsdale, C. (2011). Prosocial and antisocial behaviour in sport: The role of coaching style, autonomous vs. controlled motivation, and moral disengagement. *Journal of Sport & Exercise Psychology, 33*, 527–547.

Lonsdale, C. Hodge, K., & Rose, E. A. (2008). The behaviour regulation in sport questionnaire (BRSQ): Instrument development and initial validity evidence. *Journal of Sport & Exercise Psychology, 33*, 527–547.

Nicholls, J. G. (1989). *The Competitive Ethos and Democratic Education*. Cambridge, MA: Harvard University Press.

Ntoumanis, N., Taylor, I. M., & Thogersen-Ntoumani, C. (2012). A longitudinal examination of coach and peer motivational climates in youth sport: Implications for moral attitudes, well-being, and behavioural investment. *Developmental Psychology, 4*, 213–223.

Reinboth, M., & Duda, J. L. (2006). Perceived motivational climate, need satisfaction and indices of wellbeing in team sports: A longitudinal perspective. *Psychology of Sport and Exercise, 7*, 269–286.

Roberts, G. C. (2012). Motivation in sport and exercise from an achievement goal perspective: After 30 years, where are we? In G. C. Roberts & D. C. Treasure (Eds.), *Advances in Motivation in Sport and Exercise* (pp. 5–58). Champaign, IL: Human Kinetics.

Ryan, R. M., & Deci, E. L. (2017). *Self-Determination Theory: Basic Psychological Needs in Motivation, Development, and Wellness*. New York, NY: The Guilford Press.

Sheridan, D., Coffee, P., & Lavallee, D. (2014). A systematic review of social support in youth sport. *International Review of Sport and Exercise Psychology, 7*, 198–228.

Smith, N., Tessier, D., Tzioumakis, Y., Quested, E., Appleton, P., Sarrazin, P., Papaioannou, A., & Duda, J. L. (2015). Development and validation of the Multidimensional Motivational Climate Observation System. *Journal of Sport & Exercise Psychology, 37*, 4–22.

Smith, N., Tessier, D., Tzioumakis, Y., Fabra, P., Quested, E., Appleton, P. et al. (2016). The relationship between observed and perceived assessments of the coach-created motivational environment and links to athlete motivation. *Psychology of Sport and Exercise, 23*, 51–63.

9

DEVELOPING SELF-CONFIDENCE IN YOUNG ATHLETES

Robin S. Vealey, Melissa A. Chase, and Robin Cooley

Self-confidence is the belief that one has the internal resources, particularly abilities, to achieve success. The term sport-confidence has been used to describe a sport-specific confidence, which is an athlete's belief that she or he has the ability to perform successfully in sport (Vealey, 1986). Much of the study of self-confidence and sport-confidence has emanated from self-efficacy theory, where self-efficacy is defined as beliefs in one's capabilities to organise and execute the courses of action required to produce specific attainments (Bandura, 1997). A term related to confidence, perceived competence, refers to people's perceptions about how much ability they have in a certain achievement domain (e.g. football). So while perceived competence focuses on the skills individuals perceive they possess, self-confidence focuses on people's beliefs about what they can do with the skills that they have (e.g. perform successfully).

The aforementioned terms all have *beliefs about one's ability* in common, and whether discussing self-confidence, self-efficacy, or perceived competence, one thing is certain – belief, most commonly described in terms of confidence, is critical for young athletes. Throughout this chapter, we use these multiple conceptual approaches to organise our knowledge about confidence in young athletes and share insights into how confidence can be enhanced among young athletes. Specifically, the purposes of this chapter are to (a) explain why confidence is important, (b) provide a developmental perspective on how confidence is developed, and (c) to prescribe strategies sport psychologists, practitioners, and parents can use to enhance the confidence of young athletes.

Why is confidence important for young athletes?

Research supports that young athletes perform better in such sports as tennis (Hatzigeorgiadis, Zourbanos, Mpoumpaski, & Theodorakis, 2009), baseball (George,

1994), wrestling (Treasure, Monson, & Lox, 1996), distance running (Martin & Gill, 1995), swimming (Miller, 1993), and gymnastics (Weiss, Wiese, & Klint, 1989) when they have higher levels of self-confidence or self-efficacy. This relationship begins early, as young children higher in perceived physical competence performed better on fundamental motor skills (ball dribble, softball throw, broad jump) compared to children with lower perceived competence (Ulrich, 1987).

But how exactly does confidence enable young athletes to perform better? Self-efficacy theory states that self-confidence influences how young athletes behave, think, and emotionally respond in various situations (Bandura, 1997). Behaviourally, levels of confidence or self-efficacy influence young athletes' motivation in terms of the choices they make, the effort they expend, the persistence they show in the face of difficulty, and the resilience they demonstrate in rebounding from failure. An important choice for children is their decision to begin and continue sport participation. Chase (2001) found that 13–14-year-old girls and boys high in self-efficacy had stronger motivation to participate in sport in the future as compared to low self-efficacy children. This finding is important because it is this age group that is at high risk of dropping out of youth sport. Confidence seems to be especially important for bolstering children's motivation to try hard and persist in sport skill learning. For instance, high school baseball players higher in self-efficacy have been shown to expend more effort in hitting compared to others (George, 1994), and both self-efficacy (Allison, Dwyer, & Makin, 1999) and perceived competence (Khodaverdi, Bahram, Khalaji, & Kazemnejad, 2013) have been shown to significantly predict the adoption of, and adherence to, physical activity in school-based and recreational sport for children.

Confidence also arouses positive emotions, whereas a lack of confidence is often accompanied by negative emotions such as anxiety, depression, and dissatisfaction (e.g. Martens, Vealey, & Burton, 1990; Vealey & Campbell, 1988). Perceived physical competence has been linked to positive emotions in youth sport, such as feeling pride, satisfaction, and enjoyment (e.g. Ebbeck & Weiss, 1998). Thus, strong beliefs about personal competence and ability produce adaptive emotional states, whereas a lack of confidence (or beliefs about incompetence and lack of ability) is emotionally painful and leads to ineffective actions and thoughts.

Finally, confident individuals are more skilled and efficient in using cognitive resources that are necessary for sport success (they think better). Attributions are reasons that young athletes identify to explain why they succeed and fail, and the attributions that they internalise strongly influence their motivation (Weiner, 1986). Young athletes high in confidence and perceived competence engage in more productive attributional patterns, by attributing their success to internal and controllable factors and their failures to controllable and changeable factors (e.g. Chase, 2001; Vealey, 1986; Vealey & Campbell, 1988). Although not studied in children, confidence has been shown to facilitate attention to the task at hand, as opposed to focusing on internal doubts and fears, which is often the result of a lack of confidence.

Building confidence in young athletes: A developmental case study approach

So confidence is a critical developmental outcome for adolescent athletes based on its influence on self-perceptions, emotions, and motivation in sport. Therefore, what do we know about building confidence in young athletes that could help coaches, teachers, and parents? Seven case studies are described to illustrate important psychosocial issues influencing confidence development in young athletes. For each case, we present what practitioners should know, and what practitioners can do, to enhance confidence in these situations. Our recommendations are based on self-efficacy theory (Bandura, 1997) as well as the sport-confidence model (Vealey, 1986).

Case 1: Importance of fundamental motor skills and physical literacy for confidence

Morgan is a 9-year-old girl who is not very physically active. She has not participated in any organised sport activities and she seldom engages in free play outside with friends. Morgan's parents sign her up for the local recreational softball league, thinking this would be a good way to get Morgan involved in sport. They are hopeful she will like it and continue to participate.

What should practitioners know?

Morgan is already at a disadvantage. She has not developed competence in the basic fundamental motor skills that are a prerequisite for successful sport participation (see also Chapter 6). Confidence for young athletes begins in early childhood when they develop a wide repertoire of movement skills by participating in games and free play. Morgan is less likely to be successful in softball because she has not developed the prerequisite skills of throwing, catching, striking, eye-tracking, and eye–hand coordination during the optimal readiness period of 2 to 9 years (Vealey & Chase, 2016). And because perceived competence is important for motivation, Morgan's lack of skills may lead her to conclude that softball is not much fun and to drop out.

An important goal for all children is the attainment of physical literacy, which is the physical competence and confidence to maintain physical activity at an individually appropriate level throughout life (Whitehead & Murdock, 2006). Physical literacy provides a range of movement skills and the perceived competence so that adolescents can try and succeed in different sports and activities. It is not that Morgan began youth sport participation too late. Rather, the problem is that she had not been physically active and involved in any sort of physical free play activities in which she could have developed the fundamental motor skills that would help her succeed in softball. So it is not a simple matter of her 'lacking confidence', as some would observe. It is more that she never developed the confidence that comes with early motor skill development (Balyi, Way, & Higgs, 2013).

What can practitioners do?

Morgan has had a late start, but her parents and coaches can work with her individually to build the fundamental skills (overhand throwing, catching, batting, ball tracking) needed for softball. It may be that Morgan can catch up, but it typically takes more effortful practice once children are past the optimal period for learning fundamental skills (Vealey & Chase, 2016). Parents should provide children access to outside play areas, obstacle courses, physical activity equipment for play and games, and multiple physical activities during the early and middle childhood years. Coaches should spend time during each practice helping youth athletes develop and refine the fundamental skills critical for each sport, knowing that competence creates confidence.

Case 2: Developmental changes in perceived competence

Hannah is a physically active 8-year-old who loves ice skating and playing ice hockey. For years, she has begged her mother Kim to 'watch me' and then exclaims 'Wasn't that good, Mom?' Kim notices that Hannah is spending more time with her friends as opposed to wanting to skate with her and she tells Kim that she is worried that she is not as good as some of her friends. Hannah tells her mother, 'I thought I was fast, but I'm not near as fast a skater as Jordan. I feel nervous now when I play hockey.'

What should practitioners know?

Hannah is going through a typical developmental progression in her assessment of her own competence as a skater/hockey player. First, children become more accurate in assessing their personal competence as they age (Horn, 2004). Young children (3–7 years) often have inflated levels of perceived competence in relation to their actual competence. By middle childhood (8–10 years), children have developed cognitively to the point where they more realistically assess their own competence. During adolescence (11–18 years), young athletes typically have developed a mature ability to accurately assess their competence.

Second, children use different sources of information upon which to base their confidence as they age (Horn, 2004; Chapter 4). Very young children (4–7 years) base their confidence on effort, task accomplishment, and feedback from significant adults. During middle to late childhood (7–12 years), peer comparison becomes a very important source (and parent evaluation becomes a lesser source) of confidence for young athletes. Hannah is becoming more accurate in her self-appraisal of competence, and she is focusing more on peer comparison to assess her skills as opposed to feedback from her mom. By adolescence, Hannah will be able to use multiple sources of information as sources of confidence, including peer comparison, her own personal standards, and feedback from parents and coaches.

What can practitioners do?

Parents should not worry too much about young children's inflated levels of perceived competence. This is probably valuable to drive their development of fundamental motor skills. Practitioners should note that middle childhood (ages 8–11 years) is a time of vulnerability for many young athletes because they become more aware of their lack of ability and they are now assessing their competence in relation to their peers. Parents and coaches can emphasise personal goals and individual improvement, and encourage children to stay involved in sport. Coaches should socially engineer the youth sport environment during this time by constantly rotating warm-up partners and training groups to avoid ability grouping and cliques.

Kim could help Hannah set and work towards individual performance goals, such as skating faster times or mastering more advanced technique, and emphasise this personal focus as opposed to worrying about how fast her teammates skate. With regard to Hannah's nervousness, Kim can explain that the 'butterflies' we feel in our stomach before competing are natural and can even help our performance by getting our bodies ready to perform. Young athletes need this perspective that nervousness is not a lack of confidence, but rather a physiological response of readiness to compete.

Case 3: Maturational influences on confidence and importance of mastery orientation

Isaac is an early-maturing 12-year-old basketball player, and he is significantly taller, stronger, and more physically developed than other boys his age in his basketball league. Isaac's coach plays him exclusively in the post position (close to the basket) to take advantage of his height. Because of his physical advantages, success comes more easily to Isaac and he does not work on fundamentals or focus on individual development.

What should practitioners know?

Isaac is confident right now, but he is headed for a fall. Because of their early success, early-maturing boys receive a lot of recognition and attention from coaches, which fuels their confidence and motivation in sport (Fairclough & Ridgers, 2010). But often, early-maturing adolescent boys are 'caught' as later-maturing boys catch up in biological maturation, which is a blow to the confidence of boys like Isaac. In addition, early-maturing boys often end up as shorter adults compared to late-maturing boys, which disadvantages them in sports like basketball in the later high school years.

What can practitioners do?

Practitioners should emphasise a personal mastery approach with individual performance goals for early-maturing boys, and insist on the refinement of basic fundamental skills in daily practice. This will enable them to compete more confidently when they are caught by the later-maturing boys. Practitioners should also avoid pigeonholing young athletes into specific sport positions based on body types, because athletes' postpubescent heights and builds may not fit the position they were forced into when they were younger. Isaac's coach is actually hurting Isaac's chances of playing high school basketball because he will not have the perimeter shooting or dribbling skills needed to play outside of the post. Thus, Isaac will quickly lose his confidence in his basketball ability, unless he is encouraged to learn a variety of skills.

Case 4: Learned helplessness

Dylan is a 10-year-old age group swimmer on a summer swim team at the local pool. Coach Ledecky observes that Dylan is reluctant to participate and acts as though he does not want to be there. He always moves to the back of the line when the team practice racing starts off the blocks, and he shows very little effort to improve or learn the butterfly and backstroke. He repeatedly says he cannot do these strokes, and seems extremely embarrassed when he makes mistakes or is unable to master the dolphin kick needed for the butterfly event. When Coach Ledecky helps him with his technique work in a separate lane, Dylan says, 'Yeah, I did it, but you made it easy and I can't do it in a race.'

What should practitioners know?

Dylan is displaying learned helplessness, in which young athletes feel incompetent and powerless to improve. Dylan's helplessness is not just because of his lack of competence, but particularly caused by his maladaptive attributional patterns. Previously in the chapter, we explained that attributions affect confidence and motivation because they are the reasons young athletes identify as to why they succeed or fail. When Dylan fails, he attributes it to his lack of ability and he does not feel he can get any better. When Coach Ledecky attempts to bolster his confidence with drills that enable him to succeed, Dylan rejects her success by saying that Coach Ledecky is making it easy. So Dylan's learned helplessness hampers his confidence and motivation to get better because he does not believe he can.

What can practitioners do?

Coach Ledecky can be encouraged to talk to Dylan privately, and discuss Dylan's beliefs that he is not good at swimming. Coach Ledecky can explain to Dylan that he has the ability to learn skills, but it takes practice. While other children may be more skilled than Dylan right now, Coach Ledecky should work to convince Dylan to focus on his own improvement and on taking small steps to master the butterfly and backstroke. They can develop a list of swimming performance goals for Dylan and meet weekly to discuss progress and strategies for these goals. Most importantly, Coach Ledecky should emphasise to Dylan that practice and effort will pay off.

It takes time, but with a supportive coach or teacher, learned helplessness can be overcome. Along with practising skills in specially designed drills, coaches must also work with athletes to retrain their thinking towards a renewed sense of personal controllability over their progress (Rees, Ingledew, & Hardy, 2005). Other strategies include explaining (a) the commonality of the issue (e.g. Other swimmers struggled with butterfly when they first started), (b) the developmental process (e.g. Give yourself time to learn the kick and the arm stroke – then we'll put them together), (c) strategy (e.g. Focus on your specific performance and process goals each practice), and (d) effort and persistence (e.g. Keep working, and in time it will all come together in your stroke).

Case 5: Coach expectancy and feedback

Leo is a 14-year-old late-maturing boy on the first-year baseball team at his high school. His skills are not bad, but he lacks strength and power because of his physical immaturity. Leo feels that Coach Jeter does not provide him much individual feedback and attention. Leo also notices that Coach Jeter tells him 'Good job' sometimes, even when he just makes a routine play. Yet when other players make the same play, the coach will stop them and explain how they can improve the skill. Leo wonders if he should stick with baseball as he does not feel very confident about his skills.

What should practitioners know?

The support of significant adults is a key source of confidence for young athletes (Bandura, 1997; Harter, 1978; Vealey, Hayashi, Garner-Holman, & Giacobbi, 1998). Coaches, in particular, influence youth athletes' confidence through modelling and leadership, trust, encouragement and rewards, and performance feedback (e.g. Vella, Oades, & Crowe, 2011). But sometimes, even well-meaning coaches can hurt athletes' confidence through negative expectancy effects.

Research on coaches has shown that the expectations that coaches form about the abilities of individual athletes have the potential to determine the level of achievement that each athlete ultimately reaches (Horn, Lox, & Labrador, 2015). In Leo's case, it seems as though Coach Jeter has assessed Leo's ability as lower than other players on the team, and perhaps without meaning to, Coach Jeter is not providing contingent and appropriate feedback to Leo to enable him to improve and build greater confidence. Lower-expectancy athletes often receive less specific and prescriptive feedback, and may receive inappropriate praise for mediocre performance. Leo feels less competent and confident when Coach Jeter tells him 'good job' for an average performance play.

What can practitioners do?

Youth sport coaches can do several things to avoid the negative expectancy trap. First, coaches should maintain high but realistic expectancies for all athletes based on their unique skill levels. Coach Jeter should be aware of maturation and how it influences the build and performance of high school athletes. Leo will mature and develop strength and power to go along with his baseball-specific skills. Second, Coach Jeter should focus on the interpersonal coaching skill of providing specific, information-loaded instruction and feedback to all of his athletes. 'Way to read the bunt and charge it' is more effective than the general 'Good job' because it provides specific competency information to Leo. Third, Coach Jeter should keep his expectations for athletes performance-based, as opposed to person-based. Personal characteristics include body size and shape, gender, style of dress, race, physical attractiveness, and family background, and these characteristics often bias coaches against certain athletes. Coaches should assess performance daily, and keep their expectations for athletes flexible and open to constant change to accurately assess adolescent athletes' developing abilities.

Case 6: Importance of developing and reinforcing a growth mindset in young athletes

Andrew started playing tennis at a young age, and has continued into junior tennis. His parents have always praised him for winning matches and they obsess about his junior rankings. Coach Federer wants to help Andrew make some changes in his backhand technique, which Coach Federer believes will allow Andrew to be more successful at higher levels of competition. Andrew is resistant to the change because he fears he will lose his ranking by working to improve a new technique.

What should practitioners know?

Although confidence is based on beliefs about abilities, an athlete can believe his ability is either (a) fixed and unchanging (fixed mindset) or (b) something that can continually be improved and developed (growth mindset) (Dweck, 2006). It appears that Andrew has developed a fixed mindset, and this mindset is reinforced (perhaps even was created) by the way his parents praise him. The aim in a fixed mindset is to achieve validation. The young athlete thinks, 'You value me for my ability. I better not do anything to disprove that.' This is why Andrew resists change in an effort to hold on to his ranking and his ability to win matches right now. A fixed mindset is sensitive to mistakes, vulnerable to setbacks, and leads to unstable confidence. Andrew would be advantaged in developing more of a growth mindset, which is focused on achieving improvement and pursuing additional mastery experiences.

Research shows that individuals develop fixed mindsets when they are praised for their abilities or outcomes (as in the case of Andrew). Children who were praised for their abilities chose easier options and gave up earlier than children who were praised for their effort (Dweck, 2006). So the way adults praise young athletes can make or break their motivational mindset. Praising winning might make Andrew happy and proud for a short while. But when he loses, his confidence will spiral down because his fixed mindset will lead him to interpret losing as an indication that he lacks talent and will lose the approval of his parents.

What can practitioners do?

Coach Federer and Andrew's parents should focus on praising Andrew for controllable achievements like effort, practice, persistence, and mental skill, *not* for performance outcomes. While Andrew should be recognised for his accomplishments, excessive praise of outcomes should be avoided, as it often leads to pressure. So instead of saying to Andrew, 'Way to be a winner!' it would be better to say, 'Your practice on your kick serves really showed today – great job.'

Coach Federer could also help Andrew develop a growth mindset about mistakes, explaining that mistakes are part of learning and important for development. He could use the example of the great tennis champion Pete Sampras, who changed his backhand technique as a junior player, and after struggling initially with the change, went on to be a multiple Grand Slam winner. Coach Federer could suggest that Andrew use a mistake ritual (e.g. brushing off your shoulder, tapping his racquet on the ground) as a symbolic reminder to accept the mistake and immediately focus on the next point. Coach Federer could debrief with Andrew after each match by discussing Andrew's positive performance accomplishments as well as using the mistakes from the match to create a learning perspective and goal map for improvement.

Case 7: Performance slump and loss of confidence

Lauren is the senior setter for a top-ranked high school volleyball team. She was recognised as an All-Conference player in her junior year, but now as a senior captain is not performing as well as expected. Lauren responds by trying harder, but it is obvious her confidence has been shaken, as her performance seems hesitant instead of free and automatic. When she makes an error, she shows frustration through her on-court body language.

What should practitioners know?

The most important source of confidence for young athletes is their performance (Chase, 1998). So it is not surprising that when athletes' performance decreases, their confidence subsequently suffers. When this occurs, athletes need to focus on their physical and mental skills to develop an automatic performance response that allows them to succeed, even when their confidence is shaky. Preparation (both physical and mental) has also been shown to be an important source of competence for high school athletes (Vealey et al., 1998). Interventions with youth athletes have shown that productive self-talk (Hatzigeorgiadis et al., 2009), mental imagery (Garza & Feltz, 1998), focus training (Orlick, 2016), and appropriate goals (Harwood & Swain, 2002) can enhance performance and self-confidence.

What can practitioners do?

It may be a good idea for Lauren to spend some additional physical practice time working with a couple of her hitters to gain confidence and rhythm. Her focus in these sessions should be on process goals that describe the feeling she desires as she sets (e.g. strong and smooth) and/or instructional cues (e.g. square shoulders). Lauren should use daily imagery to mentally rehearse previous games in which she not only performed well, but also experienced enjoyment. In her imagery, she should focus on her process goals and self-talk to focus on specific aspects of her performance that she wishes to improve. She should 'fake it until she makes it' by exuding a physical body language of focus and confidence on the court, particularly in responding to mistakes. Lauren's focus should be on playing the game she loves, and competing in the moment. She can repeat 'this play' to manage her mind to stay in the moment, and not let her thoughts drift to previous mistakes or pressure to achieve future outcomes. Lauren can use her physical and mental skills to regain her performance level, and her confidence will be restored.

Conclusions

The set of case studies presented in this chapter represents a developmental progression for youth athletes to follow in developing and maintaining a stable sense of confidence. Confidence as a youth athlete has its beginnings in early childhood experiences that develop competence in fundamental motor skills. Cognitive maturation creates developmental changes in children's perceived competence, and wide variations in the physical maturation of young athletes challenge coaches to provide individualised feedback and personal mastery goals to every individual athlete. The mindset about ability that young athletes develop strongly influences their confidence and motivation, and parents and practitioners need to help athletes develop a growth mindset and engage in productive attributions for success and failure. As youth athletes continue in competitive sport, they need to develop the mental skills that help them focus under pressure and manage competitive arousal so they may productively respond to inevitable short-term lapses in confidence. The basis of confidence is beliefs about abilities to be successful, and adult practitioners must help adolescent athletes move beyond the restrictive peer comparison and counterproductive fixed mindset to realise that success can be defined in multiple ways and that personal growth and mastery are always attainable in sport and physical activity.

References

Allison, K. R., Dwyer, J. M. J., & Makin, S. (1999). Self-efficacy and participation in vigorous physical activity by high school students. *Health Education & Behavior, 26*, 12–24.

Balyi, I., Way, R., & Higgs, C. (2013). *Long-Term Athlete Development*. Champaign, IL: Human Kinetics.

Bandura, A. (1997). *Self-Efficacy: The Exercise of Control*. New York, NY: Freeman.

Chase, M. A. (1998). Sources of self-efficacy in physical education and sport. *Journal of Teaching in Physical Education, 18*, 76–89.

Chase, M. A. (2001). Children's self-efficacy, motivational intentions, and attributions in physical education and sport. *Research Quarterly for Exercise and Sport, 72*, 47–54.

Dweck, C. S. (2006). *Mindset: The New Psychology of Success*. New York, NY: Ballantine.

Ebbeck, V., & Weiss, M. R. (1998). Determinants of children's self-esteem: An examination of perceived competence and affect in sport. *Pediatric Exercise Science, 10*, 285–298.

Fairclough, S. J., & Ridgers, N. D. (2010). Relationships between maturity status, physical activity, and physical self-perceptions in primary school children. *Journal of Sports Science, 28*, 1–9.

Garza, D. L., & Feltz, D. L. (1998). Effects of selected mental practice on performance, self-efficacy, and competition confidence of figure skaters. *The Sport Psychologist, 12*, 1–15.

George, T. R. (1994). Self-confidence and baseball performance: A causal examination of self-efficacy theory. *Journal of Sport & Exercise Psychology, 16*, 381–399.

Harter, S. (1978). Effectance motivation reconsidered. *Human Development, 21*, 34–64.

Harwood, C., & Swain, A. (2002). The development and activation of achievement goals within tennis: II. A player, parent, and coach intervention. *The Sport Psychologist, 16*, 111–137.

Hatzigeorgiadis, A., Zourbanos, N., Mpoumpaki, S., & Theodorakis, Y. (2009). Mechanisms underlying the self-talk-performance relationship: The effects of motivational self-talk on self-confidence and anxiety. *Psychology of Sport and Exercise, 10*, 186–192.

Horn, T. S. (2004). Developmental perspectives on self-perceptions in children and adolescents. In M. R. Weiss (Ed.), *Developmental Sport and Exercise Psychology: A Lifespan Perspective* (pp. 101–144). Morgantown, WV: Fitness Information Technology.

Horn, T. S., Lox, C. L., & Labrador, F. (2015). The self-fulfilling prophecy theory: When coaches' expectations become reality. In J. M. Williams (Ed.), *Applied Sport Psychology: Personal Growth to Peak Performance* (7th ed., pp. 78–100). New York, NY: McGraw-Hill.

Khodaverdi, Z., Bahram, A., Khalaji, H., & Kazemnejad, A. (2013). Motor skill competence and perceived motor skill competence: Which best predicts physical activity among girls? *Iran Journal of Public Health, 42*, 1145–1150.

Martens, R., Vealey, R. S., & Burton, D. (1990). *Competitive Anxiety in Sport*. Champaign, IL: Human Kinetics.

Martin, J. J., & Gill, D. L. (1995). The relationships of competitive orientations and self-efficacy to goal importance, thoughts, and performance in high school distance runners. *Journal of Applied Sport Psychology, 7*, 50–62.

Miller, M. (1993). Efficacy strength and performance in competitive swimmers of different skill levels. *International Journal of Sport Psychology, 24*, 284–296.

Orlick, T. (2016). *In Pursuit of Excellence* (5th ed.). Champaign, IL: Human Kinetics.

Rees, T., Ingedew, D. K., & Hardy, L. (2005). Attribution in sport psychology: Seeking congruence between theory, research, and practice. *Psychology of Sport and Exercise, 6*, 189–204.

Treasure, D. C., Monson, J., & Lox, C. L. (1996). Relationship between self-efficacy, wrestling performance, and affect prior to competition. *The Sport Psychologist, 10*, 73–83.

Ulrich, B. D. (1987). Perceptions of physical competence, motor competence, and participation in organized sport: Their interrelationships in young children. *Research Quarterly for Exercise and Sport, 58*, 57–67.

Vealey, R. S. (1986). Conceptualization of sport-confidence and competitive orientation: Preliminary investigation and instrument development. *Journal of Sport Psychology, 8*, 221–246.

Vealey, R. S., & Campbell, J. L. (1988). Achievement goals of adolescent figure skaters: Impact on self-confidence, anxiety, and performance. *Journal of Adolescent Research, 3*, 227–243.

Vealey, R. S., & Chase, M. A. (2016). *Best Practice for Youth Sport*. Champaign, IL: Human Kinetics.

Vealey, R. S., Hayashi, S. W., Garner-Holman, M., & Giacobbi, P. (1998). Sources of sport-confidence: Conceptualization and instrument development. *Journal of Sport & Exercise Psychology*, *20*, 54–80.

Vella, S., Oades, L., & Crowe, T. (2011). The role of the coach in facilitating positive youth development: Moving from theory to practice. *Journal of Applied Sport Psychology*, *23*, 33–48.

Weiner, B. (1986). *An Attributional Theory of Motivation and Emotion*. New York, NY: Springer.

Weiss, M. R., Wiese, D. M., & Klint, K. A. (1989). Head over heels with success: The relationship between self-efficacy and performance in competitive youth gymnastics. *Journal of Sport & Exercise Psychology*, *11*, 444–451.

Whitehead, M., & Murdock, E. (2006). *Physical literacy and physical education: Conceptual mapping*. Retrieved from www.physicalliteracy.org.uk/conceptualmapping2006.php.

10

OPTIMISING FAMILY INVOLVEMENT IN YOUTH SPORT

Travis E. Dorsch

Youth sport cannot operate without families. Family involvement, namely that of parents, is an integral part of children's participation. In many cases, it is parents who serve as head and assistant coaches, referees, scorekeepers, concession stand attendants, and ticket-takers. Unofficially, parents also serve as chauffeurs, travel agents, nutritionists, and, in elite youth sport, agents. Overwhelmingly, these services are performed on a volunteer basis, and it is clear that youth sport would not function wholly without parent involvement. In short, youth sport is a by-product of parent involvement. To optimise the experience, researchers and practitioners have continually sought ways to enhance children's motivation in sport. Namely this has taken the form of providing best practice recommendations for coaches and administrators. Although these efforts have been fruitful in many respects, they often ignore families as the 'hidden' participants in youth sport.

Family involvement is especially salient at the earliest stages of youth sport, when parents (and sometimes guardians or grandparents) serve the multiple roles described above. Through their involvement, parents can positively and negatively influence children's developmental experiences. Accordingly, research practitioners have sought to identify how parents can best be involved in their children's sporting experiences and how they can be supported in doing this. The aim of this chapter is to outline the theoretical and research base underpinning parental involvement in sport, while providing insights into how practitioners might work with parents to enhance their involvement in youth sport (see also Chapter 27).

What is optimal parental involvement in sport?

Optimal parenting in youth sport is demonstrated via parental involvement that supports children's opportunities to achieve their potential, both in and out of sport, engage in healthy psychosocial interactions, and experience a range of positive developmental outcomes (Harwood & Knight, 2015). In their recent position paper, Harwood and Knight proposed six skills that should be fostered in parents to enhance interactions with children in youth sport:

1) Parents should help children select appropriate sporting opportunities. This is best accomplished by communicating with children about their goals for sport, providing the necessary support for participation, and placing an appropriate value on enjoyment and performance.
2) Parents should strive to understand and apply appropriate parenting styles in sport. This entails creating a healthy emotional climate, allowing children an appropriate level of autonomy, and providing a united front across both parents' parenting styles at home and in sport.
3) Parents should attempt to manage the emotional demands of sport. Indeed, sport is a context defined by emotive expression, but parents should not make their love contingent upon a child's outcomes. Instead, parents should demonstrate and foster values such as composure, sportspersonship, and teamwork.
4) Parents should strive to foster healthy relationships with significant others (e.g. parent peers, coaches, and athletes). In doing so, they must appreciate the demands associated with being a parent, coach, and athlete in youth sport, and be willing to help when called upon.
5) Parents need to manage the demands associated with youth sport. Parents should not overextend themselves or their children emotionally, financially, or physically, and each family should strategically develop personal and family strategies to manage the demands of sport.
6) Finally, parents need to adapt their children's environments across the stages of sport participation. Sport is marked by numerous transitions that must be navigated by parents, children, and families. Therefore, parents must remain cognisant of their children's changing needs across the course of a youth sport career.

Practitioners can foster these six skills by engaging in a reciprocal process of knowledge acquisition and dissemination. Specifically, they should work not just to provide knowledge *to* parents but also to learn *from* them. No two athletes, no two families, and no two sport contexts are the same; therefore, it is incumbent upon individuals who work in youth sport settings to avoid treating 'facts' as one-size-fits-all. In short, I would encourage practitioners to adopt a humanistic lens (Gordin, 2012), continually assessing the thoughts, emotions, and behaviours of the given subculture prior to designing and delivering workshops, interventions, or counselling.

Overview of relevant theoretical frameworks for examining family involvement

Youth sport is a complex setting, shaped by adults, children, communities, and the various societies in which it is enacted. Despite this, much of the research conducted in the field of sport psychology has adopted an individual lens, focusing on outcomes experienced by the children who participate (e.g. Fraser-Thomas, Côté, & Deakin, 2005). It is also important to employ a more distal lens to account for the cultural, community, team, and family contexts that surround the young athlete (e.g. Bremer, 2012; Horn, 2004; Horn & Horn, 2007). Specifically, two broad frameworks can be used to help practitioners adopt this approach when working with young athletes and their families: family systems theory and bioecological theory.

Family systems theory

Family systems theory suggests that individuals are best understood not in isolation from one another, but as a part of a larger whole: *the family system*. Individual members of a family are thought to be interconnected and interdependent; consequently, no member of the family can be understood separate from its other members. According to Von Bertanlanffy (1968), each member of a system plays a role within the system while also respecting its rules and traditions. Members of a family are expected to respond to each other in certain ways, which are determined by the nature of the relationships within the family (e.g. siblings can scratch, claw, and hit, but spouses cannot). Perhaps the most important tenet of family systems theory is that within a family, one family member's behaviour both causes, and is caused by, other family members' behaviours and experiences (Smith & Hamon, 2012).

White and Klein (2008) delineate four 'scope assumptions' of family systems theory. First, *all members of the family are interconnected*. In youth sport, this means that a child's participation also impacts the parent(s), sibling(s), and all other members of the family unit. The second assumption is that *understanding a family member is only possible by viewing the whole family*. In youth sport, to understand the thoughts, emotions, and behaviours of an athlete, one must view that athlete in the context of her/his entire family. The third assumption is that *a family affects its environment and the environment affects the family*. In youth sport, families shape – and are shaped by – the participation context. The final assumption is that *'systems' are heuristics, not real things*.

In youth sport, there are many ways to understand the experiences of athletes and families. Adopting a family systems perspective is but one way to organise these experiences into meaningful understanding. The practitioner who wishes to adopt a family systems lens can do so by working not just with the athlete, but also her parents and siblings. More importantly, the practitioner must recognise that the 'sport family' does not exist only at training and competitions. Rather, family issues can impact all aspects of sport performance *and* sport issues can permeate the family.

Bioecological theory

A family's involvement in youth sport is shaped by interpersonal, individual, and contextual factors that interact over time. Drawing from Lewin's (1935) field theory, which viewed human behaviour as an interaction of person and environment, contemporary ecologists frame human development as a function of multiple systems of influence. Four such systems are process, person, context, and time (PPCT), and taking each into account is the foundation of the PPCT framework (Bronfenbrenner, 1999, 2005; Bronfenbrenner & Morris, 1998).

Within the PPCT framework, *processes* are the social exchanges that individuals experience in their immediate social setting (Bronfenbrenner & Morris, 1998). According to Bronfenbrenner (2005), these exchanges (e.g. parent–child communication) result in gradual adaptation (i.e. development) throughout the lifespan. Indeed, as noted by Kremer-Sadlik and Kim (2007), it is the processes that occur during sport participation – not one's participation itself – that have the potential to foster positive developmental outcomes for children and families.

Person characteristics are the ascribed or achieved traits of an individual that influence his or her development (Bronfenbrenner, 1999). Tudge, Mokrova, Hatfield, & Karnik (2009) suggest that some person characteristics are external (e.g. race, sex, height), eliciting immediate responses from the outside world. For example, a youth basketball coach might have two athletes arrive at a tryout; one is nearly 2 metres tall (i.e. 6 feet 6 inches) and another is much shorter. The external characteristic of 'being tall' might elicit excitement (and favourable bias) from the coach, whether the taller athlete is more skilled or not. Person characteristics can also be internal (e.g. intelligence, determination, compassion). These characteristics might be more important to an athlete's overall development and success, but are less accessible to coaches and managers who make personnel decisions.

Context, the hallmark of most ecological perspectives, consists of four progressively more distal systems of an individual's environment (the microsystem, mesosystem, exosystem, and macrosystem) that guide one's development. For example, the parent–child relationship (microsystem), the parent–coach relationship (mesosystem), the league or community sport mission (exosystem), and society's imperative on youth sport participation (macrosystem) all influence a young athlete's sport experience. Through a family lens, it is important to note that Darling and Steinberg (1993) describe parenting as perhaps the most important 'context' of child development.

Lastly, the PPCT perspective emphasises the role of *time* in human development (Bronfenbrenner, 2005; Bronfenbrenner & Morris, 1998). Time is a necessary component of development and is therefore described by family scholars as essential in any developmental theory (Elder, 1998). Indeed, Elder and other life course theorists (e.g. Bengston, Elder, & Putney, 2005) have advised practitioners to reflect on when something occurs within the context of history (e.g. did a woman's sport participation occur before or after Title IX?) as well as within the context of the individual's life (e.g. did the sport participation occur as a young person or as an adult?).

Both of these theoretical broad frameworks can shape our understanding of youth sport and the work practitioners conduct with parents and young athletes. It is important to note, however, that they need not be used simultaneously. Indeed, my own method is often eclectic, drawing from the appropriate tenets of multiple theories (broad and narrow) to inform my research and application. The two theories presented herein are simply *potential* lenses through which to better understand the role of families in youth sport.

Applying theory and research in practice

The most important aspect of working with parents or families in youth sport is translating our growing theoretical and research evidence base into practice. In this section, I provide insights from my own research and application to illustrate how I, and other research practitioners, have attempted to do this, while sharing insights from our ongoing projects.

A case study of an American sport family

Given preliminary support for the impact of children's sport experiences on other family members (i.e. parents) across the earliest stages of youth sport (Dorsch, Smith, & McDonough, 2009, 2015), a colleague and I are currently exploring parents' sport socialisation experiences over time. Over the past seven years, we have been conducting interviews with the family's father, mother, and child, and both parents have been regularly reflecting on their experiences in journals. In these data, family members are providing a unique insight into how parents' experiences are influenced by the child's sport experiences over time.

At a general level, our preliminary findings indicate that youth sport is playing an important role in fostering the child's relationships with both parents, is impacting the substance and tenor of the child's communication with both parents, and is informing the goals both parents have for their child's overall and sport-specific development. These preliminary interpretations underscore the utility of adopting a family-focused lens when working with athletes in youth sport. One example of the importance of doing so lies in the potential for 'spillover' from the sport to home domain. Indeed, in our work, the family's commitment to youth sport is greatly influencing their scheduling and financial decision-making.

Over the first seven years of the child's sport participation, the parents have developed stronger identities as 'sport parents', begun to view sport as a forum for their child to learn life lessons, and become increasingly committed to the athletic progression of their child. In sum, it is apparent that youth sport is influencing the entire family system via the proximal processes afforded to this family by the child's sport participation. In light of this understanding, practitioners interested in the family should not only focus on the impact of family (e.g. parent and sibling) involvement on youth sport outcomes, but also the nuanced effects of sport participation on family-level processes and outcomes.

Lessons learned from my experiences as a coach, practitioner, and parent

As a sport coach and practitioner, I have learned that parents, in most cases, are allies (see also Chapter 27). Too many people view 'sport parents' as a monolithic group of crazed individuals, who are only involved because they want to see their children ascend to greatness. Largely, this caricature is perpetuated by media reports that characterise youth sport parents as a 'problem' to be fixed. Instead, I have learned that parents are a resource, albeit one that can be enhanced (see next section on parent education strategies). Indeed, the vast majority of parents share the same goal as coaches: seeing young people become more skilled athletically, while also becoming better teammates, individuals, and representatives of the next generation. I have long wondered, if parent and coach goals are generally in alignment, why is there so much vitriol in many cases between them? One answer is a potential lack of communication between coaches and parents before, during, and after a sport season. To foster such communication, practitioners could measure the quantity and quality of the communication that takes place between coaches and parents, and assess its usefulness toward achieving positive development among participating young people.

As a new sport parent, I am learning that emotion is a powerful driver of behaviour (see Chapter 27 for further information). We all want the best for our children and we all have an inalienable expectation of fairness and opportunity. When those expectations are not met (i.e. when the outcomes of our children's participation do not meet our standards), it is easy to place the blame at someone else's feet. Practitioners can play an important role in helping parents understand and accept these emotions. I like to think of myself as an expert in the content area being discussed; however, that does not mean I am impervious to the same emotions other parents feel and act upon in youth sport. So how can we teach parents to more effectively cope with – and then act upon – their emotions in youth sport? The answer, I argue, lies in parent education.

Parent education programmes

The previous question has been the catalyst for my early career research at Utah State University. One thing that strikes me is that, although many practitioners are quick to prescribe 'fixes' for negative parent behaviour (e.g. silent Saturdays, parent contracts, signs encouraging good behaviour), evidence-based parent education programmes have yet to be systematically implemented and assessed across a wide range of youth sport settings. Below I highlight two programmatic interventions that targeted parents in youth sport, both of which may be adapted or implemented by practitioners seeking to enhance their work with parents. The first was designed, executed, and evaluated by members of my research laboratory in the United States. The second was designed and executed by Sam Thrower and his colleagues in the United Kingdom.

Programme 1

In ongoing research and outreach being conducted by my lab, youth sport administrators, coaches, and parents have expressed a desire for an evidence-based approach to parenting children in youth sport. This need is supported by anecdotal reports in the popular media that communicate children's dissatisfaction with parenting practices such as over-involvement, negative communication, and pressuring behaviours (e.g. Bigelow, Moroney, & Hall, 2001).

To address this desire, we first conducted a needs assessment in our local community. In doing so, our primary aim was to highlight these key stakeholders' perceptions of how educational programming for parents in youth sport may impact parent involvement behaviour and children's developmental experiences. Indeed, I am of the mindset as a researcher that identifying the needs of parents and stakeholders is an important first step before attempting to plan and execute an intervention. From interviews with parents, coaches, and league administrators, it became clear that the current state of youth sport necessitated a formalised parent education strategy.

Informed by this needs assessment, we designed an evidence-based education programme for parents in the local youth sport community (Dorsch, Dunn, King, & Osai, 2015). Programming included a 33-page *guide* and a 45-minute *seminar*, both of which offered evidence-based tips and strategies for parenting in youth sport. While the *guide* was constructed to offer parents a self-paced curriculum, the *seminar* was designed to offer best practices to parents in a more directed, face-to-face setting.

Seven distinct categories of parent involvement serve as the framework for our educational programming:

1) The *youth sport participation* section highlights the reasons children participate in youth sport, as well as the reasons they drop out (see, e.g., Babkes & Weiss, 1999; Fredricks & Eccles, 2005).

2) The *developmental outcomes* section highlights the developmental processes children experience as they ascend in youth sport (see, e.g., Côté, Baker, & Abernethy, 2007).

3) The *participation rates* section underscores the unlikelihood of children participating in various sports in high school, college, and/or professionally (see, e.g., Aspen Institute, 2015; NFSHA, 2014).

4) The *communication* section offers parents strategies for communicating with their children, other parents, and coaches in youth sport (see, e.g., Knight & Holt, 2014; Dorsch, Smith, Wilson, & McDonough, 2015).

5) The *working with coaches* section offers parents tips from athletes and coaches on how and when to interact with a child's coach (see, e.g., Gould, Lauer, Rolo, Jannes, & Pennisi, 2006).

6) The *sport parent behaviour* section provides parents with tools for becoming effectively involved in their children's sport experiences (see, e.g., Dorsch, et al., 2015; Wuerth, Lee, & Alfermann, 2004). Specifically, it outlines a range of parent verbal sideline behaviours and their potential consequences, and highlights what children report wanting and not wanting from parents before, during, and after competitions (Harwood & Knight, 2015).

7) The *positive sport parenting* section focuses on supportive parenting strategies, meeting the emotional demands of sport, forging healthy relationships, and choosing appropriate sport settings for children (see Holt & Knight, 2014 for review).

In our pilot study, parents exposed to the intervention had children with enhanced perceptions of parent support, parent–child warmth, child enjoyment, and child competence from pre- to post-season. Further children's perceptions of parent pressure, parent–child conflict, and child stress all decreased from pre- to post-season (Dorsch, King, Dunn, Osai, & Tulane, 2017). Given such positive findings, practitioners might benefit from drawing on this intervention to structure their own work with parents, while also crafting more culturally or developmentally specific parent education programmes as required.

Programme 2

In the United Kingdom, Sam Thrower and his colleagues conducted initial research to identify tennis parents' education and support needs across contexts and developmental stages (Thrower, Harwood, & Spray, 2016a). Observational and interview data suggested a need to provide tennis parents with education in four areas:

1) Introductory needs: Parents need to understand how their involvement is influenced by their tennis knowledge, financial and time demands, and their personal reasons for involvement.
2) Organisational needs: Parents need to understand how the national, regional, or local governing body's organisational system works, and the ability to organise their child's competitions.
3) Development needs: Parents need to understand child and talent development, and the ability to make informed decisions with their child about her/his tennis involvement.
4) Competition needs: Parents need to understand how to communicate with their child and fulfil their pre-match, in-match, and post-match roles.

The authors recommended that practitioners meet these needs differently across an athlete's stages of development, a take-home message being that parents' needs can only be met if engaged in a supportive learning environment that provides them with structured education.

Thrower, Harwood, and Spray (2016b, 2017) subsequently delivered face-to-face and online interventions with parents of youth tennis players. Their face-to-face programme included seven workshops designed to run over a 12-week period for tennis parents with children between the ages of 5 and 10 years. Results of the work suggest the programme was effective in enhancing tennis parents' perceived knowledge, effect, and skills across a range of learning objectives. A subsequent online intervention showed similarly promising results, particularly with respect to improvements in sport parenting efficacy. However, the researchers noted that the effectiveness of any intervention is determined by parents' motivation to learn as well as continual support from key stakeholders such as administrators and coaches. In practice, this means interventions are not a quick fix. Rather, practitioners should attempt to build programmes that are sustainable and meaningful in their outcomes.

Conclusion

As I stated at the outset, youth sport cannot operate without families. It is therefore necessary for practitioners to understand and account for the role of family involvement in youth sport. Hopefully within this chapter I have offered some useful insights into how best to optimise family and parent involvement. If and when this mission is accomplished, parents will no longer be relegated to 'hidden' participants in youth sport; rather, they can be utilised as necessary contributors to a successful youth sport experience.

References

Aspen Institute (2015). *Sport for all, play for life: A playbook to get every kid in the game*. Retrieved from http://aspenprojectplay.org/sites/default/files/Aspen%20Institute%20Project%20 Play%20Report.pdf.

Babkes, M. L., & Weiss, M. R. (1999). Parental influence on children's cognitive and affective responses to competitive soccer participation. *Pediatric Exercise Science, 11*, 44–62.

Bengston, V. L., Elder Jr, G. H., & Putney, N. M. (2005). The life course perspective on ageing: Linked lives, timing, and history. In M. L. Johnson (Ed.), *The Cambridge Handbook of Age and Aging*. Cambridge, UK: Cambridge University Press.

Bigelow, B., Moroney, T., & Hall, L. (2001). *Just Let the Kids Play: How to Stop Adults from Ruining Your Child's Fun and Success in Youth Sports*. Deerfield Beach, FL: Health Communications.

Bremer, K. L. (2012). Parental involvement, pressure, and support in youth sport: A narrative literature review. *Journal of Family Theory & Review, 4*, 235–248.

Bronfenbrenner, U. (1999). Environments in developmental perspective: Theoretical and operational models. In S. L. Friedman & T. D. Wachs (Eds.), *Measuring Environment across the Life Span: Emerging Methods and Concepts* (pp. 3–28). Washington, DC: American Psychological Association.

Bronfenbrenner, U. (2005). *Making Human Beings Human: Bioecological Perspectives on Human Development*. Thousand Oaks, CA: Sage.

Bronfenbrenner, U., & Morris, P.A. (1998). The ecology of developmental process. In R. M. Lerner (Ed.) & W. Damon (Series Ed.), *Handbook of Child Psychology*, Vol. 1: *Theoretical Models of Human Development* (5th ed., pp. 993–1027). New York, NY: Wiley.

Côté, J., Baker, J., & Abernethy, B. (2007). Practice and play in the development of sport expertise. In R. Eklund & G. Tenenbaum (Eds.), *Handbook of Sport Psychology* (3rd ed., pp. 184–202). Hoboken, NJ: Wiley.

Darling, N., & Steinberg, L. (1993). Parenting style as context: An integrative model. *Psychological Bulletin, 113*, 487–496.

Dorsch, T. E., Dunn, C. R., King, M. Q., & Osai, K. V. (2015). *Parent Guide: Evidence-Based Strategies for Parenting in Organized Youth Sport*. Logan, UT: Utah State University Families in Sport Lab.

Dorsch, T. E., King, M., Dunn, C. R., Osai, K. V., & Tulane, S. (2017). The impact of evidence-based parent education in organized youth sport: A pilot study. *Journal of Applied Sport Psychology, 29*, 199–214.

Dorsch, T. E., Smith, A. L., & McDonough M. H. (2009). Parents' perceptions of child-to-parent socialization in organized youth sport. *Journal of Sport & Exercise Psychology, 31*, 444–468.

Dorsch, T. E., Smith, A. L., & McDonough, M. H. (2015). Early socialization of parents through organized youth sport. *Sport, Exercise, and Performance Psychology, 4*, 3–18.

Dorsch, T. E., Smith, A. L., Wilson, S. R., & McDonough, M. H. (2015). Parent goals and verbal sideline behaviour in organized youth sport. *Sport, Exercise, and Performance Psychology, 4*, 19–35.

Elder, G. H. (1998). The life course as developmental theory. *Child Development, 69*, 1–12.

Fraser-Thomas, J., Côté, J., & Deakin, J. (2005). Youth sport programs: An avenue to foster positive youth development. *Physical Education and Sport Pedagogy, 10*, 19–40.

Fredricks, J. A., & Eccles, J. S. (2005) Family socialization, gender, and sport motivation and involvement. *Journal of Sport & Exercise Psychology, 27*, 3–31.

Gordin, R. D. (2012). Dr. Rich Gordin. In M. Aoyagi & A. Poczwardowski (Eds.), *Expert Approaches to Sport Psychology: Applied Theories of Performance Excellence* (pp. 37–49). Morgantown, WV: Fitness Information Technology.

Gould, D., Lauer, L., Rolo, C., Jannes, C., & Pennisi, N. (2008). The role of parents in tennis success: Focus group interviews with junior coaches. *The Sport Psychologist, 22*, 18–37.

Harwood C. G., & Knight, C. J. (2015). Parenting in youth sport: A position paper on parenting expertise. *Psychology of Sport and Exercise, 16*, 24–35.

Holt, N. L., & Knight, C. J. (2014). *Parenting in Youth Sport: From Research to Practice*. Abingdon, UK: Routledge.

Horn, T. S. (2004). Lifespan development in sport and exercise psychology: Theoretical perspectives. In M. R. Weiss (Ed.), *Developmental Sport and Exercise Psychology: A Lifespan Perspective* (pp. 27–71). Morgantown, WV: Fitness Information Technology.

Horn, T. S., & Horn, J. L. (2007). Family influences on children's sport and physical activity participation, behaviour and psychosocial responses. In G. Tenenbaum & R.C. Eklund (Eds.), *Handbook of Sport Psychology* (3rd ed., pp. 685–711). Hoboken, NJ: Wiley.

Knight, C. J., & Holt, N. L. (2014). Parenting in youth tennis: Understanding and enhancing children's experiences. *Psychology of Sport and Exercise, 15*, 155–164.

Kremer-Sadlik, T., & Kim, J. L. (2007). Lessons from sports: Children's socialization to values through family interaction during sports activities. *Discourse & Society, 18*, 35–52.

Lewin, K. (1935). *A Dynamic Theory of Personality*. New York, NY: McGraw-Hill.

National Federation of State High School Associations (NFSHSA). (2014). High School Athletics Participation Survey. Retrieved from www.nfhs.org /content.aspx?id=3282.

Smith, S. R., & Hamon, R. R. (2012). *Exploring Family Theories* (3rd ed.). New York, NY: Oxford.

Thrower, S. N., Harwood, C. G., & Spray, C. M. (2016a). Educating and supporting tennis parents: A grounded theory of parents' needs during childhood and early adolescence. *Sport, Exercise, and Performance Psychology, 5*, 107–124.

Thrower, S. N., Harwood, C. G., & Spray, C. M. (2016b). *Educating and supporting tennis parents: An exploratory online education programme*. Manuscript submitted for publication.

Thrower, S. N., Harwood, C. G., & Spray, C. M. (2017). Educating and supporting tennis parents: An action research study. *Qualitative Research in Sport, Exercise and Health, 9*, 600–618.

Tudge, J. R. H., Mokrova, I., Hatfield, B. E., & Karnik, R. B. (2009). Uses and misuses of Bronfenbrenner's bioecological theory of human development. *Journal of Family Theory & Review, 1*, 198–210.

Von Bertanlanffy, L. (1968). *General Systems Theory*. New York, NY: Braziller.

White, J. W., & Klein, D. M. (2008). *Family Theories* (3rd ed.). Thousand Oaks, CA: Sage.

Wuerth, S., Lee, M. J., & Alfermann, D. (2004). Parental involvement and athletes' career in youth sport. *Psychology of Sport and Exercise, 5*, 21–33.

11

PSYCHOLOGICAL CHARACTERISTICS OF DEVELOPING EXCELLENCE

An educationally sound approach to talent development

Áine MacNamara and Dave Collins

Talent development in sport is often accused of elitism, with its traditional focus on identifying and then developing those athletes thought to possess the potential to achieve at the highest level, but to the detriment of the majority of young players who will not progress along this competitive pathway. Reflecting the well-documented limitations of this approach (e.g. Collins & Bailey, 2015), in this chapter we discuss how ensuring *all* young athletes are equipped with necessary psycho-motor and psycho-behavioural skills offers benefits for both elite and lifelong participation in sport and physical activity. Ensuring the development and deployment of these skills, which act as the building blocks of development, is a particularly important consideration given the growing physical inactivity and obesity epidemic being experienced worldwide.

Of course, the 'lifelong' aspect of this proposition will necessitate a relatively fluid movement between different forms of participation throughout the lifespan; a young person may begin their participation at a recreational level before moving into more competitive settings. Alternatively, an athlete should be able to maintain their post-retirement involvement in sport at more participatory levels if they so choose. Our hypothesis is that, built on a common foundation of fundamental skills, individuals will be empowered to progress back and forth between different types of activity contexts. As such, focusing on the development, deployment, and refinement of psycho-behavioural and psychomotor skills during the early stages of the pathway should be a key consideration for practitioners and a focus for the early stages of talent development (see also Chapter 6).

Building on this contention, several authors (Collins et al., 2012; Collins, Martindale, Button, & Sowerby, 2010; Giblin, Collins, Kiely, & MacNamara, 2014) advocate for a new approach to talent development that enables a flow between different, but interrelated, motives for involvement, namely participation (i.e.

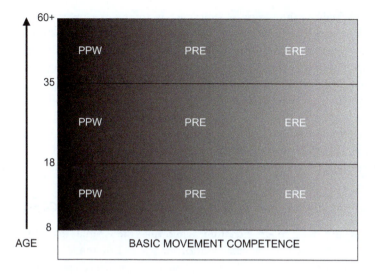

FIGURE 11.1 The Three Worlds Continuum

Source: Reproduced from *Participant Development in Sport: An Academic Review* with kind permission of The National Coaching Foundation (brand name Coaching UK). All rights reserved. Coaching UK subscription and membership services provide a range of benefits to coaches, including insurance and information services. For further details, please ring 0113-290 7612 or visit www.sportscoachuk.org.

Participation for Personal Wellbeing – PPW), personal excellence (i.e. Personal Referenced Excellence – PRE), and elite excellence (i.e. high-level sporting achievement; Elite Referenced Excellence – ERE). These authors stress the need to equip young people with the skills (i.e. psychomotor, psycho-behavioural), as well as actual and perceived competence, that can then be used to facilitate opportunities to progress back and forth between these different types of activities. Bailey and colleagues (2010) called this the Three Worlds Continuum (Participation – Personal Excellence – Elite Excellence; Figure 11.1), and such a structure can beneficially form the foundation of the talent development pathway. With this in mind, the purpose of this chapter is to explore the psycho-behavioural factors that promote this 'flow' and illustrate ways in which they may best be developed.

Equipping young people for challenge and choice

This skills approach to talent development recognises that progression and development in sport is likely to be non-linear and dynamic, with individuals choosing to engage in sport and physical activity for different motives at different points in their life (Abbott & Collins 2004; MacNamara, Button, & Collins, 2010a, 2010b). Indeed, and in contrast to the elitism arguments that have bedevilled talent development, this approach reflects an educational perspective as well as offering parallel benefits for a much broader scope of important issues, including lifelong physical activity promotion and generic achievement. In fact, the psycho-behavioural skills shown to facilitate the pursuit of excellence in sport also support achievement in non-sporting domains (Abbott & Collins, 2004; Holt & Dunn, 2004). In short, psycho-behavioural skills form part of the fundamentals that underpin learning, development, and performance in a variety of spheres and thus can underpin the achievement of many desirable targets.

It would seem sensible, therefore, for practitioners and stakeholders in talent development to consider the mechanisms that underpin progression and transfer in, and between, sporting activities as a primary focus of their practice. Accordingly, we begin this chapter by presenting the case for the role of Psychological Characteristics of Developing Excellence (PCDEs) as a key building block for athletic development.

Psychological Characteristics of Developing Excellence (PCDEs)

There is already a robust literature supporting the central role that psycho-behavioural factors play in elite performance (e.g. Ericsson & Charness, 1994, Durand-Bush & Salmela, 2002; Moore, Collins, Burtwitz, & Jess, 1998). In terms of talent development, MacNamara, Button, and Collins' (2010a; 2010b) retrospective studies of elite sport performers identified a range of psychological factors that aided the realisation of potential. MacNamara et al. (2010a) termed these psycho-behavioural characteristics *Psychological Characteristics of Developing Excellence* (PCDEs), a term encompassing both the trait characteristics (the tendency to …) and the state-deployed skills (the ability to … when …) shown to play a crucial role in the realisation of potential. As such PCDEs are not just mental skills, such as imagery or goal setting, but also include attitudes, emotions, and desires such as commitment (see Table 11.1). PCDEs allow young performers to optimise development opportunities (e.g. first-time appearances at a new level of competition, significant wins and losses), adapt to setbacks (e.g. injury, slumps in performance), and effectively negotiate key transitions (e.g. selection, demands for increased practice) encountered along the pathway to excellence.

If individuals are to fulfil their potentials, they must possess and systematically develop the necessary PCDEs that allow them to interact effectively with the developmental opportunities they are afforded within their performance environment (Côté, 1999; Simonton, 1999). As a result, the focus of the learning environment must reflect this developmentally appropriate agenda, incorporating a long-term focus with the emphasis on developing, testing, and refining the skills required for both current (getting involved) and future (staying involved) engagement (Collins, MacNamara, & McCarthy, 2016). A psychologist, teacher, coach, or parent can oversee this developmental process. However, what is most important is that all are involved in a coherent strategy to encourage, test, and refine the skills.

Applied example 1: Developing the PCDEs in an academy environment

Given the obvious importance of the PCDEs (plus the confidence to apply them), developing the skills is a central part of our work in sports academies. In one

TABLE 11.1 Psychological Characteristics of Developing Excellence

---

- Commitment
  - Arrives early to training
  - Works hard at own level
- Focus and Distraction Control
  - Remains focused under distraction
  - Displays a consistent pre-performance routine
- Realistic Performance Evaluation
  - The ability to analyse what you do well and what you do not
  - The ability to attribute success and failure appropriately
- Self-Awareness
  - Awareness of adaptive and maladaptive influences on performance
- Coping with Pressure
  - Reacts appropriately to mistakes and criticism
  - Shows confidence to thrive under pressure
- Planning and Self-Organisation
  - The ability to balance lifestyle commitments
  - The ability to prioritise different activities
- Goal Setting
  - The ability to set short, medium, and long-term goals
  - The ability to set appropriate goals
- Quality Practice
  - The ability to maximise understanding in training
  - Shows an understanding of why you are doing what you are doing
- Effective Imagery
  - Using imagery to rehearse new skills
  - Using imagery to simulate new environments
- Actively Seeking Social Support
  - Knows when and how to seek out support from others

Source: Adapted from MacNamara & Collins, 2010a, 2010b.

particular context in which we work, our aim is that young athletes have experienced input and application for all of the PCDEs by the age of 16. This curriculum prepares them for what is the sharp end of the pathway, when pressures really arise, and decisions on retain/release place a real emphasis on their performance.

Numerous principles apply to this curriculum. Firstly, the approach is skills-based, using a careful periodisation of challenge and support to teach-test-tweak the skills, then repeat in a positive spiral. Secondly, the skills are taught through a combination of formal, informal, and procedural methods. Through this medium, young athletes experience a gradual development of skills, which are then tested against realistic (rather than contrived) challenges. After each challenge, coaches and other practitioners engage the athletes in review, developing their own capacity to evaluate and self-manage in tandem with structured feedback. Given the need for reflection and refinement, this approach is built around a periodised use of challenge, allowing sufficient time for athletes to learn from, develop and refine, and, crucially, secure confidence in their capacity to use the skills.

The formal delivery component will usefully involve both psychologist and sports coach (at the least) in presenting the skill. Of course, in a team sport situation this represents numerous challenges since the provision of support is a complex issue and a range of individual differences mediate the impact of mental skills training (see Chapters 5 and 25 for further details). As such, the need for an individualised and gradual approach to the development and deployment of PCDEs is another important feature of this approach. This is backed up by a variety of informal interactions, with coach, psychologist, parent, other support specialists, and even fellow players modelling effective application of the skill to realistic challenges. The procedural part also helps to keep the skills at the forefront, and embed them within the culture of life for the young player. For example, post-game debrief procedures will expect 'Realistic Performance Evaluation' as a normal feature.

Thirdly, the skills are taught, deployed, and culturally encouraged in the sport setting. As we say elsewhere in this chapter, this does not mean that the young performers are not encouraged to deploy the skills in other areas of their life (see Chapter 12). Indeed, getting this to happen becomes a rare problem as the performers gain confidence in their mental expertise. We do feel, however, that presenting the skills against the environment they are to be used in helps to maximise transfer. In simple terms, athletes see the skills as an essential part of their sport, rather than an additional skill that *might* be useful. Likewise, the environment must ensure that the skills are developed as a key part of the coaching framework and not seen as an additional and separate process.

Table 11.2 presents a section of the curriculum, in this case aimed at 9- and 10-year-old footballers. The principles espoused in the preceding paragraph should be clear within the activities suggested.

Players at this age will only be working on a subset of the full PCDE curriculum. As described in this chapter, a number of different features of good practice are embedded within the simple expectations. At later stages, formative evaluations are completed twice a year using the PCDEQ2 (Hill, MacNamara & Collins, 2017), which provides a self-rating on different elements (both positive and negative) of the characteristic psycho-behaviours. Importantly, these self-ratings are triangulated with coach evaluations, performance data, and school reports, providing a comprehensive picture of each player's development in this crucial domain and a useful resource for reviewing and refining the player's Individual Development Plan (IDP) in conjunction with key stakeholders. Action plans can

TABLE 11.2 A section of the U9/10s psychology curriculum from a premiership academy

Topic	Support	Challenge
Grit (Determination)	• **Session** on combining imagery and goal setting to improve performance • Coach selects and player presents good practice	• X Country run 4 times per season • Timed skills tests 4 times per season • Keepy-uppy challenge (home practice-group performance) • Behaviour goals for school and home
Coach-led Goal Setting	• Session on SMART goals • Coach models use in games and training	• Coach works with players to set goals for Grit challenges • Three levels goals at U10

then be contextualised against genuine performance challenges, further promoting application and enhancing motivation.

The nature of the challenge is also worth exploring from a practitioner perspective. When designing challenging periods, examples can be as simple as encouraging/holding back athletes to compete at levels above or below their current age grading, either through training or exposure in competitions. This can be achieved by drip feeding players into senior level competitions or training for short periods of time, and/or with specific targets set. Even simply warming up at major senior events with senior athletes or participating in an element of their technical skillset at intervals independent of the competition event itself (penalty kicking at half time for example) can have a significant impact on psychological development such as confidence. Care is needed to ensure genuine challenge and growth from this process; in recent times, over-management of athlete journeys has been a strong but often detrimental focus for development systems, with eliminating stress a priority. With this caveat addressed, we suggest that a well-planned, well-managed, periodised, and individualised challenge strategy has strong merit in the long-term development of more psychologically robust athletes.

Coherence: Aligning key stakeholders on the talent development pathway

Although there is considerable recognition that coherence is a characteristic of an effective talent pathway (Martindale, Collins, & Abraham, 2007; Henriksen, 2015), ensuring that coherent support networks exist in the talent development environment is a neglected area of both research and application (Webb, Collins, & Cruickshank, 2016). Martindale and colleagues identified five principles of effective talent development environments: (a) long-term aims and methods, (b) coherent support networks and messages, (c) emphasis on appropriate development over early success, (d) individualised and ongoing development, and (e) an integrated, holistic, and systematic approach. To meet our present concern of coherence, it is important that the key stakeholders (i.e. school, family, sport) work together to facilitate a logical, intentional, and progressive talent development pathway (Webb et al., 2016). Good management in these cases will ensure a degree of consistency so that developing athletes are directed along coherent lines and philosophies, while letting coaches apply their individual stamp within set conditions.

Given that young athletes, especially those identified as having the greatest potential, will encounter a variety of coaches (i.e. school, club, county, academy, international), it is essential that there is coherence in the approaches being undertaken. This parameterisation, what Webb et al. (2016) call the 'Goldilocks zone', is best achieved through a subtle blend of direction, epistemological alignment, and discussion between all concerned. Getting the parents on side is an important though often neglected part of this, and offers a strong base to the pathway when done early (see also Chapters 10 and 27). Parents play a significant and impactful role in the development of young athletes, especially during the early phases of development, and are an important influence on the young athlete (e.g. Côté, 1999; Wuerth, Lee, & Alfermann, 2004). Therefore the management and optimum use of parents should be a key consideration for talent development pathways (Gould, Dieffenbach, & Moffett, 2002).

Based on research in other fields, it appears that a lack of coherence could impact athlete success because of mixed messages, confused agendas, and lack of clear direction and directives. For example, there are often epistemological and behavioural mismatches between short- (e.g. youth success) and long-term (e.g. senior success) objectives and this can have significant implications for the development of young athletes. Indeed, the ability of youth coaches to genuinely work towards long-term aims (perhaps to the detriment of underage success) is constrained if their role is evaluated on results and short-term success. As such, it is important that there is organisational support for genuine talent development and a clear understanding of the aims and objectives of each stage of the talent pathway. Accordingly, for the most optimum results, all individuals involved in the Talent Development (TD) pathway should be aligned in their aims and objectives and this coherence should be characterised by consistency in the perceptions and behaviours of key stakeholders (see Chapter 20).

Of course, this approach does not propose that young athletes encounter 'iden-tikit' coaches along their pathway; Webb et al.'s (2016) 'Goldilocks' system is apparent in pathways where athletes engage with different types of coaches (but not too different), are exposed to different types of coaching methods (but not too different), and participate in different types of coaching and competition environments (but not too different). Essentially, all those working on the talent development pathway share and buy into a specific model of what should be happening during each phase of development.

Applied example 2: Working with parents to enhance coherence

This short example builds from example number 1 above, focusing on work in the sport/academy setting. There is clear recognition of the important role that parents play in the development process (see Chapter 10). Unfortunately, however, sport in general has often focused on the negative consequences of involving parents rather than on developing and exploiting the significant positives that are available (see Chapter 27).

In part, the need for some sort of parental education process is obvious. Even if parents have been through an academy process themselves, and even if that has occurred in the particular sport and recently enough to be representative, there is no reason to assume that they will have a deep understanding of what is involved, nor why or how it will be accomplished in this particular setting. Indeed, research has demonstrated small but significant and impactful differences between sport, coach, and parent in their knowledge of the TD process (Pankhurst & Collins, 2013; Pankhurst, Collins, & MacNamara, 2013). Even more notable were the differences demonstrated in what each stakeholder thought the others believed! At the same time, there is a real risk of patronising parents; the use of terms such as 'parent training', indeed even parent education, can come over badly, destroying the very relationships the process is meant to build.

So, reflecting these, and building on the advantages of coherence described earlier, benefits and concerns are optimised through early introduction and subsequent involvement of parents in the PCDE development process. Returning to any earlier example, 'Realistic Performance Evaluation' is proceduralised by encouraging parents to use the 'three good, three to work on' style when questioning their child post event. In similar fashion, 'Seeking and using social support' is enhanced by encouraging 'How can I help' type questioning by family and friends. Through simple and straightforward processes like this, the most appropriate supportive culture can be encouraged.

Applied example 3: Developing the potential of young people

Physical education and youth sport are prime examples of interventions that could prepare children for lifelong engagement along the Three Worlds Continuum. Consequently, we argue that talent development initiatives should be primarily focused on *education* rather than *activity* or *identification*. Giblin et al. (2014) term this Deliberate Preparation, where participation and performance in sport and physical activity can derive from a common, robust foundation of psychomotor and psychological skills.

One example of a talent development initiative that recognised the importance of Deliberate Preparation and PCDEs was the Developing the Potential of Young People in Sport (DPYPS) programme, developed in conjunction with Sport Scotland (Abbott, Collins, Sowerby, & Martindale, 2007; Collins et al. 2010). The DPYPS approach utilised a dual curriculum encompassing both psycho-behavioural and psychomotor skills, and was aimed at pupils in primary school and the early years of secondary school. Essentially, the skills offered within the DPYPS programme are those psychological and psychomotor fundamentals that underpin learning, development, and performance across performance domains and along the Three Worlds Continuum.

Unfortunately, there is a general international movement away from unified and collaborative provision towards separate policy delivery for mass participation and performance sport. In fact, almost all structures, systems, and initiatives are built on a twin-track approach and presented as structurally distinct and incompatible; clearly this lack of organisational 'buy-in' makes it difficult to implement a Three Worlds Continuum (see Collins & Bailey, 2015), though the presumptions of this approach should be seen as the best way forward.

The psychomotor activities within DPYPS were designed to initially promote a basic moves vocabulary (e.g. the ability to catch) before encouraging the combining of basic moves into increasingly complex coordinative structures (e.g. the ability to run, catch, *and* throw a ball). Subsequent involvement in diversified activities encouraged individuals to adapt coordinative structures to various conceptual and perceptual demands; this gradually moves from small sided games to child-appropriate versions of the game itself, thus aiding motivation and a feeling of progress. By providing for learning experiences in fundamental components such as jumping, running, hopping, and balance, it was hoped that DPYPS would offer young children the basic skills they need for successful early experiences and subsequent development in sport, be it at elite levels, participatory levels, or as health-related physical activity. But just as importantly, taking these activities forwards into 'full games' serves to empower and enthuse youngsters to get and stay involved. Their own perceptions of confidence are crucial in this respect.

The interlinked psycho-behavioural curriculum provided children with the PCDEs (e.g. goal setting, imagery, realistic performance evaluations, focus, and distraction control) that have been shown to facilitate learning and performance across all sporting domains and beyond. Although some schools and teachers develop such skills as a natural part of their pedagogical approach, the need for systematic education and practice is clear. The psycho-behavioural activities were presented to children developmentally, and in practice worked both as classroom activities and as an integrated part of teaching methodology. This included a series of activities presented across and within three levels to allow them to be matched to the students' capabilities. At level one, children were encouraged to realise their level of competence and to self-reinforce. At level two, children were encouraged to begin to take responsibility for their own development. At level three, children were encouraged to aspire to excellence by achieving autonomous development. To illustrate how this worked in practice, exemplars of imagery activities at each of the three levels are presented below:

- *Level one imagery (Figure 11.2).* Children were presented with practical tasks that promote the use of imagery. The tasks highlight how imagery, if used alongside practice, can help build confidence and improve performance.
- *Level two imagery (Figure 11.3).* At this level, children were presented with practical tasks that promoted the use of controlled imagery during practice and competition.

Using Imagery to Improve Confidence and Performance

Part one

Pupils look at the star shape below and 'image' following the route to successfully draw the star in one movement. The pupils are told to have a go drawing the star and reflect on how imagery helped.

Part two

Pupils watch a video of an athlete who is imaging running around a slalom course (the Illinois agility run) and then reflect on the athlete's use of imagery.

The pupils then image successfully completing the slalom course below before running the slalom course and reflecting on whether imagery helped them.

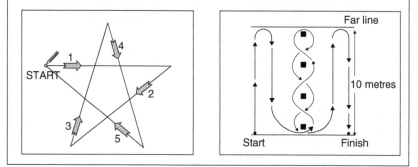

FIGURE 11.2 Example of level one psycho-behavioural activity designed to promote imagery

Source: Reprinted with permission from Abbott, A., Collins, D., Sowerby, K., & Martindale, R. (2007). Developing the potential of young people in sport (Edinburgh, sportscotland).

- *Level three imagery (Figure 11.4).* Level three was presented at a sport-specific level that provided coaches with guidance on how to promote the PCDEs developed at level one and two within their sport-specific context. In this example, the coach identifies the behaviours athletes in their sport need to show in order to use controlled imagery (i.e. athlete behaviour; what will we see your athletes doing during training and competition to show they are using controlled imagery). Systems and coach behaviours that can be employed to promote imagery use are then developed.

The impact of the DPYPS programme was seen not only in the sporting context: there were also reports of benefits of the DPYPS approach carrying over into other dimensions of excellence. For example, following the intervention the children were able to transfer the skills acquired though the DPYPS programme to other arenas and challenges (Abbott et al., 2007; Chapter 12). Specifically, the generic approach to development and participation that characterised DPYPS was

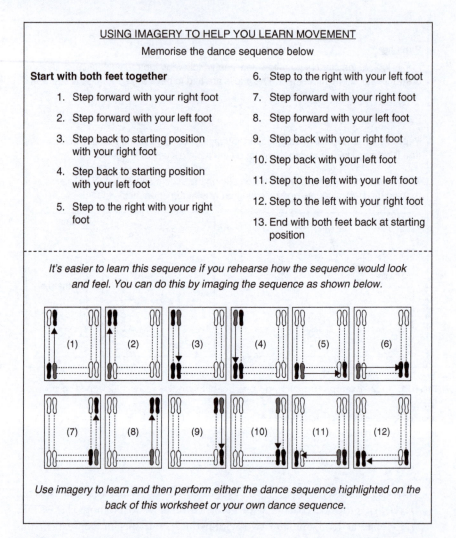

FIGURE 11.3 A sample of level two psycho-behavioural activity designed to promote imagery

Source: Reprinted with permission from Abbott, A., Collins, D., Sowerby, K., & Martindale, R. (2007). Developing the potential of young people in sport (Edinburgh, sportscotland).

cited as a particular strength since it encouraged children to adapt the PCDEs they acquired to various sporting and non-sporting activities. The generic benefits of the DPYPS approach were in keeping with the notion that individuals will move between different motives for participation as they progress along the Three Worlds Continuum.

Athlete Behaviour	Coach System	Coach Behaviour
When learning a new skill, the athlete mentally rehearses the new skill before physically trying the skill	a. Use video/demonstration to provide a prompt for imagery b. Give the athlete time to incorporate the new skill into their imagery script c. Allow the athlete to spend time imaging as well as doing the new skill	a. Reinforce the role of imagery b. Emphasise that to learn effectively you need to focus on relevant cues c. Praise athletes who spend time mentally preparing

FIGURE 11.4 Potential systems and coach behaviours that promote imagery use in a specific sport
Source: Reprinted with permission from Abbott, A., Collins, D., Sowerby, K., & Martindale, R. (2007). Developing the potential of young people in sport (Edinburgh, sportscotland).

Conclusion

In this chapter we have proposed that equipping young people with PCDEs, and promoting and reinforcing their application through a variety of means, enables individuals to pursue the intertwined targets of lifelong physical activity and sporting excellence. In fact, a significant body of evidence highlights how the attributes underpinning successful involvement in performance sport appear to be the very same factors that empower an individual to choose to be physically active throughout their life. Focusing on the development, deployment, and refinement of PCDEs (as well as psychomotor and perceptual-cognitive skills) as a central component of talent development should therefore ensure that both agendas (lifelong physical activity and sporting prowess) can be achieved through the same route (cf. Bailey et al., 2010). This educational-based approach would also counter the 'exclusive and anti-educational' criticisms often levelled at talent development initiatives as well as offering a more empirically driven and evidence-based approach than many of the short-term talent development models currently in vogue in sport.

References

Abbott, A., & Collins, D. (2004). Eliminating the dichotomy between theory and practice in talent identification and development: Considering the role of psychology. *Journal of Sports Sciences, 22*, 395–408.

Abbott, A., Collins, D., Sowerby, K., & Martindale, R. (2007). *Developing the Potential of Young People in Sport.* Retrieved from www.sportscotland.org.uk/documents/resources/developingthepotentialofyoungpeopleinsport.pdf.

Bailey, R., Collins, D., Ford, P., MacNamara, A., Toms, M., & Pearce, G. (2010). *Participant Development in Sport: An Academic Review.* Leeds, UK: sportscoachUK.

Collins, D., & Bailey, R. (2015). A sporting utopia: Easing the essential tension in sport policy. In R. Bailey and M. Talbot (Eds.), *Elite Sport and Sport-for-All: Bridging the Two Cultures* (pp. 134–146). Abingdon, UK: Routledge.

Collins, D., Bailey, R., Ford, P., MacNamara, A., Toms, M., & Pearce, G. (2012). Three worlds: New directions in participant development in sport and physical activity. *Sport, Education and Society, 12*, 225–243.

Collins, D., MacNamara, Á., & McCarthy, N. (2016). Putting the bumps in the rocky road: Optimizing the pathway to excellence. *Frontiers in Psychology, 7*, 1482.

Collins, D., Martindale, R. J. J., Button, A., & Sowerby, K. (2010). Building a physically active and talent rich culture: An educationally sound approach. *European Physical Education Review, 16*, 7–28.

Côté, J. (1999). The influence of the family in the development of talent in sport. *The Sport Psychologist, 13*, 395–417.

Durand-Bush, N., & Salmela, J. H. (2002). The development and maintenance of expert athletic performance: Perceptions of world and Olympic champions. *Journal of Applied Sport Psychology, 14*, 154–171.

Ericsson, K. A., & Charness, N. (1994). Expert performance: Its structure and acquisition. *American Psychologist, 49*, 725–747.

Giblin, S., Collins, D., MacNamara, Á., & Kiely, J. (2014). 'Deliberate Preparation' as an evidence-based focus for primary physical education. *Quest, 66*, 385–395.

Gould D., Dieffenbach K., & Moffett, A. (2002). Psychological characteristics and their development in Olympic champions. *Journal of Applied Sport Psychology, 14*, 172–204.

Henriksen, K. (2015). Developing a high-performance culture: A sport psychology intervention from an ecological perspective in elite orienteering. *Journal of Sport Psychology in Action, 6*, 141–153.

Hill, A., MacNamara, A, & Collins, D. (2017). Initial development and validation of the Psychological Characteristics for Developing Excellence Questionnaire version 2 (PCDEQ2). Manuscript Submitted for Publication.

Holt, N., & Dunn, J. (2004). Toward a grounded theory of the psychosocial competencies and environmental conditions associated with soccer success. *Journal of Applied Sport Psychology, 16*, 199–219.

MacNamara, Á., Button, A., & Collins, D. (2010a). The role of psychological characteristics in facilitating the pathway to elite performance. Part 1: Identifying mental skills and behaviours. *The Sport Psychologist, 24*, 52–73.

MacNamara, Á., Button, A., & Collins, D. (2010b). The role of psychological characteristics in facilitating the pathway to elite performance. Part 2: Examining environmental and stage related differences in skills and behaviours. *The Sport Psychologist, 24*, 74–96.

Martindale, R. J. J., Collins, D., & Abraham, A. (2007). Effective talent development: The elite coach perspective within UK sport. *Journal of Applied Sports Psychology, 19*, 187–206.

Moore, P., Collins, D. J., Burwitz, L., & Jess, M. (1998). *The Development of Talent Study (DOTS)*. London: English Sports Council.

Pankhurst, A. & Collins, D. (2013). Talent identification and development: The need for coherence between research, system and process. *Quest, 65*, 83–97.

Pankhurst, A., Collins, D., & MacNamara, A. (2013). Talent development: Linking the stakeholders to the process. *Journal of Sports Sciences, 31*, 370–380.

Simonton, D. (1999). Talent and its development: An emergenic and epigenetic model. *Psychological Review, 106*, 435–457.

Webb, V., Collins, D., & Cruickshank, A. (2016). Aligning the talent pathway: Exploring the role and mechanisms of coherence in development. *Journal of Sports Sciences, 34*, 1799–1804.

Wuerth, S., Lee, M., & Alfermann, D. (2004). Parental involvement and athletes' career in youth sport. *Psychology of Sport and Exercise, 5*, 21–33.

12

'BETTER PEOPLE MAKE BETTER ATHLETES'

Promoting a positive youth development approach with young athletes

Scott Pierce

Over the past ten years, the New Zealand men's rugby team, the All Blacks, have a winning percentage of over 85 per cent, which makes them one of the 'winningest' professional sports team in the world. During this time, the team have been guided by the philosophy that 'Better People Make Better All Blacks' (Hodge, Henry, & Smith, 2014). The leadership group of the All Blacks have put a similar emphasis on developing successful people by promoting attributes such as personal responsibility as they have on developing successful rugby players by promoting attributes of effective decision making (Kerr, 2013). For coaches and applied practitioners working with teams and athletes at the youth level, the message should be clear – if personal development can be a major focus for sport programmes at the most elite level, then personal development should be a major focus for sport programmes and for athletes at the youth level!

This chapter seeks to help practitioners, coaches, and sporting organisations create a dedicated approach to developing youth as people, as well as athletes. This chapter will, first, synthesise the research in sport-based positive youth development (PYD) to show what is known about how to develop life skills in young athletes. Following this, the research and anecdotal coaching and psychological skills training experiences will be integrated in three sections that provide strategies and recommendations to help young people develop life skills. The first section will encourage practitioners to get to know who their athletes are as individuals. The second section will outline how interactions and experiences in the youth sport context can be utilised and structured to explicitly and implicitly develop life skills in young athletes. The third section will emphasise the need to expand applied sport psychology and coaching practices beyond the sports field to help young people transfer life skills to other areas of life.

What does research in sport psychology tell us about developing young athletes as people?

Over the past 30 years, researchers have scientifically challenged the assumption that sport builds character in young people. The good news is that sport can help to develop psychological skills and attributes for young people to utilise in other areas of their lives (e.g. school, workplace). The reality is that this development does not occur automatically. It is imperative that adults involved in youth sport are aware that life skills development is not guaranteed, but that they play a pivotal role in helping this occur (Gould & Carson, 2008).

What are life skills?

Life skills have been defined as 'those internal personal assets, characteristics, and skills such as goal setting, emotional control, self-esteem, and hard work ethic that can be facilitated or developed in sport and transferred for use in non-sport settings' (Gould & Carson, 2008, p. 60). These skills have been categorised as behavioural (e.g. being assertive) or cognitive (e.g. making effective decisions); and interpersonal (e.g. communicating effectively with peers and adults) or intrapersonal (e.g. setting personal goals) (Danish, Forneris, Hodge, & Heke, 2004). To add to these action- able life skills, sport has the capability to create dispositional changes in athletes (e.g. greater self-confidence) that can facilitate holistic personal change and trans- form how these athletes view themselves as people outside of sport (Chinkov & Holt, 2016).

It is important to note that the aforementioned life skills are not dissimilar to the psychological skills identified as being beneficial for individual athletes and teams to produce gold medal and world championship success at the most elite level. For example, Gould and Maynard (2009) identified the attributes necessary for success at the Olympic level. Such attributes included: psychological states or attributes (e.g. confidence, emotional control, self-awareness), cognitive and behavioural strategies (e.g. goal setting, mistake management plans, enjoyment strategies), and personal dispositions (e.g. optimism, trait hope, adaptive perfectionism). Similarly, the world champion New Zealand All Blacks created a culture around personal and collec- tive responsibility, leadership, and expectations for excellence (Hodge et al., 2014) and Super Bowl and collegiate national championship winning American football coach, Pete Carroll, has consistently emphasised the promotion of optimism and personal responsibility in his athletes and teams (Voight & Carroll, 2006). With such commonality between desirable life skills and the psychological skills required to succeed in sport, it is easy to see why *better people might make better athletes.*

How are life skills learned?

The challenge for coaches, applied practitioners, and sport organisations is knowing how to develop these skills and attributes in young people. Researchers have been investigating this issue and have identified three key considerations:

1) Research across youth development has made it clear that young people are active producers of their own development (Larson, 2011). Each young athlete will join a team or club with their own existing personality and life skills, an established social support system, and their own experiences that will influence if and how life skills will be learned in sport (Gould & Carson, 2008; Pierce, Gould, & Camiré, 2016).

2) Youth sport is an extracurricular activity that provides young people with unique positive and negative experiences (Fraser-Thomas & Côté, 2009). These experiences and athletes' subsequent life skill development will be influenced by the coach's philosophy and characteristics and how he/she coaches for performance enhancement and personal development (Gould & Carson, 2008; Pierce et al., 2016; Turnnidge, Côté, & Hancock, 2014).

3) For a psychological skill to be classified as a life skill, it must be transferred to other life domains and create personal change in the young person (Pierce et al., 2016). Youth will experience multiple life domains outside of sport where they will be confronted with contextual factors that will help or hurt their ability to successfully transfer life skills from sport. Furthermore, youths' perceptions of domains outside of sport will influence if and how life skills are transferred (Pierce et al., 2016).

These three major areas of consideration are presented in Figure 12.1 and will be explored in the following sections of this chapter. Specific examples and anecdotal experiences are provided to help practitioners, coaches, and sport organisations understand and promote life skills development and transfer.

Get to Know the Person and the Athlete	Utilise and Structure Sport to Develop People and Athletes	Work Beyond the White Lines: Encourage Life Skills Transfer
□ Identify athlete's age and level of cognitive maturity	□ Identify a philosophy for how to help youth develop life skills	□ Identify contexts where youth can transfer life skills o Build coalitions with schools
□ Identify athlete's existing psychological skills and life skills o Motivation o Self-awareness o Reflection	□ Commit to developing strong coach–athlete relationships	o Recruit teachers and parents as advocates
□ Learn athlete's autobiographical story	□ Create a balance between support and challenge for teaching life skills	□ Create life experiences with transfer opportunities
	□ Design approaches to directly teach life skills o Define and discuss skills o Set standards to reinforce skills	□ Help athletes reflect on what life skills they possess and how they can be applied in various domains
	□ Design approaches to indirectly teach life skills o Provide opportunities to use and experience skills in sport	

FIGURE 12.1 Practical strategies for coaches, practitioners, and sport organisations to develop psychological skills as life skills

Developing life skills in practice

Get to know the person and the athlete

Children do not enter sport as blank slates (Gould & Carson, 2008). Before a coach or practitioner begins working with young athletes, the children will already have developed a unique set of cognitive and behavioural skills, as well as the intrapersonal and interpersonal skills that they use in sport and life. Children will also vary in the level and quality of social support (e.g. family, friends, and mentors) and their autobiographical experiences (e.g. socioeconomic background), which will influence how they perceive the value and applicability of life skills. Getting to know the young athletes as people is a key first step in helping them grow as an athlete and a person.

One major consideration is the age and maturity of the young athletes. The age and maturity of the child impacts what and how much can be learned and developed from a sport programme. The First Tee golf programme has been found to successfully develop transferable life skills in young golfers (Weiss, Stuntz, Bhalla, Bolter, & Price, 2013), and provides an insightful example of how to build a developmentally appropriate life skills programme. Specifically, the multi-tiered programme introduces the rules of golf and promotes the development of 'a game plan for golf and life' to the beginning 7-year-old participants. As participants become older and more mature, more complex life skills are introduced (e.g. interpersonal communication for 9-year-olds; resilience and conflict resolution skills for 13-year-olds) (The First Tee, 2016). In my experience as a volunteer coach for The First Tee programme, this approach proved valuable in first creating a motivational climate for developing life skills and then introducing more complex skills as children begin to understand the nature of the skill and have experiences in sport and life where they can apply the skill. To continue to integrate the development of sport skills with life skills across sports, it is important for coaches and practitioners to become aware of developmental changes in young people (see Chapters 4 and 5) and align sport and life skill development with these stages.

Another major consideration is understanding the psychological make-up of the young athlete (Gould & Carson, 2008). Although there is no perfect recipe of psychological attributes that will ensure young athletes develop life skills that transfer to life domains, several attributes can be influential. Through my scientific study and applied consulting at youth sport camps, I have learned from young athletes about some key skills that facilitate the growth of life skills. These attributes are highlighted through the case studies of two young male athletes experiencing an intensive wrestling camp. One athlete entered the camp *motivated to learn* how to become a better person, was *aware* that life skills could be developed through the wrestling camp, and engaged in regular *reflection* about what he was learning in sport and how it could be applied to life. Another athlete entered the camp motivated only to learn how to become a better wrestler, was unaware that life skills could be developed through sport, and did not reflect about learning life skills. Although both athletes believed they developed life skills from the camp, the first athlete experienced greater depth and scope in the life skills that he gained and the camp had a more positive long-term impact (Pierce, Gould, Cowburn, & Driska, 2016). Thus, to maximise life skill development it seems pertinent that coaches and practitioners first work to ensure young athletes are motivated and open to learning about life skills, aware of the potential for developing life skills, and reflective in their learning and growth, before promoting these attributes in young athletes.

Finally, the personal background and autobiographical story of each child needs to be a major consideration of coaches and practitioners (Martinek, Schilling, & Johnson, 2001). A number of years ago, I worked with a junior high school (age 11 to 13 years) American football programme in a city in Midwestern United States. The programme involved young males from diverse backgrounds, and my role as an applied practitioner focused on helping the athletes develop mental skills to succeed on the field and in the classroom. After the two-year programme, the school administrators shared data of high retention rates on the football team and improved grades in the classroom that they attributed to the mental skills programme. Reflecting on the programme as a practitioner, the key to this success was getting to know these young men on a personal level, and using this as a foundation to teach mental skills for sport and life. One participant shared his story of coming from a single parent home, often being teased by his classmates, and having a passion for the arts and acting as much as football. We built a strong relationship where I was committed to listening and learning about his experiences and challenges across all areas of his life, and discussing how psychological skills (e.g. goal setting and optimism) could be applied to all the areas of his life (e.g. home, classroom, acting, and football). During the programme, it was clear that he appreciated the attention and referred to me as his 'ride or die, brother' (a culturally specific title for a dedicated confidant). This highlighted that a key to helping this young man develop life skills was understanding and supporting his unique background before helping him apply the mental skills to areas of life (e.g. acting) that were important for him.

Utilise and structure sport to simultaneously develop people and athletes

Youth sport is a developmental context that has great potential to contribute to the development of transferable life skills in young people. If systematic and deliberate in their approach, practitioners, coaches, and sporting organisations can utilise and structure youth sport to simultaneously develop psychological skills for sport and for life domains. To do this, coaching philosophies and characteristics, direct approaches for teaching life skills, and indirect approaches for teaching life skills should be considered.

Coaches and practitioners should seek and create philosophies that focus on developing athletes as people, and then match their actions and behaviours to that philosophy (Camiré, Trudel, & Forneris, 2012). An example of a life skills-focused philosophy comes from a coach who has spent the past 40 years running a youth sport camp designed to teach life skills. Over time, the coach developed the belief that he is a 'planter of seeds' and his purpose in life is 'to plant the field (develop young people through youth sport) and get the seeds in the ground and plant not one but 100 acres (develop 100s of young people through his camps)' (Gould, Pierce, Cowburn, & Driska, 2017). Coaching philosophies develop with time and experience. Adults working in youth sport should begin to conceptualise their beliefs and guiding principles about how they view their role in helping young athletes develop life skills, to begin to formulate a philosophy to guide their practice.

Along with a coaching philosophy for teaching life skills, the coach/practitioner–athlete relationship is a key foundation to developing athletes as people. The old saying states that 'they don't care what you know until they know that you care', and this holds true for how children view adults in youth sport. Having consulted with athletes at the youth, high school, and collegiate level, it is clear that young athletes need to know that an adult cares about their life, in and out of sport, if they are to accept and embrace their guidance with psychological skills and life skills. Working with one collegiate head coach, I observed a concerted effort to begin daily interactions with student-athletes by focusing on topics and life outside of sport (e.g. family, school). It is not surprising that his current and former student-athletes describe him as a coach who cares and someone who has helped shaped who they are as athletes and people. Unfortunately, I have also observed approaches where practitioners have prioritised the financial bottom line over building relationships and caring about the young athletes and have struggled to grow and maintain sport psychology services for youth. From my viewpoint, the practitioner was more eager to show what they knew rather than show that they cared.

To connect sport skills to life skills, coaches should seek to understand how sport connects with each athlete's life. They should seek to ask questions about school/academics, meet and interact with family, learn about hobbies and interests outside of sport, and have a personal and professional relationship with each athlete to maximise their ability to help the development of life skills. A major consideration for the practitioner should be the balance of supporting and challenging the athlete. Young people can learn life skills when they are placed in adverse conditions (e.g. strict rules for time management; Pierce, Gould, Cowburn, et al., 2016) or even mentored with a 'tough-love' approach (Flett & Brown, 2016). It is, however, imperative that the coach is supportive and prioritises athlete wellbeing while maintaining standards and disciplining athletes when required. One needs to be acutely aware that parents and athletes may be resistant to the use of structured adversity in youth sport so practitioners must have a clear rationale for challenging young people to develop life skills that is clearly articulated to athletes and their families.

Life skills can be taught to athletes in numerous different ways. Coaches can directly teach skills by explicitly stating what the skills are and how they can be used in life (e.g. give a team talk on how to use goal setting in sport and life), and coaches can indirectly teach skills by structuring the sport environment in a way that implicitly helps athletes learn skills for sport and life (e.g. present athletes with problems in practice sessions to improve communication and decision making) (Gould & Carson, 2008; Turnnidge et al., 2014). Effective youth sport practitioners make the commitment to systematically structure their programmes to use a combination of both approaches to help young people grow as athletes and as people.

Numerous youth sport programmes integrate these approaches in innovative ways. One key to this integrative approach is choosing skills that have clear links between sport and multiple areas of life. The First Tee golf programme has nine core values that are easily linked to golf and life domains. For example, honesty is vital in golf where athletes keep their own score and in the classroom where students require honesty in test-taking situations (The First Tee, 2016). Similarly, the wrestling camp described earlier seeks to teach seven key life skills (hard work, discipline, dedication, responsibility, accountability, sacrifice, and service) that are applicable to wrestling and life, and integrate direct and indirect teaching approaches to teach each skill. For instance, when responsibility is the focus, direct teaching approaches are used, in the form of a lecture that defines personal responsibility and the need for it in sport and life, personal stories, examples, and metaphors from camp staff, and the reinforcement of camp rules related to personal responsibility. Additionally, the camp environment is set up to indirectly teach the skill of responsibility; campers are deducted points in the camp point system when they do not follow the rules implicitly related to responsibility, punished with extra workouts if they do not keep their dorm rooms clean, and required to take responsibility for their learning (Pierce, Gould, Cowburn, et al., 2016).

In addition, effective youth sport programmes reinforce and reward the successful use of the skills on and off the field. For example, the Ohio State University (OSU) LiFEsports programme is designed to teach life skills to at-risk youth through sport (OSU LiFEsports, 2016). In the successful university football programme, players get rewarded for good performance with famous Ohio State Buckeye helmet stickers. Subsequently, in the LiFEsports programme, the same respected stickers are used as 'boosters' to reward the use of life skills that have been taught in the programme. While every youth sport coach or practitioner may do it in their own innovative way, both direct and indirect approaches can and should be used to explicitly and implicitly help athletes learn and develop life skills.

Work beyond the white lines: Encourage life skills transfer

A reporter once asked American college football coach Amos Alonzo Stagg if he had a successful season. 'I won't know how good a job I did for 20 years,' he stated, 'that's when I'll see how my boys turned out' (Batterson, Foth, & Foth Aughtmon, 2015). The goal of developing life skills in young athletes is a long-term process and coaches or practitioners may not even witness the positive outcomes for their athletes. This does not mean, however, that their role is limited to the sports field or court. Coaches, practitioners, and sporting organisations can play a pivotal role in helping youth transfer life skills from sport to other life domains.

Coaches and practitioners should actively help athletes identify the life domains where they will have opportunities to transfer life skills and the key factors in these environments that support the transfer of life skills (Pierce, Gould, & Camiré, 2016). One beneficial approach for practitioners is to teach skills and explicitly encourage their use across life domains. Researchers have promoted effective strategies for connecting with the school setting and have encouraged practitioners to embrace the classroom as a life domain to transfer life skills. For instance, when teaching goal setting, practitioners can work with young people to simultaneously set goals to improve sport performance and academic performance. Anecdotally, continually promoting the use of skills in sport and the classroom has been a valuable technique to help athletes enhance their awareness of life skills and their confidence in transferring life skills across domains.

Practitioners can also build coalitions with schools to promote a similar culture for developing and transferring life skills and find advocates and mentors (e.g. teachers) in the school system that can reinforce and support life skills messages from sport (Martinek & Lee, 2012). Parents are another key social support system for facilitating the transfer of life skills. Many effective youth sport programmes make a committed effort to providing parents with programme information (e.g. OSU LiFEsports, 2016). The process of life skills transfer can benefit from practitioners providing parents with information about the life skills being taught and encouraging them to be advocates of the life skills outside of sport.

Life skill transfer opportunities can also be created for young athletes. At high school and collegiate level sport, community service and outreach has been recognised and utilised as a common approach to promote the transfer of life skills. I have worked with athletes and teams who have served at homeless shelters and food kitchens, as well as meeting, mentoring, and playing with sick children in the wider community. This engagement and outreach can provide young athletes with opportunities to put interpersonal skills into action outside of the sport context and to gain a new appreciation for helping and working with others. In the OSU LiFEsports programme, a leadership group of former campers has been established (OSU LiFEsports, 2016). This approach is effective as the group meets regularly after the camp, provides athletes with opportunities to reflect on the life skills learnt in sport, provides young people with opportunities to transfer skills, and helps them identify if and how the skills are being transferred to other life domains.

The key to these approaches is the reflection and discussion about what life skills are being applied in the experiences, how the skills connect to those learned in sport, and how the experience may have changed or shaped the athletes as people. Coaches and practitioners should seek innovative approaches for reminding and reinforcing athletes of the life skills that were learnt through sport. For example, the wrestling camp discussed earlier promotes personal journals to encourage the continued learning and transfer of life skills (Pierce, Gould, Cowburn, et al., 2016), and uses social media (e.g. Facebook) to connect with the athletes outside of camp and reinforce the messages that were taught.

Conclusion

Young people who learn cognitive, behavioural, intrapersonal, and interpersonal skills through sport not only put themselves in an excellent position to be better athletes but also put themselves in an excellent position to be better people. This chapter encourages practitioners, coaches, and sporting organisations to get to know their athletes, utilise and structure sport to develop key psychological skills, and promote the transfer of skills from sport to life to ultimately develop better people and better athletes. This insight from scientific research and anecdotal applied experiences in sport psychology was shared with the goal of providing practitioners and coaches with the tools to help young athletes develop life skills as well psychological skills for sport performance. Although it is a significant commitment to invest in young athletes and systematically structure the youth sport experience, better people and better athletes can be developed simultaneously, and I would argue this should be an integrated goal for all practitioners working with youth athletes.

References

Batterson, M., Foth, R., & Foth Aughtmon, S. (2015). *A Trip around the Sun: Turning Your Everyday Life into the Adventure of a Lifetime*. Ada, MI: Baker Publishing.

Camiré, M., Trudel, P., & Forneris, T. (2012). Coaching and transferring life skills: Philosophies and strategies used by model high school coaches. *The Sport Psychologist, 26*, 243–260.

Chinkov, A. E., & Holt, N. L. (2016). Implicit transfer of life skills through participation in Brazilian Jiu-Jitsu. *Journal of Applied Sport Psychology, 28*, 139–153.

Danish, S., Forneris, T., Hodge, K., & Heke, I. (2004). Enhancing youth development through sport. *World Leisure Journal, 46*(3), 38–49.

Flett, R., & Brown, R. (2016). A balancing act: Benefits and concerns of a tough-love approach to coaching inner-city females. *Journal of Exercise, Movement, and Sport, 48*, 86.

Fraser-Thomas, J., & Côté, J. (2009). Understanding adolescents' positive and negative developmental experiences in sport. *The Sport Psychologist, 23*, 3–23.

Gould, D., & Carson, S. (2008). Life skills development through sport: Current status and future directions. *Sport & Exercise Psychology Reviews, 1*, 58–78.

Gould, D., & Maynard, I. (2009). Psychological preparation for the Olympic games. *Journal of Sport Sciences, 27*, 1393–1408.

Gould, D., Pierce, S., Cowburn, I., & Driska, A. (2017). How coaching philosophy drives coaching action: A case study of renowned wrestling coach J. Robinson. *International Sport Coaching Journal, 4*, 13–37.

Hodge, K., Henry, G., & Smith, W. (2014). A case study of excellence in elite sport: Motivational climate in a world champion team. *The Sport Psychologist, 28*, 60–74.

Kerr, J. (2013). *Legacy: What the All Blacks Can Teach Us about the Business of Life*. London: Legacy Constable & Robinson.

Larson, R. W. (2011). Positive development in a disorderly world. *Journal of Research on Adolescence, 21*, 317–334.

Martinek, T., & Lee, O. (2012). From community gyms to classrooms: A framework for values-transfer in schools. *Journal of Physical Education, Recreation & Dance, 83*, 33–51.

Martinek, T., Schilling, T., & Johnson, D. (2001). Transferring personal and social responsibility of underserved youth to the classroom. *Urban Review, 33*, 29–45.

OSU LiFEsports (2016). *Ohio State University LiFEsports: Learning in fitness and education.* Retrieved from www.osulifesports.org/.

Pierce, S., Gould, D., & Camiré, M (2016). Definition and model of life skills transfer. *International Review for Sport and Exercise Psychology, 10*, 186–211.

Pierce, S., Gould, D., Cowburn, I., & Driska, A. (2016). Understanding the process of psychological development in youth athletes attending an intensive wrestling camp. *Qualitative Research in Sport, Exercise and Health, 8*, 332–351.

The First Tee (2016). *The First Tee.* Retrieved from www.thefirsttee.org/Club/Scripts/Home/home.asp.

Turnnidge, J., Côté, J., & Hancock, D. J. (2014). Positive youth development from sport to life: Explicit or implicit transfer? *Quest, 66*, 203–217.

Voight, M., & Carroll, P. (2006). Applying sport psychology philosophies, principles, and practices onto the gridiron: An interview with USC football coach Pete Carroll. *International Journal of Sports Science & Coaching, 1*, 321–342.

Weiss, M. R., Stuntz, C. P., Bhalla, J., Bolter, N. D., & Price, M. S. (2013). 'More than a game': Impact of the First Tee life skills development programme on positive youth development: Project introduction and first year findings. *Qualitative Research in Sport, Exercise and Health, 5*, 214–244.

SECTION III
Key considerations during adolescence

13

SPORT PSYCHOLOGISTS ASSISTING YOUNG TALENTED ATHLETES FACED WITH CAREER TRANSITIONS

Paul Wylleman

> *The Norwegian Martin Odegaard created a first on Europe's football fields. With his 15 years and 300 days Odegaard became the youngest European Championship qualification player ever.*
>
> (Sporza, 2014)
>
> *16-year old swimmer Nyls Korstanje is not allowed to go to the European Championship short course.*
>
> (NOS, 2015)

From a psychological point of view, the opportunity to be selected for the first time at senior European level can be understood as containing the basis for a developmental conflict between what athletes perceive themselves to be, and what they want, or what they perceive they ought to be (Alfermann & Stambulova, 2007). As this conflict generally implies a need for 'change in assumptions about oneself and the world … [and] a corresponding change in one's behaviour and relationships' (Schlossberg, 1981, p. 5), it requires athletes to cope with a process of transition. For our two young talented athletes referred to above, this transitional process will consist for Martin of adapting to the world of senior players, while for Nyls it will entail coping with a developmental conflict instigated by the non-occurrence of an anticipated transition.

The purpose of this chapter is to explore how sport psychologists can support young talented athletes faced with transitional challenges. After a brief overview of research on transitions, examples of transitions faced by young talented athletes and interventions to be used by sport psychologists are described. In conclusion, some suggestions are provided for sport psychologists working with talented athletes faced with transitional challenges.

A holistic perspective on transitions

Sport psychologists' initial interest in transitions grew out of research conducted during the 1970–80s on retired professional/elite athletes and the occurrence of dropout in youth sport.[1] In both cases, an often definite, unexpected, unprepared, and 'before one's time' withdrawal from competitive sport made athletes prone to problems of coping and adjustment. Around this time, Schlossberg and colleagues' Model of Human Adaptation to Transition (Schlossberg, 1981) was also developed and a clear definition of a transition was formulated. As highlighted in the introduction, this definition recognised transitions as processes of changes influenced by the interaction of the individual's characteristics and perception of the transition, and the characteristics of the pre- and post-transition environments. Moreover, it was shown that the non-occurrence of an event could also lead to a transition. Extending Schlossberg's model, sport-specific models of transitions, such as Taylor and Ogilvie's (2001) career termination, were subsequently formulated.

Further, during the 1990s, researchers revealed that athletes faced a mix of two types of transitions during their athletic career, which could be categorised by their degree of predictability: normative transitions and non-normative transitions. Normative transitions are generally predictable and anticipated as part of a definite sequence of age-related biological, social, and emotional events or changes, and generally related to the socialisation process and to the organisational nature of the setting in which the individual is involved (e.g. school, family, sport). In contrast, non-normative transitions do not occur in a set plan or schedule but are the result of important events that take place in an individual's life and are therefore generally unpredicted, unanticipated, and involuntary.

This categorisation led to the development of models describing not only normative transitions but also normative career stages, such as Stambulova's (2000) analytical six-stage model (e.g. the beginning of the sports specialisation, the transition to high-achievement sports and adult sports) and Salmela's (1994) three normative career stages model (i.e. from initiation to development, from development to perfection, from perfection to career termination). Moreover, as research showed that transitions were not only athletic-related, but also occurred in other developmental contexts (e.g. psychological, psychosocial; Wylleman, Lavallee, & Alfermann, 1999), sport psychologists were encouraged to take a 'whole career/whole person approach' when considering the transitions athletes faced (Wylleman & Lavallee, 2004).

Building upon research with student-athletes, elite athletes, and former Olympians, and complemented with experiential knowledge from applied sport psychology and career/lifestyle service provision, Wylleman and Lavallee (2004) presented a model integrating normative transitions occurring throughout the athletic career ('lifespan' approach) at athletic as well as psychological, psychosocial, and academic/vocational level ('holistic' approach). In line with its use in research (e.g. Bruner, Munroe-Chandler, & Spink, 2008; Debois, Ledon, & Wylleman, 2015; Tekavc, Wylleman, & Cecić Erpič, 2015) and in the provision of athlete career support (e.g. Bouchetal Pellegri, Leseur, & Debois, 2006; EU guidelines on dual career of athletes, 2012), this model was further specified and elaborated into the Holistic Athletic Career model (HAC; Wylleman & Rosier, 2016).

The Holistic Athletic Career model

As illustrated in Figure 13.1, the top layer of the HAC model represents the stages and transitions talented athletes will face in their athletic development and includes the initiation stage during which young athletes are introduced to organised competitive sports (from about 6 to 7 years of age); the development stage during which athletes are recognised as being talented, leading up to an intensification of the level of training and participation in competitions (from about 12 to 13 years of age); the perfection or mastery stage which reflects athletes' participation at the highest competitive level (from about 18 to 19 years of age); and the discontinuation stage entailing elite athletes' transiting out of competitive sports (from 28 to 30 years of age).

The second layer describes the developmental stages and transitions occurring at the psychological level and is based on different conceptual frameworks on psychological development (see Chapter 4 for further details). The stages of psychological development include childhood, adolescence, and (young) adulthood. The third layer represents athletes' psychosocial development relative to those individuals who are perceived as being significant during that particular stage. These include, for example, the parents, coaches, and peers during the initiation and development stages (see Chapters 10, 18, and 19 for further details). The fourth layer reflects the stages and transitions at the academic level, including the transition into primary education/elementary school, the stage of secondary education/high school, and

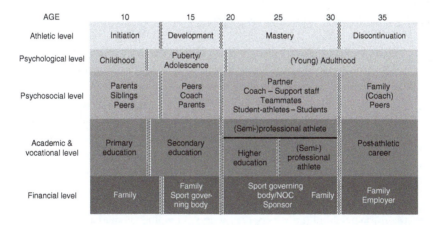

FIGURE 13.1 A holistic perspective on transitions faced by athletes at athletic, psychological, psychosocial, academic–vocational, and financial levels
Note: A dotted line indicates that the age at which the transition occurs is an approximation.
Source: M. Raab, P. Wylleman, R. Seiler, A.-M. Elbe, & A. Hatzigeorgiadis (Eds.), *Sport and Exercise Psychology Research: From Theory to Practice* (pp. 270–288). Oxford, UK: Elsevier Inc. Reproduced with permission.

the transition into higher education (college/university). As vocational training and the development of a professional occupation may also have a strong influence on a talented athlete's sport career, the talented athletes may also transit from secondary into the status of (semi-)professional athlete. The final level represents several sources of financial support that can impact talented athletes' development. These include, for example, the financial support of the family at the beginning (as well as at the end of the athletic career) and that of the sport governing body, national Olympic committee, and/or sponsors.

While the HAC model recognises that inter-individual commonalities or regularities occur at multiple levels throughout athletes' development, it also allows for inter-individual differences related to intra-individual plasticity or malleability in development, as well as varying contextual characteristics. For example, within the HAC, it is acknowledged that the ages at which transitions occur will vary between athletes across and within different sports (e.g. entering senior international level competition by female gymnasts in comparison to male beach volleyball players).

Applying the HAC model

Using the HAC model, the transitions that 8- to 12-year-old talented tennis players[2] may face can be delineated to the end of the initiation stage and the development stage. To gain a better understanding of these transitions, 12-year-old talented tennis players who entered a talent development programme of a tennis federation were asked to reflect on the first months following their transition into an elite training centre. They were encouraged to explore their experience across each of the levels of the HAC model and highlight any changes:

- *Athletic level:* The players perceived a clear increase in frequency, intensity, and types of training, and matches which were of a higher competitive level than they were used to before joining the talent programme.
- *Psychological level:* The players indicated that although the changes at athletic level increased their motivation to play tennis, it also required them to have a stronger focus during the daily training sessions. Tennis was becoming more and more a part of their identity, especially as they perceived a strong change in the importance awarded to tennis in comparison to non-tennis-playing activities.
- *Psychosocial level:* These young players changed from their home-town school to the topsportschool (i.e. a secondary school providing talented athletes from different sports with a restricted study programme allowing for two daily training sessions), which included joining a boarding school. Consequently, the players found themselves working with new coaches, becoming part of one or more new peer groups (i.e. other tennis players at the centre, other talented athletes at the topsportschool or boarding school), and sometimes establishing new friendships. At the same time, they also experienced clearly being away for home and a change in frequency of being in contact with their parents and family.

- *Academic level:* The combination of study and tennis was emphasised every day, including after-school homework, distance learning, and support provided by the (boarding) school.
- *Financial level:* For the players' parents this transition included on the one hand having to invest more in their child's intensified involvement in tennis (i.e. financing costs related to the topsportschool and the boarding school), but at the same time experiencing greater financial support from the federation in relation to costs of the coach, and travelling and playing in competitions abroad.

As a follow-up, the players were also asked how they perceived they coped with these changes. While they reported to have generally coped well with the changes at athletic (i.e. playing more and high-level matches) and academic level (i.e. adapting to the new school), the changes related to the psychological level (i.e. the non-tennis-related activities) and the psychosocial level (i.e. being away from home, establishing new friendships) were perceived as being of a greater challenge.

Providing support to athletes facing transitional challenges

After using the HAC model to analyse the transitions young talented athletes face, the question is, what support could sport psychologists provide? Sport psychologists require a specific array of competencies to work with young talented athletes facing transitions, including a knowledge base on transitions, intervention skills, and competencies for interdisciplinary teamwork as part of career and transition support programs.

Knowledge on transitional challenges faced by athletes

Taking time to develop an intricate knowledge of each level of the HAC model will help ensure practitioners can effectively understand and subsequently support athletes' transitions. Further, consideration of possible (non-normative) transitions alongside these levels may also be useful. For example, although sport psychologists are generally knowledgeable about athletes' development at athletic level, intricate knowledge about the structural, organisational, and policy aspects of competitive (elite) sports, and consequently the impacts of these within the athletic level, may elude them. Becoming knowledgeable about the different criteria and steps in the selection process for entry into a talent development programme, as well as the organisational requirements of being part of such a programme (e.g. the reduced possibilities for young players to interact and relate daily outside of the structured training and school programme), is pertinent to enable practitioners to adequately prepare athletes for changing requirements and athletic demands.

Similarly, sport psychologists will benefit from getting (newly) acquainted with stage-like conceptual frameworks that reflect on the developmental tasks and crises (e.g. cognitive readiness, identity formation, relationship formation) that athletes confront during the different life stages (e.g. childhood, adolescence) (see Chapters 4 and 5). Knowledge of athletes' psychosocial development, including the interaction between young athletes' interpersonal relationships (e.g. coaches, parents, physiotherapist, sport psychologist) and social networks (e.g. peers) and the occurrence of transitions and stages (e.g. Wylleman, De Knop, Verdet, & Cecić Erpič, 2007) will also be useful. Sport psychologists may find it more challenging to be well informed about the educational system and the financial implications related to young talented athletes' development but such information is valuable. Particularly, practitioners should seek to understand the way in which young athletes can (not) combine an athletic career with school (the dual career) (EU guidelines on dual career of athletes, 2012; Stambulova & Wylleman, 2015), as well as understanding athletes' (sometimes strong) dependency on financial support from parents and family as well as sports federations and programmes, to be able to excel.

Beyond the HAC levels, sport psychologists should also ensure a strong knowledge of the different transition models. Two complementary models can be used. In first instance, models describing the prevalence of transitional challenges (Alfermann & Stambulova, 2007) such as the HAC model or its precursor (the lifespan model; Wylleman & Lavallee, 2004), which 'directs applied sport psychologists to create a holistic view of the athlete and his or her social environment … important in individual counselling interventions' (Alfermann & Stambulova, 2007, p. 716). Adjacent to these models, sport psychologists can also get a (better) feel for the interactive and interdependent nature of transitions and stages, by way of biographies or biopics that generally describe the transitional challenges athletes faced during different stages of talent development, what effect these had, and the ways in which they were able to cope.

In the second instance, sport psychologists can use models that provide insight into the process of the actual transitional challenge (Alfermann & Stambulova, 2007), such as the athletic career transition model (Figure 13.2; Stambulova, 2003). This model reveals that the process of the transitional challenge starts for athletes with the demands posed to them in order to progress in their development (e.g. at athletic level) and which then stimulates them to mobilise resources to find ways to cope.

The demands athletes experience in transitions include all factors that may interfere with the development of the athlete (e.g. a dual career, being a last year junior), while resources include all internal and external factors that may facilitate the coping process (e.g. parental support, effective use of competencies, financial support). The balance between demands and resources and the effective use of resources will determine the extent to which athletes are able to cope with the transitional challenge. If effective, the process of coping can lead to a successful transition; if not, to a crisis-transition whereby the use of psychological intervention may still help athletes to cope successfully with the transition; if once again not, athletes may be confronted with, for example, a decline in athletic performance, overtraining and injuries, or even clinical issues.

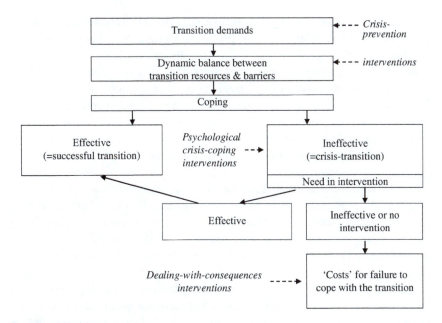

FIGURE 13.2 The Athletic Career Transition Model
Source: 'Symptoms of a crisis-transition: A grounded theory study' by N. Stambulova, in N. Hassmen (Ed.), *SIPF Yearbook 2003* (pp. 97–109). Örebro, Sweden: Örebro University Press.

Interventions for athletes facing transitional challenges

As transitions can be seen as turning points 'at which talent may be derailed or may flourish' (Dweck, 2009, p. xii), they have the power to lead to a transitional crisis. Sport psychologists should therefore have the competencies to use interventions aimed at assisting young talented athletes, in the first instance to prevent, and in the second instance to cope with, transitional crises.

Crisis-prevention interventions

Crisis-prevention interventions support young athletes in planning to mobilise resources to cope with transitional challenges ahead. In this way, they provide for the reported long-term career development needs of younger talented athletes coming through the elite athlete system (North & Lavallee, 2004). Using a hands-on approach, Bouchetal Pellegri et al. (2006) developed a methodology to assist athletes in identifying and planning how to cope with major career stages and transitions (past, present, and future). Using interview and pencil-and-paper tasks (e.g. completing a multi-year planning exercise), the athlete is guided to reflect on transitional challenges (e.g. athlete's identity, past and actual life), their life framework and plans (i.e. sport, education, occupation), and on their needs and resources relative to these plans and situated within concrete planning (i.e. daily, annual, multiyear) (e.g. Debois, Ledon, & Wylleman, 2015). Along a similar line, Stambulova (2012) developed the '5-steps career planning strategy' in which athletes first use an age-lifeline to delineate their athletic career. Second, athletes are asked to write down the most important parts of their current life and rank them in view of subjective importance, time expended on them, and their stress level. Athletes then focus on lessons learned and on the coping resources they have developed through these events. Lastly, athletes set and prioritise goals, analyse resources and barriers, plan action, and finally balance current and future priorities.

Using a three-stage approach, Wylleman, Kahan, and Beyens (2006) developed an intervention that consists of preparing young talented athletes to cope efficiently and effectively with a specific transitional challenge or stage. In the first stage, practitioners educate athletes about (future) transitions, and support them in identifying and, when required, developing those competencies that will be required at the time of the onset of a transitional challenge (Wylleman, 2016). Stage two occurs when young athletes are faced with a transitional challenge. Sport psychologists provide support to the athletes by way of assisting them in developing their support network, mobilising their coping resources, and buffering the impact of transition-related stress. In the third and final stage, sport psychologists can assist young athletes in identifying and developing the resources to cope successfully with the consequences of the transition. This may include counselling or therapeutic interventions by psychologists who have the competencies not only to use a developmental and holistic perspective, but also to consider the significance, relevance, and requirements of talent development and competitive sport in their interventions.

Crisis-coping interventions

Sport psychologists with a counselling or clinical psychology background also need to have the competencies of applying crisis-coping interventions to assist athletes when faced with a transitional crisis. These interventions (e.g. cognitive-behavioural therapy, rational-emotional behaviour therapy, cognitive restructuring) are aimed at reducing anxiety, distress, maladaptive cognitions, and possible depression, as well as at developing coping and problem-solving skills, self-instructional training, and reordering life priorities, preparing athletes not only to cope with the consequences of a crisis, but also to increase their competencies with which to minimise the possibility or actually avoid a new crisis (Lavallee, Sunghee, & Tod, 2010). The intervention of 'account-making' has shown its effectiveness in counselling athletes in transition (Lavallee et al., 2010). Asked to relate their (possibly traumatic) experiences within their own account or story with emphasis on why these experiences happened and on how these may impact their future development, (clinical) sport psychologists can offer young athletes support, validate their feelings, and assist them in reconstructing their new identities and life stories in view of future activities and career development. To increase the effectiveness of this approach, psychologists should not only have but also apply a strong contextual knowledge base of talent development and competitive sport (e.g. using examples of transitional challenges faced by well-known elite-level athletes).

Interdisciplinary teamwork as part of career and transition programmes

A significant development facing sport psychologists is that their services are becoming more and more an integrated part of career and transition programmes for athletes (Stambulova, Alfermann, Statler, & Côté, 2009). Acknowledging the multilevel challenges faced by transitional athletes, these programmes usually combine workshops with seminars and face-to-face counselling (conducted by counselling or clinical psychologists), and the provision of interdisciplinary support services related to the different levels of development. These programmes are generally aimed at 16+ year-old athletes in talent development programmes and at elite junior athletes in preparation for their transition to the senior ranks. The areas covered can include (a) mental health issues; (b) lifestyle skills related to time management, media, problem-solving, transitions, organisational issues, stress management, relationships, self-regulation, and attitude towards drug taking, racism, and discrimination; (c) education at primary and secondary level, including flexible study and exam schedules, tutoring, distance learning; (d) career management generally focused upon junior elite athletes, and including job application and job placement strategies, networking, ICT and language, and internships. To create an optimal support system, most talent development programmes also provide financial support (e.g. reimbursement of medical and psychological support, school tuition fees).

The multitude of areas covered in these programmes reflects the holistic nature of the transitional challenges young athletes may face during their athletic development. It is also indicative of the need for psychologists not only to be aware of their relevance, but also to be knowledgeable about these different areas (e.g. the restrictions young athletes face to finance psychological support, the role of the sport governing body in the selection of talented athletes, the possibilities for a dual career of elite sport and study).

Being an integral part of support programmes for talented athletes provides sport psychologists with two challenges. First, as transitions are generally related to multilevel challenges, optimal support provision will generally involve different experts (e.g. medical doctors, physiotherapists, lifestyle coaches, counselling and clinical psychologists) directed by the talent programme manager, head coach, or technical director. This approach is a reflection of the 'athlete centred – coach directed – expert supported' systems established in elite as well as talent programmes (Wylleman & Hendriks, 2015). This requires sport psychologists to have the competencies to work within an interdisciplinary team. This, however, may be challenging because sport psychologists (a) have generally been educated and are experienced in interacting directly (and often solely) with the athletes themselves, rather than interacting primarily with the experts in the interdisciplinary team; and (b) do not always have sufficient knowledge of the disciplines of the other experts involved, nor the skills (e.g. how to share information within the boundaries of ethical codes by way of progress reports), attitude (e.g. trust to allow another expert to act as case manager of an athlete's therapeutic plan), or experience to collaborate with other specialists; and (c) may not always (want to) understand or be able to cope with the overlap that can exist between them and other experts when providing athletes with support on a specific topic (e.g. time management skills, which are in the remit of sport psychologists, lifestyle coaches, and academic tutors).

Experiential knowledge of elite sport shows that the quality of the participation of psychologists in interdisciplinary teams is strongly related to, among others, (a) the vision of the national coaches/technical directors, the initiatives taken, and the continued support to make interdisciplinary collaboration a focal point (i.e. requirement) of the support team, (b) psychologists' willingness to invest (i.e. time, expertise) in the meetings of the interdisciplinary team, (c) the competencies of psychologists to reflect on, and (when possible) integrate and relate to, the advice of other experts during the support and/or consultations they provide to young athletes, and (d) the perception of psychologists to be a valued part of the advice formulated by the interdisciplinary team.

Conclusions

Using the HAC model to take a developmental and holistic perspective to working with talented athletes reveals that, rather than being a seemingly continuous 10-year period (Sosniak, 2006), the athletic career is constituted by transitions (and stages) occurring at different levels of development. Transitions have the power to become turning points at which their talent can flourish or be derailed (Dweck, 2009) or, put more generally, transitions can exert a strong influence on young talented athletes' development. With this in mind, I wonder how Martin and Nyls, our young talented athletes from the beginning of this chapter, actually experienced their transitional challenges. Were they prepared for or supported during this transition? Did it actually influence their development, and if so, at what level?

Well so far … although Bayern Munich, Manchester United, Arsenal, and Ajax wanted Martin, he signed a six-year contract with Real Madrid. However, after playing only one match in the Primera Division and then joining Madrid's second team, he is now on loan playing in the Dutch league with SC Heerenveen where he enjoyed a very warm welcome (NOS, 2016). As Nyls continued to progress, he was eventually selected for the Dutch national team with which he won a silver medal at the World Championships Short Course 4 × 50 metre relay (NOS, 2017).

In conclusion, although a need for more evidence-based research and transition-specific tools still exists, it is clear that support for and during transitions is an essential part of many talent development programmes. In fact, specialising in the provision of such support is a clear way ahead for sport psychologists providing, within an interdisciplinary approach, tailor-made support to (former) talented and (retired) elite athletes with the clear aim of optimising their holistic development.

Notes

1 For a more detailed description and related references see Wylleman & Rosier (2016).
2 This example is based on research into young tennis players' perceptions of the transition into the elite sports school of the Flemish tennis federation (Wylleman, Kahan, & Reints, 2007).

References

Alfermann, D., & Stambulova, N. B. (2007). Career transitions and career termination. In G. Tenenbaum and R. C. Eklund (Eds.), *Handbook of Sport Psychology* (3rd ed., pp. 712–736). New York, NY: Wiley.

Bouchetal Pellegri, F., Leseur, V., & Debois, N. (2006). *Carrière Sportive: Projet de vie*. Paris: INSEP-Publications.

Bruner, M. W., Munroe-Chandler, K. J., & Spink, K. S. (2008). Entry into elite sport: A preliminary investigation into the transition experiences of rookie athletes. *Journal of Applied Sport Psychology, 20*, 236–252.

Debois, N., Ledon, A., & Wylleman, P. (2015). A lifespan perspective on the dual career of elite male athletes. *Psychology of Sport and Exercise, 21*, 15–26.

Dweck, C. S. (2009). Foreword. In F. D. Horowitz, R. F. Subotnik, & D. J. Matthews (Eds.), *The Development of Giftedness and Talent across the Life Span* (pp. xi–xiv). Washington, DC: American Psychological Association.

EU guidelines on dual careers of athletes (2012). *Recommended policy actions in support of dual careers in high-performance sport*. Retrieved from http://ec.europa.eu/sport/news/20130123-eu-guidelines-dualcareers_en.htm.

Lavallee, D., Sugnhee, P., & Tod, D. (2010). Career termination. In S. J. Hanrahan & M. B. Andersen (Eds.), *Routledge Handbook of Applied Sport Psychology: A Comprehensive Guide for Students and Practitioners* (pp. 242–249). New York, NY: Routledge.

North, J., & Lavallee, D. (2004). An investigation of potential users of career transition services in the United Kingdom. *Psychology of Sport and Exercise, 5*, 77–84.

NOS (2015). *16-jarige Korstanje mag niet naar EK kortebaan*. Retrieved from http://nos.nl/artikel/2072537-16-jarige-korstanje-mag-niet-naar-ek-kortebaan.html.

NOS (2016). *Nederlands kwartet 'in de wolken' na zilver op WK*. Retrieved from http://nos.nl/video/2147128-nederlands-kwartet-in-de-wolken-na-zilver-op-wk.html.

NOS (2017). *Heerenveen bevestigt komst toptalent Ødegaard*. Retrieved from http://nos.nl/artikel/2152244-heerenveen-bevestigt-komst-toptalent-oedegaard.html.

Raab, M., Wylleman, P., Seiler, R., Elbe, A.-M., & Hatzigeorgiadis, A. (Eds.), *Sport and Exercise Psychology Research: From Theory to Practice* (pp. 270–288). Oxford, UK: Elsevier Inc.

Salmela, J. H. (1994). Phases and transitions across sports career. In D. Hackfort (Ed.), *Psychosocial Issues and Interventions in Elite Sport* (pp. 11–28). Frankfurt: Lang.

Schlossberg, N. K. (1981). A model for analyzing human adaptation to transition. *The Counseling Psychologist, 9*, 2–18.

Sosniak, A. (2006). Retrospective interviews in the study of expertise and expert performance. In K. A. Ericsson, N. Charness, P. J. Feltovich, & R. R. Hoffman (Eds.), *The Cambridge Handbook of Expertise and Expert Performance* (pp. 287–302). New York, NY: Cambridge University Press.

Sporza (2014). *Noorse wonderboy van 15 jaar is jongste EK-kwalificatiespeler ooit*. Retrieved from http://sporza.be/cm/sporza/voetbal/Euro2016/1.2118698.

Stambulova, N. B. (2000). Athletes' crises: A developmental perspective. *International Journal of Sport Psychology, 31*, 584–601.

Stambulova, N. (2003). Symptoms of a crisis-transition: A grounded theory study. In N. Hassmen (Ed.), *SIPF Yearbook 2003* (pp. 97–109). Örebro, Sweden: Örebro University Press.

Stambulova, N. (2012). Working with athletes in career transitions. In S. Hanton & S. Mellalieu (Eds.), *Professional Practice in Sport Psychology: A Review* (pp. 165–194). Abingdon, UK: Routledge.

Stambulova, N., Alfermann, D., Statler, T., & Côté, J. (2009). ISSP position stand: Career development and transitions of athletes. *International Journal of Sport & Exercise Psychology*, 7, 395–412.

Stambulova, N., & Wylleman, P. (2015). Dual career development and transitions. *Psychology of Sport and Exercise, 21*, 1–3.

Taylor, J., & Ogilvie, B. C. (2001). Career termination among athletes. In R. N. Singer, H. A. Hausenblas, & C. M. Janelle (Eds.), *Handbook of Sport Psychology* (2nd ed., pp. 672–691). New York, NY: Wiley & Sons.

Tekavc, J., Wylleman, P., & Cecić Erpič, S. (2015). Perceptions of dual career development among elite level swimmers and basketball players. *Psychology of Sport and Exercise, 21*, 27–41.

Wylleman, P. (2016). *From junior to senior: A developmental and holistic perspective.* Presentation at the Tennis Europe Coaches Conference 'Transitioning successful juniors into professional tennis players'. Wilrijk, Belgium: Tennis Vlaanderen.

Wylleman, P., De Knop, P., Verdet, M. C., & Cecić Erpič, S. (2007). Parenting and career transitions of elite athletes. In S. Jowett & D. Lavallee (Eds.), *Social Psychology in Sport* (pp. 233–248). Champaign, IL: Human Kinetics.

Wylleman, P., & Hendriks, M. (2015). *The organisation and provision of performance behaviour support to Dutch Olympic athletes.* Presentation at the 2015 European Congress of Psychology. Milano, Italy: EFPA.

Wylleman, P., Kahan, N., & Beyens, K. (2006). *Perception of young tennis players of the transition into the elite sports school of the Flemish tennis federation.* Presentation at the 26th International Congress of Applied Psychology. Athens, Greece: IAAP.

Wylleman, P., Kahan, N., & Reints, A. (2007). *Players and coaches' perceptions of transitional changes after selection for an elite sports tennis school.* Presentation at the 12th European Congress of Sport Psychology. Halkidiki, Greece: FEPSAC.

Wylleman, P., & Lavallee D. (2004). A developmental perspective on transitions faced by athletes. In M. Weiss (Ed.), *Developmental Sport and Exercise Psychology: A Lifespan Perspective* (pp. 507–527). Morgantown, WV: Fitness Information Technology.

Wylleman, P., Lavallee, D., & Alfermann, D. (Eds). (1999). *Career Transitions in Competitive Sports.* FEPSAC monograph series. Lund: European Federation of Sport Psychology FEPSAC.

Wylleman, P., & Rosier, N. (2016). A holistic perspective on the development of elite athletes. In M. Raab, P. Wylleman, R. Seiler, A.-M. Elbe, & A. Hatzigeorgiadis (Eds.), *Sport and Exercise Psychology Research: From Theory to Practice* (pp. 270–288). Oxford, UK: Elsevier Inc.

14

SELF-IDENTITY AND YOUNG ATHLETES

Britton W. Brewer, Albert J. Petitpas, and Judy L. Van Raalte

Adolescence is a period of pronounced growth and development. From a psycho-social standpoint, identity formation is a key developmental task of adolescence (Erikson, 1959). Sometimes labelled 'self-identity', identity refers to 'a clearly delineated self-definition ... comprised of those goals, values, and beliefs which the person finds personally expressive, and to which he or she is unequivocally committed' (Waterman, 1985). As a pursuit to which some adolescents commit strongly, sport participation can intersect with the process of identity development. The purpose of this chapter is to examine theory and research pertaining to the relevance of self-identity to young athletes and to offer recommendations for sport psychology practice with young athletes. Before considering contemporary perspectives on self-identity in sport, however, it is useful to provide brief overviews of the self and how it develops.

Background on the self

More than a century ago, the theoretical writings of James (1890) and Cooley (1902) laid a strong foundation for subsequent inquiry pertaining to the self. James conceptualised self-esteem as the ratio of one's successes to one's pretensions (i.e. expectations or aspirations) and distinguished between the *I-self* (i.e. the 'self-as-knower', or the part of the individual that has self-awareness and actively engages in knowing about one's own personal attributes) and the *Me-self* (i.e. the 'self-as-known', or what the knower knows about oneself in terms of personal qualities). Highlighting the role of social factors in the development and maintenance of the self, Cooley described the *looking glass self*, in which one's sense of self is strongly influenced by reflected appraisals of others' attitudes towards the self.

Building upon the work of James (1890) and Cooley (1902), scientific investigation of the self exploded in the latter half of the twentieth century and continued to expand in the early twenty-first century. A search of the PsycINFO database in 2011 revealed at least 50 descriptors with the *self* prefix and more than 260,000 abstracts featuring terms with the *self* prefix (Leary & Tangney, 2012). In response to conceptual confusion resulting from the abundance of *self* compounds and disparate uses of the term in the literature, Leary and Tangney defined the self as 'a mental capacity that allows an animal to take itself as the object of its own attention and think consciously about itself' (p. 6). This definition integrates multiple previous meanings attributed to the term and conceptualises the self as involving attentional, cognitive, and executive processes and being 'intimately linked to … but not an inherent part of' (p. 9) emotional and motivational systems.

Compatible with Leary and Tangney's (2012) conceptualisation, self-identity is currently viewed as a mental construct that is socially constructed and is a force for action. This view implies that self-identity is represented in memory, accessible through introspection, strongly influenced by the sociocultural context, and a mediator of behaviour (Oyserman, Elmore, & Smith, 2012). The properties ascribed to self-identity help explain how the self can be both stable *and* dynamic, giving individuals a sense of continuity while allowing their conceptions of themselves to change as they are exposed to contextual influences over time.

Development of the self

Changes in self-representations throughout childhood and adolescence parallel normative changes in cognitive capabilities and the socialising environment (see Chapters 4 and 5). Among the developmental trends of particular relevance to self-identity are: (a) increased differentiation of aspects of the self, as indicated by self-evaluations that vary across content domains (e.g. academic aptitude, sport performance) and social settings (e.g. family, peers); (b) increased integration of aspects of the self, as illustrated by the ability to incorporate disparate and potentially contradictory aspects of the self (e.g. good at kicking and bad at catching) into a unified self-concept; and (c) progression from temporal self-comparisons (e.g. 'I'm taller than I used to be') to social comparisons (e.g. 'I'm not as fast as Susie') to self-ideal comparisons (e.g. 'I'm not as tolerant a person as I would like to be') as sources of self-evaluation and self-regulation. These trends give rise to the notion that instead of possessing a unitary self, people have multiple selves that vary over time and across domains and settings (Harter, 2002). Although there are age-related differences in the specific content domains that are prominent components of the self-concept, evaluation of one's capabilities in the physical and athletic realms is salient across the lifespan (Harter, 1990).

Social and cognitive factors affect the development of the self across the lifespan. Development of self-identity, however, is especially salient during late adolescence (Erikson, 1959). Erikson proposed that as late adolescents begin to separate themselves from parental influences, they forge new and unique patterns of self-identification (or ego identity) by choosing freely from alternative identities and committing to those that are consistent with their abilities, interests, needs, and values. For example, a young woman might choose to pursue a career in music, rather than follow her family's expectation to go into the medical field. Extending Erikson's concept of ego identity, Marcia (1966) described identity foreclosure as a state in which individuals firmly commit to an occupation or ideology without first exploring meaningful alternatives.

Self-identity and sport participation

As a potential mediator of behaviour (Oyserman et al., 2012), self-identity has received considerable attention in the sport psychology literature. In particular, researchers have focused on the constructs of identity foreclosure and athletic identity, examining associations between the two constructs and outcomes of potential relevance to developing athletes.

Identity foreclosure

Citing the influence of situational factors such as recognition for sport accomplishments, extensive time demands of sport participation, and emphasis on conformity and compliance rather than independence and autonomy in the sport environment, Petitpas and his colleagues (Pearson & Petitpas, 1990; Petitpas & Champagne, 1988; Petitpas & France, 2010) have long considered athletes to be at increased risk for identity foreclosure. Given the strong commitment inspired and often required by involvement in sport and the concomitant lack of opportunity or inclination for exploration of alternative occupational identities, athletes with identity foreclosure are susceptible to problems in career development and adjustment to sport transitions (Petitpas & France, 2010) (see Chapter 13 for further details). Research has shown that athletes report higher levels of identity foreclosure than their non-athlete peers (Linnemeyer & Brown, 2010) and that identity foreclosure is inversely related to career maturity in college student–athletes (Murphy, Petitpas, & Brewer, 1996).

Athletic identity

As the sport-related component of self-concept, athletic identity refers to 'the degree to which an individual identifies with the athlete role' (Brewer, Van Raalte, & Linder, 1993, p. 237). In addition to the strength of identification with the athlete role, various properties, processes, and products can be considered in relation to athletic identity. Properties refer to descriptive characteristics of athletic identity, such as the salience of the identity compared to other competing identities and the extent to which one's self-worth is contingent on performance and involvement in the athlete role. Processes pertain to dynamic elements that act upon and produce systematic changes in athletic identity. Athletic identity processes include social reinforcement for sport involvement and self-presentation, which is manifested in terms of presenting oneself to others as an athlete. Products correspond to outcomes in which athletic identity is thought to play a contributing role. Associations have been documented between athletic identity and outcomes in the realms of academics, burnout, career development, psychological adjustment to sport transitions, and substance use.

Academics

A growing body of research suggests that maintaining a strong athletic identity may not be wholly compatible with academic pursuits. Not only may some athletes attempt to 'just pass' their course work and sacrifice their ability to succeed academically to allow them to pursue sport and educational goals (Cosh & Tully, 2014), negative correlations have been documented between athletic identity and academic adjustment (Melendez, 2009), belief in the importance of academics (Hale & Waalkes, 1994), general academic skills, mathematical ability, problem-solving (Fraser, Fogarty, & Albion, 2008), and susceptibility to stereotype threat (Feltz, Schneider, Hwang, & Skogsberg, 2013).

Burnout

Based on a series of informal interviews with adolescent athletes, Coakley (1992) proposed that a unidimensional self-identity was one of several factors that increased the likelihood that young athletes would experience burnout. Research testing Coakley's hypothesis has yielded equivocal results, with studies reporting both positive (e.g. Martin & Horn, 2013) and negative (e.g. Baysden, Brewer, Petitpas, & Van Raalte, 1997) associations between athletic identity and burnout. Explanations for the inconsistency of the findings across studies include variability in the extent to which the samples included burned out participants (Black & Smith, 2007) and the positive associations between athletic and both harmonious and obsessive passion, which have negative and positive associations, respectively, with burnout (Martin & Horn, 2013).

Psychological adjustment to sport transitions

In a review of the literature on athletic identity in sport psychology, Ronkainen, Kavoura, and Ryba (2016) concluded that 'athletic identity can be a positive source of meaning and self-esteem, but also highly problematic for wellbeing when sport is not going well or the career is abruptly terminated' (p. 57). Thus, although positive associations have been documented between athletic identity and indicators of favourable psychological adjustment such as self-esteem (Martin, 1999), influence of sport on quality of life (Groff, Lundberg, & Zabriskie, 2009), and athlete satisfaction (Burns, Jasinski, Dunn, & Fletcher, 2012), sport transitions that threaten performance of the athlete role may be especially difficult for individuals who are strongly identified with that role (Pearson & Petitpas, 1990; Chapter 13). Athletic identity has been considered in relation to adjustment to such sport transitions as career termination, deselection, and injury. Athletic identity is, therefore, relevant not only to sport transitions typically faced by older athletes, such as adjustment to sport career transitions (for a review, see Park, Lavallee, & Tod, 2013) and career development, but also to sport transitions commonly experienced by young athletes, namely deselection and injury.

Deselection. Being deselected or 'cut' from sport team can be a difficult situation for athletes to experience. Grove, Fish, and Eklund (2004) reported a potentially adaptive response of adolescent athletes who, when deselected from a team, decreased their athletic identity. Divesting from a threatened identity may help protect self-esteem and minimise the disappointment associated with not achieving important goals.

Injury. Individuals strongly identified with the athlete role are at elevated risk for playing their sport in pain (Weinberg, Vernau, & Horn, 2013), incurring injury (McKay, Campbell, Meeuwisse, & Emery, 2013), and experiencing psychological distress after injury occurrence (Manuel et al., 2002). Although young athletes high in athletic identity are more likely than those low in athletic identity to adhere to post-injury rehabilitation programmes (Brewer et al., 2003), they are also more likely to *overadhere* to rehabilitation (Podlog et al., 2013) and place themselves at risk for delayed recovery. As with deselection, people decrease their identification with the athlete role after ACL surgery, especially when rehabilitation has not been progressing well (Brewer, Cornelius, Stephan, & Van Raalte, 2010), potentially protecting themselves from the threat of not being able to participate in sport to the degree desired.

Substance use

Associations between athletic identity and use of recreational and performance-enhancing substances have been documented in several studies. Murray (2001) obtained a positive relation between athletic identity and alcohol consumption among female college students. Further, Grossbard et al. (2009) found that among athletes entering college, the correlation between athlete drinking norms and drinking behaviour was significantly more positive for athletes high in athletic identity than for those low in athletic identity. With respect to performance-enhancing drugs (see Chapter 17), university student-athletes high in athletic identity were more likely to report being willing to use drugs if they were guaranteed a medal than those low in athletic identity (Hale & Waalkes, 1994) and bodybuilders who acknowledged using anabolic steroids had higher levels of athletic identity than those who denied use of anabolic steroids (Smith & Hale, 1997).

Recommendations for practice

Despite the potential importance of self-identity as a mediator of important outcomes of relevance to young athletes, relatively few studies have examined the effects of psychological interventions on self-identity. Fischer (1994) found that compared with student-athletes who received no treatment, student-athletes who received a time management intervention reported higher identification with the student role and lower identification with the athlete role. Similarly, participants in a six-week residential programme designed to facilitate the 'reinvention, education, appraisal, and preparation' (Woods, Kirrane, & Buckley, 2003) of deselected young athletes reported reductions in athletic identity. Consistent with the findings of Woods et al., length of participation in a counselling programme developed to facilitate the combination of university studies and elite sport involvement was inversely related to athletic identity (Torregrosa, Mateos, Sanchez, & Cruz, 2007). More recently, Rakauskienė and Dumčienė (2012) found that a brief educational counseling intervention designed to boost physical activity increased the athletic identity of adolescents. Thus, it appears that sport-related self-identity is sensitive to the effects of psychosocial interventions.

Petitpas and France (2010) offered practical suggestions for working with athletes in identity foreclosure. Adapted to young athletes with patterns of self-identity that may pose problems in their academic, athletic, career, physical, or psychosocial development, it is recommended that practitioners: (a) understand the role sport participation plays in the identity of young athletes; (b) do not directly challenge the efficacy of an exclusive commitment to sport roles; (c) help young athletes move from extrinsic motivation to intrinsic motivation to engage in exploratory behaviour; (d) work with coaches and administrators to understand and plan appropriate educational strategies for young athletes; and (e) establish strong counselling relationships with young athletes and assist them through a process of self-disclosure, feedback, and awareness. Each of these recommendations is considered in turn.

Understand the role that sport participation plays in the identity of young athletes

It is important for young people to find their passion. When the passion is sport, it is likely that this passion will become a major part of one's identity. The sport identity is reinforced by both the intrinsic rewards of being able to master something in one's environment and the external rewards that accrue from being successful at sport (Petitpas & Champagne, 1988). Sport participation continues to be one of the most revered activities among youth and an activity that garners extrinsic reinforcement from peers and adults. A passion for sport can be a great motivator, so much so that some children and families commit only to one sport and 'put all their eggs in one basket'. Although commitment to sport is a necessary ingredient to athletic accomplishments, young athletes can reach or pass a point of diminishing returns. Research on the dangers of early sport specialisation suggests that most successful athletes participated in several sports before making a commitment to one, typically around the age of 15 (see Chapter 6).

Although 'sampling' is an important component of the athlete development life cycle, many gifted young athletes experience pressure from club coaches to specialise. Sport psychology professionals need to build relationships with young athletes that begin with an empathic understanding of their unique situations. Once empathy is established, sport psychology professionals can introduce young athletes to both the psychological and physical advantages of involvement in multiple sports and other forms of physical activity (see Chapters 6 and 11) by sharing stories and print media that highlights the sport history of successful athletes within the young athlete's primary sport interest. Attempts by sport psychology professionals to encourage young athletes to sample other sports before empathic understanding has been established can compromise the credibility of practitioners and cause young athletes to avoid adults who encourage diversification.

Do not directly challenge the efficacy of an exclusive commitment to sport roles

Most athletes will reach a point in their athletic development in which their level of aspiration will exceed their physical abilities. For example, many young athletes will aspire to play sport professionally or participate in the Olympics, but only a small number will achieve this goal. Although many young athletes have unrealistic expectations for their sports participation, organisations like Play It Smart and Academics in Motion advise 'do not squash the dream' (National Football Foundation, 2004). Instead, they allow the dream to be the desired outcome, but place emphasis on the nutritional, physical, academic, and self-management skills and knowledge that would be required to achieve the dream. Developing a goal ladder to identify the things that are needed physically, emotionally, and academically for athletic success can take advantage of athletes' passion and help them develop important life skills that can be transferred to other non-sport endeavours (The First Tee, 2016). For example, to be prepared to practise well, young athletes need to understand the importance of recovery time, both physically and emotionally, in preparing their bodies to perform optimally. Learning how to balance rest and play not only promotes healthy development, but also reduces the likelihood of burnout. Sport psychology professionals can also provide parents and coaches with information on the importance of encouraging their children to participate in a variety of sports and physical activities before specialising in one sport.

Help young athletes move from extrinsic motivation to intrinsic motivation to engage in exploratory behaviour

The importance of exploratory behaviour in identity development is described above. Individuals who are exposed to new experiences and involved in a range of activities inside and outside of sport are more likely to identify their interests, values, needs, and skills (Linnemeyer & Brown, 2010). Sport participation can expose young people to different people and experiences, but parents and coaches can facilitate their children's development by making exploratory behaviour an explicit component of sport participation (France, Petitpas, & Van Raalte, 2016). Children who travel to competitions can learn about the people and culture of new places by visiting a college or place of interest (e.g. civil rights museum or a sport hall of fame). Sport psychology professionals could solicit the support of coaches and parents in creating discovery games in which young athletes accrue points for finding items of interest when visiting new competition locations. Further, encouraging young people to reflect on their experiences and share their thoughts and questions with adults and peers can gain self-knowledge and identify activities that are intrinsically motivating (Sedikides & Skowronski, 1995).

Work with coaches and administrators to understand and plan appropriate educational strategies for young athletes

Although many coaches and sport administrators believe that participation in sport provides young people with the skills they need to have a productive adulthood, there is growing evidence that these benefits are most likely to occur in sport environments that explicitly help young people identify life skills and discuss how these skills can be used in school, at home, and in other nonsport settings (Bailey, Hillman, Arent, & Petitpas, 2013; Chapter 12). Parents, coaches, and sport administrators can focus on what athletes need to do to continue to progress athletically, academically, and personally. Several organisations, including The First Tee and Project Rebound, have adopted the 'Good, Better, How' feedback model developed by Nilsson and Marriott (2005) and used it to help coaches and athletes build self-efficacy. For example, after every practice and game, coaches and parents separately identify what the athlete did well to keep the attention on the success experiences that promote self-efficacy. The emphasis on success experiences creates a positive tone and sets the stage for the identification of specific skills that could be improved and the specific strategies to improve them. Good, Better, How feedback prevents coaches and others from an exclusive focus on the corrections of errors. In addition, coaches and parents can explicitly discuss how specific skills acquired through sport can be applied in other life settings.

Establish strong counselling relationships with athletes and assist them through a process of self-disclosure, feedback, and awareness

Coaches and teachers have been identified as having the most non-parental adult influence on children (Smokowski, Reynolds, & Bezruczko, 1999). Young athletes typically look towards coaches to provide not only sport-specific technical information, but also for advice on a variety of topics. Coaches and sport administrators who view their role as youth development specialists strive to build relationships with youth that are based on empathy, high positive expectations, and advocacy (France et al., 2016). The old adage that 'Kids don't care what you know until they know that you care' has been supported by research (Bailey et al., 2013). Communicating high positive expectations to a young athlete who does not believe that the coach understands what he or she is going through can discount the athlete and have the opposite impact than what was intended by the coach (France et al., 2016).

Conclusion

Development of self-identity is a prominent task of late adolescence. Self-identity, the formation of which is strongly influenced by cognitive and social factors, is thought to play a mediating role in several processes of relevance to young athletes. Athletes are susceptible to identity foreclosure, in which they commit strongly to the athlete role without adequately exploring other identities. Strong identification with the athlete role may have ramifications for the academic performance, burn-out, career development, psychological responses to sport transitions (e.g. career termination, deselection, injury), and substance use of young athletes. Fortunately, self-identity is malleable and responsive to psychological interventions designed to affect the academic, career, psychosocial, and sport outcomes of young athletes. Taking self-identity into account when intervening psychologically with young athletes has the potential to enhance the effectiveness of those interventions.

References

Bailey, R., Hillman, C., Arent, S., & Petitpas, A. (2013). Physical activity: An underestimated investment in human capital. *Journal of Physical Activity & Health, 10*, 289–308.

Baysden, M. F., Brewer, B. W., Petitpas, A. J., & Van Raalte, J. L. (1997). Motivational correlates of athletic identity [Abstract]. *Journal of Applied Sport Psychology, 9*, S67–S68.

Black, J. M., & Smith, A. L. (2007). An examination of Coakley's perspective on identity, control, and burnout among adolescent athletes. *International Journal of Sport Psychology, 38*, 417–436.

Brewer, B. W., Cornelius, A. E., Stephan, Y., & Van Raalte, J. L. (2010). Self-protective changes in athletic identity following ACL reconstruction. *Psychology of Sport and Exercise, 11*, 1–5.

Brewer, B. W., Cornelius, A. E., Van Raalte, J. L., Petitpas, A. J., Sklar, J. H., Pohlman, M. H., Krushell, R. J., & Ditmar, T. D. (2003). Age-related differences in predictors of adherence to rehabilitation after anterior cruciate ligament reconstruction. *Journal of Athletic Training, 38*, 158–162.

Brewer, B. W., Van Raalte, J. L., & Linder, D. E. (1993). Athletic identity: Hercules' muscles or Achilles heel? *International Journal of Sport Psychology, 24*, 237–254.

Burns, G. N., Jasinski, D., Dunn, S. C., & Fletcher, D. (2012). Athlete identity and athlete satisfaction: The nonconformity of exclusivity. *Personality and Individual Differences, 52*, 280–284.

Coakley, J. (1992). Burnout among adolescent athletes: A personal failure or social problem? *Sociology of Sport Journal, 9*, 271–285.

Cooley, C. H. (1902). *Human Nature and the Social Order.* New York, NY: Scribner's.

Cosh, S., & Tully, P. J. (2014). 'All I have to do is pass': A discursive analysis of student-athletes talk about prioritizing sport to the detriment of education to overcome stressors encoun-tered in combining elite sport and tertiary education. *Psychology of Sport and Exercise, 15*, 180–189.

Erikson, E. H. (1959). Identity and the life cycle: Selected papers. *Psychological Issues, 1*, 1–171.

Feltz, D. L. Schneider, R., Hwang, S., & Skogsberg, N. J. (2013). Predictors of collegiate student-athletes susceptibility to stereotype threat. *Journal of College Student Development, 54*, 184–201.

Fischer, K. E. (1994). *The effects of learned time management skills on the academic and sport identi-ties of NCAA Division III women student-volleyball athletes.* Unpublished doctoral disserta-tion, Ohio State University, Columbus, OH, USA.

France, T., Petitpas, A., & Van Raalte, J. (2016). Coaching for positive youth development. In P. Davis (Ed.), *The Psychology of Effective Coaching and Management* (pp. 155–166). New York, NY: Nova Science.

Fraser, L., Fogarty, G., & Albion, M. (2008). Is there a basis for the notion of athletic identity? In N. Vidouris & V. Mowrinski (Eds.), *Proceedings of the 43rd Annual Australian Psychological Society Conference* (pp. 164–168). Hobart, Tasmania: Australian Psychological Society.

Groff, D. G., Lundberg, N. R., & Zabriskie, R. B. (2009). Influence of adapted sport on quality of life: Perceptions of athletes with cerebral palsy. *Disability and Rehabilitation, 31,* 318–326.

Grossbard, J. R., Geisner, I. M., Mastroleo, N. R., Kilmer, J. R., Turrisi, R., & Larimer, M. E. (2009). Athletic identity, descriptive norms, and drinking among athletes transitioning to college. *Addictive Behaviours, 34,* 352–359.

Grove, J. R., Fish, M., & Eklund, R. C. (2004). Changes in athletic identity following team selection: Self-protection versus self-enhancement. *Journal of Applied Sport Psychology, 16,* 75–81.

Hale, B. D., & Waalkes, D. (1994). Athletic identity, gender, self-esteem, academic importance, and drug use: A further validation of the AIMS [Abstract]. *Journal of Sport & Exercise Psychology, 16,* S62.

Harter, S. (1990). Causes, correlates and the functional role of global self-worth: A life-span perspective. In R. J. Sternberg & J. Kolligian (Eds.), *Competence Considered* (pp. 67–97). New Haven, CT: Yale University.

Harter, S. (2002). The development of self-representations during childhood and adolescence. In M. R. Leary & J. P. Tangney (Eds.), *Handbook of Self and Identity* (pp. 610–642). New York, NY: The Guilford Press.

James, W. (1890). *The Principles of Psychology.* New York, NY: Holt.

Leary, M. R., & Tangney, J. P. (2012). The self as an organizing construct in the behavioural and social sciences. In M. R. Leary & J. P. Tangney (Eds.), *Handbook of Self and Identity* (2nd ed., pp. 1–18). New York, NY: The Guilford Press.

Linnemeyer, R. M., & Brown, C. (2010). Career maturity and foreclosure in student-athletes, fine arts students, and general college students. *Journal of Career Development, 37,* 616–634.

Manuel, J. C., Shilt, J. S., Curl, W. W., Smith, J. A., DuRant, R. H., Lester, L., & Sinal, S. H. (2002). Coping with sports injuries: An examination of the adolescent athlete. *Journal of Adolescent Health, 31,* 391–393.

Marcia, J. E. (1966). Development and validation of ego-identity status. *Journal of Personality and Social Psychology, 3,* 551–558.

Martin, E. M., & Horn, T. S. (2013). The role of athletic identity and passion in predicting burnout in adolescent female athletes. *The Sport Psychologist, 27,* 338–348.

Martin, J. J. (1999). Predictors of social physique anxiety in adolescent swimmers with physical disabilities. *Adapted Physical Activity Quarterly, 16,* 75–85.

McKay, C., Campbell, T., Meeuwisse, W., & Emery, C. (2013). The role of risk factors for injury in elite youth ice hockey players. *Clinical Journal of Sport Medicine, 23,* 216–221.

Melendez, M. C. (2009). Psychosocial influences on college adjustment in Division I student-athletes: The role of athletic identity. *Journal of College Student Retention, 11,* 345–361.

Murphy, G. M., Petitpas, A. J., & Brewer, B. W. (1996). Identity foreclosure, athletic identity, and career maturity in intercollegiate athletes. *The Sport Psychologist, 10,* 239–246.

Murray, A. E. (2001). A comparison of athletic identity, gender role orientation, and drinking behaviour in women from the United States and Australia. *Journal of Undergraduate Research, 4,* 71–79.

National Football Foundation–Center for Youth Development through Sport. (2004). *Play It Smart Programme training manual*. Unpublished manuscript, Springfield College, MA.

Nilsson, P., & Marriott, L. (2005). *Every Shot Must Have a Purpose*. New York, NY: Gotham Books.

Oyserman, D., Elmore, K., & Smith, G. (2012). Self, self-concept, and identity. In M. R. Leary & J. P. Tangney (Eds.), *Handbook of Self and Identity* (2nd ed., pp. 69–104). New York, NY: The Guilford Press.

Park, S., Lavallee, D., & Tod, D. (2013). Athletes' career transition out of sport: A systematic review. *International Review of Sport and Exercise Psychology, 6*, 22–53.

Pearson, R., & Petitpas, A. (1990). Transitions of athletes: Developmental and preventive perspectives. *Journal of Counseling and Development, 69*, 7–10.

Petitpas, A. J., & Champagne, D. E. (1988). Developmental programming for intercollegiate athletes. *Journal of College Student Development, 22*, 454–460.

Petitpas, A. J., & France, T. (2010). Identity foreclosure in sport. In S. J. Hanrahan & M. B. Andersen (Eds.), *Routledge Handbook of Applied Sport Psychology: A Comprehensive Guide for Students and Practitioners* (pp. 471–480). Abingdon, UK: Routledge.

Podlog, L., Gao, Z., Kenow, L., Kleinert, J., Granquist, M., Newton, M., & Hannon, J. (2013). Injury rehabilitation overadherence: Preliminary scale validation and relationships with athletic identity and self-presentation concerns. *Journal of Athletic Training, 48*, 372–381.

Rakauskienė, V., & Dumčienė, A. (2012). The impact of educational counseling on the alteration of athletic identity among adolescents. *Sportas, 4*, 49–56.

Ronkainen, N. J., Kavoura, A., & Ryba, T. V. (2016). A meta-study of athletic identity research in sport psychology: Current status and future directions. *International Review of Sport Psychology, 9*, 45–64.

Sedikides, C., & Skowronski, J. (1995). On the sources of self-knowledge: The perceived primacy of self-reflection. *Journal of Social and Clinical Psychology, 14*, 244–270.

Smith, D. K., & Hale, B. D. (1997). An exploratory study of exercise dependence in bodybuilders [Abstract]. *Journal of Sports Sciences, 15*, 104–105.

Smokowski, P. R., Reynolds, A. J., & Bezruczko, N. (1999). Resilience and protective factors in adolescence: An autobiographical perspective from disadvantaged youth. *Journal of School Psychology, 37*, 425–448.

Torregrosa, M., Mateos, M., Sanchez, X., & Cruz, J. (2007). *Evaluation of a programme to combine elite sport and university education*. Presentation at the 12th European Congress of Sport Psychology, Halkidiki, Greece.

The First Tee. (2016). *Coach Guide to Life Skills Experience: Ace level*. Unpublished manuscript. St. Augustine, FL: Author.

Waterman, A. S. (1985). *Identity in Adolescence: Processes and Contents*. San Francisco, CA: Jossey-Bass.

Weinberg, R. S., Vernau, D., & Horn, T. S. (2013). Playing through pain and injury: Psychosocial considerations. *Journal of Clinical Sport Psychology, 7*, 41–59.

Woods, C. B., Kirrane, M., & Buckley, F. (2003). Not making the grade in the Premiership: The impact of a post de-selection programme on the athletic identity of young soccer players. In R. Stelter, D. Alfermann, S. Biddle, H. Ripoll, G. Roberts, R. Seiler, & N. Stambulova (Eds.), *New Approaches to Sport and Exercise Psychology* (p. 187). Copenhagen: FEPSAC.

15

STRESS, EMOTIONS, AND COPING IN YOUTH SPORT

Peter R. E. Crocker, Katherine A. Tamminen, and Erica V. Bennett

Millions of adolescents are involved in organised competitive sport throughout the world. Competitive sport, by its very nature, imposes many threats and challenges on these young people. There are many sources of stress, including high training demands, injury and fear of injury, interpersonal conflict with coaches, teammates, officials, and opponents, parental and coach pressure to perform, personal performance expectations, performance errors, poor equipment and training facilities, an over-emphasis on winning, sport organisation politics, as well as conflict between sport and other social and academic goals (Crocker, Tamminen, & Gaudreau, 2014; Nicholls & Polman, 2007). Also we must not lose sight of the fact that adolescence is a period characterised by physical and cognitive maturation, changing social roles and obligations, increased curiosity about and involvement in romantic relationships, growing peer relationships, and increasing independence from parental control (Compas, Connor-Smith, Saltzman, Thomsen, & Wadsworth, 2001; Seiffge-Krenke, 2011) (see Chapters 4 and 5). These events result in many conflicts with social and personal goals that activate a range of positive and negative cognitions, emotions, and behaviours. Thus, effective stress and emotional regulation skills are necessary if the adolescent athlete is to successfully manage the many challenges thrown their way.

The purpose of this chapter is to provide an overview of the current knowledge about the importance of the stress, emotion, and coping process in adolescent athletes. In the first section we will focus on theoretical and conceptual issues that underpin research, intervention, and best practices in facilitating successful adaptation in competitive sport. We cover select research that examines questions related to how athletes cope, the effectiveness of coping skills interventions, and the role of parents and significant others in shaping how adolescent athletes cope. In the second section we present a case study of an athlete, Marcella, to illustrate how to translate research into practice.

Stress, coping, and emotion

Conceptual foundations

Sport research over the last 30 years investigating stress, coping, and emotion has emphasised a cognitive-evaluation viewpoint (Vallerand & Blanchard, 2000). A prominent theoretical framework is Richard Lazarus' cognitive-motivational-relational (CMR) theory (Lazarus, 1999, 2000; Nicholls & Thelwell, 2010). Lazarus (2000) argued that stress is an unfolding and dynamic transactional process between the athlete and the situation. CMR theory holds that an adolescent athlete will appraise athletic demands in relation to their potential impact on personal and social goals and values. Athletes may perceive situations as threatening, harmful, challenging, or beneficial. Another aspect of appraisal is deciding what can be done to manage the demands (coping options). The evaluation of demands and coping options will generate emotions and influence attempted actions (coping) to change the situation and/or regulate emotional responses.

As adolescent athletes achieve or are thwarted in their pursuit of important goals, they will experience a range of emotions. Emotions are a complex psycho-neuro-physiological reaction and represent a critical feature of the stress process that motivate and regulate cognitions, physiology, action tendencies, and behaviours (Lazarus, 1999). Emotions can be considered in two categories: primary emotions and self-conscious emotions. Primary or basic emotions are thought to represent those states that were largely shaped by evolution, and have specific neural, expressive, and physiological mechanisms and responses (Ekman & Cordaro, 2011). Basic emotions often include fear, happiness/joy, sadness, anger, surprise, anxiety, and disgust (see Crocker, 2015). In contrast, self-conscious emotions are dependent on self-awareness and require more elaborate cognitive processing than basic emotions. Common self-conscious emotions present in sport are pride, shame, guilt, envy, jealousy, and embarrassment (see Sabiston & Castonguay, 2015). Overall, both basic and self-conscious emotions need to be regulated to help adolescent athletes achieve successful functioning in demanding sport environments because emotions can have an impact on performance and social functioning (Hanin, 2000).

An example of how emotions are generated and influence the experiences of adolescent athletes is the case of fear. Fear is a common emotion in situations that are potentially dangerous. Years ago the first author worked with high-performance youth gymnasts. One gymnast had a bad fall while performing a backflip on the balance beam but she did not sustain any serious injuries. In subsequent training attempts on the beam the athlete could not initiate the skill. She stated that she knew she had the physical skill but she was so afraid of falling. Fear was evident in her face. Her pupils were dilated, respiration rate was high, and she was shaking; when she stepped off the beam it was soaking wet where she was standing. She wanted to do any other gymnastic skill except the backflip on beam. This example captures many of the key features of the stress and emotion process. The fall triggered the realisation that there was a real physical risk and threat to her personal physical wellbeing. Going back on the beam and being required to attempt the skill automatically generated fear appraisals, producing prototypical facial expressions as well as the neural-physiological reactions and action tendencies associated with fear. The athlete also considered her coping options, such as disengaging from the task. Such instances of emotional reactions are not uncommon in competitive sport and highlight the need to help adolescent athletes regulate such emotions and develop effective stress and emotion management skills.

If young athletes are to effectively manage the stressful demands of competitive sport then they must develop, modify, or enhance various coping and emotion regulation skills (Crocker et al., 2015). Many different types of automatic and controlled processes can be used in emotional regulation. A central process that is extensively studied in sport is coping (Uphill & Jones, 2012). Coping refers to a conscious, effortful process that involves cognitive and behaviour responses used to regulate not only emotions but also cognitions, behaviour, and the environment during stressful transactions (Lazarus, 2000). Although not extensively studied in sport, it is thought that developmental changes in adolescence will result in a shift towards a greater use of cognitive strategies by middle adolescence, ages 15 to 18 years (Holt, Hoar, & Fraser, 2005). This is likely due to maturation of cognitive systems and social cognitive skills such as increased use and organisation of abstract thinking and perspective taking (Seiffge-Krenke, 2011). Developmental maturation should increase the likelihood that older adolescents will more effectively handle the stressful demands of competitive sport (Nicholls, Perry, Jones, Morley, & Carson, 2013).

There are numerous coping strategies that adolescent athletes use in a purposeful goal-directed manner to manage stress. These strategies include, but are not restricted to, increasing effort, seeking social support, avoidance, cognitive reappraisal, distraction, imagery, wishful thinking, changing tactics, confrontation, arousal control, breathing control, suppression of thoughts, and planning (see Crocker et al., 2015; Nicholls & Polman, 2007). Given the large number of potential specific coping strategies, researchers have attempted to classify these strategies into more macro-analytic categories. Although these classification systems vary widely, in sport research there are three common systems. The most dominant classification includes problem-focused, emotion-focused, and avoidance coping (Lazarus, 1999; Crocker et al., 2015). Problem-focused coping functions to change the environmental demands and/or the response of the athlete; emotion-focused coping functions to regulate emotional distress; and avoidance coping involves attempts to remove oneself mentally or physically from the stressful situation. A second popular classification is a three-dimensional model proposed by Gaudreau and Blondin (2004), who proposed task-oriented coping (strategies that deal with situation and cognitions/emotions associated with the stress process), disengagement-oriented coping (avoidance and active withdrawal strategies), and distraction-oriented coping (focusing on information unrelated to the stressful situation).

What makes the study of stress and coping in adolescent athletes so challenging is that there are countless specific strategies that can be used in each stressful encounter. It is apparent that all of these strategies may not be adaptive over extended periods of time; yet athletes may use any of these strategies to either change a troubled athlete–person environment or modify the emotional experience. For example, a swimmer may avoid thinking about a poor race to reduce the distress associated with failing to achieve an important achievement goal. Although this strategy may provide temporary relief, it is likely to be maladaptive over the long term because the athlete fails to learn from the experience and may neglect to develop effective strategies to enhance race performance. Even strategies that intuitively appear to be adaptive may be maladaptive in some cases. For example, many athletes report increasing effort to deal with performance difficulties. However, changing individual or team tactics might be the better option in some situations. Athletes are often able to anticipate upcoming stressors and can engage in anticipatory coping such as planning ahead, time management, increasing effort, or prioritising tasks and goals (see McDonough et al., 2013; Tamminen & Holt, 2010). These strategies might not be effective if something unexpected occurs.

Coping can also be studied from a team-based perspective. Communal coping (Lyons, Mickelson, Sullivan, & Coyne, 1998) requires that the team members believe that they must act together to manage a stressor, act to communicate strategies, and work together for the overall team benefit (see Tamminen & Gaudreau, 2014). Another form of team-based coping is extrinsic emotional regulation that deals with how athletes regulate their own and others' emotions (Tamminen & Crocker, 2013). An athlete's emotional expressions and reactions are likely to impact teammates' (and opponents') emotions and behaviours; coaches' emotional reactions are also likely to directly impact the emotions and performance of their athletes. Being aware of how emotional reactions influence others can lead to the thoughtful regulation of one's own emotional displays to facilitate team performance and social functioning (Tamminen & Crocker, 2013).

As adolescence is a period of development where athletes face increasing demands in their personal and competitive lives, researchers have examined changes in the stressors and coping that young athletes report across brief competitive periods (Nicholls, 2007) and across an entire competitive season (McDonough et al., 2013; Tamminen & Holt, 2010). This research indicates that stressors and coping fluctuate over time and in conjunction with important competitive periods. Researchers have also found that coping in sport is associated with the developmental status of athletes, such that older adolescent athletes with greater conscientiousness and greater emotional maturity use more task-oriented coping in sport (Nicholls et al., 2013; Nicholls, Levy, & Perry, 2015). These differences in coping likely reflect increases in adolescents' cognitive capacity for coping and increases in the diversity of coping strategies.

The research literature shows clear relationships between coping, emotions, and wellbeing in adolescent athletes. Researchers have shown that coping skills training can help adolescent athletes manage stress. For example, Crocker, Alderman, and Smith (1988) found that an eight-week coping skills programme reduced negative thoughts to a video-taped performance stressor and led to increased service reception performance in high-performance Under 19 volleyball players. Nicholls (2007) also described a coping training programme with an adolescent international golfer that educated the athlete about coping strategies and developing awareness about effective and ineffective coping strategies. The athlete perceived the programme improved coping in competition. Another study of a six-session experiential training programme intervention demonstrated significant improvements in the coping self-efficacy, positive affect, and overall happiness of rugby athletes during their transition from high school to university (Laureano, Grobbelaar, & Nienaber, 2014).

Understanding the role of important others such as coaches and parents can help us understand how athletes learn to cope more effectively with stressors in sport. Tamminen and Holt (2012) reported that athletes learned about effective coping in sport through trial and error and by reflecting on their past coping attempts. Parents and coaches supported athletes' learning about coping by establishing a supportive relationship with the athlete, prompting athletes to think about ways of coping with stressors, questioning and reminding athletes about past coping efforts, initiating informal conversations about coping, and by sharing their own experiences with the athlete. This research highlights the value of improving social relationships between athletes, coaches, and parents as a means to helping athletes deal with stress and enjoy more positive sport experiences (see Chapters 10, 18, 19, and 27 for further details).

The importance of parental support, pressure, and the socialisation of coping among youth athletes was revealed in a recent study by Tamminen, McEwen, and Crocker (2016). Parents' socialisation of task-oriented or engagement coping (e.g. providing explicit instructions about using engagement coping strategies to deal with sport stressors) was associated with athletes' use of engagement coping. Disengagement coping, on the other hand, was associated with athletes' perceptions of parental pressure, and negatively associated with perceptions of parental support. Furthermore, athletes with the lowest disengagement coping scores reported high parental support and their parents also reported low socialisation of disengagement coping. Clearly parental behaviour has a major impact on how adolescent athletes manage stressful sport events.

Coaches also play an important role in helping athletes deal with stressors in sport (Tamminen & Holt, 2012). Athletes' perceptions of coach autonomy support are associated with task-oriented coping and goal achievement, while perceptions of unsupportive coaching are associated with the use of disengagement-oriented coping (Nicolas, Gaudreau, & Franche, 2011). Chapter 19 provides more evidence of the importance of supportive behaviours by coaches in the lives of adolescent athletes. Thus, emphasising supportive coach and parental behaviours in helping athletes cope with stressors in sport will improve the sport experiences of young athletes.

Application of research in practice

To illustrate the complexity of the stress and coping process in youth sport, we provide the experiences of an elite high school soccer player named Marcella. This case study is based on the first author's experiences with several athletes who have experienced very similar stress experiences. Following the case study, we discuss some intervention strategies that could have helped Marcella effectively manage stress and provide suggestions for practitioners working with adolescent athletes.

Case study

Marcella is a 17-year-old high school senior who plays soccer at an elite level on an age-graded team of 16 to 18 year olds. Marcella's coaches have told her that she has a shot at a university varsity sport scholarship if she continues to work on developing her skills. This means a lot to Marcella; if she does not get a scholarship, she might not be able to attend university. Marcella's parents are pushing her to train hard so she gets a scholarship. They insist that she put in extra hours of training so that she can better impress the scouts who come watch her play. They continuously remind her that she needs to outplay her teammates to show that she is the best. Marcella has mixed feelings about all this pressure. At one level she feels like she would rather play soccer for fun, but at another level she does not want to let her parents down and miss the chance to go to university. She often feels overwhelmed and anxious about these goals. Her parents notice that Marcella does not seem to be acting like herself, but she brushes them off and tells them she is fine.

Because of her skill level, Marcella's coaches have assigned her to be the team captain for the season. When she suggests to them that she might not be ready for this role, they tell her that she will experience challenges, but that this is ok and they will help her deal with these difficulties. Marcella is ambivalent; she is excited to take on this new challenge, but fears that she will let her coaches down. Marcella lacks confidence in her ability to be a captain and fears some teammates do not respect her. There have been several conflicts with teammates; when this happened, Marcella broke down, started crying, and left practice. Marcella tried talking to her teammates to make amends, but they were not receptive. Since then, she has been extra cheerful at practice in hopes that her teammates will respond positively. She also tries to avoid her teammates outside of practice and games when possible. The pressure causes her to ruminate often, get distracted at school, and she frequently wakes up in the middle of the night. Marcella does not know what she should do, so she distracts herself by keeping busy and training harder.

From our experiences, Marcella's case is not that unusual in elite sport. Many athletes face multiple stressors related to performance, role, and social expectations. In Marcella's case there are several interrelated environmental stressors coupled with her lack of effective coping skills that prevent her from effectively managing the stress process. She is feeling great pressure to get a scholarship and this pressure is compounded by her role as a captain. Clearly she is evaluating these pressures as being very threatening. In addition, there are a number of social relationships (with parents, coaches, and teammates) that are appraised as threatening. Overall, the coping strategies she is using are primarily avoidance in nature and are not effective.

Intervention strategies

Based on our experiences with similar cases, we provide some suggestions that can help athletes like Marcella deal with these performance and social stressors. Clearly Marcella is having difficulties in managing dysfunctional thoughts and emotions. We have developed an intervention for her guided by the cognitive-motivational-relational framework (Larazus, 2000) as well as the empirical literature on effective stress management strategies in sport (Crocker et al., 2015; Rumbold, Fletcher & Daniels, 2012). The first step in the intervention would be to educate Marcella about the transactional stress, emotion, and coping process. This psycho-education component involves educating her about the general factors (appraisal, coping, and emotion) in terms that she can understand and are directly relevant to her situation. For example, explaining that stress is a process that involves physiological (e.g. increases in arousal, muscle tension), psychological (e.g. perceptions of threat, negative rumination, changes in confidence), emotional (e.g. anxiety, guilt), and behavioural (e.g. avoidance, trying too hard) components. It is helpful to normalise her reactions, emphasising that her stress reactions are typical in difficult sport situations (Meichenbaum, 2007). Having Marcella recognise how her thoughts and coping responses impact her personal stress process is a critical step in enabling her to develop awareness of the (in)effective coping strategies she has employed, allowing her to think about how she might proceed in the future when similar stressors reoccur.

Marcella would need to develop new and enhanced coping and emotion regulation strategies (see Rumbold et al., 2012). This consists of developing problem- and emotion-focused coping strategies that would be most effective. For example, to help her cope with the goal of obtaining a university sport scholarship, Marcella could practice goal-setting to manage her emotions (Burton & Weiss, 2008). She could develop new challenging yet realistic short-term and process-oriented goals for practices and competitions (e.g. increasing shooting accuracy from 15–20 metres by 20 per cent over the next month by improving technical skill), which would allow her to more effectively focus on her training efforts. This form of goal-setting will help her gain control over her actions and focus on what needs to be done. Removing a focus that is solely on an outcome (e.g. getting the scholarship) can result in less performance pressure.

To reduce the stress associated with the captaincy role, the coaches might provide some education and reading materials about being an effective captain. The National Federation of State High School Association in the US, for example, offer a free online course to provide leadership training for high school sport captains (https://nfhslearn.com/courses/61028/captains-course). Marcella could also develop specific coping skills such as self-talk, imagery, and arousal control (see Rumbold et al., 2012). For example, Marcella could keep track of how she speaks to herself when facing challenges pertaining to being the captain of the team, followed by attempts to reframe negative self-talk to neutral and positive instructional and motivational self-talk. Using imagery skills, she could imagine scenarios in which she would successfully lead her teammates in a practice drill or even have everyday conversations with them. To manage the anxiety she experiences, which often leads to negative thoughts and behaviours, Marcella could also practise arousal regulation techniques such as breathing exercises and progressive muscle relaxation. Collectively, these coping strategies could help Marcella effectively manage her stressors.

A third step of the intervention could include sessions with Marcella's parents and coaches with the aim of educating them about the stressors often faced by adolescent athletes, as well as on the role they could play in modelling effective coping behaviours (Nicolas, Gaudreau, & Franche, 2011; Tamminen & Holt, 2012). Especially important would be getting these significant others to reduce the frequency they talk about the importance of earning a scholarship while simultaneously reducing uncertainly about doing so, as importance and uncertainty have been found to be two key sources of stress for young athletes (Gould, Horn, & Spreemann, 1983; Martens, 1987). Educating significant others is often a difficult step as it involves the cooperation of coaches and parents, and also involves the consent of Marcella. From our experiences, involving parents and coaches is an important step in successful interventions. Her parents and coaches could be guided in how to initiate informal conversations with Marcella where they could provide her with the opportunity to discuss the challenges she is facing, ask her how she has coped with stressors in the past and whether these strategies have been (un)helpful, and to suggest ways in which she can think about coping. Depending on the social dynamics and cooperation of coaches, it might also be possible to work with the team to learn how to use communal coping strategies to deal with team-level stressors. This can help reduce the pressure on Marcella and also increase the performance and social functioning of the team.

Collectively, the coping skills learnt by Marcella, her parents, and coaches should provide Marcella with an opportunity to learn how to effectively deal with stressors in (and outside) the sport domain. It is likely that Marcella's coping efforts will change and develop over time as a result of her ongoing personal and skill development and thus the learning of coping skills will need to be continuous (see Nicholls et al., 2013).

Conclusion

This chapter has provided an overview of some of the main theories and current research on stress, emotion, and coping among adolescent athletes. It is important for practitioners, coaches, and parents to remember that adolescence is a time of learning and development, and that adolescent athletes are being confronted with a number of new situations and stressors as they begin competing at higher levels, as they train and compete with new teammates and coaches, and as they face more intense competition demands. These stressors will generate different types of basic and self-conscious emotions that will impact performance, social functioning, and wellbeing; thus athletes need to develop effective stress and emotion regulation strategies. Athletes should try to use a variety of coping strategies to deal with the pressures they face in sport, some of which will be effective, while others will not be, depending on the situational demands. It is important that athletes are supported in trying new coping strategies and that they are able to reflect on their coping efforts to develop an awareness about what coping strategies are effective for them in dealing with stress. Helping athletes to reflect and develop awareness of their coping abilities can ultimately lead to better coping and emotional regulation, better performance and goal achievement, and importantly, happier and healthier athletes.

References

Burton, D., & Weiss, C. (2008). The fundamental goal concept: The path to process and performance success. *Advances in Sport Psychology, 3*, 339–375.

Compas, B. E., Connor-Smith, J. K., Saltzman, H., Thomsen, A. H., & Wadsworth, M. E. (2001). Coping with stress during childhood and adolescence: Problems, progress, and potential in theory and research. *Psychological Bulletin, 127*, 87–127.

Crocker, P. R. E. (2015). Basic emotions. In R. E. Eklund & G. Tenenbaum (Eds.), *Encyclopedia of Sport and Exercise Psychology* (Vol. 1, pp. 67–70). Thousand Oaks, CA: Sage.

Crocker, P. R. E., Alderman, R. B., & Smith, F. M. R. (1988). Cognitive affective stress management training for high performance youth volleyball: Effects on affect, cognition, and performance. *Journal of Sport & Exercise Psychology, 10*, 448–460.

Crocker, P. R. E., Tamminen, K. A., & Gaudreau, P. (2015). Coping in sport. In S. Hanton & S. D. Mellalieu (Eds.), *Contemporary Advances in Sport Psychology: A Review* (pp. 28–67). Abingdon, UK: Routledge.

Ekman, P., & Cordaro, D. (2011). What is meant by calling emotions basic? *Emotion Review, 3*, 364–371.

Gaudreau, P., & Blondin, J.-P. (2004). The differential associations of dispositional optimism and pessimism with coping, goal attainment, and emotional adjustment during a sport competition. *International Journal of Stress Management, 11*, 245–269.

Gould, D., Horn, T., & Spreemann, J. (1983). Sources of stress in junior elite wrestlers. *Journal of Sport Psychology, 5*, 159–171.

Hanin, Y. (2000). *Emotions in Sport*. Champaign, IL: Human Kinetics.

Holt, N. L., Hoar, S., & Fraser, S. (2005). How does coping change with development? A review of childhood and adolescence sport coping research. *European Journal of Sport Science, 5*, 25–39.

Laureano, C., Grobbelaar, H. W., & Nienaber, A. W. (2014). Facilitating the coping self-efficacy and psychological wellbeing of student rugby players. *South African Journal of Psychology, 44*, 483–497.

Lazarus, R. S. (1999). *Stress and Emotion: A New Synthesis*. New York, NY: Springer.

Lazarus, R. S. (2000). Cognitive-motivational-relational theory of emotion. In Y. L. Hanin (Ed.), *Emotions in Sport* (pp. 39–63). Champaign, IL: Human Kinetics.

Lyons, R. F., Mickelson, K. D., Sullivan, M. J. L., & Coyne, J. C. (1998). Coping as a communal process. *Journal of Personal and Social Relationships, 15*, 579–605.

Martens, R. (1987). *Coaches Guide to Sport Psychology*. Champaign, IL: Human Kinetics.

McDonough, M., Hadd, V., Crocker, P. R. E., Holt, N. L., Tamminen, K. A., & Schonert-Reichl, K. (2013). Stress and coping among adolescents across a competitive swim season. *The Sport Psychologist, 27*, 143–155.

Meichenbaum, D. (2007). Stress inoculation training: A preventative and treatment approach. In P. M. Lehrer, R. L. Woolfolk, & W. S. Sime (Eds.), *Principles and Practice of Stress Management* (3rd ed., pp. 497–516). New York, NY: Guilford Press.

Nicolas, M., Gaudreau, P., & Franche, V. (2011). Perception of coaching behaviors, coping, and achievement in a sport competition. *Journal of Sport & Exercise Psychology, 33,* 460–468.

Nicholls, A. R. (2007). A longitudinal phenomenological analysis of coping effectiveness among Scottish international adolescent golfers. *European Journal of Sport Science, 7,* 169–178.

Nicholls, A. R., Levy, A. R., & Perry, J. L. (2015). Emotional maturity, dispositional coping, and coping effectiveness among adolescent athletes. *Psychology of Sport and Exercise, 17,* 32–39.

Nicholls, A. R., Perry, J. L., Jones, L., Morley, D., & Carson, F. (2013). Dispositional coping, coping effectiveness, and cognitive social maturity among adolescent athletes. *Journal of Sport & Exercise Psychology, 35,* 229–238.

Nicholls, A. R., & Polman, R. C. J. (2007). Stressors, coping and coping effectiveness among players from the England under-18 rugby union team. *Journal of Sport Behavior, 30,* 119–218.

Nicholls, A., & Thelwell, R. (2010). Coping conceptualized and unraveled. In A. Nicholls (Ed.), *Coping in Sport: Theory, Methods and Related Constructs* (pp. 3–14). New York, NY: Nova Science.

Rumbold, J. L., Fletcher, D., & Daniels, K. (2012). A systematic review of stress management interventions with sport performers. *Sport, Exercise, and Performance Psychology, 1,* 173–193.

Sabiston, C. M., & Castonguay, A. (2015). Self-conscious emotions. In R. C. Eklund & G. Tenenbaum (Eds.), *Encyclopedia of Sport and Exercise Psychology* (pp. 623–626). Thousand Oaks, CA: Sage.

Seiffge-Krenke, I. (2011). Coping with relationship stressors: A decade review. *Journal of Research on Adolescence, 21,* 196–210.

Tamminen, K. A., & Crocker, P. R. (2013). 'I control my own emotions for the sake of the team': Emotional self-regulation and interpersonal emotion regulation among female high-performance curlers. *Psychology of Sport and Exercise, 14,* 737–747.

Tamminen, K., & Gaudreau, P. (2014). Coping, social support, and emotion regulation in teams. In M. Beauchamp & M. Eyes (Eds.), *Group Dynamics in Sport and Exercise Psychology: Contemporary Themes* (pp. 222–239). New York, NY: Routledge.

Tamminen, K. A., & Holt, N. L. (2010). Female adolescent athletes' coping: A season long investigation. *Journal of Sports Sciences, 28,* 101–114.

Tamminen, K. A., & Holt, N. L. (2012). Adolescent athletes' learning about coping and the roles of parents and coaches. *Psychology of Sport and Exercise, 13,* 69–79.

Tamminen, K. A., McEwen, C. E., & Crocker, P. R. E. (2016). Perceptions matter: Parental support, pressure, and the socialization of adolescent athletes' coping. *International Journal of Sport Psychology, 47,* 335–354.

Uphill, M. A. & Jones, M. V. (2012). The consequences and control of emotions in elite athletes. In J. Thatcher, M. V. Jones, & D. Lavallee (Eds.), *Coping and Emotion in Sport* (2nd ed., pp. 213-235). Abingdon, UK: Routledge.

Vallerand, R. J., & Blanchard, C. M. (2000). The study of emotion in sport and exercise. In Y. L. Hanin (Ed.), *Emotions in Sport* (pp. 3–37). Champaign, IL: Human Kinetics.

16

MANAGING INJURIES AMONG YOUNG ATHLETES

Urban Johnson and Andreas Ivarsson

Developmental sport psychologists emphasise using theories, designs, and methods that capture age-related differences in cognitions, perceptions, and behaviours in physical activity contexts (Weiss & Raedeke, 2004). Being able to describe and explain the course of development in a particular psychological construct provides researchers and practitioners with information for developing interventions that are age appropriate and effective for evoking behavioural change (e.g. prevention intervention and healthy rehabilitation from injury and return to participation).

According to Wiese-Bjornstal (2003) children and adolescents have rarely been studied in sport injury psychology research. This is worrying because tendencies seen in the literature (e.g. Patel & Nelson, 2000) show that about 50 per cent of youth sport athletes experience at least one injury during each athletic season. Of those injuries about two-thirds are classified as minor (i.e. less than one week rehabilitation). Several researchers have discussed potential risk factors for injuries. For example, Junge, Runge, Juul-Kristensen, & Wedderkopp (2016) reported that girls (8–15 years) were exposed to an increase risk for overuse knee injuries in comparison to boys. Other risk factors, suggested by Junge, were previous knee injury, participation in certain sports, and participation in sport more than twice a week.

Given the high prevalence of sport injuries in youth sports and also the negative consequences of becoming injured it is important to develop strategies for both injury prevention as well as support during rehabilitation. In this chapter we provide a review of research in this area, as well as presenting our applied experiences from working with youth athletes, both with injury prevention as well as injury rehabilitation. The specific target population in our previous work has been youth athletes (aged 15–19 years), thus this chapter will be directed towards this specific age group of athletes.

Injury prevention in young athletes

Pre-injury research overview

Given the high injury rates associated with participation in youth sports, it is important to develop preventive strategies for sport injuries. To develop functional preventive strategies it is important to understand what factors might increase the risk of becoming injured. In prediction as well as prevention research the majority of published studies have focused on physiological and/or biomechanical factors and their relation to sport injuries (e.g. Almeida, Olmedilla, Rubio, & Palou, 2014). However, during the last few years, researchers and practitioners have more frequently started to acknowledge psychological factors in relation to sport injuries. Wiese-Bjornstal (2010), for example, emphasised the importance of combining biological and behavioural, as well as social sciences, together into a biopsychosocial perspective, to advance the knowledge of different questions related to sport injury.

To understand how psychological factors can be related to injury risk, several theoretical models have been developed (e.g. Appaneal & Perna, 2014). The most frequently adopted model is the *model of stress and athletic injury* (Williams & Andersen, 1998). In the model it is suggested that injury risk may be influenced by the athlete's stress responses. The stress responses will, in turn, have a bi-directional relationship with the athlete's appraisal of a potential stressful situation (e.g. practice, competition). Both the magnitude of the stress responses as well as the athlete's appraisal of the potential stressful situation are suggested to be influenced by the interplay between various psychosocial factors, which in the model are divided into three categories: (a) personality factors (e.g. trait anxiety), (b) history of stressors (e.g. negative life event stress, daily hassles), and (c) coping resources (e.g. social support). In this model, intervention strategies are suggested to buffer/reduce the stress response to subsequently decrease injury risk. However, Appaneal and Perna (2014) suggested that psychological, physiological, and attentional mechanisms, as well as behavioural mechanisms associated with the stress response, should be addressed together in injury prediction research.

Based on the psychological risk factors associated with increased risk for sport injuries, several prevention programmes have been developed and tested. In a recent meta-analysis, the result showed that all intervention programmes included in the analysis ($N = 7$) had positive results (i.e. fewer injuries in the experimental group compared to the control group), with Cohen's d effect sizes ranging from 0.12 to 1.28 (Ivarsson et al., 2017). Three of those seven studies focused on youth sport (football and ballet). The psychologically based prevention programmes used with youth athletes were mindfulness acceptance training (Ivarsson, Johnson, Andersen, Fallby, & Altmyr, 2015) and psychological skills training (Edvardsson, Ivarsson, & Johnson, 2012; Noh, Morris, & Andersen, 2007). Even though there have been different conceptual approaches to injury prevention interventions, the studies all draw on applied programmes targeting stress management techniques (e.g. relaxation, goal setting) as well as self-reflection. Based on the content in those three studies, combined with the authors' applied experiences of working with injury prevention, our aim is to present strategies that might help athletes to reduce the risk for sport injuries.

Application of research in practice

As reported, high stress levels and elevated stress responses are two psychological variables that have been related to an increased risk for sport injuries (Ivarsson et al., 2017). It has, therefore, been suggested that preventive strategies should be directed towards reducing those variables.

For athletes: Practise to be present

One concept that has been implemented in injury prevention research is mindfulness (Ivarsson et al., 2015). Mindfulness has been described as 'openhearted, moment-to-moment, non-judgmental awareness' (Kabat-Zinn, 2005, p. 24). In relation to stress, a number of studies have shown that mindfulness practice can positively influence individuals' appraisals of stressful situations (e.g. Weinstein, Brown, & Ryan, 2009) and their stress responses (e.g. Cozolino, 2010). The reduced magnitude of stress responses is, for example, related to improved abilities to pay attention to stimuli that are important in the moment (e.g. slip from a tackle). Also, mindfulness training has been found to improve human beings' decision-making capacity, which can be related to a decreased injury risk by, for example, a reduction in impulsive behaviours (i.e. behaviours in which the young athlete reacts before reflecting about the consequences).

One mindfulness training approach, developed for the sport context, is the Mindfulness Acceptance Commitment (MAC) approach (Gardner & Moore, 2007). Different versions of the MAC approach have been successfully implemented in youth sport populations (Moore, 2009). To help young athletes to be mindfully present a number of strategies can be implemented:

1) Athletes should be encouraged to reflect about what they should be paying attention towards during practice and games/competitions, as well as how and why they may react as they do in different situations. Additionally, discussions about how often athletes have thoughts about stress that are related to the past or the future provide a good illustration of how being present might help to decrease their levels of stress. In such a discussion it is important that athletes have the opportunity to reflect on different situations they have experienced and particularly times during games or competitions when they did not succeed at being present (e.g. thinking about upcoming exams perhaps rather than their current competition). Gaining extended knowledge about themselves and how they react in different situations is usually a good start towards behavioural change. One practical instrument that can be used in this process of self-reflection is video-recorded sequences from games/competitions where

the athlete has the opportunity to see how they react in different situations (e.g. Edvardsson et al., 2012).

2) Help athletes to be present during sport activities by focusing on relevant behaviours. More specifically, in Ivarsson et al.'s (2015) study, the youth foot-ballers were asked to develop a goal-setting plan for their sport activity. In that goal-setting work the participants were asked to formulate specific behaviours that they thought were related to the specific goals. Reflecting on the inter-vention, the footballers explained that identifying these specific behaviours felt good because it gave them something concrete to pay attention to when they started to lose focus.

3) Young athletes can also be encouraged to find short time periods in a day when they try to be mindful and present. Having the opportunity to get 'micro pauses' in everyday life is related to decreased stress levels that, in turn, can decrease the risk of becoming injured. This can be facilitated in many different ways. One example is to provide the athlete with audio-recorded mindfulness scripts. Such scripts can nowadays be easily downloaded onto a mobile phone.

To increase the chance of successfully implementing such strategies it is important that the athletes are active participants in the discussions. Such active engagement is essential because every person is unique and must, therefore, be encouraged to reflect on the situations when being present would be beneficial for them. It might be a challenge for young athletes to be active participants in discussions, particularly if the implementation of the strategies is performed in a larger group (e.g. team). Thus, it may be beneficial for practitioners to form smaller groups in which athletes can reflect together about different topics, such as behaviours that are important in their specific sport or position in a team. During these reflections, it is also impor-tant that the practitioner guides the group so that all athletes get the opportunity to be involved in the discussions/reflections but avoids long presentations, which may limit athlete discussions or engagement.

For coaches: Create an open and non-judgemental environment

One procedure that has been suggested to have a stress-reducing effect is having the opportunity to share experiences by telling stories. However, to obtain positive effects, stories need to be told in a relationship that is non-judgemental and based on empathy and kindness (Andersen & Ivarsson, 2016). This suggestion is based on the results from research conducted in the area of interpersonal neurobiology, which has concluded that if the relationship between two humans is based on a supportive and non-judgemental foundation, it is likely that people will change for the better (Siegel, 2010). More specifically, it is likely that when an athlete interacts with someone who is empathic and supportive, a story that may have initially been associated with stress and negative emotions can be reframed to have a more pos-itive ending. Further, when an athlete feels their story is received by another who is interested, empathic, and supportive, it is likely they will experience positive emotions, such as relief and comfort, because they feel someone cares and understands. Thus, the creation of youth sport climates in which such relationships can exist between coaches and athletes is important. To help coaches develop such a climate there are several things that we would recommend in the context of injury prevention:

1) Coaches are encouraged to reflect on how they behave in different situations and why they behave in this particular way. Our experiences are that coaches often think they behave in a specific way but when reflecting on their behaviours (perhaps using video-recorded sequences from their coaching) they discover in many cases that their perceptions of their behaviour and their actual behaviour do not match. By extending understanding about their own behaviours coaches can, hopefully, create a less stressful and injury-free environment.

2) After reflections about their actual behaviours it is important for coaches to reflect on how these fit with their beliefs and norms. In such reflection it can be beneficial for the coach to formulate his/her coaching philosophy together with behaviours that manifest the philosophy. If the coach wants to facilitate the development of a supportive and non-judgemental climate where the athletes feel that it is ok to share their stories it is important that the coach listens to the athletes when they are talking and show they are supportive. Showing mutual respect for each other also helps to reduce unnecessary tension, which potentially buffers against subsequent injury risk.

One potential challenge that practitioners might experience when implementing self-reflection exercises for coaches is that many of them are inexperienced in such exercises. This might lead to problems in convincing the coaches that it is important to reflect on how different behaviours can influence the athletes. To encourage coaches to engage in these types of exercises it is important to explain how behaviours can be related to different outcomes for the athlete (e.g. performance, injury risk, stress responses). In doing this, coaches can come to understand the multiple benefits that both they and their athletes can gain through coach self-reflection.

Injury rehabilitation in youth sport

Post-injury research overview

Research regarding the psychological aspects of athletic injury has predominately focused on negative responses that arise due to physical inactivity. For example, negative responses such as tension, low self-esteem, depression, and anxiety immediately following injury and during rehabilitation have been identified in numerous studies (Brewer, 2001). As such, it is perhaps unsurprising that an athlete's ability to cope with post-injury stress has been shown to influence recovery and progression through a rehabilitation programme (Bianco, 2001).

Negative psychological responses can also occur when the athlete receives clearance to return to active sport (Morrey, Stuart, Smith, & Wiese-Bjornstal, 1999). More specifically, common risk variables in relation to return from injury are: perception of negative influence of injury on current life situation (Johnson, 1996), low confidence (Langford, Webster, & Feller, 2009), a fluctuating mood level (Webster, Feller, & Lambros, 2008), and anxieties associated with re-injury; feelings of isolation; insufficient social support; pressures to return to sport; and finally, self-presentational concerns about the prospect of appearing unfit, or lacking in skill in relation to competitors (Podlog, Dimmock, & Miller, 2011).

As with adults, some young athletes experience psychosocial problems that might delay or even prevent their return to sport. Common features include stress related to personal loss or change, self-esteem reliant on athletic prowess, and a narrow range of interest beyond athletics (Pillemar & Micheli, 1988; e.g. Chapter 14). In a study by Johnson, Carlsson, Hinic, & Lindwall (2003) it was shown that young athletes (15.8 years) exhibit lower scores for basic self-esteem compared with injured adult athletes (24.2 years). It was speculated that when young athletes lose control over their bodies (e.g. through a sport injury), their self-worth is diminished since their self-esteem is greatly dependent on their physical appearance (Fox, 1997; see Chapter 9 for further insights). Further, the younger athletes indicated lower task orientation scores than the adult athletes, which could reveal an unclear view of what is expected to occur during the rehabilitation period due to a lack of prior experience of being injured. Research shows that both first-time injured and younger athletes experience the rehabilitation period as more stressful and display less self-confidence and lower mood levels than formerly injured adult athletes (Johnson, 1996).

The Integrated Model of Response to Sport Injury

One central theory, especially well suited for a lifespan perspective to injury rehabilitation, is the Integrated Model of Response to Sport Injury (Wiese-Bjornstal, Smith, Shaffer, & Morrey, 1998). This model describes numerous factors that contribute to and influence the cognitive appraisal process when injured. In the model the authors suggest that personal factors (e.g. athletic identity and physical health status) and situational factors (e.g. level of competition and coach influence) moderate athletes' thought processes related to injury. Athletes' cognitive appraisal (e.g. belief and attribution and sense of loss or relief) is then assumed to influence emotional responses (e.g. tension, anger, depression) and ultimately behavioural responses (e.g. risk-taking behaviour and adherence to rehabilitation). Thus, the injury process is presumed to be dynamic, changing in magnitude and direction over time. This dynamic aspect of the injury experience has its underpinnings in the stress and coping literature (Folkman & Lazarus, 1984), which claims that cognitive appraisal is critical to understanding an individual's psychological response to injury.

In the following section, components of the post-injury psychological response, as outlined in the Integrated Model of Response to the Sport Injury, are used to analyse and illustrate how research can be applied in practice to facilitate young athletes' rehabilitation and recovery from injury.

Application of research in practice

In the Integrated Model of Response to Sport Injury (Wiese–Bjornstal et al., 1998) two responses are outlined: emotional and behavioural. Both have major implications for helping the injured young athlete during their rehabilitation process.

For athletes: Develop strategies to deal with negative emotions

Negative emotional reactions are common among injured athletes. Examples of common reactions are frustration, anger, and depression. These types of reactions might inhibit the athlete's adherence to the rehabilitation programme because the athlete may be distracted by her or his emotions, focusing on these rather than the rehabilitation programme. To deal with such emotional reactions, for example uncertainty about future and depressive symptoms, it is important to be accustomed with functional techniques that could reduce negative emotional reactions. Some examples of approaches practitioners can implement to help injured athletes deal with negative emotional reactions are presented below:

1) A prime intervention strategy would be to educate the injured athlete about what to expect during rehabilitation and what is to be expected from them (Johnson et al., 2003). Detailing expectations will give athletes a clear picture of the rehabilitation period (strengthening task orientation; see Chapter 8), which is particularly important given that most of them will have limited prior experience of rehabilitation settings. This strategy will eventually lead to increased self-efficacy and reduced feelings of uncertainty because the young athlete knows what to expect.

2) Goal-setting can also be beneficial (Santi & Pietrantoni, 2013). During the rehabilitation period, it can be difficult for athletes to know if they are making any actual progress. For this reason, it is important to formulate a realistic goal-setting plan for the rehabilitation period together with the physiotherapist and/or doctor. By monitoring and evaluating the goals, the athlete will notice small improvements in their rehabilitation that might have otherwise gone unnoticed. These small improvements may help the young athlete feel more positive and confident in the rehabilitation process, which can facilitate motivation for rehabilitation.

For significant others: Provide a supportive environment

One behavioural response that is occasionally observed among young athletes is inadequate adherence to rehabilitation. This could be due to immature or unclear expectations of how to behave in a potentially new situation (being injured). In a situation where the young athletes exhibit such a response, it is valuable if the treating physiotherapist (or other medical personal), together with the athlete's coach or perhaps parent, educates the athlete about the physiological and psychological responses that can be expected during rehabilitation. Such knowledge will help the athlete anticipate demands and develop/identify effective coping skills to use during rehabilitation. The development of sufficient coping skills will, in turn, increase the chance of athletes feeling that they are able to adhere to the rehabilitation programme.

In line with the above suggestions, educational and motivational efforts, such as motivation-based interventions, have demonstrated good results in research. One particular approach that has been especially effective is motivational interviewing (MI; Breckon, 2015). MI is based on the foundation that the interaction between the therapist and participant should be one of collaboration, evocation, and autonomy (Moyers & Rollnick, 2002). MI is directed towards autonomous motivation, and this approach has been found to be effective in terms of behaviour change (Hardcastle, Taylor, Beiley, Harley, & Hagger, 2013). When the treating physiotherapist meets young injured athletes, it is especially important to communicate with words that they will recognise, using clear and specific language and explanations, as well as providing feedback that is specific and given in close proximity to the physical training during rehabilitation.

Another behavioural response that is important to consider when dealing with young athletes is the synchronisation of different social and physical support systems surrounding the injured athlete. Hallqvist (2012) sought to determine who is responsible for providing children and young athletes with psychosocial support when facing serious sports injuries. Through interviews with coaches, parents, and physiotherapists, all parties underlined that communication between the different parties was a major problem and that the role of a coordinator was missing. In essence, coaches felt that they lacked education and time to appropriately support the injured athletes, parents generally described being disappointed regarding the care their child received, and physiotherapists felt that because rehabilitation is often presented as a substitute for the athletes' training/competition they had to bear a greater responsibility for the process and that this responsibility extended beyond their training.

As Hallqvist's (2012) study highlights, young injured athletes face several psychosocial challenges during rehabilitation, with many individuals involved in the athletes' life in various ways and with varying responsibilities. From our perspective the young athlete is in a potentially vulnerable situation as they are partly in the hands of other controlling authorities. With this in mind, an important practical starting point is to develop constructive and systematic communication between the different parties involved in the athlete's life (e.g. coach, parents, and physiotherapist) to increase the likelihood of a healthy rehabilitation. Developing such communication might be a challenge, but if all the individuals understand that they are working towards the same goal (i.e. to create a positive climate for the young athlete) our experiences are that it is possible.

Conclusion

Previous research has identified that, when working with young athletes, psychological factors related to both injury risk and injury rehabilitation should be considered. Coping with emotional responses (e.g. stress symptoms; see Chapter 15) seems to be particularly important to decrease the risk of becoming injured and also increase the chance for a successful rehabilitation. Several conditions make the experience of being injured particularly challenging for young athletes, such as immature coping strategies, lack of a functional social support system, and high/ exclusive athletic identity (see Chapter 14). For practitioners and significant others it is important to provide social support, and for all persons around young athletes to help athletes develop both emotional and behavioural strategies to improve their abilities to deal with life event stressors.

References

Almeida, P. L., Olmedilla, A., Rubio, V. J., & Palou, P. (2014). Psychology in the realm of sport injury: What it is all about. *Revista de Psicologia del Deporte, 23*, 395–400.

Andersen, M. B., & Ivarsson, A. (2016). A methodology of loving kindness: How interpersonal neurobiology, compassion and transference can inform researcher–participant encounters and storytelling. *Qualitative Research in Sport, Exercise and Health, 8*, 1–20.

Appaneal, R. N., & Perna, F. M. (2014). Biopsychosocial Model of Injury. In R. Eklund & G. Tenenbaum (Eds.), *Encyclopedia of Sport and Exercise Psychology* (pp. 74–77). Thousand Oaks, CA: Sage.

Bianco, T. (2001). Social support and recovery from sport injury: Elite skiers share their experiences. *Research Quarterly for Exercise and Sport, 72*, 376–388.

Breckon, J. (2015). Motivational interviewing, exercise, and nutrition counseling. In M. B. Andersen & S. J. Hanrahan (Eds.), *Doing Exercise Psychology* (pp. 75–100). Champaign, IL: Human Kinetics.

Brewer, B. W. (2001). Psychology of sport injury rehabilitation. In R. N. Singer, H. A. Hausenblas, & C. M. Janelle (Eds.), *Handbook of Sport Psychology* (2nd ed.) (pp. 787–809). New York, NY: John Wiley & Sons.

Cozolino, L. (2010). *The Neuroscience of Psychotherapy: Healing the Social Brain* (2nd ed.). New York, NY: Norton.

Edvardsson, A., Ivarsson, A., & Johnson, U. (2012). Is a cognitive-behavioural biofeedback intervention useful to reduce injury risk in junior football players? *Journal of Sport Science and Medicine, 11*, 331–338.

Folkman, S., & Lazarus, R. S. (1984). *Stress, Appraisal and Coping*. New York, NY: Springer.

Fox, K. R. (1997). The physical self and processes in the self-esteem development. In K. R. Fox (Ed.), *The Physical Self: From Motivation to Well-Being* (pp. 111–140). Champaign, IL: Human Kinetics.

Gardner, F. L., & Moore, Z. E. (2007). *The Psychology of Enhancing Human Performance: The Mindfulness-Acceptance-Commitment (MAC) Approach*. New York, NY: Springer.

Hallqvist, C. (2012). *Ansvaret för barn och ungdomars psykosociala stöd i samband med allvarlig idrottsskada* (Unpublished master's dissertation). Linneaus University, Växjö, Sweden.

Hardcastle, S. J., Taylor, A. H., Bailey, M. P., Harley, R. A., & Hagger, M. S. (2013). Effectiveness of a motivational interviewing intervention on weight loss, physical activity and cardiovascular disease risk factors: A randomized controlled trail with a 12-month post-intervention follow-up. *International Journal of Behavioral Nutrition and Physical Activity, 10,* e40.

Ivarsson, A., Johnson, U., Andersen, M. B., Fallby, J., & Altemyr, M. (2015). It pays to pay attention: A mindfulness-based programme for injury prevention with soccer players. *Journal of Applied Sport Psychology, 27,* 319–334.

Ivarsson, A., Johnson, U., Andersen, M. B., Tranaeus, U., Stenling, A., & Lindwall, M. (2017). Psychosocial factors and sport injuries: Meta-analyses for prediction and prevention. *Sports Medicine, 47,* 353–365.

Johnson, U. (1996). The multiply-injured versus the first-time injured competitive athletes during rehabilitation of long-term sport injury: A comparison of non-physical characteristics. *Journal of Sport Rehabilitation, 5,* 293–304.

Johnson, U., Carlsson, B., Hinic, H., & Lindwall, M. (2003). Psychological reactions to injury among competitive athletes, youth athletes and exercisers compared to a non-injured reference group. In G. Patriksson (Ed.), *Aktuell Beteendevetenskaplig Idrottsforskning. SVEBIs årsbok, 2003* (pp. 37–48). Lund, Sweden: SVEBI.

Junge, T., Runge, L., Juul-Kristensen, B., & Wedderkopp, N. (2016). Risk factors for knee injuries in children 8 to 15 years: The CHAMPS study DK. *Medicine & Science in Sports & Exercise, 48,* 655–663.

Kabat-Zinn, J. (2005). *Coming to Our Senses: Healing Ourselves and the World through Mindfulness.* New York, NY: Hyperion.

Langford, J. L., Webster, K. E., & Feller, J. A. (2009). A prospective longitudinal study to assess psychological changes following anterior cruciate ligament reconstruction surgery. *British Journal of Sports Medicine, 43,* 377–381.

Moore, Z. E. (2009). Theoretical and empirical developments of the Mindfulness-Acceptance-Commitment (MAC) approach to performance enhancement. *Journal of Clinical Sports Psychology, 4,* 291–302.

Morrey, M. A., Stuart, M. J., Smith, A. M. P., & Wiese-Bjornstal, D. M. (1999). A longitudinal examination of athletes' emotional and cognitive responses to anterior cruciate ligament injury. *Clinical Journal of Sport Medicine, 9,* 63–69.

Moyers, T. B., & Rollnick, S. (2002). A motivational interviewing perspective on resistance in psychotherapy. *Journal of Clinical Psychology, 58,* 185–193.

Noh, Y.-E., Morris, T., & Andersen, M. B. (2007). Psychological intervention programmes for reduction of injury in ballet dancers. *Research in Sports Medicine, 15,* 13–32.

Patel, D. R., & Nelson, T. L. (2000). Sport injuries in adolescents. *Medical Clinics of North America, 84,* 983–1007.

Pillemar, F. C., & Micheli, L. J. (1988). Psychological consideration in youth sport. *Clinics in Sport Medicine, 7,* 679–689.

Podlog, L., Dimmock, J., & Miller, J. (2011). A review of return to sport concerns following injury rehabilitation: Practitioner strategies for enhancing recovery outcomes. *Physical Therapy in Sport, 12,* 36–42.

Santi, G., & Pietrantoni, L. (2013). Psychology of sport injury rehabilitation: A review of models and interventions. *Journal of Human Sport & Exercise, 8,* 1029–1044.

Siegel, D. J. (2010). *The Mindful Therapist: A Clinician's Guide to Mindsight and Neural Integration.* New York, NY: Norton.

Webster, K. E., Feller, J. A., & Lambros, C. (2008). Development and preliminary validation of a scale to measure the psychological impact of returning to sport following anterior cruciate ligament reconstruction surgery. *Physical Therapy in Sport, 9,* 9–15.

Weinstein, N., Brown, K. W., & Ryan, R. M. (2009). A multi-method examination of the effects of mindfulness on stress attribution, coping, and emotional wellbeing. *Journal of Research in Personality, 43,* 374–385.

Wiese-Bjornstal, D. M. (2003). From skinned knees and Pee Wees to menisci and masters: Developmental sport injury psychology. In M. R. Weiss (Ed.), *Developmental Sport and Exercise Psychology: A Lifespan Perspective* (pp. 525–568). Morgantown, WV: Fitness Information Technology.

Wiese-Bjornstal, D. M. (2010). Psychology and socioculture affect injury risk, response, and recovery in high-intensity athletes: A consensus statement. *Scandinavian Journal of Medicine and Science in Sports, 20*, 103–111.

Weise-Bjornstal, D. M., Smith, A. M., Shaffer, S. M., & Morrey, M. A. (1998). An integrated model of response to sport injury: Psychological and sociological dimensions. *Journal of Applied Sport Psychology, 10*, 46–69.

Weiss, M. R., & Raedeke, T. D. (2004). Developmental sport psychology: Research status on youth and directions toward a lifespan perspective. In M. R. Weiss (Ed.), *Developmental Sport and Exercise Psychology: A Lifespan Perspective* (pp. 1–26). Morgantown, WV: Fitness Information Technology.

Williams, J. M., & Andersen, M. B. (1998). Psychosocial antecedents of sport injury: Review and critique of the stress and injury model. *Journal of Applied Sport Psychology, 10*, 5–25.

17

PREVENTING DOPING IN YOUTH SPORT

Susan H. Backhouse, Kelsey Erickson, and Lisa Whitaker

A personal introduction

I (Susan) participated in sport from an early age; it was fun and I loved being active with my friends. Over time, however, training for competition superseded playing sport for fun. I stopped playing hockey and netball, and specialised in throwing the discus. My own participation fuelled my interest in watching others compete, and I vividly remember being amazed by Ben Johnson's margin of victory in the men's 100 metre final at the 1988 Seoul Olympics. However, it soon became apparent that Ben Johnson had used a prohibited substance to assist him in achieving Olympic gold. Eventually, it came to light that he was not alone in the use of chemical assistance, leading to that race becoming known as the 'dirtiest race' in history. Ben, like many other young athletes across the globe, will not have set out to dope. Rather, across his lifespan a complex interplay of individual, social, and environmental factors will have promoted the violation of the anti-doping rules of sport.

At the age of 18, my discus coach – who was very outspoken on the prevalence of doping in track and field – asserted that I would not succeed at the highest levels of my sport without the use of performance-enhancing drugs (PEDs). Despite espousing this belief, he never explicitly encouraged me to use prohibited substances. Meanwhile, my sense of self was not wrapped up in being a discus thrower; I had an identity beyond sport and I recognise now that this served to protect me. Additionally, I had a family and peer network who condemned such behaviour, and I had never encountered drugs being used, nor knew how to get hold of them. I did not make it as an Olympic discus thrower, but my passion for sport, and positive early life experiences, led me to volunteer to support UK Athletics on their anti-doping policy and support team. Over a decade later, and still driven by a desire to protect the rights of athletes to compete in a sport where prohibited substances are the exception rather than the norm, I remain committed to this pursuit as a researcher-practitioner.

Doping remains one of the greatest threats to sporting integrity and the welfare of athletes across the performance and participation pathways. Consequently, there is a growing interest on the part of researchers, the public, and anti-doping policy makers alike related to the causes, correlates, and consequences of doping in sport. Underlying this interest is a pressing need to intervene in an evidence-informed way to prevent this complex behaviour. Practitioner psychologists are well placed to support the creation of a sporting milieu that protects and promotes clean sport (i.e. doping-free) across the lifespan. However, we must not wait until the elite level to start discussing the prevailing anti-doping issues; clean sport environments will only be created if coaches and parents start fostering anti-doping attitudes and sporting integrity when athletes are young.

With the applied practitioner in mind, this chapter aims to create a shared understanding of some of the factors influencing (anti-) doping within the context of youth sport. To achieve this, the chapter consists of three sections. The first section considers the prevalence of doping in youth sport, and synthesises the research on the correlates of this behaviour. This will alert the practitioner to the signs of doping vulnerability. The second section considers the role of socialisation and significant others in amplifying or dampening the correlates of doping within youth sport. In outlining this, the practitioner will be made aware of the importance of working with and through parents and coaches to protect the welfare of athletes. The final section promotes the role of the sport and exercise psychologist in doping prevention, offering evidence-informed recommendations and strategies that will help our profession to play an active role in the prevention of doping in sport. In doing so, they will serve to protect athletes' rights to participate in clean sport, and safeguard their long-term health and wellbeing.

What does research in sport psychology tell us about doping in youth sport?

Should we be concerned about doping in youth sport?

The simple answer is yes, we should. Typically, adolescent use of PEDs ranges from 1–5%, although studies focused on the use of anabolic androgenic steroids (AAS) suggest that prevalence is higher (e.g. 11%) (Backhouse, Whitaker, Patterson, Erickson, & McKenna, 2015). However, these estimates should be viewed with caution because doping is a silenced behaviour (i.e. a behaviour that often goes unreported). Although silenced, the published list of sanctioned athletes on the UK Anti-Doping website reinforces the view that we should care, because doping is evident even in school sport. Over the last four years, five schoolboys have been banned from competition because of the use of PEDs (e.g. AAS and growth hormones).

At a global level, the Russian under-18 ice hockey team was abruptly removed from the 2016 World Championship over what officials acknowledged were concerns that they might test positive for (prior) use of the recently prohibited substance meldonium. Meldonium is used to treat a lack of blood flow to parts of the body (ischaemia) and is typically prescribed in cases of angina or heart failure. The World Anti-Doping Agency (WADA) found evidence of its use by athletes with the intention of enhancing performance by virtue of improving exercise capacity by carrying more oxygen to muscle tissue. However, meldonium is not approved by the Food and Drug Administration for use in the United States and is not authorised in the rest of Europe. Therefore, in January 2016 this product was moved from the WADA monitoring programme to its Prohibited List.

The use of meldonium in youth sport raises serious questions about the safeguarding mechanisms in place for young athletes. Why are fit young men taking a drug designed to treat patients with heart problems, such as angina? The literature points to a number of reasons for using PEDs, including improving sports performance (Gradidge, Coopoo, & Constantinou, 2011), physique modification (e.g. gain muscle mass, lose weight, lose body fat; Rees, Zarco, & Lewis, 2008), coping with pressure (e.g. financial or emotional; Nolte, Steyn, Krüger, & Fletcher, 2014) and periods of instability (e.g. suffering an injury; Bloodworth, Petróczi, Bailey, Pearce, & McNamee, 2012). These performance- and image-enhancing reasons are also reflected in adolescents' beliefs about PED use (Backhouse et al., 2015). Therefore, in addition to a strong punitive stance, anti-doping researchers (e.g. Barkoukis, Lazuras, Tsorbatzoudis, & Rodafinos, 2013) have argued for the merits of a preventative stance by fostering young athletes' anti-doping attitudes, diminished willingness to dope, and efficacy to resist doping-related temptations early in their sporting careers.

What makes young athletes vulnerable to doping?

The use of PEDs is more prevalent among males than females (e.g. Sagoe, Torsheim, Molde, Andeassen, & Pallesen, 2015). Underpinning this elevated risk is the observation that male adolescents, compared to females, have more positive attitudes towards doping (Bloodworth & McNamee, 2010) and believe AAS will have a larger impact on sport performance and physique (Sagoe et al., 2015). In comparison, contrasting findings exist in relation to the impact of age or sports participation on PED use (Backhouse et al., 2015). For example, some studies have shown that AAS use is greater in those who participate in organised sport (e.g. Hua & Braddock, 2008; Lorang, Callahan, Cummins, Achar, & Brown, 2011), with student-athletes three times more likely to dope than non-athletes (Mallia, Lucidi, Zelli, & Violani, 2013). Yet others have found AAS users are less likely to participate in school-sponsored team sports (e.g. Elliot, Cheong, Moe, & Goldberg, 2007) and more likely to be involved with fitness and physical training in informal recreational contexts (e.g. Thorlindsson & Halldorsson, 2010).

Existing evidence remains largely centred around doping attitudes and subjective norms as predictors of intentions to dope given researchers' historical reliance on the theory of planned behaviour for exploring doping behaviour (Ntoumanis, Ng, Barkoukis, & Backhouse, 2014). Specifically, research has consistently found

TABLE 17.1 Examples of doping correlates and anti-doping correlates

Examples of Doping Correlates (i.e. factors that increase vulnerability to doping)	Male gender
	Timing in career, e.g. transitions and periods of instability
	Previous use of nutritional supplements and illicit substances
	Engagement with dopers, access to drugs
	Early specialisation
	Attributing success to external factors
	Number of years in elite sport
	Influence of peers, parents, cultural norms, and sporting culture
	Dissatisfaction with one's appearance
	Dispositional risk-taking/sensation-seeking
	Exclusive athletic identity
	Poor sport performance
	Emotional pressure
Examples of Anti-Doping Correlates (i.e. factors that decrease vulnerability to doping)	Threat of drug testing, doping control, and sanctions
	Health concerns
	Stable self-esteem
	Supportive training environment
	Maintaining an identity outside of sport
	Social pressure from parents, coaches, peers
	Respect for the law
	Religiousness
	Self-affirmation

Note: For a full list see Backhouse et al. (2015).

that more favourable attitudes towards doping and greater approval perceived from significant others to dope lead to greater intentions to dope. However, other predictors of intentions to dope include such things as pressure to lose weight, drive for muscularity or thinness, inability to resist social pressure, moral disengagement, and situational temptation (Backhouse et al., 2015) (see Table 17.1). The use of nutritional supplements has also been identified as a correlate for doping in adolescence. More specifically, the habitual engagement in permitted performance-enhancing practices, such as the use of supplements, has been suggested as a 'gateway' to doping (Petróczi & Aidman, 2008).

The life cycle model of performance enhancement (Petróczi & Aidman, 2008) suggests a gradual involvement with assisted performance enhancement, moving from conscious diet to nutritional supplements to (potential) doping. Once a method of performance enhancement no longer satisfies an athlete's motivations for its use, the athlete is likely to look to another method, which would explain the potential to move along a continuum from everyday dieting to the use of PEDs. This assertion is particularly pertinent to athletes who have become accustomed to such performance-enhancing practices from a young age (Petróczi & Aidman, 2008). Therefore, we should remain cognisant of this proposal when working with adolescent athletes; can we offer the necessary resources and support to delay the onset of supplementation practices?

Do young athletes know, or care, about doping in sport?

Adolescent athletes demonstrate limited knowledge of doping, particularly with regards to which substances and methods are prohibited (Backhouse et al., 2015). This is unsurprising given that adolescent athletes commonly rely on unreliable sources of information such as the internet, coaches, parents, friends, and other athletes to gain information on doping rather than obtaining information from recommended sources such as national governing bodies (Nolte et al., 2014). Yet if we are to reduce adolescents' vulnerability to doping, their lack of knowledge and sources of credible information needs to be addressed through carefully designed prevention programmes that offer a balanced, unbiased message.

Given the importance coaches play in young athletes lives it is especially important that they better understand the causes and consequences of doping and morally commit to the principles of clean sport. This is because adolescents tend to display negative attitudes and beliefs towards doping, perceiving doping as harmful and morally wrong. They also believe that there is a high risk of being caught if an individual uses PEDs (Fürhapter et al., 2013). Taken together, these attitudes and beliefs are likely to play a positive role in preventing adolescents from using PEDs. Likewise, they offer primary factors for practitioners to capitalise on as a means to promote the value of clean sport within this athlete population.

Youth sport, (anti-)doping, and the role of athlete support personnel

Athletes exist in an environment of complex networks and relationships. Accordingly, arrays of personal, social, and environmental factors interact to affect doping behaviour (Stewart & Smith, 2010). That said, anti-doping organisations, policies, and efforts have traditionally focused on individual athletes, while seemingly disregarding the impact of the people and environment(s) surrounding them. Moreover, research has mainly centred on the role of personal variables (e.g. attitudes, beliefs) in predicting doping intentions and doping use (Ntoumanis et al., 2014). Empirical evidence on the role of socio-contextual factors is comparatively scarce and has primarily focused on the role of prevailing social norms in condoning or sanctioning doping behaviour.

The latest anti-doping rules and regulations – known as the WADA Code (WADA, 2015) – acknowledge the (potentially) significant influence of athlete support personnel (ASP) for athletes' doping behaviours. Fundamentally, the updated Code presents a paradigm shift away from the traditional athlete-centred anti-doping approach, towards a more holistic, socio-ecological approach. That is, an approach that calls for ASP[1] (e.g. applied practitioners) and sporting organisations to play an active role in the global pursuit of clean sport. Specific roles and responsibilities are ascribed to ASP, including 'to use his or her influence on *athlete* values and behaviour to foster anti-doping attitudes' (WADA, 2015, p. 114). ASP are now obliged to come forward with doping information. In choosing not to, they risk being deemed 'Complicit' to doping activity (Article 2.9, p. 23) and facing a sanction for committing an Anti-Doping Rule Violation (ADRV). Stemming from this evolution in anti-doping efforts, exploring and acknowledging the influence of particular members within an athlete's support network is essential. Among youth and young adult athlete populations specifically, parents and coaches have been identified as particularly influential for athletes' doping attitudes, experiences, and behaviours.

Parents

Parents have been identified as one of the most likely groups to lead adolescents towards doping (Laure & Binsinger, 2005), with parental pressure to be perfect (Madigan, Stoeber, & Passfield, 2016) and to win (Chan et al., 2014) identified as being particularly influential in this regard. Furthermore, when adolescent athletes believed significant others in their lives would approve of PED use, they were more likely to use doping substances (Lucidi et al., 2008). Conversely, the potential for parents to serve as protective agents against doping has been acknowledged (Erickson, McKenna, & Backhouse, 2015). Supporting this, increased parent–athlete communication about PEDs and nutritional supplements has been promoted as a useful approach to preventing their use among adolescent athletes (Dodge, 2008; Blank, Leichtfried, Müller, & Schobersberger, 2015). The likelihood of parents serving as doping deterrents appears to be enhanced when athletes believe that using PEDs would reflect poorly on significant others in their lives (Erickson, Backhouse & Carless, 2017; Chan et al., 2014).

Offering further insights, high school athletes who used PED had sharply degraded relationships with their parents compared to non-users (Laure, Lecerf, Friser, & Binsinger, 2004).

Collectively, it seems parents have the potential to influence athletes' doping attitudes and behaviours. Yet, the direction of influence appears to vary depending on parenting styles, relational factors, and parents' personal doping stances. Currently, parents are not systematically targeted through global anti-doping education. At best, they might receive a leaflet on the anti-doping rules and regulations. Given their influence, parents need to be engaged in discussion and debate on the role that they might play in the pursuit of clean sport (e.g. promote the ethos of clean sport at parent orientation meetings and ask parents to pledge their commitment to supporting their child to compete clean).

Coaches

Coaches are directly positioned to serve as role models for their athletes given their legitimate levels of authority (Yukhymenko-Lescroart, Brown, & Paskus, 2015).

Accordingly, coaches have been depicted as strongly influencing their athletes' behaviours, and the general consensus is that what a coach says carries significant weight for athletes (Carless & Douglas, 2013). Substantiating this, athletes have indicated that developing and fostering a positive coach–athlete relationship is essential to their performance and overall satisfaction in sport and beyond (Douglas & Carless, 2006). Meanwhile, doping-specific research suggests that what athletes see coaches do and what they hear them say is likely to influence the values they adopt and utilise when determining the 'rightness' of doping and behaviour in general (Mazanov, Backhouse, Connor, Hemphill, & Quirk, 2014). On the one hand, doping literature demonstrates that coaches can play a significant role in deterring athletes from using PEDs (e.g. Erickson et al., 2015; Chan et al., 2014). On the other hand, anecdotal (e.g. Russian Athletics) and empirical (Erickson et al., 2015) evidence reveals that not all coaches hold a strong stance against doping in sport, and elite and sub-elite Australian athletes (aged 16–25 years) have suggested that they might comply with their coach's instructions if told to use banned PEDs (Chan et al, 2014). Therefore, coaches represent a powerful agent in the prevention of doping in sport given they have the ability to create a culture that promotes or thwarts PED use.

In order to thwart PED use, coaches should be encouraged to use behaviours that satisfy athletes' psychological needs, recognise that their conversations create and influence culture, and understand that athletes will only internalise their coaches' moral standards if they are explicitly reinforced and modelled. Need-supportive strategies aim to foster athletes' three fundamental psychological needs: autonomy (feeling control over one's own behaviour), competence (feeling effective in producing desired outcomes), and relatedness (feeling connected with and accepted by others). Need-supportive behaviours in action would include such things as (a) coaches offering athletes meaningful choice in the activities they undertake, and (b) being encouraged to take others' perspectives into account (Reeve, 2009). This latter behaviour could reinforce anti-doping self-regulation if we raise the voice of the athlete who plays by the rules of sport and is chronically affected by the actions of those who have doped (Erickson, Backhouse, & Carless, 2016). Such behaviours can increase athletes' psychological needs satisfaction, wellbeing, and prosocial behaviour (Hodge & Lonsdale, 2011).

Seeking to understand to prevent doping in sport: The role of the sport and exercise psychologist

As a profession, we are contributing to a better understanding of why athletes dope and how doping harms them (for a review, see Backhouse et al., 2015). Accounts of doping behaviour also contribute to an awareness of circumstances that may place athletes at greater vulnerability of doping. Preventing these doping-conducive circumstances is within the realm of sport and exercise psychologists who share a professional interest in athlete's psychological functioning and overall wellbeing. Sport and exercise psychologists are well placed to support ASP to create – and reinforce – need-supportive environments, prioritising athlete welfare over winning at all costs. With an awareness of the tipping points of doping (e.g. injury, career transitions, contract renewal), we are also positioned to intervene prior to and during these potentially stressful periods to offer tailored support for athletes. Through receipt of this targeted support, athletes might avoid feeling like choosing to dope is the only way to cope with the demands of sport.

Now, more than ever, athletes rely on the expertise and guidance of a wide network of support personnel in order to maximise their performance and achieve their goals. This 'team behind the team' are able to help athletes compete, and win, without using prohibited substances. However, they can only do this if they are educated and informed about their own rights and responsibilities. More importantly, they need to internalise the role(s) that they can play in doping prevention through the training and competition environments they create and reinforce. Empirical research has demonstrated that ASP are not well versed in anti-doping rules and regulations; therefore, they put themselves and their athletes at increased risk of inadvertent doping (Backhouse et al., 2015). Moreover, although anti-doping information is available to ASP, our applied experience has consistently highlighted that they are anxious about 'getting it wrong' and incorrectly advising athletes; therefore, they distance themselves from playing an active role in doping prevention. Moreover, as long as the anti-doping education approach remains compliance driven and passive in delivery, there will continue to be a lack of readiness to act when faced with an ethical dilemma, such as an athlete's use of PEDs. As a profession, we are well positioned to support athletes and ASP to create a sporting milieu that does not facilitate PED use, or silence it. However, in order to do so we need to flex our ethical judgement when faced with the ethical dilemma of a doping athlete.

When working with athletes and ASP, practitioner psychologists operate within a professional framework, such as the Code of Ethics and Conduct (BPS, 2009). This code conveys a set of ethical principles, values, and standards that assist the profession in ethical decision-making. It acknowledges that psychologists are 'likely to need to make decisions in difficult, changing and unclear situations' (p. 4). As such, the society 'expects that the Code will be used to form a basis for consideration of ethical questions, with the principles in this Code being taken into account in the process of making decisions, together with the needs of the client and the individual circumstances of the case' (p.4). The advisory nature of the code – evidenced through the use of the word 'should' rather than 'must' throughout the framework – provides a conundrum for the sport and exercise psychologist who consults with a young athlete who admits they have used a prohibited substance.

The conundrum arises because we are, by definition, a 'helping' profession. For example, if a distressed young athlete admits to using AAS in order to get bigger because they are scared of getting injured through their sport, *should* a sport and exercise psychologist report them to the anti-doping authorities because they have violated the anti-doping rules? Or, should they assist the athlete to cease their AAS use by developing a multi-disciplinary programme of support that offers functional alternatives to doping (e.g. a carefully planned and monitored diet and strength and conditioning programme) and builds the athlete's confidence to compete in their sport, rather than focusing on the risk of injury?

The professional's response to these questions is, to some extent, governed by their position as much as their ethical judgement. If they are employed by a signatory of the WADA code (e.g. a national governing body or international sporting federation) they are bound by the articles in the code and therefore their employers will contractually propel them to report doping in sport to the authorities. Importantly, sport and exercise psychologists who are contractually bound to report doping in sport should make this clear to the athletes that they are working with during the contracting phase of their relationship. This is vital so that the limits of confidentiality in the client–athlete relationship are transparent at the outset. In doing so, we need to recognise that this will limit the sport and exercise psychologist's ability to support the athlete to stop doping.

At the same time we should recognise that the decision not to support – and to report – might also place the athlete at greater risk of psychological harm. Athletes who are banned from their sport can feel isolated, empty, and lost, leading to significant stress and depressive symptoms. The consequences of doping in sport can be social, financial, and psychological (Georgiadis & Papazoglou, 2014). Therefore, with concern for the long-term welfare of athletes at the forefront, it is crucial that we establish a programme of support for athletes who have served a period of ineligibility from sport, whether they are planning to return to competition or not. Finally, these points notwithstanding, the sport and exercise psychologist has the potential to influence the sporting context and the doping risk, through their work with the athlete, their support network, and the governers of sport. Collectively, it is on us (the profession) to challenge sporting contexts that threaten the health and wellbeing of athletes across the lifespan.

Conclusion

Empirical research has highlighted that youth athletes are vulnerable to using PEDs, particularly when they are unable to cope with the demands of their sport. Sport and exercise psychologists offer a crucial line of defence for doping in sport, by helping athletes to ensure the demands of their sport do not exceed their own resources. Moreover, the practitioner psychologist is well placed to support the change agents, such as parents and coaches, within various sporting environments to foster a clean sport culture. Successfully tackling the issues provoking doping in sport will undoubtedly require a range of approaches, including complementary strategies addressing the individual, social, and environmental determinants of doping. Sport and exercise psychologists can, and should, play an instrumental role in addressing this array of determinants to protect the rights of athletes to compete and succeed in sport without using prohibited substances.

Note

1 In the code, ASP are defined as 'any coach, trainer, manager, agent, team staff, official, medical, paramedical personnel, parent or any other Person working with, treating or assisting an Athlete participating in or preparing for sport Competition' (WADA, 2015, p. 132).

References

Backhouse, S. H., Whitaker, L., Patterson, L., Erickson, K., & McKenna, J. (2015). *Social psychology of doping in sport: A mixed narrative synthesis*. Commissioned Report for the World Anti-Doping Agency. Montreal, Canada.

Barkoukis, V., Lazuras, L., Tsorbatzoudis, H., & Rodafinos, A. (2013). Motivational and social cognitive predictors of doping intentions in elite sports: An integrated approach. *Scandinavian Journal of Medicine & Science in Sports, 23*, 330–340.

Blank, C., Leichtfried, V., Müller, D., & Schobersberger, W. (2015). Role of parents as a protective factor against adolescent athletes' doping susceptibility. *South African Journal of Sports Medicine, 27*(3), 87–91.

Bloodworth, A., & Mcnamee, M. (2010). Clean Olympians? Doping and anti-doping: The views of talented young British athletes. *International Journal of Drug Policy, 21*, 276–282.

Bloodworth, A., Petróczi, A., Bailey, R., Pearce, G., & Mcnamee, M. J. (2012). Doping and supplementation: The attitudes of talented young athletes. *Scandinavian Journal of Medicine & Science in Sports, 22*, 293–301.

BPS. (2009). *Code of Ethics and Conduct*. Retrieved from www.bps.org.uk/system/files/documents/code_of_ethics_and_conduct.pdf.

Carless, D., & Douglas, K. (2013). 'In the boat' but 'selling myself short': Stories, narratives, and identity development in elite sport. *The Sport Psychologist, 27*, 27–39.

Chan, D. K. C., Hardcastle, S. J., Lentillon-Kaestner, V., Donovan, R. J., Dimmock, J. A., & Hagger, M. S. (2014). Athletes' beliefs about and attitudes towards taking banned performance-enhancing substances: A qualitative study. *Sport, Exercise, and Performance Psychology, 3*, 241–257.

Dodge, T. (2008). *Incorporating parents in the anti-doping fight: A test of the viability of a parent-based prevention program*. Commissioned Report for the World Anti-Doping Agency. Montreal, Canada.

Douglas, K., & Carless, D. (2006). *Performance environment research*. Retrieved from www.whatdotheyknow.com/request/280223/response/680652/attach/2/Performance%20Environment%20Study%20report%20Feb%202006.pdf.

Elliot, D. L., Cheong, J., Moe, E. L., & Goldberg, L. (2007). Cross-sectional study of female students reporting anabolic steroid use. *Archives of Pediatrics and Medicine, 161*, 572–577.

Erickson, K., Backhouse, S. H., & Carless, D. (2016). 'The ripples are big': Storying the impact of doping in sport beyond the sanctioned athlete. *Psychology of Sport and Exercise, 24*, 92–99.

Erickson, K., Backhouse, S. H., & Carless, D. (2017). Doping in sports: Do parents matter? *Sport, Exercise, and Performance Psychology, 6*, 115–128.

Erickson, K., McKenna, J., & Backhouse, S. H. (2015). A qualitative analysis of the factors that protect athletes against doping in sport. *Psychology of Sport and Exercise, 16*, 149–155.

Fürhapter, C., Blank, C., Leichtfried, V., Mair-Raggautz, M., Muller, D., & Schobersberger, W. (2013). Evaluation of West-Austrian junior athletes' knowledge regarding doping in sports. *Wiener klinische Wochenschrift*.

Georgiadis, E., & Papazoglou, I. (2014). The experience of competition ban following a positive doping sample of elite athletes. *Journal of Clinical Sport Psychology, 7*, 57–74.

Gradidge, P., Coopoo, Y., & Constantinou, D. (2011). Prevalence of performance-enhancing substance use by Johannesburg male adolescents involved in competitive high school sports. *Archives of Exercise in Health and Disease, 2*, 114–119.

Hodge, K., & Lonsdale, C. (2011). Prosocial and antisocial behaviour in sport: The role of coaching style, autonomous vs. controlled motivation, and moral disengagement. *Journal of Sport & Exercise Psychology, 33*, 527–547.

Hua, L.V., & Braddock, J. H. (2008). School sports and adolescent steroid use: National trends and race-ethnic variations. *Challenge, 14*, 29–49.

Laure, P., & Binsinger, C. (2005). Adolescent athletes and the demand and supply of drugs to improve their performance. *Journal of Sports Science & Medicine, 4*, 272–277.

Laure, P., Lecerf, T., Friser, A., & Binsinger, C. (2004). Drugs, recreational drug use and attitudes towards doping of high school athletes. *International Journal of Sports Medicine, 25*, 133–138.

Lorang, M., Callahan, B., Cummins, K. M., Achar, S., & Brown, S. A. (2011). Anabolic androgenic steroid use in teens: Prevalence, demographics, and perception of effects. *Journal of Child & Adolescent Substance Abuse, 20*, 358–369.

Lucidi, F., Zelli, A., Mallia, L., Grano, C., Russo, P. M., & Violani, C. (2008). The social-cognitive mechanisms regulating adolescents' use of doping substances. *Journal of Sports Sciences, 26*, 447–456.

Madigan, D. J., Stoeber, J., & Passfield, L. (2016). Perfectionism and attitudes towards doping in junior athletes. *Journal of Sports Sciences, 34*, 700–706.

Mallia, L., Lucidi, F., Zelli, A., & Violani, C. (2013). Doping attitudes and the use of legal and illegal performance-enhancing substances among Italian adolescents. *Journal of Child & Adolescent Substance Abuse, 22*, 179–190.

Mazanov, J., Backhouse, S., Connor, J., Hemphill, D., & Quirk, F. (2014). Athlete support personnel and anti-doping: Knowledge, attitudes, and ethical stance. *Scandinavian Journal of Medicine & Science in Sports, 24*, 846–856.

Nolte, K., Steyn, B. J. M., Krüger, P. E., & Fletcher, L. (2014). Doping in sport: Attitudes, beliefs and knowledge of competitive high-school athletes in Gauteng Province. *South African Journal of Sports Medicine, 26*, 81–86.

Ntoumanis, N., Ng, J. Y., Barkoukis, V., & Backhouse, S. H. (2014). Personal and psychosocial predictors of doping use in physical activity settings: A meta-analysis. *Sports Medicine, 44*, 1603–1624.

Petróczi, A., & Aidman, E. (2008). Psychological drivers in doping: The life-cycle model of performance enhancement. *Substance Abuse Treatment, Prevention and Policy, 3*, 1–12.

Rees, C. R., Zarco, E. P., & Lewis, D. K. (2008). The steroids/sports supplements connection: Pragmatism and sensation-seeking in the attitudes and behaviour of JHS and HS students on Long Island. *Journal of Drug Education, 38*, 329–349.

Reeve, J. (2009). *Understanding Motivation and Emotion* (5th ed.). Hoboken, NJ: Wiley.

Sagoe, D., Torsheim, T., Molde, H., Andreassen, C. S., & Pallesen, S. (2015). Attitudes towards use of anabolic-androgenic steroids among Ghanaian high school students. *International Journal of Drug Policy, 26*, 169–174.

Stewart, B., & Smith, A. C. T. (2010). The role of ideology in shaping drug use regulation in Australian sport. *International Review for the Sociology of Sport, 45*, 187–198.

Thorlindsson, T., & Halldorsson, V. (2010). Sport, and use of anabolic androgenic steroids among Icelandic high school students: A critical test of three perspectives. *Substance Abuse Treatment, Prevention, and Policy, 5*, 32.

WADA. (2015). *The Code.* Retrieved from: https://wada-mainprod.s3.amazonaws.com/resources/files/wada-2015-world-anti-doping-code.pdf.

Yukhymenko-Lescroart, M. A., Brown, M. E., & Paskus, T. S. (2015). The relationship between ethical and abusive coaching behaviours and student-athlete well-being. *Sport, Exercise, and Performance Psychology, 4*, 36–49.

18

FOSTERING ADAPTIVE PEER RELATIONSHIPS IN YOUTH SPORT

Alan L. Smith and Anthony G. Delli Paoli

For coaches and others interested in promoting developmentally sound youth sport experiences, it is important to consider the various social relationships that make up the youth sport context. More adaptive experiences, optimised learning, and high-level performance owe not only to a young athlete's individual efforts, but also to interpersonal dynamics with coaches, parents, other supporters, and teammates. Sport psychology researchers and practitioners have paid considerable attention to the role of coaches and other adults in youth sport (see Chapters 8, 19, 26, and 27) as well as strategies that can be used to promote greater consistency in performance. This work is illustrated throughout this volume and forms an important foundation for promoting a healthy youth sport context. Specific attention to peer relationships, however, offers additional pathways to fostering developmentally sound and productive sport experiences for young athletes. In this chapter we showcase the importance of peer relationships in youth sport, providing background information on the nature and salience of these relationships as well as considerations both for promoting positive relationships and for addressing relationship challenges such as conflict and social exclusion.

Definitions and background

Relationships consist of familiar individuals with a history of interactions, and possess meanings, expectations, and emotional experiences (Rubin, Bukowski, & Parker, 2006). Thus, teammates, classmates, and other near-age individuals that a young person interacts with are agents of interest when seeking to understand peer relationships. These individuals can shape how one values and commits to sport versus other activities as well as influence day-to-day experiences and outcomes in the sport setting. *Peers* are characterised as those of equal power and standing, and equal standing is typically assumed for individuals of about the same age (Smith, 2007).

As compared to their relationships with adults, young athletes have much greater balance of power in their relationships with one another and ascribe progressively more importance to peers as a source of intimacy and validation as they move into later childhood and adolescence (Smith & d'Arripe-Longueville, 2014).This noted, contextual factors such as team positions/roles (e.g. central playing positions, captainships) and different levels of ability introduce variations in power and standing among peers. In working with athletes, practitioners must be aware of such contextual factors as they relate to peer relationships. Indeed, the nature and quality of relationships among peers on a sport team can vary as a function of these factors as well as interpersonal dynamics.This makes peer relationships important to consider when looking to optimise the youth sport experience.

Most scholarly work on peer relationships has addressed two focal social constructs – popularity and friendship (see Smith, 2007; Weiss & Stuntz, 2004).

- *Popularity* is a group-oriented construct that reflects the experience of being liked or accepted by peers (Bukowski & Hoza, 1989). In the context of youth sport, concern has largely been with athletes' perceptions of acceptance by peers or relatedness within a sport/team context. An important motive for young athletes to participate in sport is the opportunity to affiliate with and be accepted by peers (Weiss & Amorose, 2008); as such this is an important consideration in optimising youth sport experiences.
- *Friendship* addresses dyadic relationships, and is the experience of closeness and mutuality between two individuals (Bukowski & Hoza, 1989).Youth sport research has explored the nature of sport friendships and their quality because friendships offer important contributions to psychological wellbeing and growth (Weiss & Stuntz, 2004).

Peer relationships research is guided by a variety of theoretical frameworks (see Bukowski & Hoza, 1989; Weiss & Stuntz, 2004) and extends to an array of peer constructs (Smith & McDonough, 2008); however, focus on popularity/acceptance and friendship can largely be traced to the conceptual writings of Harry Stack Sullivan (1953). Sullivan posited that developmental growth is afforded through coming to learn about others and their differences, and that this learning process is advanced through engagement with the larger peer group and specific friends. Importantly, Sullivan proposed these social constructs to offer unique but complementary contributions to development. Peer acceptance is viewed as salient from young childhood (e.g. age 6 years) onward through development. Beginning in middle childhood (e.g. age 8 years), interest increases in the interpersonal intimacy and validation that is afforded through specific friendships. Moving into the late childhood and adolescent years (e.g. age 12 years), when sport involvement can serve as an important context for psychosocial development, both popularity/acceptance and close friendships can be expected to shape young athletes' experiences and outcomes.

Evidence of the importance of peers within youth sport comes from a variety of research areas. Early work in the 1970s and 1980s that addressed sport participation motivation showed that being with friends and social acceptance were among the prevailing reasons that young people report for their sport involvement (Weiss & Amorose, 2008). Additionally, peers are prominent sources of the information that young athletes use to gauge their competence in sport, particularly during later childhood and early adolescence (Horn, 2004). Through the feedback they provide and the social comparisons they offer, peers play a role in athletes developing a sense of competence that fosters adaptive sport outcomes as well as sustained attraction and commitment to sport (see Chapter 9 for further information). Also, research across multiple developmental contexts for older children shows ego reinforcement, preferential opportunities to display strengths, and expression of fair play as uniquely strong friendship expectations in sport (Zarbatany, Ghesquiere, & Mohr, 1992). When considered together, these areas of research offer preliminary evidence that peer relationships matter in sport *and* sport matters to peer relationships. This has stimulated more specific empirical efforts to understand how peer relationships link to sport-related developmental and motivational outcomes.

The early empirical literature further establishes peers as warranting close attention in youth sport research and practice. This work has shown a consistent association of peer relationships with perceived and actual physical competence, suggesting that sport and physical activity involvement can serve as a form of social currency for young people (Ommundsen, Gundersen, & Mjaavatn, 2010; see Smith, 2007). Moreover, peer relationships are linked with affective and motivational outcomes in sport, such as enjoyment, sport commitment, and participation decisions (e.g. Ullrich-French & Smith, 2009; Weiss & Smith, 2002).

Research also shows peers as important to the motivational climate that prevails in sport (Keegan, Harwood, Spray, & Lavallee, 2009). The peer-initiated motivational climate can take the form of one focused on normative comparison and conflict (i.e. ego-involving) and, alternatively, one focused on relatedness support, improvement, and effort (i.e. task-involving; Vazou, Ntoumanis, & Duda, 2005). Accordingly, this climate links to important motivation-related outcomes, both adaptive and maladaptive, such as physical self-worth, intrinsic motivation, and burnout (Jõesaar, Hein, & Hagger, 2012; Smith, Gustafsson, & Hassmén, 2010; Vazou, Ntoumanis, & Duda, 2006; see Chapter 8). Considered together, this literature suggests that there is value in exploring practical strategies for fostering adaptive aspects of peer relationships and managing potentially negative aspects such as conflict or exclusion. Currently there are few intervention-focused efforts on which to base practical implications. However, the broader literature base in sport and exercise psychology and in-depth research exploring the nature of peer relationships in sport offer a basis for preliminary recommendations.

Strategies to foster adaptive peer relationships

Promoting positive peer relationships in sport

Drawing from the existing conceptual and empirical work, an overarching strategy to promote peer relationships is to address both the broader peer group and friendships. Though sport professionals (e.g. coaches, sport psychologists) and parents are not members of youth sport peer networks, they are nonetheless linked to peer networks in important ways as leaders, experts, and confidants. This positions them to pursue strategies that enhance positive peer relationships and, in turn, the quality of the youth sport experience. Importantly, in pursuing any strategies to enhance peer relationships, placing young athletes at the centre of their experience is critical. For the peer network to be leveraged to produce adaptive developmental and performance outcomes in sport, young people must be afforded sufficient authority and space to meaningfully exchange with one another. This can be accomplished, for example, during team meetings where athletes collaborate to identify how individual goals contribute to the broader goals of the team. For this to be effective, the right team climate is necessary.

In focusing on the broader peer group, setting the stage for and reinforcing an adaptive motivational climate is essential. Fostering cooperative learning opportunities and interdependent goals have been recommended as strategies for increasing the sense of peer acceptance (Ntoumanis, Vazou, & Duda, 2007; Weiss & Stuntz, 2004). For example, team members can individually consider solutions to defending an offensive scheme used by an upcoming opponent, followed by team discussion, setting practice goals, and then physically implementing the ideas and re-evaluating progress. These opportunities direct attention to group achievements, collaborative activity and problem-solving, helping one another, and valuing the array of roles that must be fulfilled for goal success.

There are multiple ways for individual group members to contribute to group success, and decision-making can be more egalitarian. Specific to promoting a task-involving peer-created motivational climate, emphasis should be placed on peers helping one another improve, accepting and valuing teammates, and recognising and promoting effort (Ntoumanis et al., 2007; Vazou, Ntoumanis, & Duda, 2005; 2006). Key adults in the youth sport setting should model these behaviours, but most importantly young athletes should be encouraged to take personal responsibility for making improvements, demonstrating supportiveness, and putting forth effort on a day-to-day basis. Coaches and sport psychologists that explicitly reinforce expressions of this personal responsibility will fuel an adaptive peer dynamic among their athletes.

These strategies for enhancing the motivational climate of youth sport are expected to increase young athletes' sense of acceptance, yet it is important to remember that physical competence is strongly tied to perceived and actual social acceptance (see Smith, 2007). Therefore, it is critical to provide young athletes the opportunity to fully develop their athletic capabilities. Expert coaching is required for continuing development of skills, ample practice time is necessary for skill mastery, and optimal challenges (challenges that are matched to athletes' competence and readiness) need to be incorporated within learning and competitive situations. Combined with open communication of roles and recognition of varying forms of contributions to group success, this offers a foundation for young athletes to develop self-confidence and a sense of purpose within the group setting. This can be challenging in high-stakes competitive settings, yet key adults can help young people frame these settings in productive ways by emphasising process over outcomes and giving feedback that orients attention on what to do rather than what not to do. The strategies broaden what it means to be successful and use the peer network to reinforce adaptive interpersonal and achievement behaviours.

Strategies should also be employed to enable athletes to cultivate friendships. Foundational research on the nature of best sport friendships can help guide this work. Weiss, Smith, and Theeboom (1996) interviewed young people, ages 8 to 16 years, about the positive and negative features of their best sport friendship. Through these interviews, a host of friendship quality dimensions emerged that showed these relationships to be important to instrumental as well as emotional/psychological aspects of sport participation. Moreover, even while focusing on best sport friendships, it was evident that these relationships include negative components that must be effectively managed if friendships are to be sustained and adaptive. The many dimensions that emerged were further examined through research designed to construct a survey measure of sport friendship quality (Weiss & Smith, 1999; 2002). As a result of this work, six identifiable and distinct dimensions of friendship quality were perceived by young athletes: (a) companionship and pleasant play, (b) self-esteem enhancement and supportiveness, (c) loyalty and intimacy, (d) things in common, (e) conflict resolution, and (f) conflict. Below we describe these dimensions and strategies for fostering positive friendship quality in sport:

- *Companionship and pleasant play* pertains to spending time together in a way that is enjoyable. Doing fun things and interacting well together characterises this dimension of friendship quality. Important to fostering this dimension of friendship quality is allowing time for young athletes to interact. For example, setting aside portions of practices for free interaction and arranging opportunities for team members to get to know one another outside of the sport setting (e.g. team meal at a restaurant after a competition) allows young athletes the opportunity to cultivate friendships.
- *Self-esteem enhancement and supportiveness* involves friends saying and doing things that boost sense of worth and encouraging one another after mistakes. The strategies described above for promoting a task-involving peer-created motivational climate afford the opportunity to develop friendships in this way as well as foster perceptions of broader peer acceptance. Additionally, providing peer-assisted learning opportunities where athletes are charged with responsibility for helping one another develop skills can also help (see Smith & d'Arripe-Longueville, 2014). This is accomplished through strategically pairing team members for cooperative learning and by communicating to team members a responsibility for helping all teammates to fulfil their respective roles and develop.
- *Loyalty and intimacy* pertains to a sense of commitment and reliable alliance as well as interactions of a close personal nature. Friends can talk about anything with one another and look out for one another's best interests. Providing opportunity for teammates to spend time together allows space for loyalty and intimacy to develop, and communicating messages about 'what makes a good

teammate/friend' to young athletes can be helpful as well. This aspect of sport friendship involves development of trust and a bond between friends and is characterised by caring. Adults in sport can model caring (see Chapter 22) and trust by communicating interest in all team members' contributions and lives outside of sport, as well as reliably fulfilling their own commitments to their athletes. Higher perceptions of a caring climate have been shown to relate with greater liking of the coach and teammates (Fry & Gano-Overway, 2010).

- *Things in common* pertains to the sharing of interests and values. As with other friendship dimensions, providing less structured opportunities for young athletes to interact allows them to get to know their teammates better and discover shared interests and values. Additionally, communicating shared/team goals and reviewing shared accomplishments and challenges highlights the common interests and experiences of team members that can serve as a foundation for building relationships.

- The final key dimensions of friendship quality are *conflict* and *conflict resolution*. Evident from Weiss et al.'s (1996) interviews with young athletes was that even best friendships involve negative behaviours, disagreements, and negative affect (e.g. anger). This is a natural feature of relationships, and it is unsurprising that a competitive and often emotionally charged context such as sport would introduce challenges to peer relationships. Successful friendships, therefore, are those that involve constructive attempts at resolving differences and are characterised by the capacity to move forward after a negative exchange.

In the following section we specifically discuss the nature of conflict in sport as well as possible strategies to address it. We additionally consider how to address social exclusion in sport, an experience that poses a challenge to developing constructive peer relationships.

Addressing conflict and social exclusion

In Weiss et al.'s (1996) interviews of young athletes, the conflict dimension of friendship was characterised as negative behaviours that cause disagreement, disrespect, or dissention, and included themes such as verbal insults, arguing, negative competitiveness, and physical aggression. Importantly, beyond behavioural aspects, interpersonal conflict is conceived as having cognitive and affective components (Paradis, Carron, & Martin, 2014). In the broader conflict literature, which has been criticised as lacking consistent and clear conceptualisation of conflict, Barki and Hartwick (2004) suggest adopting a two-dimensional framework of interpersonal conflict. First, conflict is conceived as having three core properties – disagreement, negative emotion, and interference. Indeed, disagreement in itself does not necessarily rise to the level of conflict, but can rise to this level in a context where conflict is not effectively managed. Second, interpersonal conflict in organisational settings is conceived of as pertaining to the task at hand or to the interpersonal relationship context. Task and social aspects of a sport team must be considered in any efforts to prevent or resolve conflict. This conception is supported by qualitative accounts of athletes (Holt, Knight, & Zukiwski, 2012; Paradis et al., 2014). Conflict is an inherent feature of sport settings.

Holt and colleagues conducted research that sheds light on peer conflict in adolescent and intercollegiate athletes, specifically with reference to views on managing conflict (Holt, Black, Tamminen, Fox, & Mandigo, 2008; Holt et al., 2012). Athletes view conflict as a normal feature of participation on sport teams and view relationship conflict as more problematic than task-related conflict. Emphasising the collective interests of the team in light of personal conflicts may help address more problematic types of conflict. For instance, Holt et al. (2008) found that some players are able to place the team before personal interests in order to resolve conflict and that team members will attempt to work within the peer network to resolve or mediate conflict. Unless absolutely necessary, athletes also expressed reticence to involve the coach in conflict resolution.

Due to the reluctance to involve coaches, and the potentially negative consequences of particularly relationship conflict, it is important to proactively structure a team climate that curtails unnecessary conflict and provides a structure for conflict resolution among team members. There are a few ways this can be accomplished. Drawing from the peer-created motivational climate literature (Ntoumanis et al., 2007; Vazou, Ntoumanis, & Duda, 2005; 2006), it is important to buffer ego-involving features of the climate. Ego-involving peer-created climates are those where normative ability is the primary or sole basis of an athlete's value to the group (see Chapter 8), where mistakes are criticised rather than viewed as opportunities to learn, and losing is tied with complaints and blaming. Fostering a task-involving peer-created motivational climate that emphasises improvement, acceptance, and effort is important for counteracting excessive conflict. Feedback during practice and competitive situations should acknowledge team members' efforts to reinforce these features among one another, as well as instances of noteworthy collective efforts and collaborations to meet group goals.

Holt and colleagues (2012) solicited additional recommendations directly from athletes. One suggestion was to engage in team building early in the season, with a key focus being to create open communication lines. With open communication among team members, there is greater opportunity to swiftly and effectively address conflicts that arise. Relatedly, focusing on formation of team norms early in the season is useful in establishing structure and expected behaviours of team members, which can help head off conflict (Paradis et al., 2014). An additional recommendation from athletes was to address conflict early when it does arise, so as not to have conflicts intensify or deepen over time. Another was to involve third-party mediators such as captains or more senior athletes, sport psychology consultants, or coaches (when all else fails). An advantage of having fellow athletes mediate conflicts is their unique familiarity with team peer dynamics and their more egalitarian social position.

A final recommendation is to hold team meetings where concerns are discussed, with the important caveats that these be structured team meetings rather than unstructured meetings and that they be guided by someone other than the head coach, such as a sport psychology consultant. The athletes suggested that unstructured meetings can turn into unproductive 'free-for-alls', where team members take sides rather than resolve conflict, and that athletes may be less open in coach-guided meetings where there is potential for the coach to dictate a resolution rather than work through a solution. Addressing conflict can come in proactive forms to limit their occurrence (e.g. open communication) and as resolutions that evolve from the empowerment of team members to mediate their own conflicts.

Conflict and other interpersonal dynamics within and outside sport can precipitate exclusion behaviours as well as other adverse peer-related behaviours such as teasing and bullying. Adverse peer relationships in their various forms communicate that an individual does not belong and is devalued by others (Leary, 2001). These forms can range from passive (ignoring or neglecting another individual but tolerating their presence) to overt (behaviours intended to exclude, tease, or victimise). These and other adverse events threaten an individual's inherent need for acceptance and belonging, and such a threat is tied to a range of maladaptive consequences (Baumeister & Leary, 1995). These consequences span psychological and physical wellbeing (Baumeister, Brewer, Tice, & Twenge, 2007; Cacioppo & Cacioppo, 2014; Espelage & Holt, 2001), and can foster more specific outcomes that interfere with sport performance, such as impaired attention and lack of self-awareness (Hawes et al., 2012; Twenge, Catanese, & Baumeister, 2003).

There is little research that has been conducted on these adverse peer behaviours in competitive sport; however, many of the strategies described above would be expected to limit behaviours such as social exclusion, teasing, and bullying. Caution is recommended when intervening to address adverse peer behaviours because such involvement may evoke a relived experience for athletes. Proactive approaches are likely most useful to diminish their occurrence. Pursuing interdependent goals, encouraging a task-involving peer-created motivational climate, productive efforts at skill development, opportunity for development of friendships, team building, and proactively addressing conflict will go a long way to fostering peer group acceptance and friendship quality. They can also help mitigate against formation of unproductive cliques that interfere with the task and relationship aspects of the sport environment. As a final point, athletes describe avoidance as being a common reaction in the face of conflict (Holt et al., 2012). Promoting a culture of personal responsibility and teaching athletes how to proactively (e.g. see strategies for promoting positive sport friendship dimensions) and effectively manage their relationships with teammates is a way to leverage the peer group to promote positive peer relationships and mitigate interpersonal challenges.

Conclusion

Social relationships in the youth sport context can substantively impact learning, performance, and developmental outcomes for young athletes. Sport psychologists, coaches, parents, and other adults in the youth sport context are encouraged to optimise interpersonal relationships among peers, considering matters pertaining to group acceptance as well as close friendships. This will involve both promoting positive peer relationships and working to prevent conflict and adverse peer behaviours in the youth sport setting. Importantly, attending to peer relationships in sport not only leverages a significant social network in accomplishing goals, but also places young people at the centre of the youth sport experience. This is essential to ensuring the health of youth sport and the meaningful and adaptive involvement of its core participants.

References

Barki, H., & Hartwick, J. (2004). Conceptualizing the construct of interpersonal conflict. *The International Journal of Conflict Management, 15*, 216–244.

Baumeister, R. F., Brewer, L. E., Tice, D. M., & Twenge, J. M. (2007). Thwarting the need to belong: Understanding the interpersonal and inner effects of social exclusion. *Social & Personality Psychology Compass, 1*, 506–520.

Baumeister, R. F., & Leary, M. R. (1995). The need to belong: Desire for interpersonal attachments as a fundamental human motivation. *Psychological Bulletin, 117*, 497–529.

Bukowski, W. M., & Hoza, B. (1989). Popularity and friendship: Issues in theory, measurement, and outcome. In T. J. Berndt & G. W. Ladd (Eds.), *Peer Relationships in Child Development* (pp. 15–45). New York, NY: Wiley.

Cacioppo, J. T., & Cacioppo, S. (2014). Social relationships and health: The toxic effects of perceived social isolation. *Social & Personality Psychology Compass, 8*, 58–72.

Espelage, D. L., & Holt, M. (2001). Bullying and victimization during early adolescence: Peer influences and psychosocial correlates. *Journal of Emotional Abuse, 2*, 123–142.

Fry, M. D., & Gano-Overway, L. A. (2010). Exploring the contribution of the caring climate to the youth sport experience. *Journal of Applied Sport Psychology, 22*, 294–304.

Hawes. D. J., Zadro, L., Fink, E., Richardson, R., O'Moore, K., Griffiths, B., ... Williams. K. D. (2012). The effects of peer ostracism on children's cognitive processes. *European Journal of Developmental Psychology, 9*, 599–613.

Holt, N. L., Black, D. E., Tamminen, K. A., Fox, K. R., & Mandigo, J. L. (2008). Levels of social complexity and dimensions of peer experiences in youth sport. *Journal of Sport & Exercise Psychology, 30*, 411–431.

Holt, N. L., Knight, C. J., & Zukiwski, P. (2012). Female athletes' perceptions of teammate conflict in sport: Implications for sport psychology consultants. *The Sport Psychologist, 26*, 135–154.

Horn, T. S. (2004). Developmental perspectives on self-perceptions in children and adolescents. In M. R. Weiss (Ed.), *Developmental Sport and Exercise Psychology: A Lifespan Perspective* (pp. 101–143). Morgantown, WV: Fitness Information Technology.

Jõesaar, H., Hein, V., & Hagger, M. S. (2012). Youth athletes' perception of autonomy support from the coach, peer motivational climate and intrinsic motivation in sport setting: One-year effects. *Psychology of Sport and Exercise, 13*, 257–262.

Keegan, R. J., Harwood, C. G., Spray, C. M., & Lavallee, D. E. (2009). A qualitative investigation exploring the motivational climate in early career sports participants: Coach, parent and peer influences on sport motivation. *Psychology of Sport and Exercise, 10*, 361–372.

Leary, M. (2001). Towards a conceptualization of interpersonal rejection. In M. R. Leary (Ed.), *Interpersonal Rejection* (pp. 3–20). New York, NY: Oxford University Press.

Ntoumanis, N., Vazou, S., & Duda, J. L. (2007). Peer-created motivational climate. In S. Jowett & D. Lavallee (Eds.), *Social Psychology in Sport* (pp. 145–156). Champaign, IL: Human Kinetics.

Ommundsen, Y., Gundersen, K. A., & Mjaavatn, P. E. (2010). Fourth graders' social standing with peers: A prospective study on the role of first grade physical activity, weight status, and motor proficiency. *Scandinavian Journal of Educational Research, 54*, 377–394.

Paradis, K. F., Carron, A.V., & Martin, L. J. (2014). Athlete perceptions of intra-group conflict in sport teams. *Sport & Exercise Psychology Review, 10*(3), 4–18.

Rubin, K. H., Bukowski, W., & Parker, J. (2006). Peer interactions, relationships, and groups. In W. Damon, R. M. Lerner (Series Eds.), & N. Eisenberg (Vol. Ed.), *Handbook of Child Psychology*, Vol. 3: *Social, Emotional, and Personality Development* (6th ed., pp. 571–645). Hoboken, NJ: Wiley.

Smith, A. L. (2007). Youth peer relationships in sport. In S. Jowett & D. Lavallee (Eds.), *Social Psychology in Sport* (pp. 41–54). Champaign, IL: Human Kinetics.

Smith, A. L., & d'Arripe-Longueville, F. (2014). Peer relationships and the youth sport experience. In A. G. Papaioannou & D. Hackfort (Eds.), *Routledge Companion to Sport and Exercise Psychology: Global Perspectives and Fundamental Concepts* (pp. 199–212). New York, NY: Routledge.

Smith, A. L., Gustafsson, H., & Hassmén, P. (2010). Peer motivational climate and burnout perceptions of adolescent athletes. *Psychology of Sport and Exercise, 11*, 453–460.

Smith, A. L., & McDonough, M. H. (2008). Peers. In A. L. Smith & S. J. H. Biddle (Eds.), *Youth Physical Activity and Sedentary Behaviour: Challenges and Solutions* (pp. 295–320). Champaign, IL: Human Kinetics.

Sullivan, H. S. (1953). *The Interpersonal Theory of Psychiatry*. New York, NY: Norton.

Twenge, J. M., Catanese, K. R., & Baumeister, R. F. (2003). Social exclusion and the deconstructed state: Time perception, meaninglessness, lethargy, lack of emotion, and self-awareness. *Journal of Personality and Social Psychology, 85*, 409–423.

Ullrich-French, S., & Smith, A. L. (2009). Social and motivational predictors of continued youth sport participation. *Psychology of Sport and Exercise, 10*, 87–95.

Vazou, S., Ntoumanis, N., & Duda, J. L. (2005). Peer motivational climate in youth sport: A qualitative inquiry. *Psychology of Sport and Exercise, 6*, 497–516.

Vazou, S., Ntoumanis, N., & Duda, J. L. (2006). Predicting young athletes' motivational indices as a function of their perceptions of the coach- and peer-created climate. *Psychology of Sport and Exercise, 7*, 215–233.

Weiss, M. R., & Amorose, A. J. (2008). Motivational orientations and sport behavior. In T. S. Horn (Ed.), *Advances in Sport Psychology* (3rd ed., pp. 115–155). Champaign, IL: Human Kinetics.

Weiss, M. R., & Smith, A. L. (1999). Quality of youth sport friendships: Measurement development and validation. *Journal of Sport & Exercise Psychology, 21*, 145–166.

Weiss, M. R., & Smith, A. L. (2002). Friendship quality in youth sport: Relationship to age, gender, and motivation variables. *Journal of Sport & Exercise Psychology, 24*, 420–437.

Weiss, M. R., Smith, A. L., & Theeboom, M. (1996). 'That's what friends are for': Children's and teenagers' perceptions of peer relationships in the sport domain. *Journal of Sport & Exercise Psychology, 18*, 347–379.

Weiss, M. R., & Stuntz, C. P. (2004). A little friendly competition: Peer relationships and psychosocial development in youth sport and physical activity contexts. In M. R. Weiss (Ed.), *Developmental Sport and Exercise Psychology: A Lifespan Perspective* (pp. 165–196). Morgantown, WV: Fitness Information Technology.

Zarbatany, L., Ghesquiere, K., & Mohr, K. (1992). A context perspective on early adolescents' friendship expectations. *Journal of Early Adolescence, 12*, 111–126.

19

FACILITATING COACH INVOLVEMENT WITH ADOLESCENT ATHLETES

Denise M. Hill and Richard C. Thelwell

The aim of this chapter is to examine critically how sport psychologists can support effective coach involvement with adolescent athletes, particularly those aged approximately 15 years and older. This period of mid–late adolescence (e.g. ages 15 years and older) represents a challenging and important time for athletes. In terms of their athletic progression, this stage is normally associated with the transition of investment (Côté, 1999), whereby the athlete starts to concentrate their efforts on one sport and engage in a high amount of deliberate practice to achieve their goals (Wylleman, Reinta, & De Knop, 2013). At the same time, athletes must also negotiate a number of other transitions in their life, including: psychological (adolescence into adulthood); psychosocial (source of social support from peers/coaches rather than parents); academic/vocational (from secondary to higher education or employment); and financial (to paid employment or support from their governing body; see Chapter 13). Accordingly, the athlete must cope with the pressure associated with progressing in their sport, alongside managing the demands of their changing relationships (i.e. with peers and parents), balancing their sport and life goals, and discovering their individual and athletic identity (Stambulova, 2009; see Chapter 14). It is therefore not surprising that many athletes fail to progress through this stage of development and stagnate or withdraw from their sport (Rosier & Wylleman, 2015).

Adolescence is also an important stage for positive youth development (see Chapter 12), that is, the acquisition and development of 'assets' (i.e. cognitive, emotional, and social skills) required for thriving in sport and non-sport settings (see Lerner et al., 2006). There are (at least) 40 developmental assets, which are cumulatively linked with positive athletic and interpersonal outcomes (e.g. achievement, resilience, mental toughness, and leadership), and diminished risk behaviours (e.g. doping, cheating, alcohol abuse, tobacco use, depression, antisocial behaviour, and school problems) that persist through to adulthood (see Benson, 2007). Sport can inherently provide the opportunity for the adolescent athlete to acquire devel-opmental assets and experience positive youth development if they are within an appropriate environment and have access to positive external influences/relation-ships (see Chapter 27). Hence, the coach is well placed to engender positive youth development and elicit the associated performance and interpersonal benefits with their adolescent athletes (e.g. Côté & Gilbert, 2009; Fraser-Thomas, Côté, & Deakin, 2005).

It is evident, therefore, that to facilitate effective coach involvement with adoles-cent athletes the sport psychologist can enable the coach to support their athletes through the challenging transition, and encourage positive youth development by providing an effective coaching environment and promoting a positive coach–ath-lete relationship. Consequently, in this chapter we will consider: (a) the charac-teristics of an effective coaching environment; (b) the properties of a successful/ supportive relationship between a coach and adolescent athlete; and (c) the role a sport psychologist can play in facilitating effective coach involvement with adoles-cent athletes. To provide further guidance, a case study is then presented to illustrate how we (as sport psychologists) worked with a coach to improve his involvement with adolescent athletes, and thereby enhance performance and interpersonal outcomes. The chapter concludes by offering recommendations for best practice, regarding how we believe sport psychologists should work with coaches to facili-tate coaching involvement.

Creating an effective coaching environment for adolescents

Research indicates that adolescent athletes require certain social, psychological, and coaching components within their coaching environment for it to be per-ceived as effective (see Mills & Pain, 2016). The key social components noted were task and social cohesion, which refer respectively to the extent that team members remain united in pursuit of a common performance goal, and the degree of affiliation among team members (Carron, Hausenblaus, & Eys, 2005). The main psychological components identified were the management of expec-tations, an alleviation of anxiety, and a task/mastery coaching climate that can enable the development of resilience and confidence. Finally, the coaching com-ponents acknowledged were the receipt of quality technical support, constructive feedback, a holistic/autonomous student-centred experience, access to sport sci-ence staff/role models, and a positive coach–athlete relationship (e.g. Mills, Butt, Maynard, & Harwood, 2014; Pain & Harwood, 2007). Furthermore, when the coach's perspective of an optimal coaching environment was examined, it was found that adolescent athletes benefited from a climate in which their wellbe-ing was of primary importance, they had an empowering relationship with the coach, and received a supportive, engaging, and developmental motivational cli-mate (Mills et al., 2014).

Accordingly, the psychologist can advise the coach on how to deliver an effec-tive climate for the mid–late adolescent athlete that contains the necessary social, psychological, and coaching components. First, task and social cohesion can be evoked through developing the coach's understanding of successful group formation, development, and performance (e.g. values, role clarity, and team goals; Cotterill, 2013). Second, the coach can be encouraged to communicate in a style which emphasises cooperation, self-development, and process in order to create a holistic student-centred and task/mastery coaching climate, which positively influences the athletes' wellbeing, anxiety, resilience, and confidence (e.g. Weiss, Amorose, & Wilko, 2009; see Chapter 8).

Crucially, to deliver an effective coaching environment, the coach must learn how to cope with the stressors they themselves experience, and manage their own emotions appropriately. In a recent study by Thelwell, Wagstaff, Rayner, Chapman, & Barker (2017) it was found that when the coach was 'stressed' they were perceived by their athletes as being less effective. For the most part, this was due to the stress causing a deterioration in the coach's behaviour (e.g. distracted, unorganised, and unsupportive), appearance (withdrawn, emotional, and rushed), communication (unclear, increased autocratic behaviours, and critical), and training climate (e.g. failure to manage conflict, poor decision-making, indifferent technical advice, failure to motivate, and lacking athlete focus). Thelwell, Wagstaff, Chapman, & Kenttä (2017) also noted that coaches often lack the self-awareness to recognise when they were suffering from the effects of stress, and as a result failed to employ necessary coping responses.

Consequently, one of the most important ways in which the sport psychologist can support effective coach involvement with mid–late adolescent athletes is to help coaches to become more aware of their own response to stress, and then challenge their underlying beliefs that contribute to this response. Thereafter, the coach can be guided to develop their capability to reappraise stressors (as facilitative/manageable) through strategies such as cognitive restructuring (Hanton, Wadey, & Mellalieu, 2008) and rational emotive behaviour therapy (REBT; Turner & Barker, 2014; see Chapter 24). The delivery of multi-modal psychological interventions to coaches may also be of benefit (e.g. attentional training, relaxation training, goal setting, imagery, and self-talk), as they are known to reduce the impact of stress on athletes (see Rumbold, Fletcher, & Daniels, 2012 for a review).

Developing and maintaining the coach–athlete relationship

Alongside the delivery of an effective coaching environment, the coach must also develop a high-quality relationship with their adolescent athletes to encourage the desired athletic and personal benefits. The coach–athlete relationship is considered to be any situation in which the thoughts, feelings, and behaviours of the coach and athlete are inter-related (Jowett & Cockerill, 2002). Therefore, it is reciprocal and dynamic, with both the coach and athlete influencing the quality of the relationship concurrently. Several conceptualisations of the coach–athlete relationship have been proposed (e.g. interpersonal theory, Wylleman, 2000; social exchange theories, Poczwardowski, Barott, & Jowett, 2006), though it is the

3Cs+1 model by Jowett and colleagues (Jowett, 2007; Jowett & Cockerill, 2002) that remains the most pervasive. Based on the interdependence theory (Kelley & Thibault, 1978), the 3Cs+1 model indicates that the quality of a coach–athlete relationship is based on closeness (the affective or emotional connection between the coach and athlete), commitment (the degree to which the coach and athlete wish to maintain their relationship), complementarity (the level of co-operative and corresponding behaviours within the athlete–coach dyad), and co-orientation (the extent to which the athlete and coach can infer how the other is feeling, thinking, and behaving).

If the coach–athlete relationship is effective, the mid–late adolescent is more likely to progress successfully through their challenging transition, achieve positive youth development (e.g. Vella, Oades, & Crowe, 2013), and thereby attain their sporting and interpersonal potential (e.g. Jowett & Cockerill, 2002). The athlete's level of wellbeing, intrinsic motivation (through the satisfaction of psychological needs; Felton & Jowett, 2013a, 2013b), self-efficacy, and engagement in their sport (Curran, Hill, Hall, & Jowett, 2015) is also higher when involved in a positive relationship with their coach (Hampson & Jowett, 2014). Importantly, such athletes also tend to appraise stressors as challenging rather than threatening (Nicholls et al., 2016). This is of significance when challenge appraisals are associated with positive emotions and clutch performance under pressure, while threat appraisals tend to encourage negative emotional responses and under-performance (see Lazarus, 1999).

Therefore, to facilitate coach involvement further, the psychologist can introduce the coach to strategies that can foster positive relationships with their athletes (i.e. closeness, commitment, complementarity, and co-orientation). This includes the use of the COMPASS framework (Rhind & Jowett, 2010), whereby the coach is encouraged to focus on: Conflict management (e.g. be proactive and reactive to conflict); Openness (create open communication channels); Motivation (engender a mastery/fun-orientated climate); Positivity (be adaptable and fair); Advice (offer constructive and process-focused feedback); Support (deliver reassurance and support/empathy); and Social networks (socialising and creating networks).

In addition, the extant literature has highlighted the importance of the coach addressing: (a) the athlete's psychological needs (i.e. autonomy, competence, and relatedness; see Choi, Cho, & Huh, 2013); (b) developing empathy (Lorimer & Jowett, 2010); and (c) demonstrating transformational leadership (Vella et al., 2013) to increase the quality of the coach–athlete relationship. With regards to the psychological needs, the sport psychologist can guide the coach on how to satisfy the athlete's need for autonomy, competence, and relatedness through the delivery of an autonomous-supportive coaching environment (see Chapter 8), and engendering cohesion/sense of belonging.

As empathy (i.e. the accurate perception of another's psychological condition) is a core component of effective relationships (Ickes, 2001), it is appropriate for sport psychologists to enable the coach to develop empathetic accuracy. This is achieved by encouraging the coach to adopt the appropriate type (e.g. social interaction and

openness) and volume/frequency (e.g. relevant to the athlete's needs) of communication, which promotes the social interaction/interpersonal bond required for
eliciting empathy (e.g. Rhind & Jowett, 2010) . The coach can also be supported to
request interpersonal feedback from athletes, which reinforces the accuracy of the
coach's empathy (Lorimer & Jowett, 2010).

Finally, transformational leadership is an established key antecedent of effective
coach–athlete relationships (e.g. Price & Weiss, 2013), and accordingly it is important for the sport psychologist to encourage the coach to demonstrate all relevant
transformational characteristics. This should include: eliciting inspirational motivation through creating a vision; providing an idealised influence by modelling
behaviours or values; offering individualised consideration to address the specific
needs of each athlete; and encouraging the athletes to think/behave creatively to
provide intellectual stimulation (see Bass, 1985).

Case study: Cricket

Thus far, the chapter has indicated the importance of an effective coaching environment and positive coach–athlete relationship for adolescent athletes. The mode/
methods through which the sport psychologist can support the coach to cultivate
an appropriate environment and relationship have also been provided. To supplement this theoretical discussion, the following case study is offered in which we
(as sport psychologists) indicate how we worked with a full-time cricket coach to
improve his involvement with adolescent athletes. Alongside a description of how
we supported the coach, a critical review of the consultancy process and outcomes
will be offered.

Context

Adam was an experienced cricket coach who had developed a reputation for providing an effective coaching environment for adolescent athletes. Indeed, many
of his athletes had progressed through the academy on to the professional ranks.
However, for the first time in Adam's career, the youth players were not making
the upward transition and his superiors and players were questioning his approach.
Adam explained that he found this group of players more challenging than others,
because they were slow to respond to his instructions and were not progressing at
the expected rate. He felt he did not possess a positive relationship with any of the
players, and he was experiencing high levels of negative affect (e.g. frustration and
anger) which he had to expend considerable effort to control. We noted that such
emotional labour might have contributed to Adam's increasing sense of emotional
exhaustion and signs of burnout (Lee & Chelladurai, 2016). It was therefore unsurprising that Adam confessed to the occasional loss of emotional control, whereby
he had demonstrative outbursts with his players (see Larner, Corbett, Thelwell, &
Wagstaff, 2017). He had also started to question his level of emotional intelligence
(Salovey & Mayer, 1990), for while he recognised his emotions were unhelpful,

he felt unable to manage them. This culminated in Adam experiencing a lowered level of coach efficacy (i.e. perceived ability to affect the learning/performance of athletes), which contributed further to the lack of player progression, as Adam suggested the players were becoming increasingly defensive/unresponsive to his progressively ineffective and unpredictable coaching behaviour.

Intervention

Stage 1

Using the work of Augustine and Hemenover (2009), we explored Adam's subjective appraisals of the situation. The results suggested an increased perception of pressure due to the players' inability to respond to his instructions and failure to progress as anticipated. Secondly, we explored Adam's primary appraisal, which indicated that he did not want to show emotions to the players and instead used 'expressive suppression' that signified the masking of his felt emotions via his facial expressions. As this was consuming his cognitive resources and decreasing psychological functioning, it was likely to have contributed to his decreasing capability to cope with his role, deliver high-quality training sessions, and sustain emotional control. Finally, through the examination of secondary appraisals, we identified that the emotional demands of the situation were perceived as debilitating, the suppression of emotions was too much of a personal cost to Adam, and the displaying of those emotions was becoming a cost to the athletes. Adam possessed an athlete-centred philosophy, as he was sensitive to the psychosocial demands that the multi-level transition placed on his athletes, and to the importance of positive youth development. However, due to the inability to manage his own emotions effectively, he lacked the psychological capacity to monitor and identify the needs of his athletes and respond appropriately.

Stage 2

To support Adam, we adopted an emotional management approach that reflected Visek, Harris, and Blom's (2009) educational consultation model (see Chapter 21). That is, he was initially encouraged to enhance his emotional intelligence by reflecting on the internal (self) and external (in others) emotions that were unhelpful to athlete progress. Thereafter, we introduced Adam to rational emotive behaviour therapy (REBT) so he could reappraise the environmental stressors and restructure/manage his emotional response to the pressurised situation (see Chapter 24). This allowed Adam to gain emotional control, remove the need to suppress his debilitative emotions, and increase his psychological capacity (Turner & Barker, 2014).

Thereafter, and using his preference for providing an athlete-centred approach, we explored how Adam could use the information available to him to assist his decision-making and ensure the athletes were engaged and responsive to his message. The first key development was to encourage an accurate appraisal of the situation, which required Adam to develop communication channels between himself and the athletes. He could then receive athlete feedback regarding their preferred method and style of communication, and discuss why certain approaches were or were not appropriate. Subsequently, Adam adapted his communication style in response to the changing needs of the athletes.

Having established the athletes' preferred approach to communication, the next phase was to understand why the athletes were not engaging with Adam's coaching instructions and progressing as expected. Here, we explored the learning styles literature (e.g. Occhino, Mallett, Rynne, & Carlisle, 2014), and as a result advised Adam to rely more on the use of self-discovery, simplicity, and personalisation in his delivery, and he was encouraged to challenge himself via the adoption of an individualised approach to his communication with the athletes.

The above programme of work remains ongoing, but via the use of social validation approaches (Page & Thelwell, 2013) it appears Adam is more confident in his ability to manage his emotions and understand the emotions of others. More importantly, by developing communication channels and maintaining emotional control, he perceives that he has a greater capacity to identify signals from the athletes and, when necessary, adapt the delivery style of his coaching. He has also noticed some changes (albeit subjectively) to how athletes have engaged with his sessions, as the athletes are asking more questions and the intensity of training has increased. The players are also providing regular feedback regarding their own development and the broader training environment. As Adam summarised:

> I've tried to make sure I'm using the emotion and thought change skills [REBT]. I feel more confident and I'm starting to get more in tune with what they [the players] are thinking. I think the relationships are getting better and they seem to want to communicate with me … as I do with them.

Although the intervention is proving to be effective, it must be stated that we encountered initial resistance from Adam when presenting the intervention. Specifically, by employing an educational model we offered Adam extensive information regarding the aim, purpose, and nature of our intervention. However, on reflection, we delivered the message in a manner that fell in to the 'expert trap' (Miller & Rollnick, 2013). That is, we implied implicitly that our sport psychology expertise could provide the answer to his current coaching issues, rather than utilise Adam's expertise – along with our own – to develop an intervention in partnership. As this 'expert' approach is seldom successful when trying to evoke change, and had clearly disempowered/demotivated Adam, the situation was quickly rectified. We ensured that Adam led the intervention process, while we played a more supportive, counselling, and facilitative role, and only offered our technical sport psychology expertise (i.e. mental skills strategies) when this direct guidance was necessary.

Conclusions and lessons learned

There are many challenges for those who coach adolescents, as they need to support an athlete who is negotiating a challenging transition and develop a high-quality coach–athlete relationship. Moreover, the adolescent athlete requires an effective coaching environment that addresses specific social, psychological, and coaching components. Throughout the chapter, and as illuminated through the case study, a sport psychologist can play a crucial part in enabling the coach to attend effectively to these requirements and subsequently elicit the aspired athletic and interpersonal developments for their adolescent athletes.

One of the main challenges for the coach of this age range is the need to be highly responsive to the changing psychosocial needs of the athletes. It was evident in our case study that Adam fell foul to such athlete unpredictability; he adopted a coaching approach that had proved to be successful in the recent past but was not appropriate for this new group of athletes. It is critical, therefore, that as well as providing the coach with guidance regarding the development of an effective coaching climate and relationship with the athlete, the sport psychologist needs to support the coach to become a reflexive practitioner, so they can monitor and modify their coaching approach when necessary.

Throughout the chapter, it has been noted that the sport psychologist is well placed to offer the coach a wealth of theoretical, evidence-based guidance to support their work with adolescent athletes, though *how* this information should be delivered to the coach requires further consideration. As explored within the case study, we initially delivered the educational material in a disempowering manner that placed the sport psychologist as the expert. Thus, both the coach and sport psychologist must facilitate a working relationship based on reciprocity, where both sets of knowledge and expertise inform the delivery of a coaching environment.

Finally, although the evidence reviewed in the chapter identifies the need for coaches to adopt an athlete-focused approach, we advocate that the coach must also become self-focused at times. As observed with Adam, when the psychological capacity of the coach is reduced due to the negative effects of stress, they become unable to maintain their normal standards of delivery. Therefore, a fundamental role for the sport psychologist is to encourage the coach to become more self-aware of their response to stress and facilitate the development of psychological skills they can use to regulate their own emotions. The coach will then be able to maintain the psychological state required to produce optimal involvement with their adolescent athletes.

References

Augustine, A. A., & Hemenover, S. H. (2009). On the relative effectiveness of affect regulation strategies: A meta-analysis. *Cognition and Emotion, 23,* 1181–1220.

Bass, B. M. (1985). *Leadership and Performance beyond Expectations.* New York, NY: Free Press.

Benson, P. L. (2007). Developmental assets: An overview of theory, research, and practice. In R. K. Silbereisen & R. M. Lerner (Eds.), *Approaches to Positive Youth Development* (pp. 33–58). Thousand Oaks, CA: Sage.

Carron, A. V., Hausenblaus, H. A., & Eys, M. A. (2005). *Group Dynamics in Sport* (3rd ed.). Morgantown, WV: Fitness Information Technology.

Choi, H., Cho, S., & Huh, J. (2013). The association between the perceived coach–athlete relationship and athletes' basic psychological needs. *Social Behavior and Personality, 41,* 1547–1556.

Côté, J. (1999). The influence of the family in the development of talent in sport. *The Sport Psychologist, 13*, 395–417.

Côté, J., & Gilbert, W. (2009). An integrative definition of coaching effectiveness and expertise. *International Journal of Sports Science & Coaching, 4*, 307–323.

Cotterill, S. (2013). *Team Psychology in Sports: Theory and Practice.* Abingdon, UK: Routledge.

Curran, T., Hill, A. P., Hall, H. K., & Jowett, G. E. (2015). Relationships between the coach-created motivational climate and athlete engagement in youth sport. *Journal of Sport & Exercise Psychology, 37*, 193–198.

Felton, L., & Jowett, S. (2013a). 'What do coaches do' and 'how do they relate': Their effects on athletes' psychological needs and functioning. *Scandinavian Journal of Medicine & Science in Sports, 23*, 130–139.

Felton, L., & Jowett, S. (2013b). Attachment and wellbeing: The mediating effects of psychological needs satisfaction within the coach–athlete and parent–athlete relational contexts. *Psychology of Sport and Exercise, 14*, 57–65.

Fraser-Thomas, J. L., Côté, J., & Deakin, J. (2005). Youth sport programs: An avenue to foster positive youth development. *Physical Education and Sport Pedagogy, 10*, 19–40.

Hampson, R., & Jowett, S. (2014). Effects of coach leadership and coach–athlete relationship on collective efficacy. *Scandinavian Journal of Medicine & Science in Sports, 24*, 454–460.

Hanton, S., Wadey, R., & Mellalieu, S. D. (2008). Advanced psychological strategies and anxiety responses in sport. *The Sport Psychologist, 22*, 472–490.

Ickes, W. (2001). Measuring empathetic empathy. In J. A. Hall & F. J. Bernieri (Eds.), *Interpersonal Sensitivity Theory and Measurement* (pp. 219–241). Mahwah, NJ: Lawrence Erlbaum.

Jowett, S. (2007). Interdependence analysis and the 3+1Cs in the coach-athlete relationship. In S. Jowett & D. Lavallee (Eds.), *Social Psychology in Sport* (pp. 15–27). Champaign, IL: Human Kinetics.

Jowett, S., & Cockerill, I. M. (2002). Incompatibility in the coach–athlete relationship. In I. M. Cockerill (Ed.), *Solutions in Sport Psychology* (pp. 16–31). London: Thomson Learning.

Kelley, H. H., & Thibault, J. W. (1978). *Interpersonal Relations: A Theory of Interdependence.* Michigan, MI: Wiley.

Larner, R. J., Corbett, J., Thelwell, R. C., & Wagstaff, C. R. D. (2017). A multi-study examination of organizational stressors, emotional labour, burnout, and turnover in sport organizations. *Scandinavian Journal of Medicine & Science in Sport*. Epub ahead of print. doi:10.1111/sms.12833.

Lazarus, R. S. (1999). The cognition-emotion debate: A bit of history. In T. Dalgeish & M. Power (Eds.), *Handbook of Cognition and Emotion* (pp. 3–19). Chichester, UK: Wiley & Sons.

Lee, Y. H., & Chelladurai, P. (2016). Affectivity, emotional labor, emotional exhaustion, and emotional intelligence in coaching. *Journal of Applied Sport Psychology, 28*, 170–184.

Lerner, R. M., Lerner, J. V., Almerigi, J., Theokas, C., Phelps, E., Naudeau, S., ... von Eye, A. (2006). Towards a new vision and vocabulary about adolescence: Theoretical and empirical bases of a positive youth development perspective. In L. Balter & C. S. Tamis-LeMonda (Eds.), *Child Psychology: A Handbook of Contemporary Issues* (pp. 445–469). New York, NY: Taylor & Francis.

Lorimer, R., & Jowett, S. (2010). Feedback of information in the empathic accuracy of sport coaches. *Psychology of Sport and Exercise, 11*, 12–17.

Miller, W. R., & Rollnick, S. R. (2013). *Motivational Interviewing: Helping People with Change.* New York, NY: Guilford Press.

Mills, A., Butt, J., Maynard, I., & Harwood, C. (2014). Identifying factors perceived to influence the development of elite football academy players in England. *Journal of Sports Sciences, 30*, 1593–1604.

Mills, A., & Pain, M. (2016). Creating effective development environments for the adolescent athlete. In R. C Thelwell, C. Harwood, & I. A. Greenlees (Eds.), *The Psychology of Sports Coaching: Research and Practice* (pp. 21–37). Abingdon, UK: Routledge.

Nicholls, A. R., Levy, A. R., Jones, L., Meir, R., Radcliffe, J. N., & Perry, J. L. (2016). Committed relationships and enhanced threat levels: Perceptions of coach behavior, the coach–athlete relationship, stress appraisals, and coping among athletes. *International Journal of Sports Science & Coaching, 11*, 16–26.

Occhino, J., Mallett, C., Rynne, S., & Carlisle, K. (2014). Autonomy-supportive pedagogical approach to sports coaching: Research, challenges and opportunities. *International Journal of Sports Science & Coaching, 9*, 401–416.

Page, J., & Thelwell, R. (2013). The value of social validation in single-case methods in sport and exercise psychology. *Journal of Applied Sport Psychology, 25*, 61–71.

Pain, M., & Harwood, C. (2007). The performance environment of the England youth soccer teams. *Journal of Sports Sciences, 25*, 1307–1324.

Poczwardowski, A., Barott, J. E., & Jowett, S. (2006). Diversifying approaches to research on athlete–coach relationships. *Psychology of Sport and Exercise, 7*, 125–142.

Price, M. S., & Weiss, M. R. (2013). Relationships among coach leadership, peer leadership, and adolescent athletes' psychosocial and team outcomes: A test of transformational leadership theory. *Journal of Applied Sport Psychology, 25*, 265–279.

Rhind, D. A., & Jowett, S. (2010). Relationship maintenance strategies in the coach-athlete relationship: The development of the COMPASS model. *Journal of Applied Sport Psychology, 22*, 106–121.

Rosier, N., & Wylleman, P. (2015). A cross-cultural study into the junior-senior transition of (pre-) Olympic athlete. *IOC Olympic Studies Centre.*

Rumbold, J. L., Fletcher, D., & Daniel, K. (2012). A systematic review of stress management interventions with sport performers. *Sport, Exercise, and Performance Psychology, 1*, 173–193.

Salovey, P., & Mayer, J. D. (1990). Emotional intelligence. *Imagination, Cognition and Personality, 9*, 185–211.

Stambulova, N. (2009). Talent development in sport: The perspective of transitions. In T. M Hung, R. Lidor, & D. Hackfort (Eds), *Psychology of Sport Excellence* (pp. 63–74). Morgantown, WV: Fitness Information Technology.

Thelwell, R. C., Chapman, M., Wagstaff, C. R. D., & Kenttä, G. (2017). Examining coaches' perceptions of how their stress influences the coach-athlete relationship. *Journal of Sports Sciences, 35,* 1928–1939.

Thelwell, R. C., Wagstaff, C. R. D., Rayner, A., Chapman, M., & Barker, J. (2017). Exploring athletes' perceptions of coach stress in elite sport environments. *Journal of Sports Sciences, 35*, 44–55.

Turner, M. J., & Barker, J. B. (2014). Using rational emotive behavior therapy with athletes. *The Sport Psychologist, 28*, 75–90.

Vella, S. A., Oades, L. G., & Crowe, T. P. (2013). The relationship between coach leadership, the coach–athlete relationship, team success, and the positive developmental experiences of adolescent soccer players. *Physical Education and Sport Pedagogy, 18*, 549–561.

Visek, A. J., Harris, B. S., & Blom, L. C. (2009). Doing sport psychology: A youth sport consulting model for practitioners. *The Sport Psychologist, 23*, 271–291.

Weiss, M. R., Amorose, A. J., & Wilko, A. M. (2009) Coaching behaviours, motivational climate, and psycho-social outcomes amongst female adolescent athletes. *Pediatric Exercise Science, 21*, 475–492.

Wylleman, P. (2000). Interpersonal relationships in sport: Uncharted territory in sport psychology research. *International Journal of Sport Psychology, 31*, 555–572.

Wylleman, P., Reinta, A., & De Knop, P. (2013). A developmental and holistic perspective on athletic career development. In P. Sotiriadou & V. De Bosscher (Eds.), *Managing High Performance Sport* (pp. 159–182). New York, NY: Routledge.

20

ORGANISATIONAL CULTURE AND INFLUENCE ON DEVELOPING ATHLETES

Kristoffer Henriksen, Louise K. Storm, and Carsten H. Larsen

A day in the office

Today I[1] attend the badminton national team training. I have no specific appointment but simply drop in to observe training. I notice how the atmosphere is relaxed and the coaches are laughing, but as the training starts coaches and athletes become more serious. A key characteristic of this training group is the integration of senior and junior national team athletes ranging in age from 16 to 32, which creates a good learning environment. A singles coach working with a youth national team player catches my eye. The young player is in a training match against an older, more experienced player. I am not interested in the drill itself or in the athlete's performance, but rather in the behaviour and communication of the coach. I notice that, in each pause, the coach takes his time to talk to the player. He does not instruct the player on what to do, but rather asks questions about what happens on the court and possible strategies to respond. He does not praise the player when he scores a point, nor does he seem preoccupied with the result. Rather he praises the player when he provides good reflections about how to handle the challenges and adversity he encounters. Through his behaviour and communication, the coach creates a climate of equality and openness, where young athletes are stimulated to reflect and contribute. I understand that in this environment the athletes learn to autonomously make decisions and handle adversity during matches. Before I leave, I approach the coach and we shortly discuss my observations and remind each other why his strategies are appropriate and important.

In this chapter we will argue: (a) that a preoccupation with individual talented athletes should be supplemented with an understanding of the environment in which they develop; (b) that a strong and coherent organisational culture of a youth club or team is a, if not *the*, key factor in successful athlete development; (c) that such an organisational culture can, and must, be deliberately developed and maintained by the coach and management through cultural leadership; and (d) that a key task of the sport psychology practitioner is to make the coach conscious of his role as a culture leader and thus build mentally strong athletes *through* supporting the coach's cultural leadership. This chapter consists of two major sections. The first section is a general review on the holistic ecological approach, organisational culture, and influences on developing athletes. The second section details a specific case example regarding the influence of cultural leadership in youth sport based on the authors' applied work.

Setting the scene: A holistic and ecological approach

As a relatively new perspective on talent development in sport, the holistic ecological approach (HEA) shifts the attention from the individual athlete to the environment in which he or she develops (Henriksen, Stambulova, & Roessler, 2010a). This perspective expands our understanding of what it takes for a young athlete to make it to the elite senior level. The HEA highlights two interconnected ways of analysing talent development environments. First, there is a focus on the *structure* of the environment, particularly the roles and cooperation of key individuals (e.g. parents and coaches). Environments are most successful in supporting athletes when the efforts of different parts of the environment (e.g. school, club coaches, national team coaches, parents, and others) are integrated rather than fragmented or in opposition. Second, there is a focus on the organisational culture (Schein, 1990) of the team, with organisational culture being defined as a set of shared assumptions that define appropriate behaviour for various situations.

According to Schein (1990), all groups are faced with two basic tasks. First the group must 'survive' and grow through adapting to the constantly changing external environment. For instance, changes in legislation may allow/force football clubs to identify talented players at an earlier age, and increased competition between clubs may drive clubs to sharpen their profile or offer extra benefits for young athletes. In such change, the group must negotiate their core mission, goals, and means to accomplish the goals. Second, the group develops through internal integration, which involves establishing a common language, group boundaries, and criteria for allocating status and reward. Organisational culture emerges as a set of solutions, actions, and values that, in contributing to the group's ability to solve these two tasks, become integrated to a degree where they are no longer questioned. The interactions of the group members constantly shape and refine the culture, while at the same time the culture stabilises these interactions.

Schein (1990) further describes that organisational culture consists of three levels with varying degrees of visibility: (1) cultural artefacts, which are visible manifestations such as stories and myths told in the environment, clothing, buildings, and organisation charts (e.g. stories about particularly games or team members); (2) espoused values, which are the social principles, norms, goals, and standards that the organisation shows to the world (i.e. what the members of the culture say they do); and (3) basic assumptions, which are underlying reasons for actions.

These basic assumptions comprise the core of the culture and are no longer questioned but are 'taken-for-granted, underlying, and usually unconscious assumptions' (Schein, 1990, p. 112) that strongly influence what the members of the culture (athletes, coaches, managers) actually do. For example, basic assumptions might include the answers to questions such as whether members are encouraged to compete or to cooperate, whether the club or team values openness and cooperation with its surroundings or remains closed, whether talent is perfectible or fixed, and whether athletes should focus on one sport or would benefit from broader sports profiles.

Research findings: A strong culture creates strong athletes

Numerous in-depth case studies of successful talent development environments have shown that while each environment is unique, they also share a number of features. Successful athletic talent development environments (ATDE) are characterised by proximal role modelling; an integration of efforts among the different agents (family, coaches, management etc.); inclusive training groups rather than early segregation; a focus on long-term developmental rather than early success, and a broad sampling basis (e.g. Henriksen, Stambulova, & Roessler, 2010a; 2010b; 2011; Larsen, Alfermann, Henriksen, & Christensen, 2013; Martindale & Mortimer, 2011). These findings provide an important note of caution to many contemporary talent development programmes, which, according to our experience, often seem to promote early specialisation and the organisation of selected talented athletes in small elitist training groups at an early stage (see Chapters 6 and 11 for further information). For the present chapter, however, the most important common feature of successful ATDEs is a strong and coherent organisational culture, with corresponding espoused (e.g. desired) and enacted (e.g. lived or demonstrated) values. Such alignment of desired values and demonstrated actions ensures a stable environment and is an important factor in explaining the success of certain athletic development environments (Henriksen, 2010).

The coaches are central in the processes of creating and maintaining a strong and coherent organisational culture. As an example, in the case of the Danish national 49er sailing team, autonomy and a long-term focus were considered key attributes of a prospective winner in sailing and the coaches expected the young athletes to take responsibility for their own development. In this environment the young athletes were always welcome at the elite athletes' meetings during training camps; however, they were never formally invited. They had to ask when and where the meetings were held. As one young athlete said, 'You are there on your own initiative. Developing your talent is your own responsibility. No one invites you or holds your hand. You have to kick the door in, and that is how it should be' (Henriksen, 2010, p. 78). In this way, the basic assumption of the environment ('the individual athlete must take responsibility for his/her own excellence') was reflected in the practices (no invitations for meetings) and the team culture was reflected in the athletes who developed autonomy and responsibility.

In a recently explored case – a Norwegian handball club (Storm, 2015) – the organisational culture was characterised by a consistent learning focus for the young athletes. The young athletes were encouraged to learn by taking chances. The coach continuously said to the athletes in the environment, 'If you haven't made a mistake today you haven't done enough.' This was not just an espoused value; it was also an integrated part of the coach's own practice. For example, during a match he did not change his strategy even though the team started to lose. Several young players were on court, with the intent that they would learn about how to handle stressful situations. The coach was aware that his trust in them was crucial for them to develop these skills and he was willing to risk a bad result in the short term in order to fulfil his value regarding long-term development. In this way, the coach deliberately maintained the consistency between espoused (if you haven't made a mistake today you haven't done enough) and enacted values (the young players remain on court in pressure situations).

By contrast, a study of a less successful golf team in a Danish sport college (Henriksen, Larsen, & Christensen, 2014) revealed a fragmented culture in which espoused values did not correspond to actions. Particularly, the behaviour and the communication of the coach were inconsistent. For example, the coaches often preached the importance of eating healthily, warming up, and training in a structured manner. At the same time, however, they would often show up at training eating a pizza when the school kitchen served fish, take part in training without warming up themselves, and arrive late at training. The incoherence between the espoused and enacted values created an unclear culture and left the athletes in this environment with too few supporting guidelines in terms of how to develop as a golfer, resulting in the athletes developing autonomy, but also a lack of responsibility.

To sum up, the organisational culture in which athletes are located will influence the development of their psychological characteristics, as well as their opportunities for development and learning. The coach is in a key position to create and maintain an organisational culture that supports the development of desired attributes in the athletes. However, for such attributes to be developed it is critical that coaches demonstrate consistency between the espoused and enacted values defining the culture.

The organisational culture and the sport psychology practitioner

The holistic ecological perspective has implications for the practitioner (see Box 20.1). On a general level, a practitioner adopting this perspective will acknowledge that the athlete is embedded in an environment and aim to involve individuals in this environment (coaches, managers, teammates etc.) in his or her interventions. Further, the practitioner will support the development of a holistic package of psychosocial skills that will be of use for the athletes in their sport and other life spheres (Martindale & Mortimer, 2011). On a more specific level, we also suggest that the practitioner aims to improve not only the psychological skills of the individual athletes but also the functioning of the environment. This work will typically include two key foci. First, the practitioner should work to create an

---

BOX 20.1 TYPICAL PROBLEMS IN CONSULTING VS. CONSULTING FROM A HOLISTIC ECOLOGICAL APPROACH

Typical problems in sport psychology consulting in youth sport:

- Classroom teaching: The athletes are too often removed from their sport context, making it difficult to transfer new skills to training and competition.
- Focus on the individual athlete without involving the context: The consultant does not involve coaches or parents, making it difficult for the athletes to find someone to discuss ideas and exercises with.
- Focus on the sports persona: The consultant often limits his focus to only mental skills.
- Curriculum design: Interventions are planned like a school curriculum and planned as a series of workshops on key mental skills, rather than integrated in daily training.

Holistic ecological approach to sport psychology consulting in youth sport:

- Integration in everyday training environment: The consultant acknowledges that athletes are embedded in an environment and that learning is situated; psychological skills training is integrated in sport-specific drills.
- Environment involved: The consultant involves coaches, older athletes, and others to reinforce learning.
- Athlete as a whole human being: The consultant aims to support the development of a holistic skills package that is of use for the athletes both in and out of sport.
- Organisational culture as a target: The practitioner looks beyond the individual athletes and their mental skills and aims to create and maintain a strong and coherent organisational culture.

---

integrated environment with good working relations among the environment's different agents. Second, practitioners should aim to create and maintain a strong and coherent organisational culture that provides stability and clarity for the group and allows people to focus on the task.

Organisational culture leadership and the coach

An organisational culture can be more or less functional depending upon the task of the team or club. For example, some elite sport teams may benefit from an organisational culture characterised by a here–and–now performance focus, internal competition, and a clear hierarchy. On the contrary, a talent academy is likely to benefit from an organisational culture that values long-term development focus, sharing knowledge, and room for unstructured play-like activities. From a holistic ecological perspective, a key function of the practitioner is to make the coach aware of how he or she, through cultural leadership, influences the psychological characteristics of the young athletes in his or her team. In line with cultural sport psychology, we perceive cultural leadership to be related to cultural sensitivity (Schinke, McGannon, Parnham, & Lane, 2012). To be successful as a cultural leader, the coach is dependent on his or her ability to act in a culturally sensitive manner (McGannon & Johnson, 2009) and willingness to confront one's own background, biases, and interests in a self-reflexive manner (Schinke et al., 2012). The coach has a position of power in the environment, and according to Schein, such a position has a substantial impact on the development of the culture. Culture is constantly reenacted and created by people's interactions with each other and shaped by people's own behaviour (Schein 2010, p. 3). Through their interactions, often guided by the coach, the underlying assumptions of the group are taught to new team members as the correct way to perceive, think, feel, and act in relation to different challenges. For present purposes we examine the role of organisational culture and how coaches may increase awareness of their role as cultural leaders.

In our applied work, we are inspired by Schein's (2010) perspective on cultural leadership in the daily life of the organisation and how leaders (in this case coaches) often unknowingly (and culturally insensitively) teach the members of the team how to think feel and act. We perceive cultural leadership to be the deliberate use of what Schein refers to as cultural embedding mechanisms. We have adapted these to sport and present them in Table 20.1. Through the mechanisms depicted in Table 20.1, the coaches communicate their values and expectations towards the athletes. Cultural leadership takes place all the time, but in our experience coaches are not always aware of their roles as cultural leaders. Thus, when aiming to improve organisational culture, our role as sport psychologists will often centre around teaching coaches to be more aware of the ways in which their actions communicate values and expectations.

Schein (1990) contended that because culture provides meaning and stability to its members, these members may be resistant to change, making cultural change difficult. In our work on organisational culture and leadership we therefore always pay deliberate attention to the change process, and we are inspired by Lewin (1947) who suggested three stages in change process: the unfreeze stage, the change stage, and the refreeze stage.

- In the *unfreeze* stage, the members' survival anxiety must be greater than the learning anxiety that is also involved in all change processes to be motivated to change. We will therefore increase survival anxiety by presenting data to suggest that a change is necessary (e.g. because of an economic threat or a reduction in performance), and also work to reduce learning anxiety by creating a sense of psychological safety, for example through providing a compelling vision of the future and through positive role models.

TABLE 20.1 Examples of cultural embedding mechanisms

What the coach takes an interest in, pays attention to, and controls/oversees on a regular basis	A powerful mechanism for a coach to communicate what he believes in and what he strives for, especially when consistent and systematic.
	What is the first question a coach poses when seeing the athletes after a break? What does he comment on in training? How does he measure success (result statistics or effort)?
How coaches react to critical incidents	Critical incidents and crises in a broad sense make people more susceptible to learning and change. A coach's actions in such situations are a powerful signal of his priorities and goals.
	What does the coach do the first time the team's star player is late for training (are we equal)? What is the coach's reaction after a series of losses? Or when the team is financially threatened?
How coaches allocate resources	The allocation of resources shows a coach's priorities. In a limited budget, does he prioritise an extra training camp or a fancier location for the camps; an expensive star player or a strong community?
How coaches allocate rewards and status	The allocation of reward and status in a team shows what behaviours the coach values from the athletes. Rewards can be recognition, finances, one-on-one attention from the coach etc.
	Who are allocated these resources? The athletes who are currently best, who put in the greater effort, or those who are most loyal to the team?
How coaches select, promote, and deselect	A subtle yet potent way to communicate values and expectations. Who wins a spot on selected teams? Who is selected captain? Is it all about results or more about effort?
The deliberate use of role models	The coach's own visible behaviours serve as a clear communication of his values. The strategic use of role models in daily training serves the same purpose. Is the coach always on time?
	Is the coach equally present in all parts of the training (also warm up and cool down)? Would a coach ever check his smart phone during training?
The use of mottos, posters, organisation charts, and rituals.	These factors are secondary but they send a strong signal if aligned with the first six mechanisms. What is the club motto? What is posted on the walls in the training facility or on the home page?

Source: Adapted from Schein, 2010.

- In the *change* stage, the members learn new behaviours, agree upon new team values, or acquire new psychological skills.
- In the *refreeze* stage, the new behaviours are gradually internalised into the members' self-image and incorporated into relationships and habits (see Henriksen, 2015 for an example).

The key idea is that, although practitioners may often find themselves jumping straight to the change phase (and educating coaches or athletes, delivering workshops etc.), the key to success, in our view, lies in creating a solid sense of necessity to change (unfreeze) and in making sure acquired skills and perspectives are incorporated into behaviour and into the basic assumptions that govern the behaviour of the members in the team (refreeze).

Insights from the field

Before we present a case to illustrate the work we have done in this area, we will shortly summarise what we mean when we talk about *sport psychology interventions aimed at organisational culture*. Such interventions: (a) aim to improve athletes' psychological skills through improving the organisational culture; (b) take their point of departure from an analysis of strong and weak points of the current team culture; (c) keep a main focus on the role of the coach as a cultural leader and aim to reinforce his/her awareness of this role; (d) ensure support from the wider environment (management, medical staff, or other stakeholders); (e) target all levels of the culture (artefacts, espoused values, and basic assumptions); and (f) take a long-term perspective and prioritise unfreeze, change, and refreeze phases.

An applied case: Developing a culture for goal directedness in soccer

In the following section we provide an example of a sport psychology intervention with a group of under-17 players in a football academy in Denmark. The coach approached us with a wish for a typical workshop series for his players. He had observed that the players were very results focused (and not sufficiently process focused), and that they very rarely had specific goals or focus points for a training session. As a result, his observation was that the intensity and quality of training, unless incorporating competition, was too low. In drills that were designed as a competition, intensity was typically high but this intensity was not directed at specific learning outcomes. The coach asked for a workshop series on goal setting and on the importance of athletes taking responsibility for their own development.

The practitioner presented his reservations towards workshops out of context (lack of transfer, learning not situated in the football context) and introduced the idea of looking at the team culture (we used the word team culture instead of the more theoretical concept of organisational culture) to understand the players' focus and behaviour, and to develop him as a cultural leader. He found the personal development aspect on his own role as a coach interesting and agreed.

Unfreeze: Getting everyone on board

The unfreeze stage consisted of assessing the need and making the need explicit to the whole team in order to develop survival anxiety and reduce learning anxiety. The practitioner conducted short (10–20 minutes) interviews with selected players, coaches, and managers about their perceptions of the daily training and competition environment. The practitioner also made sure to include gatekeepers in the interviews (key players, manager, head coach of the senior team) and take time during the interviews to explain the overall rational. Additionally, several informal visits to the club in order to observe the players were also conducted.

The observations and interviews confirmed the coach's concerns. The athletes described how they were uncertain about their overall development path and were often less than fully focused in training because they did not see a clear link between the individual drills and their individual strengths, weaknesses, and focus areas as players. The managers confirmed that such awareness was key to making a successful transition to the club's senior teams.

In a meeting with the coach and athletes the practitioner presented the main results from the individual interviews with an emphasis on the athletes' own descriptions of unhealthy competition, a lack of goals, and a resulting loss of focus. The athletes fell silent and nodded in agreement. The coach then made a presentation about the attitude that is necessary to maximise potential, and the senior head coach supported this by explaining that these mental qualities were an important marker in his team selection. Together, these talks created a sense that a change was necessary (survival anxiety). Finally, a key senior player talked about how he used goal setting as a key to personal improvement. His talk served to reduce learning anxiety through role modelling and a compelling vision of the future. Overall, in this stage we deemed it critical to demonstrate a genuine interest in the team and to secure buy-in from all stakeholders who might at a later stage become a barrier for the project.

Change: Learning to set goals in context

The change stage started with a short presentation by the practitioner about the finer points of goal setting. After this, the players would work with goal setting in different ways, but always on the pitch. For the first three weeks the coach would, in selected exercises or drills, bring a number of small (business card size) laminated papers each describing a possible goal for the session. These could be tactical, technical, communication, or attitude goals. The cards were distributed on the ground and the players were asked to select one or two goals for the session. Some days the athletes would then read their cards out loud to their teammates and after the exercise they would be asked to evaluate how well they managed to (a) keep a focus on that goal; and (b) accomplish the goal. Other days, the players would pair up and simply present their goals and evaluate together.

After this initial introduction, the coach asked the players to formulate their own goals, first for a specific exercise, then for a whole training session, and finally for longer periods. In every session he asked them to evaluate how the goals affected their focus and learning outcomes. The practitioner's role was rarely to address the players, but more often to prepare the coach for the talks about goals followed by an evaluation of his engagement and successful creation of a culture for goal direct-edness. When the players on rare occasions seemed disengaged, the coach despair-ingly doubted the work and asked the practitioner to take more responsibility and address the players directly. However, this would have worked against the purpose of the project because our aim was to empower the coach as a cultural leader. An informal talk over a cup of coffee about team culture, the purpose of the work, and the slow nature of all learning was usually enough to motivate the coach to keep up his efforts.

Refreeze: Into the daily practices

The main purpose of the refreeze stage was to integrate the new behaviours around goal setting in the daily team practices. It is not easy to distinguish between the change and the refreeze stages because change is on-going. But, in the refreeze phase the focus is on moving from espoused to enacted values and incorporating the new values and behaviours in the team's identity as basic assumptions.

In this stage, the focus was directed explicitly towards the coach's role in creat-ing a culture for working deliberately with goals situated in real-life contexts. The practitioner supervised the coach for a six-month period. In this period the practi-tioner and coach discussed, based on cultural embedding mechanisms described in Table 20.1, how the coach could work deliberately with his role as a cultural leader. Some of the key focus points are described below:

- The first focus point was how the coach paid attention to goal setting and focus in training. While observing his practice the practitioner would often challenge him to take a stronger interest in the athletes' use of goals. For a start he would ask players about their goals for specific training days and drills and demonstrate a genuine interest in how the players evaluated their training. Later he would involve them in setting goals for matches.
- Second, the role of critical incidents was discussed and it was agreed that the coach would focus on situations when the team did not reach its process goals. Before, the coach would have been satisfied if the team reached their result goals and dissatisfied if the team lost. Now he would always evaluate process before results, and discuss a potential adjustment of process goals disregarding if the team lost or won.
- Third the coach agreed to allocate more resources and status to those players who worked most ambitiously with goal setting in the daily training. Such resources could be one-on-one talks with the coach and first access to massage

after matches. He even (after initial resistance and admittedly only to a certain degree) let the starting line-up reflect the athletes' efforts and goal directedness in training rather than current performance level and explained this when presenting the line-up.

- Fourth, the practitioner urged him to reinforce the project using role models. On two occasions he invited players from the senior elite team to demonstrate how they work with goals in training.
- Finally, discussions focused on how to use cultural artefacts to support the process. The coach designed a motivational poster about the importance of goals and hung it in the locker room.

Although this intervention was successful, in the refreeze stage a major challenge is reversal to the old culture. This typically happens during times of poor results or changes in staff and players. In this particular case, the club hired a new assistant coach, who reinforced behaviours that were not aligned with the desired culture. This required the practitioner to commit time to educating the new assistant coach about the process and his role in it.

Reflections

Sport psychology interventions are not uniform. They may target several levels, including the individual, the team, and the organisation. In this chapter we have argued that practitioners, in their efforts to be of service for youth athletes, should widen their focus, look beyond the psychological skills of the individual athletes, and include the optimisation of a team's or club's organisational culture in their mission. Based on the holistic ecological approach to talent development in sport (Henriksen et al., 2010a), we have argued that a team's organisational culture influences young athletes, or in popular terms that the characteristics of culture become the character of the developing athletes. We have further argued that the coach plays a vital part in creating and maintaining a team's organisational culture. For these reasons we have finally argued that the practitioner should aim to make coaches more aware of their role as cultural leaders when working with young (and senior) athletes.

A typical curriculum-based workshop intervention can make it difficult for young athletes to transfer acquired skills from the classroom to the training pitch. In contrast, improving young athletes' psychological skills through the coach's cultural leadership and the team's organisational culture is more likely to produce a long-term change in the way athletes approach their training and competitions. We realise such a shift is not easy. It requires educational institutions to include a stronger focus on organisational and cultural psychology in their programs. It requires practitioners to broaden their understanding of their own role. And it requires that coaches and managers take more responsibility for development of the athletes' psychological skills and see practitioners not only as service providers for their athletes, but also as important sparring partners for themselves. Nevertheless, based on our experience and the scientific literature, such efforts can have substantial impacts on the lives of young athletes.

Note

1 Throughout the chapter we present cases. The cases are based on the applied experiences of the first and last author. However, to protect the identity of teams and athletes, the cases are contructed, often drawing on more than one real-life experience. The term 'I' is used throughout the chapter in reference to the individual consultant conducting the work.

References

Henriksen, K. (2010). *The ecology of talent development in sport: A multiple case study of successful athletic talent development environments in Scandinavia* (Unpublished doctoral thesis). Institute of Sport Science and Clinical Biomechanics, University of Southern Denmark, Denmark.

Henriksen, K. (2015) Developing a high-performance culture: A sport psychology intervention from an ecological perspective in elite orienteering. *Journal of Sport Psychology in Action, 6,* 141–153.

Henriksen, K., Larsen, C. H., & Christensen, M. K. (2014). Looking at success from its opposite pole: The case of a talent development golf environment in Denmark. *International Journal of Sport and Exercise Psychology, 12,* 134–149.

Henriksen, K., Stambulova, N., & Roessler, K. K. (2010a). A holistic approach to athletic talent development environments: A successful sailing milieu. *Psychology of Sport and Exercise, 11,* 212–222.

Henriksen, K., Stambulova, N., & Roessler, K. K. (2010b). Successful talent development in track and field: Considering the role of environment. *Scandinavian Journal of Medicine & Science in Sports, 20,* 122–132.

Henriksen, K., Stambulova, N., & Roessler, K. K. (2011). Riding the wave of an expert: A successful talent development environment in kayaking. *The Sport Psychologist, 25,* 341–362.

Larsen, C. H., Alfermann, D., Henriksen, K., & Christensen, M. K., (2013). Successful talent development in soccer: The characteristics of the environment. *Sport, Exercise and Performance Psychology, 13,* 190–206.

Lewin, K. (1947). Frontiers in group dynamics: Concept, method and reality in social science; social equilibria and social change. *Human Relations, 1,* 5–41.

Martindale, R. J. J., & Mortimer, P. (2011). Talent development environments: Key considerations for effective practice. In D. Collins, A. Button, & H. Richards (Eds.), *Performance Psychology: A Practitioner's Guide* (pp. 65–84). Edinburgh, UK: Elsevier.

McGannon, K. R., & Johnson, C. R. (2009). Strategies for reflective cultural sport psychology research. In R. J. Schinke & S. J. Hanrahan (Eds.), *Cultural Sport Psychology* (pp. 57–75). Champaign, IL: Human Kinetics.

Schein, E. H. (1990). Organisational culture. *American Psychologist, 45,* 109–119.

Schein, E. H. (2010). *Organisational Culture and Leadership.* Hoboken, NJ: John Wiley & Sons.

Schinke, R., McGannon, K., Parham, W., & Lane, A. M. (2012). Toward cultural praxis and cultural sensitivity: Strategies for self-reflexive sport psychology practice. *Quest, 64,* 34–46.

Storm, L. K. (2015). *'Coloured by culture': Talent development in Scandinavian elite sport as seen from a cultural perspective* (Unpublished doctoral dissertation). Institute of Sport Science and Clinical Biomechanics, University of Southern Denmark, Denmark.

SECTION IV
Working with young athletes

21

KEY CONSIDERATIONS FOR APPLIED SERVICES WITH YOUNG ATHLETES

Brandonn S. Harris, Lindsey C. Blom, and Amanda J. Visek

Given their ongoing physical, emotional, psychological, and social development, working with young athletes requires approaches and adaptations to service delivery that are different to those provided to adults. But, how does one provide meaningful, effective sport psychology services to children and adolescents? In our early work, answering this question was difficult. There was a void in the literature when it came to addressing the unique aspects of providing sport psychology services to children and adolescents. Based on our experiences, along with the scholarly work of our colleagues, we saw this as an opportunity to fill a significant gap in the extant literature and provide novel and seasoned practitioners with the tools to effectively navigate and work with young athletes.

To that end, we developed the Youth Sport Consulting Model (YSCM; Visek, Harris, & Blom, 2009), an educational consulting framework that coalesces our applied sport psychology experiences, along with Orton's (1997) stages of group development and the work of Poczwardowski, Sherman, and Henschen (1998). The YSCM provides specific recommendations to planning, implementing, and evaluating sport psychology services using a start-to-finish approach (see Figure 21.1 and Visek et al., 2009 for a full review).

In addition to the YSCM, we recognised the practitioner's need for a robust yet easy framework for navigating the complexity of multiple relationships among a young athlete, the practitioner, coach(es), and the parent-guardians. Therefore, we developed the Youth Sport Psychology Consultation Triangle (YSPCT; Figure 21.2; Blom, Visek, & Harris, 2013), a family-systems adaptation of Wylleman's (2000) athletic triangle that integrates the sport psychology practitioner and describes the role each dyad (i.e. coach–parent, parent–practitioner, and coach–practitioner) plays in addressing the overall wellbeing and interests of the young athlete. The YSPCT is useful for understanding the interplay of dynamic interactions and how to establish transparent working relationships based on open communication.

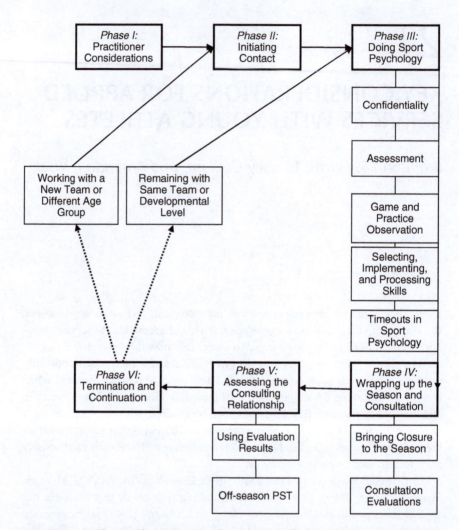

FIGURE 21.1 The Youth Sport Consulting Model (YSCM; Visek et al., 2009) is designed to assist practitioners in their sport psychology consultations with youth sport teams and participants. The YSCM begins in the upper left corner of the figure and continues sequentially clockwise. Bolded blocks indicate major phases within the Youth Sport Consulting Model (YSCM); secondary blocks that appear either below or above the bolded blocks highlight important considerations within each phase. Dashed arrow lines signify bi-directional opportunities that may potentially exist for the youth sport psychology practitioner.

Source: Reprinted with permission from Visek, A. J., Harris, B. S., & Blom, L. C. (2009). Doing sport psychology: A youth sport consulting model for practitioners. *The Sport Psychologist*, *23*, 271–91.

FIGURE 21.2 The Youth Sport Psychology Consultation Triangle
Source: Reprinted with permission from Blom, L. C., Visek, A. J., & Harris, B. S. (2013). Triangulation in youth sport: Healthy partnerships among parents, coaches, and practitioners. *Journal of Sport Psychology in Action, 4,* 86–96.

Drawing on the YSCM and the YSPCT frameworks, in this chapter we address select relational, ethical, and logistical considerations that are key to providing effective services to young athletes.

Developing healthy relationships

When working with young athletes, taking the time to routinely educate parents and coaches throughout the consultation process is critically important to establishing good rapport and developing healthy working relationships (Blom et al., 2013; Lafferty & Triggs, 2014; see Chapters 26 and 27). Not doing so can create confusion, miscommunication, and unintended obstacles, thereby impeding a young athlete's progress towards achieving her or his goals. Research has shown children in counselling improve significantly when strong partnerships are formed between the parents and the child regarding the goals of treatment, and when parents are taught how to control their own emotions, communicate effectively, and reinforce the child's target behaviours (Barrett, Dadds, & Rapee, 1996).

Parental involvement

Sport psychology is a relatively young discipline and most parents are unlikely to have experienced structured, formal sport psychology work themselves (see also Chapter 27). As such, many parents are likely to be unfamiliar with the ins and outs of sport psychology. Thus, allowing their child to engage in such services could be anxiety producing. It is vital for practitioners to work to alleviate parental concerns and be transparent throughout the consulting process. Under most circumstances, parental guardians are a tangential part of the working relationship and their child athlete is the primary client.

Parental involvement can vary on a continuum from not involved at all (e.g. parent just dropping off the client or client arriving to sessions alone) to very involved (e.g. parent sitting through the entire session). It is important to discuss the advantages of different levels of involvement with both the athlete and parent(s). We recommend discussing and deciding on the best level of parental involvement very early in the consultation process, remembering legally parents often have the right to be involved in all aspects of the services provided if the client is a minor. We typically find a moderate level of involvement at the start of the relationship to be quite effective. For example, an average 50-minute appointment might be structured in the following way:

- To start, the young athlete and her mother join the practitioner for about 5–10 minutes. The practitioner reminds the athlete and mother about the goals from last week and asks the mother if she has any observations to share related to these goals. The practitioner may also ask the mother to share any other relevant information that would facilitate an effective and helpful session for her child.
- After discussion, the mother excuses herself and the practitioner and athlete work together for the next 30–40 minutes. During the last 2–5 minutes, they discuss how to summarise and debrief the session with the mother, also identifying any important things for the mother to know to help the athlete work towards her goals over the next week.
- The mother is invited to return to the session for the last 3–5 minutes for the session briefing, ideally shared by the athlete.

The involvement of the parent in the above example allows the mother to learn about the session topic and ways to help her child without distraction or interference in the active portion of the appointment.

Lafferty and Triggs (2014) developed a stage-based Working with Parents in Sport (WWPS) model as a guide to effectively sharing information with parents (stage 1) and directly or indirectly helping parents manage their own sport-related behaviours (stage 2) to support their young athlete. This model provides a complementary framework for effectively working with the young athlete's parents. Lafferty and Triggs also developed a figure summarising key issues and problems parents may experience. Although parents are not the direct client, understanding their experiences as a sport parent can help assist the practitioner in understanding a young athlete's sport experiences and how best to engage parents in their efforts to support their young athlete's goals (see Chapters 10 and 27).

By utilising the frameworks discussed thus far, parents are likely to be more supportive of their child receiving sport psychology services and in turn more likely to proactively support the young athlete's development in a healthy, positive manner (Hawley & Weisz, 2005). We recommend educating parents about the consultation process, perhaps even having a separate educational session with them at the start of the consulting relationship to delineate their role(s) in this process.

This conversation may be particularly important for those parents who may not know how engaged they should be in this experience, and/or what being engaged would consist of. Having this discussion also allows for the consultant to follow up with parents to address any future concerns or non-engagement by revisiting these ground rules or expectations given they were established early in the consultation process. Indeed, consultants can explain to parents that they too play an important role in their child's sport development by imparting practical ways parents can support their young athlete, which can also help ease any anxiety or apprehension they may have of allowing their child to receive services.

Coach involvement

Keeping with a recommended player-centered approach (e.g. Visek et al., 2009), we encourage practitioners to allow the young athlete to determine the degree of inclusion of the coach, which can range from not at all involved to sitting in on session appointments. Early on, it is important to determine the level of involvement to reduce the chance of any misunderstandings about the coach's role. It may also be helpful to remind the young athlete that the decision she or he makes is not final and can be adjusted at any time. Although it is less awkward to bring a coach into the sport psychology consultation down the road than it is to remove a coach, either is possible. Inclusion of the coach is often ideal (e.g. they can remind and help the athlete to implement psychological skill strategies during practices and competitions); however, it is not always realistic, practical, and/or helpful, depending on the circumstances (e.g. a lack of coach support for psychological skills training).

If coaches were to be involved in consultations, we would recommend a similar approach to that described above to manage parental involvement. Specifically, we would recommend a conversation with the coach at the onset of the consultation in which the amount and type of involvement would be addressed. This would help delineate the expectations for the coach, consultant, and athlete(s) so that each stakeholder's roles are defined prior to the start of service provision, making this easier to monitor and re-evaluate throughout the consultation as necessary. Ultimately, if the coach is not directly part of the consulting relationship, indirectly she or he is still an important stakeholder, profoundly influencing a child's overall sport experience (Blom et al., 2013;Visek et al., 2015). In accordance with the consultant and parent/guardian, once the young athlete makes an initial decision, the psychological skills training plan can be developed with the coach's role keenly in mind.

Ethical issues

In this section, we provide brief overviews and our best practice recommendations for attending to the main ethical issues, including gaining parental consent and athlete assent, as well as issues surrounding confidentiality. In addition, based on our experiences, we discuss ethical issues relating to making referrals and the use of technology.

Consent and assent

A critical component to providing services to young athletes involves informed consent and assent. Legally, consent from a parent or legal guardian is usually required in order for a minor to receive psychological services of any kind. Similarly, the Association for Applied Sport Psychology's ethics code, based on the American Psychological Association's ethics code, indicates that practitioners have an obligation to protect the rights and dignity of those we serve (AASP, n.d.). Obtaining a minor's assent to services supplements the parental-guardian consent process by engaging a young athlete in the decision-making process from the start. Of note, it is important to ensure the content that is included in the consent process is explained in an age- and developmentally appropriate manner for the athlete so that she or he understands assent and the components addressed within its process, such as her or his rights and confidentiality (Blom, Visek, & Harris, 2014). Please refer to Chapters 4 and 5 for a full discussion of pertinent developmental considerations.

Confidentiality

Balancing the rights and dignity of a young athlete with the legal rights of her or his parents can be challenging. Navigating this process effectively is important because confidentiality is the cornerstone of a trusting and effective therapeutic relationship (Belitz & Bailey, 2009). In so doing, we have found it helpful to discuss different degrees of confidentiality with the young athlete and her or his parent(s) prior to and/or during the consenting and assenting process to identify which approach is best for their collective needs. For example, the practitioner, parent(s), and young athlete may agree to:

1) *Complete confidentiality* – no information is disclosed to the parent(s) and/or coach without an explicit request from the athlete.
2) *Limited confidentiality* – the information to be shared is jointly agreed upon by all those involved. Limited confidentiality can also be agreed upon in which the decision to share information is left to the discretion of the practitioner.
3) *No confidentiality* – all information is freely shared with the parent(s) and even the coach with written permission. (Peterson, 2004)

In our experiences, maintaining some degree of confidentiality facilitates a more effective working relationship and helps to create a healthy, trusting, and safe environment for a young athlete to share their experiences freely. Regardless of how the practitioner, parent(s), and young athlete decide to arrange confidentiality, it is also important to discuss the limits of confidentiality as it pertains to abuse (e.g. duty to warn, harm to self or others), including legal mandates (subpoenas or mandatory reporting).

Technology

Given the rapid advances in technology, text messaging and social media are often preferred methods of communication among young people (Windham, 2008). We have noticed that our adolescent athletes will use e-mail and text messaging to provide updates on their sport performances and their progress in using sport psychology skills. Video conferencing using FaceTime, Skype, Google Hangout, and other related platforms are also useful for connecting and providing consultation from a distance. We have found connecting with our athletes using technology has strengthened our working relationships with them. Not surprisingly, research has shown that young people that communicate more regularly with schoolteachers and can text them report feeling more connected (Pollock & Amaechi, 2013). Likewise, it is common for parent(s) to provide performance updates via e-mail and text messaging and to schedule their child's appointments using these methods. Reciprocally, we respond using these same modes of communication to confirm appointments and send reminders.

Our experience with incorporating technology into sport psychology practice has proven to be useful. However, all modes of technology have limitations (e.g. varying levels of security) and risks. For example, breeches in confidentiality, despite the use of firewalls, are always possible (Bradley, Hendricks, Lock Whiting, & Parr, 2011). With various forms of social media, electronic communication, and videoconferencing available for distance consultation, it is important that practitioners only utilise those methods of technology in which they have appropriate training and competence to do so (see Standard 26 of the AASP ethics code). Such training can be accomplished through workshops and other continuing education opportunities oftentimes offered through various organisations. This ensures that those advantages associated with technology are reaped, while minimising any potential harm that could arise from their noted limitations. With each of the benefits and potential ethical concerns associated with technology use, we recommend addressing these important issues first during the consent/ assent process verbally and in written form via the consent and assent forms and again as needed.

Referral

Oftentimes, the sport psychology practitioner is one of the safest and most comfortable persons for a young athlete to talk to and explore her or his interests, needs, and challenges. Because the practitioner does not make playing time decisions, is not associated with an athlete's school or academic progress, and is a continuous advocate encouraging the athlete's parent(s) to support her or him, the relationship is seen as trusting and secure. In fact, the ability for practitioners to speak the athletes' language through sport can be a powerful tool in first establishing and sustaining a strong relationship.

However, there are times in which it will be necessary for a practitioner to make a referral because the needs of the athlete are outside the practitioner's expertise and scope of practice. If a young athlete is apprehensive or anxious about talking with and receiving services from someone else, the process of referring can be challenging. When the need for referral becomes apparent, it is important to discuss the reasons for this with the athlete as well as the parent(s) and to have an established list of recommended, local providers (e.g. school counsellors, child psychologists, sports medicine and strength and conditioning facilities, nutritionists). It is possible for a young athlete to initially have feelings of abandonment, even simply at the idea of referral. Contrastingly, it is possible that because transitions in sport are commonplace (e.g. changes in coaches, teammates, and teams), some athletes may actually cope well with referral and even the termination of sport psychology services, when it becomes appropriate. We have found it helpful and encourage practitioners to explore with the athlete the benefits of support beyond the practitioner or as an adjunct to doing sport psychology. When possible, we also recommend practitioners discuss the potential for a referral or termination of services several sessions before it occurs. This can help support the athlete in preparing for and adjusting to a new service provider.

Special considerations

In this section, we highlight a few special considerations that have facilitated positive, effective sport psychology practices for us and that we have found to be helpful in developing rapport and maintaining strong partnerships with young athletes. These include practitioner characteristics that can influence athlete perceptions of effectiveness, tips for working in the field, keeping young athletes engaged in meaningful psychological skills practice between appointments, and how to discreetly collect fees for service.

Practitioner characteristics

There are known characteristics of practitioners that athletes perceive to be effective. Although the sport psychology literature in this area focuses on the perceptions of college-level athletes, in our own applied practice we extrapolate from these scholarly findings below while also drawing on the child counselling literature. For example, a practitioner with positive interpersonal skills (e.g. friendly, approachable, trustworthy, can maintain confidentiality) is consistently rated as highly preferable among athletes (Lubker, Visek, Geer, & Watson, 2008; Lubker, Visek, Watson, & Singpurwalla, 2012). Although collegiate athletes have indicated preference for working with female practitioners (Lubker et al., 2012), presumably because of their stereotyped association with empathy and compassion, the counselling research findings are mixed with respect to children. Studies have indicated preference for same sex and same ethnicity (Esters & Ledoux, 1999), while others indicate no preference for ethnicity except in cases where children are strongly identified with their culture (Bigfoot-Sipes, Dauphinais, LaFromboise, Bennett, & Rowe, 1992).

Given the sport context, athletes also regarded having knowledge of sport, including a background in sport, as particularly important. As would be expected, practitioners dressed in sport attire were perceived to have more sport knowledge (Lubker, Watson, Visek, & Geer, 2005). In cases in which the athlete first meets the practitioner, acting in ways expected of sport-related professionals and doing things such as speaking the child's sport language goes a long way towards building rapport. In fact, the counselling literature states that when an unfamiliar adult behaves in ways that a child expects, rapport is more easily established (Gurland & Grolnick, 2003). An important component to developing a positive relationship also includes honouring a young athlete's autonomy and supporting her or his choices (Gurland & Grolnick, 2003). One way for practitioners to do this and determine the athlete's needs and goals is through informal and formal means of assessment. For more information on the assessment of young athletes' needs and developing a psychological skills training programme based on these assessments, we refer readers to Chapter 6, as well as to Harris, Blom, and Visek's (2013) applied practice paper on using assessment in youth athletics.

Field work

With some young athletes, there will be opportunities to observe them during practice and competition and/or to hold sport psychology sessions directly on the field in the athlete's sport environment. These situations present a unique opportunity for the practitioner to get a first-hand account of how a young athlete performs and copes behaviourally. Practitioners doing work in the field often grapple with deciding what kind of clothing is appropriate in out-of-office sport settings, where to position themselves in the sport environment, and how to be present without drawing inappropriate attention or interfering with the sport activities taking place. In our experience, being inconspicuous and blending into the spectating audience is often most appropriate when we are simply observing a young athlete practice or compete. When we will be intentionally interacting with a young athlete, we will position ourselves in a place that facilitates communication while also causing the least amount of disruption to the normal structure of practices and competitions. When deciding the clothing most appropriate for these settings, we typically wear casual, comfortable sport attire similar to that of a coach.

An additional consideration involving ethical implications includes the potential for others to draw conclusions about the existence of a professional, working relationship between the consultant and youth athlete. Being present at practices or competitions, along with any observable communication between the practitioner and athlete-client, could lead others to inquire about or assume the presence of a consulting relationship. This potential threat to confidentiality should be addressed with the young athlete and their parents before engaging in field work to ensure all stakeholders are aware of this potential outcome, as well as discussing agreed upon ways to manage this when in public.

Assigning sport psychology homework

When young athletes are learning new skills, informing them of the need to practise what they are learning is helpful towards acquiring and mastering new psychological skills. For example, providing them with a handout along with an interactive worksheet or journal log to complete can be a useful step towards semi-structured practice of the skills outside of sport psychology appointments. In non-sport settings, activities like these were more efficiently used when the child was highly motivated to achieve her or his goals, was aware of the benefits of the assignment, and when parent(s) encouraged completion of the activity (Houlding, Schmidt, & Walker, 2010).

Activities like this could be viewed by the young athlete as a varying form of homework, which can have a negative connotation for many children. In our work, we have found reframing homework-related activity as 'challenges' increases the likelihood it will be completed. Encouraging the use of Android and iOS applications (apps) on smart phones and tablets is an interactive approach for young athletes to practise their sport psychology skills. For example, apps provide a convenient and engaging method for young athletes to journal about their sport experiences (e.g. Thought Diary Pro, iCBT), record notes from practices and competitions to share with the practitioner at a follow-up session, and to acquire and reinforce new psychological skills (e.g. Calm.com, Headspace, iPerformance, Focus to Win, iPeakCoach, GetPsyched).

Practitioners should be aware that a young athlete's age could influence whether she or he completes assigned sport psychology challenges. Specifically, adolescents in non-sport settings have demonstrated low completion of homework-related activities (Houlding et al., 2010), presumably because there is less adult oversight of such activities during the teenage years. That said, sport psychology challenges are more likely to be of interest to a young athlete given their sport relevance; therefore, completion may not be as challenging to achieve particularly when using state-of-the-art technology with parental approval and support.

Service fees

Providing sport psychology services for young athletes can range from being a service-oriented professional activity (e.g. academia) usually offered at gratis to a profitable fee-for-service (e.g. private practice). Our experiences include providing pro bono and for-profit services. Our for-profit fees vary considerably based on comparable hourly rates consistent with our city's cost of living. When needed, we will use a sliding scale to make services more accessible, taking into consideration factors such as a family's financial means, competition level of a young athlete, and other sport-related training costs (e.g. speciality coaching, distance travelling for sport psychology services). We discreetly collect payment for services from the parent or guardian at the end of the appointment once the athlete has exited the room to avoid any undue awkwardness that could result from an exchange of money in the young athlete's presence. For us, online money transfer systems such as PayPal or placing a box by the door for payments have proven helpful.

Conclusion

Providing services to young athletes is a growing area of applied practice. Doing so effectively requires developmentally, age-appropriate adaptations for athletes to develop the psychological skills needed for enhancing their sport performance and wellbeing. Acquiring these skills early in life benefits young athletes socially and interpersonally within their sport experiences, as well as in a more holistic manner in other life domains (e.g. family and social interactions, academics, extracurricular activities); this may likely even track into their adolescence and adult lives. Moreover, athletes who have had early, positive experiences are more likely to seek services later, when needed, and experience fewer obstacles (e.g. stigma) in doing so (Wrisberg, Loberg, Simpson, Withycombe, & Redd, 2010).

References

Association of Applied Sport Psychology [AASP]. (n.d.). *Ethics code: AASP ethical principles and standards.* Retrieved from http://appliedsportpsych.org/about/ethics/code.

Barrett, P. M., Dadds, M. R., & Rapee, R. M. (1996). Family treatment of childhood anxiety: A controlled trial. *Journal of Consulting and Clinical Psychology, 64,* 333–342.

Belitz, J., & Bailey, R. A. (2009). Clinical ethics for the treatment of children and adolescents: A guide for general psychiatrists. *The Psychiatric Clinics of North America, 32,* 243–257.

BigFoot-Sipes, D. S., Dauphinais, P., LaFromboise, T. D., Bennett, S. K., & Rowe, W. (1992). American Indian secondary school students' preferences for counselors. *Journal of Multicultural Counseling and Development, 20,* 113–122.

Blom, L. C., Visek, A. J., & Harris, B. S. (2013). Triangulation in youth sport: Healthy partnerships among parents, coaches, and practitioners. *Journal of Sport Psychology in Action, 4,* 86–96.

Blom, L. C., Visek, A. J., & Harris, B. S. (2014). Ethical issues in youth sport consulting. In J. Watson & E. Etzel (Eds.), *Ethical Issues in Sport, Exercise, and Performance Psychology* (pp. 25–35). Morgantown, WV: Fitness Information Technology.

Bradley L., Hendricks, B., Lock, R., White, P., & Parr, G. (2011). E-mail communication: Issues for mental health counselors. *Journal of Mental Health Counseling, 33,* 67–79.

Esters, I. G., & Ledoux, C. L. (1999). *At-risk high school students' preferences for counselor characteristics.* Presentation at the Annual Conference of the Mid-South Educational Research Association, Point Clear, AL.

Gurland, S. T., & Grolnick, W. S. (2003). Children's expectancies and perceptions of adults: Effects on rapport. *Child Development, 74,* 1212–1224.

Harris, B. S., Blom, L. C., & Visek, A. J. (2013). Assessment in youth sport: Practical issues and best practices guidelines. *The Sport Psychologist, 27,* 201–211.

Hawley, K. M., & Weisz, J. R. (2005). Youth versus parent working alliance in usual clinical care: Distinctive associations with retention, satisfaction, and treatment outcome. *Journal of Clinical Child and Adolescent Psychology, 34,* 117–128.

Houlding, C., Schmidt, F., & Walker, D. (2010). Youth therapist strategies to enhance client homework completion. *Child and Adolescent Mental Health, 15,* 103–109.

Lafferty, M. E., & Triggs, C. (2014). The Working with Parents in Sport Model (WWPS-Model): A practical guide for practioners working with parents of elite young performers. *Journal of Sport Psychology in Action, 5,* 117–128.

Lubker, J. R., Visek, A. J., Geer, J. R., & Watson, J. C. (2008). Characteristics of an effective sport psychology consultant: Perspectives from athletes and consultants. *Journal of Sport Behavior, 31,* 147–165.

Lubker, J. R., Visek, A. J., Watson, J. C., & Singpurwalla, D. (2012). Athletes' preferred characteristics and qualifications of sport psychology practitioners: A consumer market analysis. *Journal of Applied Sport Psychology, 24,* 465–480.

Lubker, J. R., Watson, J. C., Visek, A. J., & Geer, J. R. (2005). Physical appearance and the perceived effectiveness of performance enhancement consultants. *The Sport Psychologist, 19,* 446–458.

Orton, G. L. (1997). *Strategies for Counseling Children and their Parents.* Pacific Grove, CA: Brooks/Cole.

Peterson, J. (2004). The individual counseling process. In A. Vernon (Ed.), *Counseling Children and Adolescents* (pp. 35–74). Denver, CO: Love.

Poczwardowski, A., Sherman, C. P., & Henschen, K. P. (1998). A sport psychology service delivery heuristic: Building on theory and practice. *The Sport Psychologist, 12,* 191–207.

Pollock, M., & Amaechi, U. (2013). Texting as a channel for personalised youth support: Participatory design research by city youth and teachers. *Learning, Media, and Technology, 38,* 128–144.

Visek, A. J., Achrati, S. M., Mannix, H. M., McDonnell, K., Harris, B. S., & DiPietro, L. (2015). The fun integration theory: Toward sustaining children and adolescents' sport participation. *Journal of Physical Activity and Health, 12,* 424–433.

Visek, A. J., Harris, B. S., & Blom, L. C. (2009). Doing sport psychology: A youth sport consulting model for practitioners. *The Sport Psychologist, 23,* 271–291.

Windham, R. C. (2008). The changing landscape of adolescent Internet communication and its relationship to psychosocial adjustment and academic performance. *Dissertation Abstracts International: Section B: The Sciences and Engineering, 68,* 8449.

Wrisberg, C. A., Loberg, L. A., Simpson, D., Withycombe, J. L., & Redd, A. (2010). An exploratory investigation of NCAA Division-I coaches' support of sport psychology consultants and willingness to seek mental training services. *The Sport Psychologist, 24,* 489–503.

Wylleman, P. (2000). Interpersonal relationships in sport: Uncharted territory. *International Journal of Sport Psychology, 31,* 1–18.

22

THE ROLE OF SPORT PSYCHOLOGY CONSULTANTS IN PROTECTING YOUNG ATHLETES FROM HARM

Shifting from safeguarding to an ethic of care

Gretchen Kerr, Ashley Stirling, and Ellen MacPherson

Natalie, a 10-year-old competitive artistic gymnast, stands motionless on the balance beam with tears streaming down her cheeks. She is fearful of a new skill she is attempting to learn. In her previous attempts at executing this skill, she has missed her landing and her head has come within a few inches of hitting the beam. With each unsuccessful attempt, her fear and distress intensify. Her coach is sitting nearby with full attention on Natalie and with each unsuccessful attempt the coach's frustration grows. The coach's voice becomes louder and louder and everyone else in the training facility can hear her telling Natalie, 'Don't be a baby – just do it!', and 'You're not going home until you land this.' An important competition is just a few days away and Natalie needs to perform this skill. All eyes are now on Natalie.

As the true story of Natalie illustrates, not all sport experiences are positive or growth-enhancing. Concerns about harmful experiences of young athletes in sport have been expressed for decades in the field of sport psychology. Such writings as Orlick and Botterill's *Every Kid Can Win* (1975) and Martens's (1978) *Joy and Sadness in Children's Sport* highlighted the potentially harmful experiences created for young athletes because of the over-emphasis adults place on outcome measures of performance and winning. Since that time, there has been a proliferation of scholarly work on harmful experiences, including overuse injuries, excessive stress, and burnout (Harris & Watson, 2014; Merkel, 2013), and sexual and emotional abuse (Alexander, Stafford, & Lewis, 2011; Hartill, 2013; Pinheiro et al., 2014), among other concerns. Sport psychologists can play a critical role in helping to minimise harmful experiences, while increasing positive ones.

Within sport psychology research, the voices of athletes who have had harmful sport experiences have been overshadowed by the dominant discourse of sport as inherently good (Brackenridge & Fasting, 2002; David, 2004), and references to the developmental benefits – physically, psychologically, and socially – of sport participation for young people (Janssen & LeBlanc, 2010). Although many young athletes do indeed experience benefits from their sport participation, the documented cases of athlete maltreatment and the growing body of scholarly work in this area cannot be ignored. An awareness of such work is an important starting point for all individuals, particularly psychologists, working in the field of youth sport.

Athlete maltreatment

In the early 1990s, coinciding with several media cases of sexual harm of high-profile athletes at the hands of their coaches, researchers highlighted experiences of sexual abuse and harassment in the coach–athlete relationship (Brackenridge, 2001). Subsequent attention was devoted to experiences of emotional and physical harm in the coach–athlete relationship, including reports of athletes being the recipients of hurtful, demeaning, or humiliating comments, intentional denial of attention and support, and the use of exercise as punishment (Stirling & Kerr, 2014; Kerr et al., 2016). Other forms of athlete maltreatment that occur in sport, but have received less scholarly attention, include athletes' experiences of bullying (Shannon, 2013), corruption/exploitation (Nassif, 2014), neglect, and institutional maltreatment (Stirling, 2009).

In addition to the growing attention on the issue of athlete maltreatment among the academic community, interest in the protection of children has been expressed and endorsed globally (with the exception of Somalia and the US) with the United Nations Convention on the Rights of the Child (1989). This Convention outlines the fundamental rights of children, including the right to be protected from economic exploitation and harmful work, all forms of sexual exploitation and abuse, and physical or mental violence. Internationally, sport organisations have responded with various safeguarding or child protection measures. With respect to children, specifically, the National Society for the Prevention of Cruelty to Children in the UK (2016) describes safeguarding as: protecting children from abuse and maltreatment; preventing harm to children's health or development; ensuring children grow up with the provision of safe and effective care; taking action to enable all children and young people to have the best outcomes. Among other organisations, the term child protection is more commonly used; UNICEF, for example, uses the term child protection to refer to preventing and responding to violence, exploitation, and abuse against children (The United Nations Children's Fund, 2006).

Within the sport context, policies and educational initiatives to promote safeguarding or child protection have been developed and implemented internationally. The efficacy of these measures, however, has been called into question. A recent analysis of some of the educational initiatives indicates that important constructs such as sexual, emotional, and physical abuse are defined differently across initiatives and differently from the empirical literature in the area. Without a grounding in the theoretical and empirical scholarly work, these well-meaning initiatives lack practical relevance and significance (Kerr, Stirling, & MacPherson, 2014). Further, a recent study of Canadian child protection in sport policies indicated that numerous sport governing bodies are failing to meet national safeguarding requirements (Donnelly, Kerr, Heron, & DiCarlo, 2016). Sport psychology consultants may play important roles in working with the organisations within which they are embedded, to strengthen their safeguarding policies and help to ensure their implementation.

Despite the growth of safeguarding/child protection policies, advocacy and education programmes, and coaching codes of conduct designed to protect athletes from harm, maltreatment of young athletes continues and sport organisations do not always comply with their duty to report concerns. The recent case of USA Gymnastics failing to investigate and/or report complaints about coaches sexually abusing athletes is one of many examples (Victor, 2016). In 2013, Rutgers's coach Mike Rice (Gleeson, 2013) and Oakland University's coach Beckie Francis (Jesse, 2013) were fired for emotionally abusing athletes. Taken together, the ongoing occurrences of athlete maltreatment and research evidence demonstrating the problematic nature of existing policies suggest that a different approach to preventing harm and optimising the quality of sport experiences for young people is needed.

In this chapter, we argue that sport psychologists should adopt an approach that prioritises the optimisation of the healthy development and wellbeing of young athletes. More specifically, it is our supposition that the adoption of an ethic of care perspective and the creation of caring communities by sport psychology consultants is the best way to prevent athlete maltreatment, to optimise holistic growth in young athletes, and to enhance performance.

Ethic of care

An ethic of care is a theory that emerged from the work of feminists in the 1980s (Noddings, 2005) and is based upon a relational view of individuals. This relational view holds that we are social beings with needs for dependency and interdependency (Diller, 1988); further, it assumes that our identities and individual responsibilities emerge through relationships (Held, 2006). As Noddings (2012) writes, 'Every human life starts in relation, and it is through relations that a human individual emerges' (p. 771). The starting point for discussion in care ethics is the relation rather than the individual or the collective (Buber, 1965) and as Tronto (2010) writes, our need for care challenges the notion of human beings as autonomous and independent.

Care theorists (Gilligan, 1982; Noddings, 2005) view relationships as webs of connection and interconnection rather than the more traditional view of relationships as structures of power and inequality. And yet, there is recognition that some relationships, such as that between a coach and athlete or between a sport psychologist and athlete, are characterised by inherent power imbalances; care theorists argue, however, that power, inequality, and interconnection can occur simultaneously in relationships:

> ...the vision that self and other will be treated as of equal worth, that despite differences in power, things will be fair; the vision that everyone will be responded to and included, that no one will be left alone or hurt. These disparate visions in their tension reflect the paradoxical truths of human experience – that we know ourselves as separate insofar as we live in connection with others, and that we experience relationship insofar as we differentiate other from self.
>
> *(Gilligan, 1982, p. 63)*

Since this theory was introduced, it has been applied widely to such fields as healthcare, education, law, psychology, business, political science, and international relations (Held, 2006; Noddings, 2005), and it is fitting to consider it in reference to the work of sport psychologists. Given the roles and responsibilities that sport psychologists play with respect to the health, growth and development, and welfare of young athletes, care should form the foundation and compass for their practices.

Caring has been referred to as a 'way of being in a relationship' (Noddings, 1992, p. 17) that fosters self-realisation, growth, development, protection, empowerment, and possibility (Jones, 2009; Noddings, 1996). Moreover, caring about someone differs substantially from caring for someone; caring for young people denotes a deeper level of involvement, engagement, and commitment to the young person's welfare and development (Armour & Jones, 1998). As Owens and Ennis (2005) posit, 'Caring about connotes a more global generality and objectification of the one receiving care, as opposed to caring for, which implies a recognition and relationality with the one receiving care' (p. 404). The purpose of the carer's work is to understand what the cared-for is experiencing and to hear and understand the needs expressed (Owens & Ennis, 2005).

Although it may be tempting to view caring for as similar to empathy, there are important differences between these two constructs; specifically, care is other-oriented whereas empathy is self-oriented. With empathy, there is an inclination to assume we know what and how the other person is feeling and, in this way, empathy is self-referencing; it also does not appropriately consider the idiosyncratic nature of experiences. Caring for, on the other hand, involves attending to the needs and interests of the other, trying to understand her or his perspectives and experiences by listening, sympathising, and accepting the cared-for as s/he is (Noddings, 2012). To highlight the differences between empathising with and caring for someone, please see Box 22.1.

We propose that an ethic of care builds upon and extends beyond a safeguarding approach in sport to reducing incidents of harm by having the adult in a position of responsibility understand the needs (e.g. physical, psychological, social) and interests of the young athlete and to commit efforts to optimising the young person's welfare and development. As a result of such an approach, safeguarding and protection

---

BOX 22.1 AN EXAMPLE OF EMPATHY VERSUS 'CARING FOR'

A sport psychologist is working with a young football (soccer in North America) goalie who has just had a dismal performance in an important game. The player allowed in several 'easy' shots which contributed significantly to the team's loss. This young athlete is feeling publically embarrassed, extremely disappointed in his performance, and is now questioning his overall athletic abilities.

An empathic approach

A sport psychologist using an empathic approach may show understanding and support by placing his or her arm around the athlete's shoulders and offering such comments as 'it's okay, you'll feel better tomorrow', 'every athlete has had this kind of experience before', or 'don't worry, in time we'll talk about what went wrong and what can be done the next time to have a better performance'. While attending to the athlete's feelings, the desired outcome of the sport psychologist's interaction is to understand the causes of the athlete's poor performance and to develop a plan to address these causes in the next game.

A 'caring for' approach

A sport psychologist using a caring for approach would focus on understanding the athlete's experiences by encouraging the athlete to talk (or otherwise express) their thoughts and feelings about the game and his performance. Rather than assuming a problem-solving and planning focus to the work, the sport psychologist would follow the direction of the athlete's preferences. For example, the athlete may reveal that he dislikes the game itself and is playing only because his father, who was a very successful football player, insisted he play. With a caring for approach, the sport psychologist would then help to enable the athlete to convey his feelings to his parent rather than trying to help improve his football performance.

---

from harm becomes a by-product of the relationship rather than the primary focus; in other words, if the sport psychologist focuses on *caring for* the young athlete, safeguarding will not necessarily rely on separate policies, procedures, or actions but, rather, will occur automatically as part of caring. Table 22.1 compares safeguarding and ethic of care approaches.

TABLE 22.1 Distinguishing characteristics of safeguarding and ethic of care approaches

Characteristics	Safeguarding	Ethic of Care
Purpose	• Protection from harm	• Self-actualisation of young person and optimisation of holistic potentials
Power Relation	• Adult is in a position of power and authority and the relationship is hierarchical	• Adult is in a position of power and authority and relationship is cooperative and collaborative
Nature of Approach	• Reactive: concern for the young person's wellbeing is motivated by instances of harm or the potential for harm	• Proactive: concern for the young person's wellbeing and safety is ongoing, within and outside of instances of harm
Emphases of Approach	• Prevention of harm to young people and intervention when harm occurs • Educate about characteristics of maltreatment (harassment, abuse, bullying, etc.), how to recognise, report, and address concerns or complaints • Focus on 'What not to do' and 'How to deal with a problem once it emerges'	• Promotion of care for young person • Focus on 'How to promote optimal development, health, and wellbeing' • Values input from athlete and dialogue about the ways in which personal needs are/are not being met • Anticipate potential issues/ obstacles to creating and sustaining a positive environment where the needs of young people are met proactively • Address potential issues with stakeholders and create solutions
Central Guiding Principle	• Concern for the young person motivates adults to protect them from harm	• Concern for the young person is an end in itself

Box 22.2 highlights the differences between a safeguarding and an ethic of care approach using the case study of Natalie that was presented at the beginning of this chapter.

Noddings (2012) argues that an ethic of care should be at the core of all educational practices. We extend Nodding's argument by proposing that such an approach should also be central to the work of those who engage with young people in sport, including coaches and sport psychology consultants. Further, the ability to care cannot be assumed to be inherent; instead, *caring for* is a skill set to be nurtured and taught. Indeed, almost all teachers, coaches, and sport psychology consultants would say they *care about* the young people with whom they work; however, as others have

BOX 22.2 AN EXAMPLE OF SAFEGUARDING VERSUS AN ETHIC OF CARE APPROACH

A safeguarding approach

In the case of Natalie outlined at the beginning of this chapter, a safeguarding approach would involve the sport psychologist playing a role in educating stakeholders – the coach in this case – that psychological and social harm is occurring and that the potential for physical harm exists should Natalie continue to practise under such distress, especially as she has come close to hitting her head in previous attempts at the skill. To protect Natalie from further harm, the sport psychologist could discourage the coach from using such demanding coaching practices and, importantly, could advise the coach on alternative, healthier coaching or pedagogical strategies by which to facilitate Natalie's skill acquisition.

An ethic of care approach

If the sport psychologist had encouraged Natalie's coach to adopt an ethic of care approach, the described scenario would have been prevented. By caring for Natalie and attending to her holistic health and development, the coach would have ascertained that she was not technically, physically, or psychologically ready to perform the skill. Sport psychologists should play a valuable role in facilitating a dialogue between the coach and Natalie about her thoughts and feelings about the skill to better understand the root of the problem; together they would then develop strategies for addressing the barriers to her progress.

highlighted (Owens & Ennis, 2005), there may not be a deep understanding of what *caring for* means and how *caring for* may be operationalised. The following section addresses ways in which sport psychologists may demonstrate *caring for* athletes and facilitate this approach amongst other stakeholders in youth sport.

Providing sport psychology support to young athletes based upon an ethic of care approach

We contend that sport psychologists are uniquely positioned to embody and promote an ethic of care approach given their professional responsibility for the well-being of young athletes. As stated in the AASP (Association for Applied Sport Psychology) ethics code, 'AASP members seek to contribute to the welfare of those with whom they interact professionally … and to perform those roles in a

TABLE 22.2 Working as a sport psychologist within an ethic of care approach

	Goal of Sport Psychologist's Work	Nature of Sport Psychologist's Work
Pre-Season	Educate Stakeholders (athletes, coaches, and parents) about the Purpose of Sport for Young People	• Purpose of sport for young people is participation, enjoyment, development of physical skills/fitness, and life skills • Performance is a by-product of participation, enjoyment, and development focus (and not the main focus)

	Establish Awareness of Roles and Responsibilities	• Roles and responsibilities of adults in sport are to form a web of support to care for young athletes:
		  – Seek to understand their perspectives, see the world through their eyes
		  – Acknowledge, accept, and value athletes' feelings
		  – Focus on needs of young people
		  – View sport as a learning environment for teamwork, collaboration, decision-making, etc. and be explicit about the ways in which these skills are helpful in other environments
		  – Maintain long-term view, e.g. how will the child's experiences today affect him/her in the longer term?

During Season	Monitor and Reinforce a *Caring for* Community amongst Stakeholders	• Assess nature of athletes' sport experiences throughout the season:
		  – In-person meetings
		  – Anonymous online opportunities
		• Teaching of mental skills for purposes of enjoyment, performance, and holistic development with explicit links to other applications (e.g. school)
		• Regular meetings with parents and coaches to reinforce purpose of sport, ethic of care approach, and address athletes' holistic development
		• Facilitate collaboration between parents, coaches, and sport administrators to promote a caring community
		• Reinforce messages through posters in training facility, newsletters, and blogs

	Intervene when the Ethic of Care Approach is Slipping	• Assume responsibility for intervening when others are demonstrating behaviours incongruent with an ethic of care approach • Teach others when and how to intervene

TABLE 22.2 *(cont.)*

	Goal of Sport Psychologist's Work	*Nature of Sport Psychologist's Work*
Post-Season	Evaluate the Season from an Ethic of Care Lens	• Assess athletes' enjoyment levels of previous season • Assess athletes' sense of being cared for within the sport environment • Assess athletes' intentions to continue sport participation • Assess development of athletes' life skills • Assess coaches' and parents' satisfaction with the season and the athletes' personal and athletic development
	Plan for Subsequent Season	• Maintain aspects appraised as strengths, improve weaknesses, and actualise opportunities for growth
	Celebrate Ethic of Care Successes	• Ensure regularly scheduled events that publicly recognise those who demonstrate the values associated with sport for young people

responsible fashion that avoids or minimises harm' (Whelan, 1996). Additionally, as many sport psychology consultants have access and presumably have established trust and rapport with the young athletes with whom they work, they are well positioned to demonstrate an ethic of care approach. As sport psychologists are, or at least should be, less invested in performance outcomes than coaches and parents of young athletes, they are better able to reinforce the purpose of more holistic development of young athletes. And finally, their access to other stakeholders in sport, including coaches, parents, and administrators, may provide valuable opportunities through which to educate about an ethic of care approach and to create a caring community *for* the athlete.

Aspects of caring about and caring for behaviours have been addressed in various forms in sport psychology literature. Orlick and McCaffrey (1991) argued that sport psychology work with children requires a special focus in part because children 'want to know that you care before they care what you know' (p. 34). Hellison (2000) highlighted the significance of contact with a caring adult for the success of children's physical activity programmes. Similarly, Petitpas, Cornelius, Van Raalte, & Jones (2005) identified genuine care for children as an essential ingredient for effective youth sport programmes. Caring may also be inferred from Jowett's (2007) 3 + 1 Cs – closeness, commitment, complementarity, and co-orientation – model of effective coach–athlete relationships. Much has been written in the sport literature about Positive Youth Development (PYD) based upon Lerner et al.'s model (Jones, Dunn, Holt, Sullivan, & Bloom, 2011), which includes caring in addition to competence, confidence, connection, and character. Several authors have also cited the centrality of being supported within a caring community for positive psychosocial development to occur (e.g. Perkins, 1997).

So, how might sport psychology consultants demonstrate an ethic of care in their work and how might they promote a community of care for young athletes? Table 22.2 illustrates some examples.

The sport psychologist who advocates the approaches suggested in Table 22.2 will inevitably face challenges, stemming primarily from the pervasive focus on performance outcomes – or winning – in youth sport. The negative consequences of over-zealous parents and 'win-at-all-costs' approaches to coaching have been well documented and extend into accounts of athlete maltreatment (David, 2004). Even the bulk of the existing literature within sport psychology focuses on mental training skills for the purpose of performance enhancement. It will therefore be no small task for sport psychologists to encourage parents, coaches, athletes, and sport administrators to focus on and adhere to the goals of sport participation, enjoyment, and holistic development for young athletes. Importantly, however, these goals do not negate an interest in performance. Instead, as indicated by the education literature (Agne, 1992), when young people feel cared for, they are more likely to enjoy the learning experience, and with enhanced enjoyment, better performances emerge. In this way, performance enhancement becomes a consequence of caring rather than the central focus.

Conclusion

For young people to experience the potential enjoyment and developmental benefits that sport can offer, they must be protected from maltreatment. Although many sport organisations have attempted to prevent harmful experiences through safeguarding measures, we suggest these do not go far enough in realising athletes' optimal growth and development as athletes and individuals. Instead, we posit that an ethic of care approach and the building of caring communities for young athletes would enhance the likelihood that sport serves as a vehicle through which holistic growth and development may occur; further, with such an approach, safeguarding and protection from harm become by-products of the experience. With an ethic of care approach, caring for the young athlete is the priority for the sport psychology consultant and is an end in itself. The sport psychology consultant, with professional responsibilities for the wellbeing of young athletes and access to athletes, coaches, parents, and administrators, is uniquely positioned to build a community of care in which all adults focus on contributing to and supporting the personal growth of young people in sport.

References

Agne, K. (1992). Caring: The expert teacher's edge. *Educational Horizons, 70,* 120–124.

Alexander, K., Stafford, A., & Lewis, R. (2011). *The experiences of children participating in organized sport in the UK.* The University of Edinburgh/NSPCC Child Protection Research Unit.

Armour, K. M., & Jones, R. L. (1998). *Physical Education Teachers' Lives and Careers: PE, Sport, and Educational Status.* London: Falmer Press.

Brackenridge, C. H. (2001). *Spoilsports: Understanding and Preventing Sexual Exploitation in Sport.* Abingdon, UK: Routledge.

Brackenridge, C., & Fasting, K. (2002). *Sexual Harassment and Abuse in Sport: International Research and Policy Perspectives.* London: Whiting & Birch.

Buber, M. (1965). *Between Man and Woman.* New York, NY: Macmillan.

David, P. (2004). *Human Rights in Youth Sport: A Critical Review of Children's Rights in Competitive Sport.* Abingdon, UK: Routledge.

Diller, A. (1988). The ethics of care and education: A new paradigm, its critics, and its educational significance. *Curriculum Inquiry, 18,* 325–342.

Donnelly, P., Kerr, G., Heron, A., & DiCarlo, D. (2016). Protecting youth in sport: An examination of harassment policies. *International Journal of Sport Policy and Politics, 8,* 33–50.

Gilligan, C. (1982). *In a Different Voice.* Cambridge, MA: Harvard University Press.

Gleeson, S. (2013). *Rutgers fires coach Mike Rice.* USA Today. Retrieved from www.usatoday. com/story/sports/ncaab/2013/04/03/amid-abuse-backlash-rutgers-fires-coach-mike-rice/2048903/.

Harris, B. S., & Watson, J. C. (2014). Developmental considerations in youth athlete burnout: A model for youth sport participants. *Journal of Clinical Sport Psychology, 8,* 1–18.

Hartill, M. (2013). Concealment of child sexual abuse in sports. *Quest, 65,* 241–254.

Held, V. (2006). *The Ethics of Care: Personal, Political, and Global.* New York, NY: Oxford University Press.

Hellison, D. (2000). Physical activity programs for underserved youth. *Journal of Science and Medicine in Sport, 3,* 238–242.

Janssen, I., & LeBlanc, A. (2010). Systematic review of the health benefits of physical activity and fitness in school aged children and youth. *International Journal of Behavioral Nutrition and Physical Activity, 7,* 1–16.

Jesse, D. (2013). *Oakland says Beckie Francis fired for mentally abusing players. USA Today.* Retrieved from www.usatoday.com/story/sports/ncaaw/2013/11/11/oakland-says-womens-basketball-coach-beckie-francis-fired-for-mentally-abusing-players/3497569/.

Jones, M. I., Dunn, J. G., Holt, N. L., Sullivan, P. J., & Bloom, G. A. (2011). Exploring the '5Cs' of positive youth development in sport. *Journal of Sport Behavior, 34,* 250–267.

Jones, R. L. (2009). Coaching as caring (the smiling gallery): Accessing hidden knowledge. *Physical Education and Sport Pedagogy, 14,* 377–390.

Jowett, S. (2007). Interdependence analysis and the 3 + 1Cs in the coach-athlete relationship. In S. Jowett & D. Lavallee (Eds.), *Social Psychology in Sport* (pp. 15–27). Champaign, IL: Human Kinetics.

Kerr, G., Stirling, A., & MacPherson, E. (2014). A critical examination of child protection initiatives in sport contexts. *Social Sciences, 3,* 742–757.

Kerr, G., Stirling, A., MacPherson, E., Banwell, J., Bandealy, A., & Preston, C. (2016). Exploring the use of exercise as punishment in sport. *International Journal of Coaching Science, 10*(2), 35–53.

Martens, R. (1978). *Joy and Sadness in Children's Sport.* Champaign, IL: Human Kinetics.

Merkel, D. L. (2013). Youth sport: Positive and negative impact on young athletes. *Open Access Journal of Sports Medicine, 4,* 151–160.

Nassif, N. (2014). Corruption in sport: The case of Lebanon. *Middle East Law and Governance, 6,* 123–140.

National Society for the Prevention of Cruelty to Children. (2016). *Safeguarding children: What organisations need to do to protect children from harm.* Retrieved from www.nspcc.org.uk/preventing-abuse/safeguarding.

Noddings, N. (1992). *The Challenge to Care in Schools*. New York, NY: Teachers College Press.

Noddings, N. (1996). The cared-for. In S. Gordon, P. Benner, & N. Noddings (Eds.), *Care-Giving: Readings in Knowledge, Practice, Ethics and Politics* (pp. 21–39). Philadelphia, PA: University of Pennsylvania Press.

Noddings, N. (2005). What does it mean to educate the whole child? *Educational Leadership, 63*, 8–13.

Noddings, N. (2012). The caring relation in teaching. *Oxford Review of Education, 38*, 771–781.

Orlick, T., & Botterill, C. (1975). *Every Kid Can Win*. Chicago, IL: Nelson-Hall.

Orlick, T., & McCaffrey, N. (1991). Mental training with children for sport and life. *The Sport Psychologist, 5*, 322–334.

Owens, M., & Ennis, C. D. (2005). The ethic of care in teaching: An overview of supportive literature. *Quest, 57*, 392–425.

Perkins, D. D. (1997). The individual, the family, and social good: Personal fulfillment in times of change. *Family Relations, 46*, 458.

Petitpas, A. J., Cornelius, A. E., Van Raalte, J. L., & Jones, T. (2005). A framework for planning youth sport programs that foster psychosocial development. *The Sport Psychologist, 19*, 63–80.

Pinheiro, M. C., Pimenta, N., Resende, R., & Malcolm, D. (2014). Gymnastics and child abuse: An analysis of former international Portuguese female artistic gymnasts. *Sport, Education and Society, 19*, 435–450.

Shannon, C. S. (2013). Bullying in recreation and sport settings: Exploring risk factors, prevention efforts, and intervention strategies. *Journal of Park and Recreation Administration, 31*, 15–33.

Stirling, A. E. (2009). Definition and constituents of maltreatment in sport: Establishing a conceptual framework for research practitioners. *British Journal of Sports Medicine, 43*, 1091–1099.

Stirling, A. E., & Kerr, G. (2014). Initiating and sustaining emotional abuse in the coach-athlete relationship: An ecological transactional model of vulnerability. *Journal of Aggression, Maltreatment & Trauma, 23*, 116–125.

Tronto, J. C. (2010). Creating caring institutions: Politics, plurality, and purpose. *Ethics and Social Welfare, 4*, 158–171.

United Nations Children's Fund (2006). *Child protection information sheet: What is child protection?* Retrieved from www.unicef.org/protection/files/What_is_Child_Protection.pdf.

United Nations High Commission for Human Rights. (1989). *Convention on the rights of the child*. Retrieved from www.ohchr.org/en/professionalinterest/pages/crc.aspx.

Victor, D. (2016). U.S.A. Gymnastics failed to notify authorities of sexual abuse allegations, report says. *The New York Times*. Retrieved from www.nytimes.com/2016/08/05/sports/olympics/usa-gymnastics-sexual-abuse-coaches.html?_r=1.

Whelan, J. (1996). *Ethics code: AASP ethical principles and standards. Association for Applied Sport Psychology*. Retrieved from www.appliedsportpsych.org /about/ethics/ethics-code/.

23

USING COGNITIVE BEHAVIOURAL THERAPY TO WORK WITH AND UNDERSTAND INDIVIDUAL ATHLETES

Paul J. McCarthy

Procrustes, a Greek mythological character, owned a small estate between Athens and Eleusis. He ensnared passers-by with a lavish dinner and a special bed for the night. He claimed that all guests, no matter their size, would fit his bed exactly. His claim omitted his actions if the guest were too short or too tall for his bed – he stretched those too short and removed the excess of those too tall. A Procrustean bed, therefore, assumes a random standard we meet abidingly. Sport psychologists supporting young athletes might unwittingly shrink or stretch the world they see into prepared categories and vocabularies because of their limited awareness, knowledge, and understanding about children and adolescents. Children and adolescents share physical, social, psychological, and emotional likenesses and differences so any issues presented by young athletes harbour this layer of complexity to which no single therapeutic approach fits precisely (Stallard, 2002; Weiss, 1991; see Chapters 4 and 5). Basic and applied research from clinical, counselling, and educational psychology offers guidance here, with several reviews showing cognitive behavioural therapy (CBT) as an effective intervention to treat a child's psychological issues (Kazdin & Weisz, 1998; Roth & Fonagy, 1996).

This chapter presents cognitive behavioural methods as I applied them to sport psychology support with two young athletes. CBT focuses on relations between what we think, how we feel, and what we do. The collaborative effort between the client and me guided how we shaped, delivered, and judged our work together. A firm emphasis working from theory to practice and practice to theory meant that we could cooperate when blending my experience with each client's. I knitted these case studies with the literature from sport psychology while noticing the gaps and seeking guidance elsewhere to meet the needs of the individual. I placed the individual at the heart of our work together. We united to understand the present, step lightly into the future, and accept the uncertainty of it.

Why choose CBT for young athletes?

Sport psychology occurs in a sociocultural context of time, place, and domain (Andersen, 2009). A sport psychologist might find herself supporting two 15-year-old athletes – a tennis player and a diver – but one competes at a regional competition and another competes at the Olympics. When we familiarise ourselves with norms, traditions, and histories of performance for different sports, we can choose how best to support the young athlete. These changing circumstances and the child's stage of development ought to guide our chosen model of therapy (e.g. cognitive behavioural therapy, rational emotive behaviour therapy). When we address the concept of child development, we consider cognitive, social, emotional, and physical entities within the therapeutic alliance (see Chapters 4 and 5 for details).

CBT interventions share core features and offer several benefits for the young athlete and sport psychologist. First, a balanced, unified intervention emerges from empirically testable models rather than joining incongruent techniques. Second, the young athlete identifies goals, practises, and checks performance with the psychologist's support. Children assume a better understanding of their issues and alternative ways to think and behave. Third, CBT intervention for children is much shorter than for adults, prompting independence and self-help through each session. Fourth, CBT involves assessment, problem formulation, intervention, monitoring, and evaluation. This objective approach means the child and psychologist check and review progress regularly by comparing current performance against baseline. Fifth, because CBT deals with present issues it appeals to the practical young person to address the issue rather than speculating about its origins. Finally, the child shares, experiments, and learns actively rather than passively. The child tests thoughts, beliefs, and assumptions with alternative explanations and strategies to appraise events. In summary, the child sharing in cognitive behaviour therapy develops cognitive and behavioural skills for self-awareness, self-understanding, and self-control. She identifies self-critical, crooked thinking and through self-monitoring, learning, and experimenting replaces these unhelpful thoughts and beliefs with more balanced and helpful ones. These cognitive and behavioural skills reassure the child to meet new challenges confidently (Greenberger & Padesky, 1995; Persons, 2008; Stallard, 2002; Stallard, 2005).

The relationship heals

Saul Rosenzweig reasoned that so universal were the shared features across psychotherapies there would be only small differences between the results of different forms of psychotherapy. Rosenzweig's (1936) paper presented a quote from Alice in Wonderland, 'everyone has won, and all must have prizes', which was the Dodo bird's verdict after judging the race in which some characters who got wet ran around a racecourse until they were dry. No one thought to measure how far each had run or for how long, so when they asked who had won the Dodo could not answer without much thought; then he declared: 'Everybody has won and all must have prizes.' An examination of 100 comparative treatments (Luborsky, Singer, & Luborsky, 1975) and 17 meta-analyses of comparisons of active treatments with each other confirmed Rosenzweig's clinically based hypothesis of 1936. The Dodo bird verdict suggests that all therapies are winners because they yield similar results. As our understanding of client–practitioner relations matures, we gain a firm foothold in therapy by recognising that the way we treat the client in the relationship *is* the treatment.

The young athlete's story emerges best when the client (i.e. the young athlete) and psychologist lead where appropriate. The client leads the direction of support, as we see in client-centred therapy (Rogers, 1951); however, young clients also seek guidance and feedback, so the input of the psychologist seems critical here. In telling this story collaboratively, the client and sport psychologist describe and then explain the issues presented. The sport psychologist guides therapy to meet the client's goals. Clients draw meaning from experience and the sport psychologist integrates empirical knowledge into this construction to present the client with an understanding of her experience that is original and precise. This mix of ingredients from the client and sport psychologist coalesces to build a model for therapy. The precise weighting of theory, research, and client experience remains unknown and unknowable but we test theories that we revise from observations and clients' comments. We begin with descriptions to explain the problem in cognitive and behavioural terms. We move toward explanatory models (e.g. a theory-based understanding of how clients uphold anxious symptoms) and possibly a historical explanation of how predisposing and protective factors contribute to develop the problem. This fluidity among client experience, theory, and research suggests a sensitive, responsive, and precise therapy underpins the work of the sport psychologist, unveiling what triggers, preserves, and predisposes the client's presenting problems.

Working alongside children and adolescents to ease distress and harness resources we begin by understanding the client. It seems obvious when we work with children in sport that we view them ostensibly as children yet this view cloaks biases and misunderstandings. We need an integrated sport science perspective to understand the complexity inherent in the child. This view should recognise physical, psychological, biological, and social differences among children (see Chapters 4 and 5). A tall, strong, motivated, and mature young female golfer that enjoys her friendships within golf at 11 years of age might be able to compete against older children and appear ready to play. But her experiences in these competitions against older adolescents might stretch her psychological, emotional, and social maturity unduly. When we grasp how children experience competitive and recreational sport alongside parents, coaches, and friends of different races and genders we improve the way we support children as sport psychologists (Knight & Harwood, 2009; Weiss, 1991).

The case of Cameron

'You're so annoying – so bloody annoying.' 'How do you mean?' I enquired. 'Well, where do you want me to start? For one, you're like my dad and my coach – you want the best for me in golf. But *you* want the best for me in a different way that doesn't involve golf and I don't even want that for myself – I hate me. Why can't you let me hate myself and just help me play golf better?'

Cameron and I exchanged these lines on the final hole of a practice round before he left to compete at an international amateur competition. Cameron's father originally contacted me to help Cameron with his tuitions for his final year as an amateur golfer. His father asked me to teach Cameron how to be a better golfer; thankfully Cameron allowed me to stay long enough to learn from him. I am not sure I helped Cameron or his father in any way but they reminded me that what they were looking for they already owned.

I acted as the middle panel in this triptych between Cameron and his father. They poured their misunderstandings and misgivings through me; yet I was the obstacle in the way. Cameron's presenting issue kept revealing new layers as our relationship unfolded. He explained originally that he 'struggled to concentrate on the golf course'. On further examination and following some time watching him in practice and competition, I saw other seized up cogs in the performance machine. Cameron understood little about the normative performance standards for amateurs and professionals playing golf. For instance, he believed and expected 90 percent of his tee shots should hit the fairway even though the best world-ranking professionals failed those standards. He held similar beliefs about approach shots to the green and putting. If he were to miss the fairway with a tee shot he assumed that his opportunity to make par or birdie evaporated. He typically responded angrily towards himself with a verbal diatribe and slamming his club back into his bag. He considered golf as a series of dependent rather than independent events, so whatever happened on one shot carried over to the next shot. The effects of his cognitive distortions and shortfalls, unhelpful emotions, and disruptive behaviour multiplied as rounds unfolded.

Together we identified predisposing factors and precipitating events. Briefly, Cameron's early experiences in golf comprised much harsh and critical feedback from his father. His core beliefs were that he was incapable and unlovable. He assumed he could protect himself from the pain of rejection by not letting people get close. He also assumed that people only accept you if you do not make mistakes. His compensatory strategies included distancing himself from others and externalising mistakes. There were also critical incidents in his golf career where he lost in the national final of two match play events.

We began our work together through formulation and psychoeducation (Persons, 2008). First, we developed a shared understanding about the interconnection between what people think, feel, and do. We noted where strong emotional change occurred and the accompanying self-critical thoughts. Cameron worsened the effects of his golf shots, focusing intensively on how the outcome did not match his perfectionistic expectations. These cognitive distortions and cognitive deficits (for example, he held few problem-solving skills) influenced his mood and behaviour. After identifying unhelpful cognitive processes, we tested and evaluated his assumptions and beliefs, which allowed him to think rationally through restructuring his assumptions and beliefs. We also attended to his core emotions, especially anger and anxiety, to explain and understand his signature expression of emotion. We monitored his affective responses on the golf course and rated the intensity of his dominant emotions and associated thoughts.

When Cameron recognised his emotional rhythm on the golf course he understood his role in preventing his aggressive outbursts. We agreed some specific goals following our work in therapy sessions. Part of the process was to reschedule events in preparation and increase those activities that allowed more pleasant emotions. To bring our work to the golf course we began with some brief exposure on practice rounds using role play, modelling, and rehearsal. Cameron often practised alongside a tour professional who modelled fitting behaviour. Reinforcement and reward were absent in Cameron's golf. For example, to his best recall he never reinforced himself (e.g. well done, you coped well there) and placed little stock in positive reinforcement from others unless they were touring professionals.

Steve, Cameron's father, kept abreast of our work, ensuring he frequently spoke with both Cameron and me. After six weeks working with Cameron, Steve confided that he might be lessening Cameron's progress as a golfer. He said, 'I see so much of me in Cameron, which is such a pity because I hoped he would have his mother's temperament – it's why we end up clashing so many times. I struggle to get the words to say what I feel because I'm washed in waves of strong emotions that I can't manage so I never seem to make my point. I read recently that communication is an outcome so I need to find a way to get to the outcome.'

We explored Steve's story and sought a way to communicate. Steve decided to write a letter to Cameron. Here's an excerpt from the letter:

> I'm sorry I was saying I wanted the best for you. I'm sorry because it was not true but I think you know that anyway. I wanted this for me. I wanted to be you and be amateur champion. I wanted you to win to make up for what I couldn't do. I don't know why I feel this way but I've convinced myself that I want what is best for you – I do; but I have to say that I want it for me too. Remember when you shouted at me 'You just want this to look good to your pals at the golf club.' And what did I say? I said 'that's rubbish, rubbish'. But I was lying. I think I have learned to accept my truths and my lies – I don't like what I see but I'm learning to accept them. The National Lead coach asked me if I was proud of you being on the national squad for golf. I told him what I have always thought: 'I don't need my son to play golf for me to be proud of him.'

Cameron read his father's letter sitting in the practice bay at the far end of the practice range an hour or so before our scheduled session. In my office, he sat down with the letter in his hand and I could see he had been crying. I was about to speak when he motioned me not to, so we sat in silence. After a minute or so through his tears he said:

> The time we have worked together has been so hard for me because I've been so angry – angry at everyone and myself. But I realise now that I'm angry to protect myself from what I'm really feeling. It took me ages to read the letter – I couldn't stop crying. I've been hiding how I really feel about my need to get everything right and not making mistakes and wanting to be the best. I'm tired of trying to jump over the high jump bar that no one could get over. I just thought if I could keep raising the bar I would think I was worth something. But it's silly; I realise that now. And my dad wrote that he doesn't need me to play golf for him to be proud of me. And somehow seeing it written down makes all the difference to me.

Cameron felt he needed to explain to his dad how he felt too. He thought a letter would work well. Here's an excerpt:

> I wanted you to be proud of me. I started playing golf because you love golf. I wanted to be the best at golf so you would be proud of me. But you know me; I'm so desperate to be the best I get it all out of proportion. I shout at you and blame you because I can't look at me. I'm frightened to find out that I'm not good enough. I'm scared I won't make it and then what are you going to think? All our dreams will be gone but I'll be the one who stole yours. Your letter made me realise exactly what I want. I was playing golf out of weakness, not out of strength. I know you're proud of me. It was nice to see that written down. I realise now that my weaknesses are my real strengths.

Cameron explained later that he did not know if what he had learned in our work together had helped him most or whether the letter assignment made the difference, but finding someone to trust, who did not blame, criticise, or judge him, was bizarre, yet beguiling. In his own words, he explained, 'I didn't know that someone could be this way and still help me – I had no experience of support of this kind before. Our work together helped me to ask the questions that most needed asking, even though I didn't know these questions at the beginning and I didn't feel I had the strength to answer them.'

Case formulation and intervention represent key processes in cognitive behavioural therapy. I sought a means to support Cameron and his father to communicate with meaning and permanency especially because of their struggle to express their thoughts and emotions clearly. Writing a letter offered a solution. The writing process permitted Cameron and his father to be heard accurately – to explain their experiences with freedom at their own pace. The healing powers of expressive writing are rooted in scientific research and form a guiding conduit in therapy (Pennebaker, 2004). Cameron and his father agreed that the letter-writing process meant choosing the right words to communicate lest they cause further offence.

CBT with children and adolescents

CBT therapists treat children and adolescents for anxiety disorders, pain, depression, disruptive classroom behaviours, and aggressive behaviours. This widely studied form of psychotherapy claims strong meta-analytic support for treating children and adolescents with these conditions (Hofmann, Asnaai, Vonk, Sawyer, & Fang, 2012). Randomised controlled trials targeting specific anxiety conditions, for example, reveal the efficacy of these targeted CBT protocols (Ollendick et al., 2015). Not only does this evidence encourage CBT interventions among young people in sport, but it also shows how to modify these interventions to match concepts and techniques to the developmental level of the child (Ronen, 1992). Within CBT, the client and psychologist reason about concrete rather than abstract conceptual thinking, so children within the concrete operational stage of cognitive development (around 7–12 years of age) should manage the basic tasks with clear and simple instructions (Harrington, Whittaker, Shoebridge, & Campbell, 1998; Verduyn, 2000).

Case study: Sarah – when perfect isn't good enough

Sarah, an 11-year-old gymnast, shuffled into my office behind her mum and dad. She seemed distracted and nervous. Her taciturnity was unbroken for some time, with some brief nodding of her head to accept my questions. Sarah met some opening questions with silence and her parents answered them in her stead. When her parents retired to the waiting area, Sarah began to speak solemnly, 'I used to be good at gymnastics – I'm not now. All I see is what I cannot do. I cannot figure it. I cannot figure out how I'm feeling and why I'm feeling the way I feel.' Her eyes filled and a tear careered down her cheek. That lone tear reflected the lonely feelings Sarah expressed about herself and the remorse she suffered. The gloomy feeling within the room resonated for some time and leaked into the sessions which followed that day. Over the following weeks, Sarah and I travelled together on her journey to appreciate herself, especially those disabling feelings that hung around the gymnasium when she trained. She hoped that I could help her with whatever ministrations were necessary. To understand Sarah's presenting issues, I shall begin by describing her case while recognising the precipitants of her feelings as well as what preserved her presenting issues.

Sarah's strain to perform well without mistakes weighed heavily on her. She performed faultlessly at school and expected a similar changeover to gymnastics, but more recently mistakes had crept in and her routine faultless gymnastic moves were lost in translation. Sarah's demand for perfection strained her relationship with gymnastics. Her dominant thoughts were unhelpful (e.g. I can't do anything right; I'll probably get this wrong again), and the associated emotions (e.g. anxiety, shame, and embarrassment) were disabling. I intended to create calm but fun and engaging support by translating abstract concepts into simple, concrete examples and metaphors from the child's life. For example, to explain automatic thoughts we used a metaphor of water flowing from a garden hose wherever it pleased (automatic thoughts). She could direct the flow by holding the hose or stem the flow at the tap (mediated). I explained how stress works for or against you like a bicycle tyre. With the right pressure you can cycle easily along the road; when the pressure is too low you feel sluggish and feel all the bumps. When the pressure is too high you bounce over humps and hollows and lose control.

Sarah worried about others' judgements of her performance. She held rigid beliefs about mistakes and poor competition scores. We created hypothetical situations to understand whether she could identify alternative attributions for events (Greenberger & Padesky, 1995). For example, 'Sally is playing tennis in the park with her brother. She sees her friend Sophie run past the court and shouts to say hello but Sophie does not stop.' I asked Sarah to think of as many explanations as she could for what happened. Sarah used thought records (Greenberger & Padesky, 1995) to explore the situation, moods, and automatic thoughts she experienced about gymnastics. She sifted the evidence to prove and disprove her hot thoughts with alternative or balanced thoughts to follow. We moved steadily through this process, constantly exploring the link between thoughts, feelings, and actions. Sarah valued the analogy of her mind resembling a beautiful garden with flowers, shrubs, and trees with some weeds (negative automatic thoughts) that she learned to remove (using thought records and action plans). She delighted in her dexterity to apply these skills to challenges at school and at home.

Concrete actions, like writing, helped draw the abstract concepts out of Sarah's head onto paper. Not only did Sarah enjoy writing stories but also she recognised how she authored her thoughts, feelings, and actions. I suggested to Sarah that her thought record sheets (Greenberger & Padesky, 1995) would help her to reel in the story casting around in her mind and she could choose how to deal with it. Writing offered her a sense of control and a guide for her actions. In addition to metaphor, I drew on concrete actions to express key constructs. For example, I used the expression 'words are knives' and demonstrated this point by showing Sarah how I could pass a knife safely to another person by holding the blade. She realised that I had a choice about whether I presented the handle (i.e. speaking respectfully and considerately) or the blade (i.e. speaking disrespectfully and inconsiderately). Sarah reflected, 'Words can hurt – but only if I choose to catch the blade.'

Millions of children and adolescents play sport at recreational and elite levels. The literature in sport psychology faintly traces the accompanying motives and emotions emerging from this involvement. For example, stress and anxiety receive much research focus among adult performers but much less among young athletes. But their understanding of sport experiences plants emotional responses that affect their reasons to commit to sport. We know that stress precedes burnout and dropout (Smith, 1986), while enjoyment prompts young athletes to engage and commit to sport (McCarthy, Jones, & Clark-Carter, 2008). Through this commitment they set foot on the path towards excellence (Côté, Baker, & Abernethy, 2007). A child's trail through sport leaves clues about how sport influences the child psychologically and socially. This psychosocial change also involves parents, peers, and coaches weaving many strands in a developmental fetter. This developmental perspective captures intrapersonal and social factors influencing affective and motivational patterns for the young athlete (Weiss & Bredemeier, 1983).

Reflections

Sport psychologists working with children in sport continually search for conditions for fruitful change. This journey seeks to help the child to understand herself better and offers a selection of methods to secure change. The former element presses upon the sport psychologist to gather a sensitive understanding of the developing child in sport. We then help the child to understand the present and assess whether change is possible and how this change will be realised. The child learns from the information bank of her past and then moves forward while acknowledging the uncertainty of the future. The latter element − offering a selection of methods to change − means taking one path without ever knowing what might have happened were we to choose another path.

These case studies echo the tapestry of challenges and threats children face in recreational and competitive sport. Although I focused on the psychological dimensions of the case study, I did so accounting for the sociocultural influences of the sport on the child as well as the physical, social, and emotional challenges they faced. Through education, support, and guidance, children learn to think, feel, and do better because when they change the way they think, they change the way they feel. This premise captures CBT and reminds us that it is the thought that counts. Rather than instilling this notion in children, I encourage its development.

These brief case studies allow us to glimpse at the work I did with two young athletes. The immediate and lasting struggle rests to reflect and distil this work for the reader. I scrimmage with words to express my recollection of consultancy but I am reminded of the words of Alexander Pope, 'What oft was thought, but ne'er so well express'd'. The CBT work attended to building a therapeutic relationship, developing a case formulation, developing an initial treatment plan, and establishing a permeable boundary between assessment and treatment, monitoring progress, and terminating the relationship. The structure and method of CBT helped these young athletes to cultivate a schema for our work together and adhere to the programme of support. The detail of this therapy weaves through our work inside and outside the consulting room but good therapeutic support depends heavily on honing the personal and professional skills of the psychologist. Practice with reflection and supervision brings these personal and professional skills to fulfilment.

References

Andersen, M. B. (2009). The 'canon' of psychological skills training for enhancing performance. In K. F. Hays (Ed.), *Performance Psychology in Action: A Casebook for Working with*

Athletes, Performing Artists, Business Leaders, and Professionals in High-risk Occupations (pp. 11–34). Washington, DC: American Psychological Association.

Côté, J., Baker, J., & Abernethy, B. (2007). Practice and play in the development of sport expertise. In R. Eklund & G. Tennenbaum (Eds.), *Handbook of Sport Psychology* (3rd ed., pp. 184–202). Hoboken, NJ: Wiley.

Greenberger, D., & Padesky, C. (1995). M*ind over Mood*. New York, NY: Guilford Press.

Harrington, R., Whittaker, J., Shoebridge, P., & Campbell, F. (1998). Systematic review of efficacy of cognitive behaviour therapies in childhood and adolescent depressive disorder. *British Medical Journal, 316,* 1559–1563.

Hofmann, S. G., Asnaani, A., Vonk, I. J. J., Sawyer, A. T., & Fang, A. (2012). The efficacy of cognitive behavioral therapy: A review of meta-analyses. *Cognitive Therapy Research, 36,* 427–440.

Kazdin, A. E., & Weisz, J. R. (1998). Identifying and developing empirically supported child and adolescent treatments. *Journal of Consulting and Clinical Psychology, 66,* 19–36.

Knight, C., & Harwood, C. (2009). Exploring parent-related coaching stressors in British tennis: A developmental investigation. *International Journal of Sports Science & Coaching, 4,* 545–565.

Luborsky, L., Singer, B., & Luborsky, L. (1975) Comparative studies of psychotherapies: Is it true that 'Everyone has won and all must have prizes'? *Archives of General Psychiatry, 32,* 995–1008.

McCarthy, P. J., Jones, M. V., & Clark-Carter, D. (2008). Understanding enjoyment in youth sport: A developmental perspective. *Psychology of Sport and Exercise, 9,* 142–156.

Ollendick, T. H., Halldorsdottir, T., Fraire, M. G., Austin, K. E., Noguchi, R. J., Lewis, K. M., et al. (2015). Specific phobias in youth: A randomized controlled trial comparing one-session treatment to a parent-augmented one-session treatment. *Behavior Therapy, 46,* 141–155.

Pennebaker, J. W. (2004). *Writing to Heal: A Guided Journal for Recovering from Trauma and Emotional Upheaval*. Oakland, CA: New Harbinger Press.

Persons, J. B. (2008). *The Case Formulation Approach to Cognitive Behaviour Therapy*. New York, NY: The Guilford Press.

Rogers, C. R. (1951). *Client-Centred Counselling*. Boston, MA: Houghton Mifflin.

Ronen, T. (1992). Cognitive therapy with young children. *Child Psychotherapy & Human Development, 23,* 19–30.

Rosenzweig, S. (1936). Some implicit common factors in diverse methods of psychotherapy. *American Journal of Orthopsychiatry, 6,* 412–415.

Roth, A., & Fonagy, P. (1996). *What Works for Whom: A Critical Review of Psychotherapy Research*. New York, NY: Guildford Press.

Smith, R. E. (1986). Toward a cognitive-affective model of burnout. *Journal of Sport Psychology, 8,* 36–50.

Stallard, P. (2002). *Think Good – Feel Good: A Cognitive Behaviour Therapy Workbook for Children and Young People.* Chichester, UK: Wiley.

Stallard, P. (2005). *A Clinician's Guide to Think Good – Feel Good: Using CBT with Children and Young People*. Chichester, UK: Wiley.

Verduyn, C. (2000). Cognitive behaviour therapy in childhood depression. *Child Psychology & Psychiatry Review, 5,* 176–180.

Weiss, M. R. (1991). Psychological skill development in children and adolescents. *The Sport Psychologist, 5,* 335–354.

Weiss, M. R., & Bredemeier, B. J. (1983). Developmental sport psychology: A theoretical perspective for studying children in sport. *Journal of Sport Psychology, 5,* 216–230.

24

RATIONAL EMOTIVE BEHAVIOUR THERAPY TO HELP YOUNG ATHLETES BUILD RESILIENCE AND DEAL WITH ADVERSITY

Andrew G. Wood, Jamie B. Barker, and Martin J. Turner

This chapter brings together the theoretical postulations and applied implications of using Rational Emotive Behaviour Therapy (REBT; Ellis, 1957) with elite youth athletes. We first provide a concise overview of REBT and the resulting impact on adolescent athletes' ability to overcome adversity and attain their respective goals. Second, we present a case study that details the application of REBT with young elite athletes. Ultimately, in this chapter we offer a novel insight into practical techniques, practitioner reflections, and key considerations for those working in youth sport looking to foster resilience.

Overview of Rational Emotive Behaviour Therapy

REBT is a psychotherapeutic intervention based on the underlying premise that 'men are not disturbed by things, but by the view which they take of them' (Epictetus, 55–135 AD). Specifically, REBT proposes that an individual's beliefs (rational versus irrational beliefs) are associated with emotions and action tendencies that are divergent in their functionality (functional versus dysfunctional) towards goal achievement. Irrational Beliefs (IBs) are characterised as extreme, inconsistent with reality, illogical, largely dysfunctional in their behavioural, emotional, and cognitive consequences, and detrimental to the individual in pursuing his/her goals. In contrast, Rational Beliefs (RBs) are flexible, consistent with reality, logical, functional in their behavioural, emotional, and cognitive consequences, and help an individual to reach his/her goals. Thus, psychological disturbances do not merely follow from one's beliefs but from a combination of thoughts, feelings, and behaviours (Ellis & Dryden, 1997).

To elaborate, IBs consist of the four core beliefs of: demandingness (e.g. 'I would like to win, therefore I must'), awfulising (e.g. 'it would be terrible if I did not win'), frustration intolerance (e.g. 'not winning would be unbearable'), and self-downing (e.g. 'not winning would make me a complete failure'). Therefore, when encountering adversity young athletes with IBs will experience unhealthy emotions (e.g. anxiety, depression, and unhealthy anger) and display maladaptive behaviours (e.g. avoidant or angry outbursts) that hinder goal achievement. In contrast, RBs are characterised as logical, empirical, and pragmatic, consisting of four core beliefs: preferences (e.g. 'I would like to win, but that does not mean I have to'), anti-awfulising (e.g. 'not winning would be bad but certainly not terrible'), frustration tolerance (e.g. 'although I would not like it, I could tolerate not winning') and unconditional self-acceptance (e.g. 'not winning does not make me a complete failure, only that I have failed this time, showing that I am a fallible human being'). In the face of adversity young athletes with RBs will experience healthy emotions (e.g. concern, sadness, healthy anger) and display adaptive behaviours (e.g. approach and assertive behaviour) that facilitate goal achievement (David, Szentagotai, Eva, & Macavei, 2005).

ABC(DE) framework to foster resilience

Resilience is defined as a 'dynamic process encompassing positive adaptation within the context of significant adversity' (Luthar, Cicchetti, & Becker, 2000, p. 543). To foster resilience in athletes practitioners are able to employ a situational ABC(DE) framework (see Figure 24.1). Specifically, people experience undesirable activating events (A; or adversity), about which they have rational and irrational beliefs (B; David et al., 2005). These beliefs then lead to four intimately interconnected levels of cognitive, emotional, behavioural, and physiological consequences (C). Therefore, in the face of failure, rejection, and poor treatment (A) it is the person's irrational or rational beliefs that determine the functionality of their response (Ellis & Dryden, 1997). REBT theory posits that IBs about adversity (e.g. failure, rejection, and poor treatment) lead to unhealthy emotions (e.g. anxiety, depression, unhealthy anger) and dysfunctional behaviours; whereas RBs about adversity lead

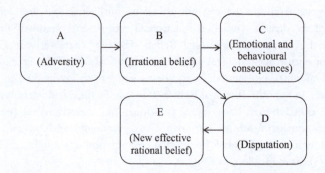

FIGURE 24.1 A schematic of the ABC(DE) framework used within the REBT process
Source: Reproduced with permission from Turner, M. J., & Barker, J. B. (2014). Using rational emotive behavior therapy with athletes. *The Sport Psychologist, 28*, 75–90.

to healthy emotions (e.g. concern, sadness, healthy anger) and functional behaviours. The ABC(DE) framework can also explain how two individuals can respond, that is think, feel, and behave differently, based on what they tell themselves about the situation (David et al., 2005).

To emphasise and support a rational philosophy practitioners use three main strategies to actively dispute (D) the athlete's IBs and replace them with more adaptive and effective rational alternatives (E). First, REBT encourages the client to seek *empirical* evidence that confirms or disconfirms the truth of the irrational belief. Second, REBT presents a *logical* argument, questioning whether their irrational belief follows from a rational preference. Finally, REBT proposes whether clients' IBs are *pragmatic*, that is asking whether holding such beliefs have been helpful or a hindrance for them (Dryden & Neenan, 2015). Ultimately, REBT provides a model of optimal human functioning (David et al., 2005) and is used to promote a rational philosophy, providing athletes with a skill set to handle challenges, unexpected obstacles, and setbacks that they will inevitably encounter in the pursuit of sporting excellence.

Irrational beliefs in youth sport

In the pursuit of performance excellence elite athletes are required to manage and respond adaptively to a variety of stressors (i.e. competitive, organisational, and personal; Hanton, Fletcher, & Coughlan, 2005), none more so than between middle to late adolescence (the investment years; Côté, 1999), where participation in competitive sport can be extremely stressful (see Chapter 15 for further information).

Elite sport may perpetuate an athlete's IBs. For example, an athlete's regular experience of bespoke training and exceptional treatment may encourage an irrational shift from 'I want to be treated fairly' to 'I have to be treated fairly' (i.e. akin to entitlement), leading to unhealthy emotions (e.g. anger) and maladaptive behaviours (e.g. angry outbursts). Although it is a transition that presents much opportunity, rather than focused on nurturing athletic development, athletes can enter into this period inherently fixated upon success, failure, and perceived self-worth. Here shifts can be made from a strong preference for success ('I more than anything want to perform well, but there is nothing to say that I must') to a demand ('I more than anything want to perform well, and therefore I must'). This has important ramifications for athletes in late adolescence who are approaching athletic, psychological, psychosocial, and academic/vocational transitions (e.g. Wylleman & Lavallee, 2004; see Chapter 13). Indeed, IBs have been associated with burnout in elite youth athletes (Hill, Hall, Appleton, & Kozub, 2008) and adult athletic populations (Turner & Moore, 2015).

To illustrate, when faced with setbacks, rejection, or ill-treatment youth athletes may become more susceptible towards harbouring IBs (e.g. 'not making selection would be awful, and this would make me a complete a failure'), in turn propagating unhealthy emotions and maladaptive behaviours. The demands of training and competition characteristic of the investment years and beyond are often at odds with those who are also considering careers and life choices out of sport (Brown, Glastetter-Fender, & Shelton, 2000). Here being ill-prepared for missing the cut can exacerbate an athlete's IBs (e.g. 'I must make it, otherwise it would be terrible and would make me a complete failure'), encouraging an irrational and motivational shift from 'want to' to 'have to'. In many ways middle to late adolescence represents an important and defining period where an athlete's ability to cope and manage stressors can restrict or strengthen their transition onto the next level, as well as acting as a precursor, shaping how they manage adversities into adulthood (Compas, Connor-Smith, Saltzman, Thomsen, & Wadsworth, 2001).

Why REBT?

REBT has a long history of application, and is well supported with children and adolescents (e.g. Gonzalez et al., 2004) to manage various challenges, such as academic underachievement, anxieties, disruptive behaviours, phobias, low frustration tolerance, depression, and childhood sexuality (David et al., 2005). Our research has supported the effects of REBT as an intervention to develop performance and psychological health using both one-to-one and group-based interventions with young athletes (e.g. Cunningham & Turner, 2016; Turner & Barker, 2013; Turner, Slater, & Barker, 2013; Wood, Barker, & Turner, 2017).

REBT is an efficacious form of cognitive behavioural therapy (MacInnes, 2004); however, it is distinct from cognitive behavioural programmes typically adopted within sport psychology (see Chapter 23 for examples). Below we detail how REBT contributes above and beyond existing interventions within sport:

1) Using the ABC(DE) framework, REBT does not dispute the situation (A) but assumes it to be true. For example, an athlete may be extremely anxious about an important upcoming competition. Here a REBT practitioner does not dispute the athlete's inference that this is 'an important competition' (A); instead REBT disputes (D) their IBs (B) about the situation (A) and replaces them with rational alternatives (E) to promote a flexible and adaptive response that facilitates goal achievement (see Turner & Barker, 2014).

2) Beliefs mediate the relationship between the environment and emotional distress; therefore, those who harbour IBs are vulnerable whereas RBs act as protective factors during stressful situations. Accordingly, if IBs are effectively disputed and replaced with rational alternatives this promotes long-term and fundamental changes in the way athletes manage and overcome adversity. The ABC(DE) model provides athletes with a tangible understanding of emotion development, which for some has been an uncontrollable 'controllable' – 'something, which just happens'. Thus, irrespective of the situation athletes are provided with an understanding and the autonomy to manage situations they encounter. This is important because as practitioners, coaches, and support staff we should not become their crutch, instead encouraging independent athletes who are able to manage any challenges they will inevitably encounter.

3) REBT encourages athletes to understand that negative emotions in relation to adversity are normal and a vital element of attaining their respective goals, permitting them to return to a normative or positive state effectively and swiftly. To explain, REBT advocates a binary distinction between helpful and unhelpful negative emotions (e.g. concern vs anxiety, healthy anger vs. unhealthy anger, sadness vs. depression; Hyland & Boduszek, 2012) instead of a positive and negative response. This offers a more credible and believable alternative for athletes when responding to adversity.

4) REBT posits Unconditional Self/Other/Life-Acceptance (USA), reaffirming that humans are too complicated to be defined by a single action, and although we do not have to like it, we can accept that humans are fallible beings (Dryden & Branch, 2008). This, in turn, reduces the harsh, extreme, and unhelpful self-criticism athletes with IBs will impose upon themselves.

Using REBT in practice

The present case details the first author's (AW) application of a one-to-one REBT intervention with a 15-year-old male cricketer. Alex (pseudonym) was playing county, school, and club cricket – approaching a stage in his cricketing development that was filled with important selection games that would have a large bearing on his transition to become a professional cricketer. Although Alex had also started to bowl, he was primarily a batsman and had been struggling for some time with his consistency, especially when playing for his county. He noted that these were the games where he felt the highest expectation to perform in front of others; this was not the case in club cricket, which was played at a lower standard and among close friends. As a result Alex reported feeling extremely anxious prior to important matches, and experienced angry outbursts after receiving unfavourable decisions by the umpire(s).

Subsequently, this was having negative effects on his performances and compromised his chances of continuing through the ranks of academy cricket. Notably, for Alex his performances and selection for respective teams were evaluated primarily based upon his batting, and paradoxically the harder he tried the harder it became to attain and impress the selectors (i.e. coaches). Alex was also concerned about the broader implications and consequences of not making it in cricket. In turn, this perpetuated the unhelpful emotions (i.e. anxiety and anger) he had been experiencing when his goals and ambitions were partially thwarted (e.g. being observed by selectors, unfair dismissal by an umpire). Specifically Alex noted:

> Especially with batters like me you are batting for your living, there are players who are literally batting for their career and it can be extremely stressful when you are failing all the time. I know three or four lads older than me that if they don't get contracts I don't know what they're gonna do for work. They have nothing other than cricket and for them it is all or nothing.

It appeared Alex was harboring IBs about success and failure and consequently placing great demands on himself (in this situation), resulting in adverse effects on his performance. The presence of unhelpful emotions and behaviours was largely indicative of the presence of IBs. To further this assessment, as a quantitative triangulation strategy on behalf of the practitioner, Alex completed the Shortened General Attitudes and Belief Scale (SGABS; Lindner, Kirkby, Wertheim, & Birch, 1999), which confirmed high irrational belief scores. Specifically, Alex's scores indicated that he was oriented around a demand for achievement, fairness, and a need for approval, all commonly associated with unhealthy anger and anxiety.

The intervention

For long-term effects REBT is purported to be most effective on a one-to-one basis, often taking between five and twelve sessions, allowing the athlete to both comprehend and put their learning into practice (Turner & Barker, 2014). Alex was an open, intelligent, and self-aware individual who was able to articulate his thoughts, emotions, and behaviours clearly. The main focus of the REBT intervention lasted for six sessions, with each session approximately 45 minutes in duration. The present case details the intervention, which was broken down into education, disputation, and reinforcement phases, while focusing on the variety of techniques that were used to reinforce Alex's new rational philosophy.

The education phase

The education phase lasted for two sessions, with one inter-session task. The main aim was to educate Alex on the ABC process, whereby his beliefs (B) rather than the adversity (A) dictated the functionality of his response (C). During our first session Alex highlighted the most recent or most poignant adversity, as well detailing the corresponding unhealthy and dysfunctional thoughts, feelings, and behaviours. As an inter-session task I asked Alex to complete an A to C diary of varying adversities (A) and the subsequent consequences (C) he experienced. At the beginning of our second session we reviewed the A–C diary and revisited the adversity he proposed during our first session. Following this, I asked Alex to detail a functional alternative response if/when he were to encounter such a situation again. This was important, because it highlighted to Alex first, that he would not necessarily feel positive about the adversity but instead experience a healthy negative emotion, and second, there was an adaptive and maladaptive manner in which he could respond to the same adversity. I often assume that this is common knowledge for athletes; however, as in Alex's case it was to be a light-bulb moment – an insight that he alone was able to manage how he adaptively responds, encouraging a sense of autonomy and control over his emotions.

Following this I began to elicit the core IBs that Alex held about the adversity. Here I asked Alex what was he telling himself about the situation that was leading him to respond in this way (i.e. unhelpful response) that hindered his goal

achievement. The process of self-reflection and open discussion can be challenging for some adolescents, and subsequently in this case I found it useful to provide
a menu of IBs that Alex may have been harbouring. For example, I asked, 'Are
you telling yourself that because you want to win that you have to?' Alternatively,
conjunctive phrasing can also be used as a useful technique to establish the core
IBs. This involves repeatedly probing an athlete's suggested adversities (Dryden &
Branch, 2008), for example:

> Practitioner: So what might the adversity be in this instance?
> Athlete: Not being selected to represent the regional side.
> Practitioner: And what does this mean?
> Athlete: It means that I am a complete failure.

In Alex's case, once the core IBs were agreed I explicitly emphasised the notion that
while the adversity may act as a trigger, ultimately it was his beliefs (B) that dictated
his response (C). The education phase can often be rushed and practitioners should
ensure the athlete grasps the ABC model before moving onto disputing IBs. In
Alex's case he was both engaged, open, and demonstrated excellent self-awareness
of his emotions; accordingly Alex quickly grasped the ABC model and we moved
onto the most challenging and important phase within REBT.

Disputation phase

The disputation phase lasted for three sessions and two inter-session tasks. The main
aim was to dispute IBs and replace them with rational alternatives. Often, termi-
nology such as 'irrational' can have negative connotations for the athletes and it was
crucial I reinforced this to Alex and normalised his position prior to the disputation
phase. To explain, I highlighted that both irrational and rational beliefs were ubiqui-
tous in humans, and that sometimes a person's beliefs unwittingly become unhelpful during situations that may block or hinder them from reaching meaningful and
important goals. In this case Alex was able to relate to this, sharing his experiences
of a common paradox – the harder and more desperate he was in his endeavours to
perform, the more he would be met with an equal and opposite force, preventing
him from reaching his potential.

During the disputation phase the practitioner is able to switch between socratic
and didactic methods (Dryden & Branch, 2008). A socratic approach involves open-
ended questions that are designed to encourage the athlete to think critically about
the respective topic (e.g. 'How has believing that you "have to" been helpful for
you and your ambitions?'), whereas a didactic method involves disputing and teaching rational principles by explanation (i.e. we know that IBs are likely to lead to
unhelpful and negative responses to adversity). A blend of both approaches was
informed largely by Alex and my professional judgement, resulting in an athlete
who was both educated and actively involved within the REBT process. During
this phase I disputed (D) his IBs empirically (e.g. 'where is it written that you must

meet others' expectations?'), logically (e.g. 'just because you want to, does that mean that you have to?'), and pragmatically (e.g. 'how helpful has it been for you to hold onto these beliefs?').

As with other adolescent athletes, Alex was open and flexible to the disputation process. Compared to older athletes I have worked with his beliefs appeared to be less engrained and presented less resistance when relinquishing his IBs and adopting new RBs (E). In turn, the disputation process was a formulaic and relatively straightforward one. Once the old IBs had been successfully disputed we created a new set of RBs, which were then unsuccessfully disputed using empirical, logical, and pragmatic arguments. For example, the practitioner would say, 'Is it true that just because you really want to win that does not mean that you have to?' This helped to reaffirm his conviction that his new RBs are true, logical, and helpful for goal attainment. The practicality and accessibility of the ABC(DE) model meant we repeated this process across a variety of challenging situations that Alex encountered. Repetition of this process meant he was able to become proficient in recognising, reappraising, and regulating his response to adversity. An example of Alex's irrational and rational beliefs about playing in an important cricket match is provided (see Table 24.1).

Disputation and reinforcing techniques

To help Alex establish a helpful and adaptive approach/response to adversity I asked him to pictorially create and label a cartoon figure that best represented this response. Certainly with young athletes I have found the use of metaphor an effective means of enhancing self-awareness and establishing their desired state. Humour is a core condition of REBT and considered to be a desirable quality of REBT practitioners, and while it should be used carefully, together we used it to help Alex to not take himself, others, and life too seriously (Dryden & Branch, 2008).

TABLE 24.1 Example irrational and rational beliefs established with Alex in reference to an important cricket match

Irrational Beliefs	Rational Beliefs
'I really want to perform well as there's gonna be selectors watching – this **means I must perform well in today's match**. If I was to have a bad game, this may mean I wouldn't be selected for the regional team and this **would be terrible**. Considering everything I have done and how well I've played all season the thought of not being selected **is intolerable** and this would **make me a complete failure**.'	'I really want to perform well in today's match as there's gonna be selectors watching, however this **doesn't mean I have to**. If I was to have a bad game, this may mean I wouldn't be selected for the regional team and **although bad it certainly wouldn't be terrible**. This wouldn't make me a failure, only that **I've had bad day**. Although it would be **uncomfortable I could live with that**, I've tolerated much harder things in my life.'

To dispute and reinforce Alex's awfulising, we used a method called the 'badness scale' that asked Alex to place a numerical percentage of badness on a scale from 0 to 100 using a variety of sport- and life-related adversities. First, I provided Alex with a list of relatively trivial adversities (e.g. being late to training, getting a cold, eating his least favourite food), and expectedly these were scored low on the badness scale. Second, I provided Alex with a range of cricket-related adversities (e.g. missing practice, losing out on selection, underperforming during an important match), and comparatively these examples were scored highly (50–100 per cent). Finally, after asking Alex if he was happy with his answers so far, I provided Alex with a range of serious adversities. It was here the penny dropped and Alex realised that there are much worse things that someone can experience, and although failing selection was bad it was never 100 per cent awful or terrible. This activity allowed Alex to take a new perspective on the challenges he encountered (e.g. an important match), removing the exaggerated consequences of failure; in turn, the less he ruminated about the prospect of failure he was able to enjoy and focus on the challenge in hand. To help reinforce this point we decided Alex would keep the badness scale within his bag and integrate it as part of his pre-match routine. In a follow-up session Alex voluntarily offered cricket-specific examples that reinforced his ability to take a new perspective and emphasised the importance of enjoying his cricket:

> There've been two examples I've reflected on since last time. I know a player who has been diagnosed with cancer and I think he is doing better now but that is a real wake up call. Another lad is James Taylor – have you seen in the news he can't play ever again, he has retired from cricket. Basically what happened was that he had a really bad heart issue and almost lost his life, I'm sure he would love to go back and just enjoy being able to play full stop. For me the enjoyment factor has to be there.

To consolidate Alex's understanding and ability to practise the principles of REBT we enacted a reversal role-play scenario called the 'Devil's Advocate'. Here I assumed the role of an athlete who was struggling with pre-performance nerves, while Alex adopted the role of the practitioner, helping to explore, elicit, and dispute my IBs. This provided a true test, allowing me to confirm Alex's understanding of the REBT process.

Finally, a new self-mantra was created, one that he would use to reinforce his new RBs around the weight of expectation he felt when being evaluated by significant others. Whilst incorporating the four core RBs, I also encouraged Alex to change the wording and add extra statements into his mantra to enhance its personal meaning:

> I would really like to meet others' expectations of me, especially if they are coaches, selectors or important people. I would be very happy if I did, but there is nothing to say that I have to. If I did not meet others' expectations, I would not like it, however it certainly wouldn't be terrible, in fact it would

only be 5% bad. I could tolerate not meeting others' expectations of me. This doesn't mean I am a complete failure, instead this means that I haven't met their expectations this time around. I can accept this and move on. Today I want to play well, simply do the best that I can and that is all I can ever do.

Practitioner considerations

IBs are deeply engrained and can often rear their heads if the process and a rational philosophy is not reinforced actively by the athlete. Therefore, from a practitioner or coaching perspective we should be willing to challenge the use of irrational language (e.g. 'I had a terrible game last week, it was awful') with our athletes. Furthermore the disputation and reinforcement of rational beliefs is not restricted to cognitive methods. Often, behavioural techniques can provide the most effective means to do so. For example, with Alex I actively encouraged him to seek important matches where he experienced selector evaluation. This provided him with an opportunity to create his own evidence that he could tolerate discomfort and manage adversity, and that it certainly was not the end of the world if he underperformed.

Alex received the intervention positively, reporting notable developments in his enjoyment of cricket and ability to control his emotions during pivotal moments of a match (e.g. walking out to open the batting). These benefits also transcended into other aspects of his life and such changes were reciprocated by Alex's father. The newly formed rational philosophy and resilience was to stand him in good stead in the upcoming seasons where Alex weathered a series of major injuries. After the main block of sessions, Alex and I would intermittently catch up to review his progress; here I acted as a sounding board to any queries or concerns he was having. Nevertheless, Alex was largely independent and was steadily progressing with his ambitions on the road to being a professional crickter.

Alternative modalities

REBT presents a formulaic but malleable intervention. Its application is not restricted to one-to-one work, but can be used in educational group-based settings (e.g. Turner et al., 2013). Furthermore, we also utilise REBT with coaches and parents of youth athletes to both help themselves and reinforce rational principles with the athletes. Considering the prevalence of emotional stress, physical exhaustion, and burnout in youth sport, coaches are in a position to create healthy environments that implicitly promote rational philosophies to sport.

Final thoughts

The application of clinical models such as REBT within sport marks a shift in perspective in exploring interventions to enhance athletes' psychological wellbeing. Using REBT, practitioners are able to reduce individuals' IBs and replace them with rational alternatives. By encouraging healthy emotions and adaptive behaviours to adversity it is likely athletes will experience improved psychological health and athletic performance. The ABC(DE) framework presents a working model of optimal human functioning, which once understood and adopted is applicable to any challenge or adversity young athletes will inevitably encounter throughout their lifespan.

References

Brown, C., Glastetter-Fender, C., & Shelton, M. (2000). Psychosocial identity and career control in college student-athletes. *Journal of Vocational Behavior, 56*, 53–62.

Compas, B. E. E., Connor-Smith, J. K. K., Saltzman, H., Thomsen, A. H. H., & Wadsworth, M. E. E. (2001). Coping with stress during childhood and adolescence: Problems, progress, and potential in theory and research. *Psychological Bulletin, 127*, 87–127.

Côté, J. (1999). The influence of the family in the development of talent in sport. *The Sport Psychologist, 13*, 395–417.

Cunningham, R., & Turner, M. J. (2016). Using rational emotive behavior therapy (REBT) with mixed martial arts (MMA) athletes to reduce irrational beliefs and unconditional self-acceptance. *Journal of Rational-Emotive & Cognitive-Behavior Therapy, 34*, 289–309.

David, D., Szentagotai, A., Eva, K., & Macavei, B. (2005). A synopsis of rational-emotive behavior therapy (REBT): Fundamental and applied research. *Journal of Rational-Emotive & Cognitive-Behaviour Therapy, 23*, 175–221.

Dryden, W., & Branch, R. (2008). *The Fundamentals of Rational Emotive Behavior Therapy* (2nd ed.). Chichester, UK: John Wiley & Sons.

Dryden, W., & Neenan, M. (2015). *Rational Emotive Behavior Therapy: 100 Key Points and Techniques.* Abingdon, UK: Routledge.

Ellis, A. (1957). Rational psychotherapy and individual psychology. *Journal of Individual Psychology, 13*, 38–44.

Ellis, A., & Dryden, W. (1997). *The Practice of Rational Emotive Behavior Therapy.* New York, NY: Springer.

Epictetus (1948). *The Enchiridion.* Indianapolis, IN: Bobbs-Merrill.

Gonzalez, J. E., Nelson, J. R., Gutkin, T. B., Saunders, A., Galloway, A., & Shwery, C. S. (2004). Rational emotive therapy with children and adolescents: A meta-analysis. *Journal of Emotional and Behavioral Disorders, 12*, 222–235.

Hanton, S., Fletcher, D., & Coughlan, G. (2005). Stress in elite sport performers: A comparative study of competitive and organisational stressors. *Journal of Sports Sciences, 23*, 1129–1141.

Hill, A. P., Hall, H. K., Appleton, P. R., & Kozub, S. A. (2008). Perfectionism and burnout in junior elite soccer players: The mediating influence of unconditional self-acceptance. *Psychology of Sport and Exercise, 9*, 630–644.

Hyland, P., & Boduszek, D. (2012). A unitary or binary model of emotions: A discussion on a fundamental difference between cognitive therapy and rational emotive behavior therapy. *Journal of Humanistics and Social Sciences, 1*, 49–61.

Lindner, H., Kirkby, R., Wertheim, E., & Birch, P. (1999). A brief assessment of irrational thinking: The Shortened General Attitude and Belief Scale. *Cognitive Therapy and Research, 23*, 651–663.

Luthar, S. S., Cicchetti, D., & Becker, B. (2000). The construct of resilience: A critical evaluation and guidelines for future work. *Child Development, 71*, 543–562.

MacInnes, D. (2004). The theories underpinning rational emotive behavior therapy: Where's the supportive evidence? *International Journal of Nursing Studies, 41*, 685–695.

Turner, M. J., & Barker, J. B. (2013). Examining the efficacy of rational-emotive behavior therapy (REBT) on irrational beliefs and anxiety in elite youth cricketers. *Journal of Applied Sport Psychology, 25*, 131–147.

Turner, M. J., & Barker, J. B. (2014). Using rational emotive behavior therapy with athletes. *The Sport Psychologist, 28*, 75–90.

Turner, M. J., & Moore, M. (2015). Irrational beliefs predict increased emotional and physical exhaustion in Gaelic football athletes. *International Journal of Sport Psychology, 47*, 187–199.

Turner, M. J., Slater, M. J., & Barker, J. B. (2013). The season-long effects of rational emotive behavior therapy on the irrational beliefs of professional academy soccer athletes. *International Journal of Sport Psychology, 44*, 429–451.

Wood, A. G., Barker, J. B., & Turner, M. J. (2017). Developing performance using rational emotive behavior therapy (REBT): A case study with an elite archer. *The Sport Psychologist, 31*, 78–87.

Wylleman, P., & Lavallee, D. (2004). A developmental perspective on transitions faced by athletes. In M. R. Weiss (Ed.), *Developmental Sport and Exercise Psychology: A Lifespan Perspective* (pp. 503–524). Morgantown, WV: Fitness Information Technology.

25

DELIVERING SPORT PSYCHOLOGY PROGRAMMES

Effective group presentations

Daniel Gould and Lauren Szczygiel

I agree to talk to a local gymnastic club about the importance of sport psychology and how these young athletes can develop their mental games. As the presentation date comes closer I ask the club owner about the ages of the athletes who will attend and I am surprised to learn that the vast majority are all under 10. I was thinking most of the gymnasts would be in the 12- to 15-year-old age range, not under 10. As I quietly panicked, thinking about how I would structure the session and what I was going to say, I wondered if these children would understand what psychology even was, a fact that became very apparent on the day of the presentation when I met with the team of 40 tiny munchkins sitting on the mat waiting to hear me.

I am in an open-air pavilion and just finished my short presentation to 75 junior elite wrestlers on the importance of developing the ability to relax and take centred breaths to refocus. They are all lying on the mat ready to take part in a 20-minute introductory progressive relaxation experience. I lower my voice and calmly begin the exercise when all of a sudden an incredibly loud bulldozer starts up next to the pavilion. I finally get the bulldozer to stop and start again when one of the athletes lets out a very loud fart! Of course, the room breaks out in laughter!

A tennis coach invited me in to talk to his team. There are 15 boys aged 14–17 years in the room. While most are engaged and are listening, two or three are pretty immature and distracting some of the others with their wisecracks. To top it all off the head coach is sitting in the back of the room and says nothing.

We bring up these three scenarios because they actually occurred. Luckily, most sessions go more smoothly or are easier to manage than these. However, any sport psychology specialist who works with young athletes needs to be prepared to give group sessions and be ready for situations such as these. Ironically, most of the applied sport psychology literature does not give us much guidance in these areas. In fact, most of the literature focuses on *what* we should say rather than *how* we should deliver it. Further, most literature focuses on one-to-one sessions, with less information available regarding working with teams or groups of young athletes.

This chapter is designed to discuss how to deliver sport psychology programmes to teams of young athletes and will focus on one important component of doing so – delivering effective group presentations. Although the focus in this chapter is on presenting to groups, in our experience the most effective interventions involve both group and individual sessions and include parents, coaches, and support staff. However, we focus on key considerations for delivering effective group presentations here because often, at least in our experience, these are desired by youth sport coaches because they are a relatively quick and cost-effective mechanism through which to expose young athletes to mental training.

The importance of group or team sport sessions

Working with groups of young athletes[1] is a key skill for practising sport psychology specialists for several reasons:

1) Group presentations are often the first exposure a young athlete has to sport psychology. Research with experienced sport psychology consultants shows that 80 per cent conduct group presentations or workshops (Gould, Murphy, Tammen, & May, 1989). If done well, group presentations can make the young athletes aware of the importance of working on their mental games and teach key skills, but if they are delivered poorly, they may be turned off sport psychology entirely.

2) Presenting to groups is an efficient way to cover a great deal of material that everyone needs. For instance, if we provide the basics of relaxation in a group session we do not need to repeat what was said in individual athlete consultations. Instead, we can spend our time with each athlete customising what was learnt to each athlete's individual unique needs.

3) Group sessions allow teams to learn from one another and to understand individual differences between teammates.

4) If you are in private practice, conducting group sessions is a great way to advertise what you do and get your name out there. Often, individual athletes or, in the case of young athletes, their parents and coaches will contact you for individual work with a young athlete because they heard you give a group session.

Research on group interventions

Although many sport psychology interventions focus on one-on-one consultations with athletes, some have assessed the effectiveness of programmes delivered to groups of young athletes (e.g. Fournier, Camels, Durand-Bush, & Salmela, 2005; Gucciardi, Gordon, & Dimmock, 2009; Wikman, Ryom, Stelter, & Elbe, 2016). An excellent example of such an intervention was conducted by Gucciardi and his colleagues (2009), who examined the effectiveness of both a mental toughness and a more traditional psychological skills training programme on three groups of 15-year-old

Australian footballers. Both interventions consisted of two weekly, two-hour group sessions that focused on either general sport psychological skills (e.g. arousal regulation, mental rehearsal, self-efficacy) or key mental toughness characteristics (e.g. resilience, self-motivation, and effort). Results revealed that both intervention groups reported positive changes in player, parent, and coach ratings of resilience, mental toughness, and flow when compared to a control group that did not receive any training.

An intervention study by Fournier and colleagues (2005) is particularly interesting because it not only looked at psychological changes as a result of intervention participation but actual performance. Specifically, studying ten national level French gymnasts (mean age of 12 years), Fournier et al. found that a 25-session five-step psychological skills training programme was associated with psychological changes and a 5 per cent performance improvement over a comparison group of gymnasts who did not participate in any psychological training. The psychological skills training sessions took place in a group format, were 30 minutes in length, and focused on relaxation, goal setting, self-talk, focusing, and imagery.

A smaller group of studies have found partial or no support for group intervention effectiveness. Wikman et al. (2016) examined the impact of a 12-week school-based relaxation intervention on facilitating recovery of young (ages 16–19 years) Danish athletes. The intervention occurred for one hour per week. Quantitative data showed no stress-recovery effects of the intervention. However, interview data from four participants indicated that the intervention was perceived to be effective. In another recent study, Ong and Griva (2016) found no effects of two group mental skills training sessions on 13-year-old rugby players' anxiety or psychological skills development. The two sessions were two hours in length and involved demonstrations of goal setting, positive thinking, and pre-performance routines/techniques.

Although a detailed review of group intervention literature is beyond the scope of this chapter, looking across the studies the results are mixed. The good news is that the majority of studies show that group interventions can positively influence young athletes' mental states and performance. However, other studies find only partial or no effects. The failure to find effects is often linked to programme length or the design of the programmes. As such, the implication of these findings is that group interventions can be effective for facilitating the psychological development of young athletes. However, such programmes must be well thought out, long enough to have impact, and carefully designed and executed.

Factors to consider when delivering group presentations

There are numerous factors to consider when planning and delivering group presentations to young athletes. We will highlight some of the most important ones below.

Your philosophy

One's professional philosophy, theoretical orientation, and beliefs drive actions when working in applied settings and it is no different when making group presentations.

Most sport psychologists working with young athletes have found it helpful to adopt a holistic view of development – a view where one considers both the athletic and the developmental needs of the young athlete (e.g. Henriksen, Larsen, Storm, & Ryom, 2014; Foster, Maynard, Butt, & Hays, 2016). Hence, although the primary focus of a presentation may be on teaching a specific psychological skill or technique (e.g. goal setting, relaxation, imagery) it is important to consider how this skill might fit into a broader context. For example, you might talk to young athletes about how relaxation can be used to deal with stress associated with a competition while at the same time trying to help them realise that sport is only one part of their life. Similarly, when teaching goal setting we might have the young athlete set a goal for their sport while simultaneously also setting one for school or some other non-sport aspect of their life.

Purpose

It may sound trivial but when asked to make a group presentation to young athletes spending time thinking about the purpose of that presentation is essential. A presentation might have numerous, often combined, purposes. For example, one might aim to establish trust with the young athletes, with the goal being to get them to believe you have something worth listening to; to learn what the young athletes are interested in; or what they think about their coaches. At other times the purpose is to teach a specific technique (e.g. how to control an image or develop a pre-performance routine), simply make athletes aware of the importance of mental skills, encourage communication and disclosure, and/or build team cohesion. The bottom line is to really spend some time thinking about what you are trying to achieve in the presentation and what you would like the audience to remember or conclude by the time you finish. Once the purposes are clearly identified, structure the presentation to achieve those purposes.

Audience, audience, audience

Presentations work best when they meet the needs of the audience. It is ironic, then, that when the organisers ask you to present they seldom tell you much about the audience. The more information you can obtain about the audience the better you can meet their needs, so it is imperative to obtain as much information as possible about who will attend. For instance, in the opening scenario of this chapter, knowing that most gymnasts were under the age of 10, the first author did not talk about sport psychology. Rather, he labelled his presentation 'Brain Power Gymnastics' and brought a foam model of the brain with him. He then focused the presentation on why our brains are important and how children can strengthen their brains just like their bodies by practising mental skills. Key points emphasised were that 'stinking' thinking hinders your brain and that it is normal to be nervous. Audience needs, as well as the purpose of the presentation and the time available, are critical in determining presentation content; it does not matter what you think athletes need or what you hope to do, the time available and athletes' developmental stage will determine what and how much content you can convey.

Presentation context and setting

Just like the audience, the more you can know about the setting you will present in the better. Will it be in a classroom with fixed seating? On the field? Are audio-visual (AV) options available? There is nothing worse than trying to have athletes work in small groups in classrooms with fixed seating or trying to talk to a team on a field next to a noisy freeway with distractions all around. Remember Murphy's law (everything that can go wrong will go wrong) and that Murphy was an optimist! Applied practitioners doing group presentations need to be flexible and able to adapt on the spot. For instance, we never go to a presentation where PowerPoint slides will be used without a paper copy of the slides or a backup plan if AV is not available. Further, recent evidence indicates that young people are often more comfortable learning about mental skills in their own sport environments (Henriksen et al., 2014) and that they are learned more successfully when developed with physical skills (McCarthy et al., 2010). Thinking about ways to present group sessions on the field or in the gym while athletes are practising their sport should be considered.

Instructional method

There are any number of instructional methods you may employ in group presentations. Each has its strengths and limitations and we contend that the practising sport psychologists working with young athletes should develop the ability to use a wide variety of methods and then let the purpose of the presentation and audience needs determine which method to use.

Formal presentations

Formal presentations are an efficient way to convey large amounts of information. The consultant also controls the content and flow of information. The downside of formal presentations can be the lack of audience engagement and involvement, especially with young athletes where attention spans are shorter. So presentations need to be delivered enthusiastically and kept fairly short. It is also important to use mini-audience engagement strategies like asking questions, having them raise their hands if they experienced some key point, write something down, etc. Finally, think of the process of presenting as a performance; working on your voice inflections, timing, body language, and ability to infuse emotion are important.

Fireside chats

A second method for working with athletes in groups is the 'fireside chat'. The fireside chat is structured but more conversational than a formal presentation. Visual aids are seldom employed. Often you might sit and talk with the athletes as a group and try to engage them in a conversation about some topic (e.g. mental preparation for nationals, how to deal with parental pressure). As the discussion progresses the facilitator stresses key points and may discuss ones the young athletes have not mentioned.

Fireside chats, while not appearing as being structured, are. The presenter has predetermined key points to cover but talks about the topic informally while working to engage the young athletes in conversations focused on it. The advantage of the fireside chat approach is that it helps place young athletes at ease because it is similar to how a coach might talk with them before or after practice. At the same time it is structured and focused on a particular topic. Disadvantages include having less control, as you do not necessarily know what the athletes will say or if they will engage.

Group exercise or activities

Young athletes often enjoy learning through doing. For this reason it is imperative that consultants have the skills needed to conduct engaging exercises along with their skills presentation. These exercises may occur on the field or off the field. Off-field exercises might include building a belief wall where the members of the team each write out reasons for why they should be confident as a team on blocks or sticky notes. The team then builds a wall with the blocks or places their individual confidence sticky notes on a wall graphically displayed on a white board. Other exercises might involve team-building activities or filling out goal forms (see Lauer, Gould, Lubbers, & Kovacs, 2010 for over 100 mental training activities developed for tennis that can be adapted to other sports).

Leading exercises is more difficult than it might initially seem. On one hand you want the exercise or activity to be fun and engaging but not so much fun that the young athletes do not recognise the psychological principles you are trying to convey. It can also be difficult to find or design your own exercises that are good at achieving the psychological points you are trying to make. Further, effectively setting up the task and debriefing after is a skill that takes practice. For example, sometimes you need to be purposefully vague setting up an exercise because you want the young athletes to work through an issue or problem (e.g. the goal might be to facilitate group communication) or need to solicit what was learned from the athletes during the debrief when the natural tendency is to tell the athletes the answers.

Guided discussions

The guided discussion method involves the sport psychology consultant acting as a facilitator leading a discussion around a topic. They differ from fireside chats in that the presenter does not necessarily have set points to convey but rather questions to pose to the group. Guided discussions are an excellent way to help athletes learn from their peers or from high-status role models. For example, the uncertainty that accompanies participation in a national championship can cause considerable anxiety and self-doubt in young athletes. We have found, however, that having a guided discussion about going to nationals is an excellent way to prepare. This typically involves the consultant interviewing older athletes or more experienced athletes relative to how they mentally prepared for nationals, what distractions arose, and what helped and hurt performance.

Demonstrations

Finally, demonstrations are an excellent mechanism for instructing young athletes. For instance, when working with baseball and softball players on the importance of establishing routines, we will often use actual players as examples. As a player hits in the batting cage we may ask him to demonstrate his routine and discuss it as he takes repeated pitches. Or when having the team identify their vision for the season and linking it to their individual goals, we may work through an example using one of the players.

Visual aids

Visual aids include things such as PowerPoint slides, flip charts, or tangible objects like trophies, an Olympic medal, or pieces of sports equipment. Given that a picture is worth a thousand words and can elicit emotions, visual aids certainly have a place when making group presentations. However, they should not be employed in all situations. For example, we have found using PowerPoint presentations when conducting captains' leadership training programmes helps standardise content across different presenters. At the same time, we have greatly reduced their use because the student-athletes feel it is too much like school.

Language, metaphors, and examples

The developmental capabilities of children differ throughout childhood and adolescence; as such the ability of children to understand psychological concepts and the language used to describe them changes as they age (see Chapters 4 and 5). For instance, when working with younger ages (e.g. 12 years and under), using simpler instructions, fewer goals, and shorter sessions is key (Foster et al., 2016). Additionally, all athletes, but particularly young athletes, better remember and understand psychological principles when they are tied to a metaphor or some mnemonic. For example, asking them what it is like if someone does not flush the toilet in the bathroom and then saying that this is what it is like when you have negative 'bad' thoughts in your head is a strategy we use. We then go on to explain how useful having a flushed toilet is and you can flush the 'bad' thoughts out of your head by taking a big breath and blowing them out. Some consultants have even found models of toilets that flush and use that as a visual aid to make the presentation more memorable. Overall, a good way to understand the language to employ and level at which to pitch psychological material is to talk to teachers who work with the age group of children you are targeting or to read the books they use for school.

Adding spice

Any audience, but particularly children and youth, have limited attentional capacities. For this reason, when presenting it is often recommended to add 'spice' roughly every seven minutes during a presentation. Spice can be saying something humorous, using a visual (e.g. changing the colour of a slide or showing an unusual photo), exaggerating a point, or telling a story. The key is to provide a short attentional break for the listener. A note of caution, however, is not to make the spice so distracting that the young athletes lose focus as to the purpose of your presentation.

Issues you may encounter and considerations you need to understand

As the opening scenarios of this chapter showed, there are numerous issues you may encounter when conducting group sessions. Further numerous considerations must be made when working with young athletes. Particularly prominent issues and considerations are discussed below.

The rule of thirds

Although it is often not discussed, most top sport psychology consultants do not connect with every athlete; some are just not interested in what we have to say. We think of this as the rule of thirds, which suggests that one-third of the audience will always be interested in what you are saying, for the other third it will greatly depend on how you present, and the final third will not be very interested. It is important to remember that this is not unusual and not to get distracted by those who do not seem interested. Focus on winning over the top two-thirds and over time some of the bottom third will realise what they are missing and be converted. And, frankly, some will not buy in despite your best efforts.

Involving parents and coaches

The more consultants can work with the young athletes' support system (e.g. parents and coaches) the more likely it is that they will be successful (see Chapters 10, 26, and 27). The question, however, is whether they should be invited to attend sessions that are given to groups of young athletes. The answer to this question is that it depends on the topic being discussed. Having parents and coaches attend can inhibit athlete discussion on many issues or increase the likelihood of athletes providing socially appropriate responses. At other times having coaches or parents attend can add to the discussion (e.g. when doing demonstrations of pre-performance routines a coach may introduce some technical behaviours that should be included). In our work, the majority of the time, we just meet with athletes but we try to let everyone know what topics we are working on.

Disruptive participants

Although the majority of young athletes are well behaved, disruptions will happen from time to time. Dealing with them can be tricky to manage because on one hand you are trying to establish a good relationship with the young athletes, but on the other hand misbehaving individuals can derail a very well-planned session. There is no magic solution to such situations. You can try to ignore the interruption in the hope that the disruptive behaviour is a one-off and that by not reinforcing it the behaviour will end. However, if such actions persist you must deal with it. Sometimes simply asking the person if they have something to say will end the problem. Other times you might say something like, 'I understand you might not be interested in what I am saying but your coach asked me to speak today and wants me to cover this information. I am okay if you are not interested but I would appreciate it if you would not interrupt the session.' In extreme cases you may ask the individual to leave the session or talk to the coach. Finally, learn to anticipate what might occur and plan for it. For example, we have often found when doing relaxation training for the first time with adolescent boys saying something like the following helps minimise disruptive behaviours: 'Okay, I am going to turn the lights out now and what typically happens is someone will fart or someone will yell out don't touch me. So let's take a minute to all have a group fart and say don't touch me. Your coach and I think you are ready and mature enough to do this so let's be disciplined and give it a good try.'

Recognising and adapting to the development level of the audience

Making group presentations targeted at young athletes is challenging because within a group there are likely to be individuals who differ greatly in cognitive, physical, and social development. Relative to what is said, a consultant must consider what children and youth at different ages can comprehend (see Chapters 4 and 5). Further, we may not always be able to differentiate what children understand versus what they have the vocabulary to express. As such, consultants must spend time really thinking about what mental skills children can understand as well as how sometimes abstract psychological content can be made more concrete. Based on the work of Orlick (1993) and her own experience, Chase (2013) also emphasises the importance of making sessions fun, individualising as often as you can, being as concrete as possible, using role models, employing multi-model instructional techniques, and being optimistic and enthusiastic in your approach. Importantly though, when discussing development and making changes to our practice, we must not restrict our thinking to prepubescent children. Adolescence is a time of great change for young people and it can be easy to forget that while they may look more adult they may not be adult in their thinking (see Chapter 5 for further information).

Recognising and adapting to the characteristics of Generation Z

Individuals born after 1996 are considered Generation Z or the Internet generation (Seemiller & Grace, 2016). These young people have grown up in a completely digital world, a world where they feel the need to be constantly connected, where their parents have often sheltered them, where they have been constantly reinforced (e.g. everyone getting trophies merely for participating), and are used to being constantly entertained and stimulated via video games and other forms of digital media. This has resulted in Generation Z youth having shorter attention spans, being more visual learners, communicating in different ways (e.g. texting versus talking), needing more reinforcement, and needing clearly prescribed expectations (Seemiller & Grace, 2016; Tulgan, 2016; Van den Bergh & Behrer, 2016). These characteristics have implications for giving group presentations for young people:

1) Presenter skills are more important than ever before because youth are used to receiving information in a slick and highly professional manner. You need to be able to deliver the goods in a professional but interesting and entertaining manner.
2) Their attention spans are likely shorter, so adding spice or doing activities between lecture points are important. At the same time, as consultants we might want to work on helping them learn to concentrate for longer time periods.
3) This generation likes to learn in small groups and engage in active learning, so using more exercises and activities is important.
4) Today's young athletes may need more reinforcement and reassurance than previous generations. That being said, consultants may also need to wean them off the need for high doses of reinforcement.
5) Infusing more visual displays and graphical illustrations will help keep the attention of Generation Z youth.

Conclusions

Working with children and youth can be one of the most rewarding professional experiences for a sport psychology consultant. However, as has been said so many times in the past, children are not miniature adults. They are qualitatively and quantitatively different and consultants must discover the best ways to provide group presentations that are developmentally appropriate for young athletes. There will certainly be challenges but, in our experience, the rewards will far outweigh the costs.

Note

1 Throughout this chapter, the term group presentation will be used to account for presentations to groups of individual/teams of athletes as well as sessions delivered to individual teams.

References

Chase, M. (2013). Children. In S. J Hanrahan & M.B Andersen (Eds.). *Routledge Handbook of Applied Sport Psychology* (pp. 377–386). New York, NY: Routledge.

Foster, D., Maynard, I., Butt, J., & Hays, K. (2016). Delivery of psychological skills training to youngsters. *Journal of Applied Sport Psychology*, *28*, 62–77.

Fournier, J. F., Calmels, C., Durand-Bush, N., & Salmela, J. H. (2005). Effects of a season-long PST program on gymnastic performance and on psychological skill development. *International Journal of Sport & Exercise Psychology*, *3*, 59–78.

Gould, D., Murphy, S., Tammen, V., & May, J. (1989). An examination of US Olympic sport psychology consultants and the services they provide. *The Sport Psychologist*, *3*, 300–312.

Gucciardi, D. F., Gordon, S., & Dimmock, J. A. (2009). Evaluation of a mental toughness training program for youth-aged Australian footballers: II. A qualitative analysis. *Journal of Applied Sport Psychology*, *21*, 324–339.

Henriksen, K., Larsen, C. H., Storm, L. K., & Ryom, K. (2014). Sport psychology interventions with young athletes: The perspective of the sport psychology practitioner. *Journal of Clinical Sport Psychology*, *8*, 245–260.

Lauer, L., Gould, D., Lubbers, P., & Kovacs, M. (2010) (Eds.). *USTA Mental Skills and Drills Handbook*. Monterey, CA: Coaches Choice.

McCarthy, P. J., Jones, M. V., Harwood, C. G., & Olivier, S. (2010). What do young athletes implicitly understand about psychological skills? *Journal of Clinical Sport Psychology*, *4*, 158–172.

Ong, N. C., & Griva, K. (2016). The effect of mental skills training on competitive anxiety in schoolboy rugby players. *International Journal of Sport and Exercise Psychology*, 1–13.

Orlick, T. (1993). *Feel Free to Feel Great: Teaching Children to Excel at Living*. Ontario, Canada: Creative Bound.

Seemiller, C., & Grace, M. (2016). *Generation Z Goes to College*. San Francisco, CA: John Wiley & Sons.

Tulgan, B. (2016). *Not Everyone Gets a Trophy: How to Manage the Millennials*. Hoboken, NJ: Wiley.

Van den Bergh, J., & Behrer, M. (2016). *How Cool Brands Stay Hot: Branding to Generations Y and Z*. London and Philadelphia, PA: Kogan Page.

Wikman, J. M., Ryom, K., Stelter, R., & Elbe, A. M. (2016). Effects of a school-based relaxation intervention on recovery in young elite athletes in high school. *Sport Science Review*, *25*, 199–224.

26

EXCELLENCE TOGETHER

Integrated sport psychology for coaches
and young athletes

Chris G. Harwood and Karl Steptoe

When working with young athletes sport psychology practitioners are only a single part of a social-environmental system influencing that individual. Parents, coaches, sport and non-sport peers, and the sport organisation form parts of the ecological system (Bronfenbrenner, 1999) around the athlete and will have an influence on the work a practitioner can conduct (see Chapters 10, 18, 19, and 27 for further information). Given the strong relationships that develop between coaches and athletes, as well as coaches' access to and engagement with young athletes, they can become a valuable ally when working with young athletes on sport psychology. As such, the aim of this chapter is to illustrate how sport psychology practitioners can integrate their services successfully with coaches and athletes in order to optimise their impact on both athlete development and the coach–athlete relationship. The first section will stress the importance of practitioner services that aim to be mutually beneficial to a young athlete's psychosocial development and wellbeing, and their athletic performance. Subsequently, and through drawing on relevant applied research, we will describe the intervention processes and practical strategies that represent how we have integrated sport psychology in sport organisations that target these self-development and performance-related needs.

Integrated service provision: Strategic considerations

Integrated services demand a particular type of sport psychology practitioner. Firstly, practitioners are likely to be embedded in the sport. They tend to work within the system and have knowledge of the sport to advanced levels. Further, they have a good appreciation of interdisciplinary sport science as well as the team working around the athlete. Finally, they are likely to have quite close professional relationships with other support staff and coaches, and healthy relationships with parents who they will see as resourceful allies to their work. This leads to a number of other key points.

Integrated services are close to the action to learn from the action

At the heart of integrative models of sport psychology is the proximity of the psychological strategy to the actual context in which psychological outcomes will affect the performance or growth of the athlete. It is imperative that those working with young athletes consider how forms of psychological skills training blend in to physical or technical practice (see Chapter 2 for an example). Sinclair and Sinclair (1994) argued that psychological skills and strategies are not add-ons to physical skills, but valued processes forming an inseparable part of the learning process. This means that those coaches, practitioners, parents, and team members working with young athletes need to intentionally value psychological strategies and reinforce their use in all contexts (see Harwood, 2009). Further, they need to be prepared to jump on the teachable moments that emerge as events naturally unfold (e.g. a coach who constructively halts a practice when they see a player negatively respond to a decision). In sum, this approach helps young athletes to develop the coping strategies needed to effectively manage the inevitable performance pressures that are a part of competitive sport.

Integrated services consider performance and development interdependently

Integrated work, however, is philosophically more than just 'training mental skills in the field'. Over the last ten years there has been a noticeable philosophical and political shift around the ethics of pursuing certain intentional outcomes for young people in sport, particularly for those ascribed as 'talented athletes'. This movement signals an era in which the psychological health and development of the young athlete – both 'in' and 'through' sport – will form a greater prominence than ever before. Fortunately, paediatric sport psychology researchers and practitioners are well placed to draw upon knowledge of both positive youth development (see Chapter 12) and psychosocial processes and characteristics of talent development, (e.g. Chapter 11) to target dual (and interdependent) objectives of positive developmental experiences and healthy career transitions for their clients.

Integration means working with significant others

The challenge for sport psychology practitioners is integrating the required services based on their scholarly knowledge, the athlete's needs, and a complex appreciation of the athlete's support systems. For example, a young athlete's coach plays a fundamental psychological role and the integrated practitioner is aware that although they cannot be around 24/7, the coach will be more available and influential. A coach's understanding of the cognitive, physical, motivational, and emotional maturity of a young athlete (see Chapter 4) and their understanding and use of psychological strategies, as well as the athlete's family environment and peer relationships, are all important parts of their psychological role. Practitioners can provide insights and help to the coach in these areas. Equally, it is valuable for the sport psychologist to understand the coach's leadership style, their values, and the quality of the coach–athlete relationship (see Chapters 19 and 20). Such factors are important in terms of optimising compatibility with the athlete's personal attributes, needs, and expectations, as well as minimising conflict (Wachsmuth, Jowett, & Harwood, 2017). In sum, using various sources of information (e.g. observation, interviews, and questionnaires; see Chapter 5) practitioners can identify young athletes' psychosocial strengths and areas for development. However, the formulation of strategies for intervention (based on theory and practical experience) will often involve coaches and parents, and indeed may be targeted at coaches and parents (see Chapters 10 and 27).

Integrated service provision in contemporary practice

With the above considerations in mind, the remainder of this chapter comprises four schemes of work, rich in their dual emphasis on development and performance, that have represented integrated psychological services with young athletes.

Scheme 1: Shaping optimal motivation in young athletes

A recurrent theme in our experience as practitioners is helping adolescent athletes to develop and maintain a high quality of motivation in sport, and to be able to process inevitable success and failure in healthy ways. In large part, our work is about helping the young athlete to develop and apply a system that creates a healthy balance in their achievement goals (see Chapter 8). This is firmly about the capacity of the athlete to draw a sense of achievement from personal improvement, learning, and ongoing growth (i.e. task/mastery goals) versus success/failure being dependent on gaining positive, external social comparisons or win/loss outcomes (i.e. ego goals; see Harwood & Swain, 2002). Such work requires a focus on optimising athletes' motivational qualities, their environment, and their interpretation of this environment.

As a first piece of advice, it is critical not to discount the importance of competitiveness in sport. Talented athletes and experienced coaches can switch off when practitioners come with messages that it is purely 'the taking part that counts'. Such messages – although well intentioned – grossly discount the personal, social, and emotional challenges that sport demands of committed athletes. When we hear parents saying 'it doesn't matter if you win or lose', we need to be very careful that this does not translate to 'competing unconditionally does not matter either'! In my (Harwood) work based around applied research in this area (see Harwood & Swain, 2001, 2002), I found it important to help young athletes develop a personal philosophy for how they would approach a match or competition. What mattered is how they competed in sport and what competing meant to them. I introduced them to the principles of a Competitive Performance Mentality (CPM; Harwood & Swain,

2002) and developed a system of training, competition planning, and performance review that served as a continuous, formulaic process to shape and maintain quality, healthy motivation. This process is explained below.

Stage 1: Understanding the CPM

Athletes with a CPM acknowledge two simple tests that their sport will always set up – the self-challenge and the game challenge. The *self-challenge* reflects the opportunity to strive to the best of one's current capacity in skills that are under the player's control. The *game challenge* reflects the test of competitively overcoming an opponent or a standard that the sport presents them with on that particular day (e.g. tennis will provide the uneven court surface, the weather, and the opponent … now go and test yourself out and see how you do). In most sports, these two challenges exist for every single competition, and either, both, or neither of the challenges may be met successfully. These points can be discussed during training sessions to share the message about what processes and goals are controllable or less controllable in competition.

Stage 2: Pre, during and post competition tools

Before every competition, it is important to commit to self-challenge goals in the form of process goals that are relevant tactically to win/compete effectively, or to develop mastery of new skills under pressure. After every competition it is important to appraise the self-challenge first (i.e. unconditional consistency of effort, self-discipline, composure following mistakes). This is the 'Me versus Me', self-referenced performance debrief that should highlight positive self-directed achievements and draw out any areas for self-development and practice. Appraisal of the game challenge includes time to reflect on one's competitive handling of critical events in the game, the strengths and weaknesses of the opposition, and situational elements that tested the athlete's resources. Ultimately, such appraisal coalesces to what athletes learnt about themselves, their opposition, and the standards posed by the challenge today. These lessons can be recorded in log books, through audio-verbal or audio-visual reflections (i.e. video diaries), or through tailored review sheets (see Figure 26.1 as a very early example of this from a 15-year-old tennis player; Harwood & Swain, 2002) and self-written newspaper article-type reflections. These processes and exercises can be worked through with the practitioner on a competition by competition basis so that the athlete becomes more confident and refines their systematic approach to competition. Importantly, this happens without even using the terms win or lose.

Stage 3: The competitive performance environment

The introduction of the CPM system to the athlete does not occur in a vacuum and, as an integrated practitioner knowledgeable of achievement goal theory, the

PERFORMANCE REVIEW SHEET

Date: 25/7/95   Tournament Event: Lois Points Open   Round: Quater 16s

Surface: hard   Opponent: ▮▮▮▮▮▮

Opponent style of play: attacking baseliner

PERFORMANCE SELF CHALLENGE GOALS:	RATING OF ACHIEVEMENT	
Keep ball deep to backhand	90	/100 Eventually match problem solving
Vary ball - use dropshots & angled balls	80	/100
Approach net when appropriate - not impatient	70	/100
Positive serves. Vary & use topspin on 2nd's - bounce high on court	75	/100

MENTAL PERFORMANCE HELPERS:	RATING OF ACHIEVEMENT	
don't worry, be happy. R.F.S.I.S.T.AN.C.e	90	/100
100% focused - plan next point before it starts	80	/100
1st point of each game, then 2nd & 3rd point etc	70	/100
run every ball down, Never give up	80	/100

DURING MATCH PROBLEM SOLVING ACTIONS	RATING OF ACHIEVEMENT	
Slowed the pace - more topspin &		/100
keeping the ball deeper to backhand		/100
side	80	/100

RATING OF COMPETITIVENESS TO MEET GAME CHALLENGE: 80 /100

RATING OF SELF-CHALLENGE SATISFACTION: 80 /100

WAS THE GAME CHALLENGE MET? (YES) NO   SCORE: 6-4 6-2

6 PERFORMANCE POSTIVES FROM THE CHALLENGES:

1. good backhand depth
2. didn't worry - enjoyed match
3. focused well
4. good movement. - chased everything
5. attacked well + kept her on move
6. defended well. This was helped by the way I ran everything down. By making her play extra shots I caused her to make more errors.

3 PERFORMANCE TRAINERS FROM THE CHALLENGES:

1. more aggressive. I was dominated early on.
2. consistant. Still cut down errors due to impatience
3. better net approaches - don't come in of balls that do not put opponent under pressure.

FIGURE 26.1 A CPM performance review sheet: 15-year-old tennis player

role of coaches and parents in reinforcing a congruent motivational climate around the athlete is pivotal. In Harwood and Swain's (2002) intervention, I worked directly with coaches on their coaching session plans with players to reiterate CPM principles and process goals, and with parents on their use of language with players before, during, and after competition. In essence, I started as the educator and facilitator but then transitioned into the background and the athlete became 'Chairperson of their Sport Board' with the aim that coach, parent, and athlete feed into developments at scheduled 'board meetings' around recent challenges and achievements.

Such work draws heavily on achievement goal theory (Nicholls, 1989) and self-determination theory (Deci & Ryan, 1985), looking to ensure that perceptions of competence, autonomy, and relatedness are all being addressed. Further, principles and practices around the CPM draw from research demonstrating the positive outcomes of high task/high ego goal profiles in athletes (Hodge & Petlichkoff, 2000) as well as from reflective practice. The system encourages athletes to value competitively striving to the best of their controllable abilities while depersonalising the battle with the opposition and reducing an extraneous focus on others' expectations. Commitment to performance planning, honest performance review, and lessons for training to facilitate the development of this growth mindset (Dweck, 1999) in sport is something I believe helps players to maintain long-term motivation and confidence through the challenges of adolescent and adult sport.

Scheme 2: Working with coaches to develop the 5Cs

Integrating psychosocial strategies into training sessions is not a process that many coaches will have expertise in. Therefore, another prominent feature of a sport psychologist's work is to help the coach consider why, how, and when they can help to ensure their training sessions yield psychological and social outcomes for their athletes, as opposed to merely technical and physical outcomes. Recent examples of this have been portrayed in work conducted in professional youth football academies (Harwood, 2008; Harwood, Barker & Anderson, 2015) where coaches underwent training in the 5Cs approach (see www.the5cs.co.uk) to enhance their confidence in developing the psychosocial qualities of their youth players. The section below outlines some of the key processes when working with coaches.

Stage 1: Education in the 5Cs

The first stage of this work incorporates education – through meetings or on pitch discussion – with coaches identifying some of the key behaviours that underpin five fundamental psychosocial qualities in players: commitment (i.e. motivational qualities), communication (i.e. interpersonal skills), concentration (i.e. position-relevant attention), control (i.e. emotional regulation), and confidence (i.e. belief in ability). Having identified core behaviours, coaches work collaboratively to consider specific coaching behaviours, strategies, and conditions they could employ in normal training that would serve to trigger and foster each one of the Cs in their players. Ideally, practitioners would work on one C at a time with coaches, considering each in detail.

Stage 2: Making PROGRESS

With coaches having deliberated personal and team/squad techniques in stage 1, introduction to the acronym PROGRESS can be further employed as a method of reflection and addition to the process of creating a 5Cs climate in a coaching session (Harwood & Anderson, 2015; see Figure 26.2). This enables coaches to recognise, for example, the importance of setting up the session with an intentional focus on a particular 'C' – for example, 'communication' before the warm up, and engaging players to talk about what effective communication means to them. It also helps coaches to recognise that peers are a valuable, natural source of social support for players and to task teammates with the role of offering reinforcement and praise to other team members when they demonstrate appropriate communication.

Promote the 'C' in the same way that coaches would introduce and value a technical or tactical skill. Provide the rationale for the 'C' and how important it is to football

Role-model the 'C' through the appropriate model behaviour as a coach. Bring the meaning of the 'C' to life by demonstrating or referring to excellent examples versus bad examples, from football or other sports

Ownership of their learning. Involve players in decisions within the session about how they can demonstrate a 'C'; allow them options to work at their own pace and to benefit from favourite drills and practices that showcase their strengths

Grow the 'C' by providing players with opportunities to practice the 'C', and then to train it in more open game situations when 'pressure' can be added to test players

Reinforce the 'C' by praising those players who respond by demonstrating the chosen 'C' skill or behaviour, and by making courageous decisions

Empower peer support by encouraging players to praise each other for positive efforts related to each 'C' in order to build individual and collective confidence

Support the supporter by acknowledging those players when they praise a peer, thereby closing the loop on a supportive peer climate around each of the 'Cs'

Self-Review. Check in with players on their levels of the 'C' and empower them to keep working hard; use monitors to review collective efforts, and apply self-reflection and learning points at the end of the session

---

FIGURE 26.2 Guidelines for making PROGRESS with the 5Cs in coaching
Source: Adapted from Harwood and Anderson, 2015.

Stage 3: Applying self and team assessments

As an extension to this work, core behaviours underpinning the 5Cs can be self-assessed by players (individually or as a team) and by coaches as part of ongoing profiling and needs analysis. In football academy work with mid-adolescents, players and coaches have independently reported their perceptions of (the player's) current ability to consistently demonstrate desired 5C behaviours/responses on a seven-point Likert-type scale (i.e. strongly disagree to strongly agree).

In feeding back (with player consent) to coaches and players, three specific outcomes can be achieved. First, the discrepancy between player and coach perceptions is highlighted, and this may trigger a subsequent need for education regarding desired 'C' standards for those players who are over-reporting abilities. In contrast, opportunities to reinforce psychological strengths in those players who are under-reporting their perceived competence are equally valued. Third, in framing the 5Cs in a scaling grid format aligned with non-league (lowest level), Championship, Premier League, and Champions League (highest level) behaviours, it offers a user-friendly visual (see Figure 26.3) and encourages both coaches and players to re-evaluate their ratings to create opportunities for growth (i.e. a young player currently rated as demonstrating Champions League level 5C behaviours would not

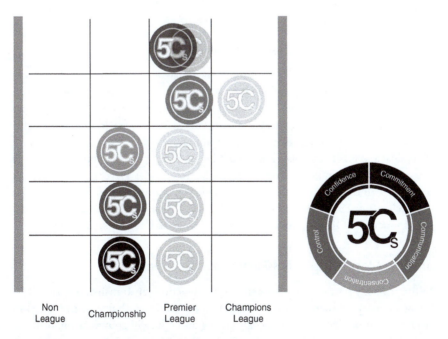

| Non League | Championship | Premier League | Champions League |

FIGURE 26.3 Case example: 5C behaviour discrepancies in coach–player perceptions grid

Note: Coach perceptions solid colour/player perceptions transparent.

presently recognise a need for development). This type of work enables the design of more individualised psychological support for training and matches. However, more importantly, it is useful for enriching coach–athlete relationships and helping players and parents to see that coaches are interested in the psychosocial facets of their development.

Scheme 3: Integrating syste matic and professional support

Increased opportunities for qualified practitioners to work in professional youth academy settings (e.g. football, rugby, cricket, tennis) reflect the multidisciplinary approach taken to the development of expertise. However, there are challenges associated with service delivery to aspiring athletes and these challenges must be negotiated through innovative and adaptive design to demonstrate the efficacy of psychological interventions. Determining role clarity and resource allocation represents an essential foundation with which to meet many of these demands, as an increasing body of academy staff (including managers/directors, coaches, sport scientists, nutritionists, welfare officers, education officers, and chaplains) all have responsibilities for player development. It is important for practitioners to specify how sport psychology services complement and add value to these roles and how meaningful provision can be made to an extensive number of potential clients (e.g. more than 150 across age group phases in a football academy, i.e. players, coaches, and parents).

Stage 1: Deploying finite resources appropriately

Using professional football as an example, an initial analysis of academy needs will help to identify those best positioned in each phase (i.e. foundation (U9–11), youth development (U12–15), and professional development (U16–23)) to shape and reinforce positive psychosocial behaviours. For example, prioritising parent education in the younger age groups may be important, with an increasing focus on individual and team-level player and coaching support as the development pathway progresses. Opportunities to work with coaches to enhance player performance can be created through: attendance at management meetings, structured observation on pitch, contribution to in-house coach professional development sessions, and the production of player profiles to inform bespoke training and match objectives.

Stage 2: Maintaining professional and scientific integrity

In the academy setting, there is a need for the practitioner to maintain a balance of being an accepted member of the support team while not being so immersed in academy culture that they cannot objectively and ethically comment on, or make contributions to, its development. For example, in one academy setting the strategic positioning of the sport psychology office away from the main academy building afforded the practitioner (Steptoe) this possibility and, in one-to-one sessions with the academy management team, discussions helped shape coherent messages regarding philosophy, standards, and expectations. Such dialogue represents the foundation of ethical psychology services within an interdisciplinary team, as decisions taken at the highest level of the academy structure permeate all levels of the player development framework.

An important foundational agreement that has to be established relates to what constitutes good psychological performance in players (i.e. how do staff infer this?). In Steptoe's case, the predominant cognitive philosophy of the practitioner demanded a concomitant interest in the assessment and development of adaptive processes (i.e. quality of thinking, decision making, problem solving, perception, and attention). In discussion with staff, however, it was accepted that evaluation of a player's psychological progression through specific support would ultimately be determined by behaviour change.

Stage 3: Ensuring behaviour change has backbone!

Where there is an understandable focus on the quality of player/athlete behaviour in coaching staff, interventions to assist cognitive-behavioural improvements need to be substantive and rigorous. Superficial, one-off pieces of work with single touch points reflective of less qualified practitioners and ill-informed coaches (e.g. the one-off motivational presentation) are unlikely to be the magic pill/cure. A request from coaches to Steptoe to input into the challenges a professional development team were having in 'starting games well' offers a great example in designing 'what to do professionally' versus 'what coaches felt might do the trick'!

A lack of concentration was considered by the coaches to be the main contributing factor to conceding goals in the first 15 minutes in five out of the last six games and the coaches' prior experiences of sport psychology (i.e. less than qualified practitioner) had led to the request for a one-off workshop to address this issue! One-to-one sessions were also suggested with those players *believed to be most culpable*; however, the potential impact of such an intervention was anticipated by Steptoe to be minimal. In a session with the head and assistant coach, the current performance issue was considered, not in terms of the sum of individual aggregated performances, but instead by the continuous interactions between team members and the wider support staff (i.e. how is performance preparation happening given all the resources available?). A system level task analysis was proposed that would reveal the co-operative interactions, bounded by unique spatial and temporal constraints, that were contributing to sub-optimal performance in the first 15 minutes of competitive matches (Ribeiro, Silva, Duarte, Davids, & Garganta, 2017).

The team (players and coaching staff) were observed over a 5½-hour period, from meeting until the end of the first quarter of the game. The aim of the analysis was to focus solely on the specific performance issue and not to interpret acts through any theoretical lens. Instead key phases of team preparation were highlighted for their contribution to effective concentration and decision making; from which opportunities for meaningful intervention could be explored. Observations were fed back

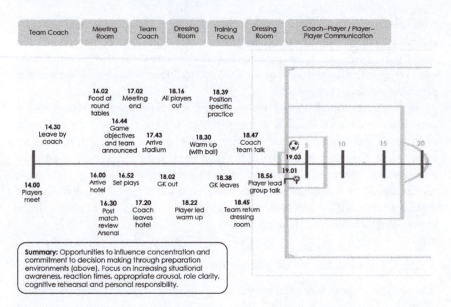

FIGURE 26.4 System level task analysis – factors contributing to performance in first 15 minutes

during a scheduled coach professional development meeting, and the presentation centred around a match-day timeline (see Figure 26.4).

All match preparation and in-game tasks were recorded (including the concession of a goal within 3 minutes) and the significant environmental and group member interaction phases were highlighted. Subsequent discussion regarding the potential impact of the team coach journey, meeting room, dressing room, warm up (training focus) environments, and in-match communication upon poor starts to games revealed threats to optimum arousal, role clarity, intrinsic motivation, reaction time, and commitment to decision making. These phases were recognised by the coaches as areas in which they could positively influence psychological performance in order to enhance team concentration in the first 15 minutes of games (see Table 26.1 for some key examples).

In sum, this example of integrated work showcases the more proximal role of the practitioner working alongside coaches and players – more akin to a performance scientist enabling conceptually valid solutions to be considered based on authentic data, as opposed to single-session team building.

Scheme 4: Creating a rational and resilient identity

Aligned with Scheme 1 (motivation), two of the personal attributes that we believe sport challenges in aspiring athletes is their self-concept and identity (see Chapter 14 for details). When young athletes begin to invest themselves in a sport, their perceptions of competence and self-identity can become narrowed and defined to their

TABLE 26.1 System level task analysis – example of identified threats and interventions to enhance commitment to decision making and team performance

Task	Key observations	Threat to presenting issue ('starting well')	Intervention (coach led)
Team Coach 1	No assigned activities	Lack of role clarity	Individual player objectives and opponent analysis to be given to players on team coach
Meeting Room	No player input to team discussion	Controlling motivational climate	Players to state their individual and team objectives
Team Coach 2	Inadequate lighting	Inappropriate arousal	Changes made to lighting and use of team videos
Dressing Room 1	Music selection <60bpm	Inappropriate arousal	Coaches to select music >80bpm in next game
Warm Up (Training Focus)	Strikers shooting from consistent feeds	Inappropriate preparation for complex environment	Confidence for strikers to be promoted from getting shot away from unexpected feed
Dressing Room 2	Communication intensity	Not prepared for processing multiple instructions	Communication intensity to match that of in-game regarding volume and quantity of messages
Coach–Player Communication	Coach instruction when in position	Reduced commitment to decision making	Monitor instructional information given to players in and out of possession

achievement in competition. Self-concept can become fragile when it is based on irrational beliefs (e.g. I'm a failure if I lose this match), a lack of recognition of personal strengths, and a unidimensional view of the young person behind the athlete. With this in mind, a progressive exercise that practitioners might employ is to help athletes construct a holistic, rational, and resilient competitive identity through the process of a four-quadrant poster. This can also be a useful collaborative exercise with the support of the coach.

Quadrant 1: Rules of engagement

As sport situations can render irrational thinking in adolescent athletes (e.g. the referee should make perfect decisions all the time), it is useful to counter this potential challenge by preparing rational thinking and acceptance in advance (see Chapter 24). Athletes can be asked to create their 'rules of engagement' for competition based on collaborative discussion around questions such as 'What are going to be the adversities and challenges that you accept that you may face in competition?'; 'What choices do you want to make in the way that you behave with yourself and others?' Such discussion stimulates thinking around rational and less rational beliefs, and challenges players to think more smartly about competition. For example, 'I know that to deal with adversity (e.g. poor line calls), I have to experience it'; 'I will make brave decisions that "stretch" my level without fear of any mistakes that I will make.' The athlete creates the rules of engagement that they sign up to so that there is no place for irrational beliefs to creep in when the going gets tough.

Quadrant 2: Signature strengths

In the next session, the athlete profiles their specific strengths from a technical, tactical, physical, psychological, and team perspective. Discussion stems from questions posed by the practitioner, such as 'What skills do you enjoy doing/executing most in competition that send a message to the opposition?' 'What attributes can you depend on in a tough situation?' 'What makes you a great teammate?' In tennis, for example, players have noted: an explosive forehand, exceptional reactions and 'good hands' at the net, positive communication with my partner at all times to keep our momentum.

Quadrant 3: Mental kitbag

Akin to the process goals linked to the self-challenge of the CPM, the mental kitbag segment focuses discussion between the athlete and practitioner on the specific mental tools that the athlete could use in competition (pre and during performance). Stimulus questions might include: 'What do you do before or during competition that helps you to optimise your strengths and meet your rules of engagement?' And, 'What mental strategies pull it all together for you?' This also allows for the process of self-awareness and gap analysis where the athlete recognises that they have developed rules of engagement and noted strengths, yet have not thought about any strategies that might assist or sustain these. Therefore, this segment of work can be as much about developing the mental kitbag and initiating planned work as it is about reinforcing what is already in the bag.

Quadrant 4: The Real Me

The final, and possibly most important, segment of work, which taps into a humanistic focus on identity and wellbeing, reflects the process of internalising how one's strengths and qualities as a person are far broader than what one demonstrates in sport competition. Instrumentally tied to fostering a healthy identity and self-concept as an adolescent, the 'Real Me' cannot be defined by the outcome of a match or race, and it is critical for young athletes to have the chance to explore those qualities, values, and experiences that make up the strengths of their 'Real Me' away from sport (e.g. in social, family, academic contexts). Sensitive discussion with the practitioner might therefore focus on identifying these qualities – from past and present experiences (i.e. the real self) and what the person would like other people to say about them behind their back. This activity forms an important assessment of the athlete's sense and breadth of identity, and it may be that further identity-based work is required to help them understand and pursue being more than just an athlete. Athletes might note personal qualities such as 'trustworthy', 'finds good in people', and 'a fun character to be around'. Most importantly for performance and development, our belief is that when an athlete recognises and attends to the strengths, qualities, and dimensions of their 'Real Me', it helps their 'Sport Performance Me'. No matter what the competitive situation, acknowledgement and recognition of their Real Me allows their inner athlete greater freedom to express itself in competition without fear. After all, there is always the Real Me to go back to.

This process can take numerous sessions, building up and evolving progressively over time as athlete and practitioner build a relationship with each other. A final poster or reminder card for a kitbag enables the athlete to see a more rounded picture guiding their mental approach to competition preparation. It may be appealing to young athletes to encourage them to offer a codename that represents their identity. Of course, all of the components to this process can be useful material to guide imagery work with the player, as well as observation, self-review and performance debriefing of the mental kitbag, strengths and stickiness to the rules of engagement.

Conclusion

In this chapter, we have offered readers a glimpse of what it is like to provide more proximal integrated services to young athletes – sometimes directly, sometimes through the coach, sometimes as part of a strategy that targets the coach–athlete relationship. The modern-day coach has a vital role in creating an environment that engenders trust and confidence in terms of balancing the pursuit of excellence in performance with attention to health, wellbeing, and development. Practitioners who integrate effectively with coaches and support staff create the opportunity to develop a practical, educational platform for athletes to engage richly with all that sport psychology has to offer. Critically, this engagement is one where young athletes view sport psychology not with any 'old school stigma' or 'cynical derogation' but with a belief that psychological skills and strategies are as relevant, natural, and invaluable as gym work, serving practice, or shooting drills.

References

Bronfenbrenner, U. (1999). Environments in developmental perspective: Theoretical and operational models. In S. L. Friedman & T. D. Wachs (Eds.), *Measuring Environment across the Life Span: Emerging Methods and Concepts* (pp. 3–28). Washington, DC: APA.

Deci, E. L., & Ryan, R. M. (1985). *Intrinsic Motivation and Self-Determination in Human Behavior.* New York, NY: Plenum Press.

Dweck, C. S. (1999). *Self Theories: Their Role in Motivation, Personality, and Development.* Philadelphia, PA: Psychology Press.

Harwood, C. G. (2008). Developmental consulting in a professional football academy: The 5C's coaching efficacy program. *The Sport Psychologist, 22,* 109–133.

Harwood, C. G. (2009). Enhancing self-efficacy in professional tennis: Intensive work for life on the tour. In T. Holder & B. Hemmings (Eds.), *Applied Sport Psychology: A Case-Based Approach* (pp. 7–32). Chichester, UK: Wiley.

Harwood, C. G., & Anderson, R. (2015). *Coaching Psychological Skills in Youth Football: Developing the 5Cs.* London: Bennion-Kearney.

Harwood, C. G., Barker, J., & Anderson, R. (2015). Psychosocial development in youth soccer players: Assessing the effectiveness of the 5C's intervention program. *The Sport Psychologist, 29,* 319–334.

Harwood, C. G., & Swain, A. B. (2001). The development and activation of achievement goals in tennis: I. Understanding the underlying factors. *The Sport Psychologist, 15,* 319–341.

Harwood, C. G., & Swain, A. B. (2002). The development and activation of achievement goals in tennis: II. A player, parent and coach intervention. *The Sport Psychologist, 16,* 111–137.

Hodge, K., & Petlichkoff, L. (2000). Goal profiles in sport motivation: A cluster analysis. *Journal of Sport & Exercise Psychology, 22,* 256–272.

Nicholls, J. G. (1989). *The Competitive Ethos and Democratic Education.* Cambridge, MA: Harvard University Press.

Ribeiro, J., Silva, P., Duarte, R., Davids, K., & Garganta, J. (2017). Team sports performance analysed through the lens of social network theory: Implications for research and practice. *Sports Medicine,* 1–8.

Sinclair, G. D., & Sinclair, D. A. (1994). Developing reflective performers by integrating mental management skills with the learning process. *The Sport Psychologist, 8,* 13–27.

Wachsmuth, S., Jowett, S., & Harwood, C. (2017). Conflict among athletes and their coaches: What is the theory and research so far? *International Review of Sport and Exercise Psychology, 10,* 84–107.

27

UNDERSTANDING AND WORKING WITH PARENTS OF YOUNG ATHLETES

Camilla J. Knight and Rachael A. Newport

Don't just tell parents that they're doing everything wrong, it's hard enough being a parent as it is, everyone judging what you're doing all the time.

For the last ten years, through my research and practice, I (Camilla) have had the privilege of talking to hundreds of parents of young athletes. I have spoken to them about their experiences, their needs, and, of course, their children. I have sat, silenced by the tears streaming down their face, as they shared the heartache of watching their child's world come crumbling down as they were cut from teams, criticised by coaches, or experienced severe injuries. I have shared in their joy as they have described seeing their child rewarded for their efforts, finally mastering a skill they have been practising for weeks, or receiving positive feedback from their coach. I've been shocked by the tales of divorce, the limited social lives, and the deterioration in parents' mental and physical health as they have committed to helping their children realise their dreams. And, too often, I've bubbled with frustration as I've heard parent after parent recall times when they were judged, ignored, or criticised as they tried their best to support their children.

Through all these stories and emotions, I constantly return to the opening quote. In 2005, my mother made this throwaway comment as we discussed my impending dissertation research on tennis parents. Over the last decade, as I have gained an increasing appreciation for just how hard it can be to parent children involved in sport, this comment has increasingly guided my work as a practitioner and a researcher. I am unashamedly parent-focused in my work; I seek to demonstrate the value and importance of parents, and, most importantly, try to create cultures that support parents as they attempt to support their children. This is not an approach that is easy, nor is it one that is always welcomed by sports organisations or coaches, but it is one that I believe is extremely important and we hope to illustrate why through this chapter.

Throughout this book numerous references are made to the importance of including parents in work with young athletes (see Chapters 11, 12, 21, and 24) and Travis Dorsch (Chapter 10) has provided excellent insights into strategies for educating parents to optimise their involvement. In the current chapter, we seek to add to Travis' work by providing insights into the experiences of parents. Particularly we are focused on exploring how an understanding of these experiences can inform the work we do with parents to help them support their children. However, we are well aware that it is not always easy for practitioners to engage with parents. Thus, we also describe some of the strategies we use when working with parents, as well as a small selection of the *numerous* lessons we have learnt (and continue to learn) through this work.

(Mis)perceptions of parents

Prior to examining the experiences of parents in sport, we believe it is important to first reflect upon what we, and others, think about parents. As practitioners, we can play an important role in advocating for parents and in helping to optimise their involvement in sport (see Chapter 10; Lafferty & Triggs, 2014; Vincent & Christensen, 2015). However, just as our consulting philosophy and theoretical orientations impact upon our work with young athletes (see Chapters 20 and 24), our perceptions of parents will impact upon how we engage with them (Knight & Harwood, 2015). A quick perusal of major media outlets provides numerous examples of inappropriate or negative parental involvement in sport (e.g. Kinder, 2014; White, 2017). Such stories are often shocking, detailing abusive and pressuring behaviours from parents towards (adolescent) referees, coaches, and children themselves, and leave the reader to question why any parent would ever behave in such a manner. As a national coach once said, 'What is it about youth sport that makes successful, rational adults lose all perspective?'

In seeking to explain such behaviours, media stories often draw on traditional explanations, including: parents being overly focused on winning, parents expecting a return on their financial/time investments, and 'failed athlete' parents living their unfulfilled dreams through their children (cf. Paton, 2014; Philipson, 2013). Similarly, when recalling their experiences, coaches often provide similar explanations for the behaviour of 'overinvolved' and 'pushy' parents (e.g. Knight & Harwood, 2009; Ross, Mallett, & Parkes, 2015). However, despite the consistency with which these explanations are provided, empirical evidence to support such statements is limited (Holt & Knight, 2014). This may be due to limitations in research itself (i.e. it is often difficult to engage with parents who demonstrate such behaviours to understand what leads to this involvement) or because such explanations generally oversimplify complex parent behaviours (see Chapter 10 for further details).

One thing that is common across such explanations of negative or inappropriate parental behaviour is that they place the blame on individual parents; the implication is that parents should know better; they should just control their emotions and keep things in perspective. However, decades of study into human and parenting behaviours (e.g. Bronfenbrenner, 1992; Grolnick, 2003; McConnell, 1974) demonstrate that parenting is much more complicated than simply knowing what to do and doing it. We cannot imagine there are many parents who do not know that tripping an opposing team member (Kinder, 2014) or screaming at child referees (White, 2017) is less than optimal behaviour, yet we still see these behaviours. Understanding the dominant narrative about parents and our limited explanations for their involvement is, in our opinion, an important first step in effectively working with parents.

Understanding parents' experiences in youth sport

So what is it like to parent a child in sport? As neither of us are parents we do not have a personal appreciation of the intensity of the emotional bond between a parent and a child, nor can we fully understand just how hard it is to juggle the various demands associated with parenting. However, if we do not attempt to understand what it is like to have a child involved in youth sport, how can we expect parents to accept or welcome our support? Fortunately, over the last ten years, there has been a growth in research examining parents' experiences in youth sport (see Holt & Knight, 2014, and Chapter 10 for further details) and it is this literature that we draw on to underpin the work we conduct with parents. As a full review of this literature is beyond the scope of this chapter, we have identified select areas that we deem particularly important for understanding parents' experiences and involvement.

Emotional demands and the parent–child relationship

In 2010, Maria Ana Parera, mother of Rafael Nadal, shared:

> …when I'm watching a match, I see from a distance whether or not he has problems, and when he does, I want the match to end. I can't watch him suffer, it's too much for me … When he wins a big one it's impressive because at home I see how much he works, how much he struggles. From the outside you only see the spectacle and, make no mistake, this world is very hard, it's full of obstacles.
> *(Rafaholics.com, 2010)*

As the mother of one of the greatest tennis players in the modern era, one might be forgiven for thinking that Maria Ana would be used to watching her son compete. However, sharing the sentiments of many parents of young athletes (cf. Clarke, Harwood, & Cushion, 2016; Harwood and Knight, 2009a; Knight & Holt, 2013a, 2013b), as a mother, Maria Ana wants to protect her son and she shares in his struggles and his disappointments.

Such empathy from parents has been identified as a contributing factor to the verbal behaviours parents display on the sideline (e.g. Holt, Tammien, Black, Sehn, & Wall, 2008) and how they react to their children's performances (e.g. Burgess,

Knight, & Mellalieu, 2016). Parents consistently indicate that watching their children compete can be very challenging, especially when they see them struggling or disappointed (Knight & Holt, 2013a). This challenge can be further exacerbated because parents know they are going to have to try and comfort their child after the competition (Knight & Holt, 2013b) and they often do not know what to say (Harwood & Knight, 2009a, 2009b).

As practitioners, when seeking to support parents, we have found it useful to first try and understand the emotions they are experiencing and then introduce different activities to help them manage their emotions (Harwood & Knight, 2015). Such strategies include:

- Helping parents to anticipate the emotions they might experience at competitions through the presentation and discussion of different scenarios. For instance, we ask parents to imagine their child being taken off for a 'poor performance' and then ask them to reflect upon the emotions they might experience. Through such reflection parents have an opportunity to understand how they might respond in different situations and identify *why* such emotions might arise.
- Working with parents to role-play different situations that are identified as particularly challenging. For instance, we act out different post-game conversations (e.g. when children have won and lost) and highlight the importance of consistency. When conducted in small groups, these activities have stimulated extensive discussion as parents develop a better understanding of their anticipated experiences.
- Giving parents general guidelines regarding what to say before, during, and after competitions. This was something that we were somewhat adverse to because of perceptions that we might be telling parents how to parent, but parents have consistently indicated that they want some guidance around this (Thrower, Harwood, & Spray, 2016). As such, we provide basic information regarding structuring pre-and post-game conversations, as well as some suggestions regarding competition behaviours. However, our first suggestion is always for parents to first talk to their individual child.
- Helping parents to develop emotional coping strategies. Parents have indicated that emotional coping strategies are one of the key ways in which they can manage the stressors they can encounter in youth sport (Burgess et al., 2016). As such, we also spend time teaching parents basic emotional coping strategies (e.g. breathing strategies, self-talk). By increasing their 'toolkit' of techniques (Harwood & Knight, 2015), we hope they feel better equipped to manage the emotional stressors they may encounter.
- When working with parents individually, we have sought to help them reappraise competitive situations by understanding what their child is gaining through challenging experiences. Evidence increasingly indicates that there is a need for children to experience some adversity to develop resilience and raising parents' awareness of this can facilitate reflection on their children's and their own experience.

Organisational demands and stressors

Over the last ten years, there has been a rapid increase in our understanding of environmental demands (stressors) that parents might experience (e.g. Clarke & Harwood, 2014; Harwood, Drew, & Knight, 2010; Harwood & Knight, 2009a, 2009b). Such research is valuable because there is consistent evidence that parenting stress is associated with more punitive behaviours (Knight, Holt, & Tamminen, 2009). Studies by Harwood and colleagues (2009a, 2009b, 2010) indicated that parents of children involved in tennis and football experience numerous stressors, arising from three main sources: competitive, organisational, and developmental. The main competitive stressors relate to the ideas outlined above pertaining to children's performance and response to performances, while organisational stressors pertain to demands that arise as result of the broader organisational aspects of youth sport, and developmental stressors are parental concerns arising in relation to their child's future.

The organisational challenges that dominate research and our conversations with parents are the large financial and time demands associated with youth sport (e.g. Clarke & Harwood, 2014; Harwood et al., 2010, Knight & Harwood, 2009a, 2009b). Such demands can result in parents experiencing guilt over the lack of time spent with other children, restricted social lives, and in some cases limited career progression (Bean, Fortier, Post, & Chima, 2014). Unfortunately, in our work with parents, there is often little we can do to directly address these stressors or concerns. However, we have found the following two activities beneficial:

- Providing parents with safe, confidential environments in which to offload about the demands they are encountering. Then engaging in supported reflection to help parents reframe their experiences and understand the many benefits their children are gaining as a result of their support and commitment.
- Facilitating parent networks to encourage life sharing, social engagements, and develop parents' access to social support. Further, through participating in these networks parents are able to see that others are also experiencing similar challenges.

Many other organisational demands can arise, including interactions with coaches, competition and training structures, and expectations of sports organisations (e.g. Clarke & Harwood, 2014; Dorsch, Smith, & McDonough, 2015; Harwood & Knight, 2009b). Given such an extensive range of organisational stressors, when seeking to work with parents we also try and include work with coaches, club managers, and sports organisations to help address some of these concerns. Consequently, we spend time:

- Encouraging parents and coaches to engage in open and honest communication. In such instances, we often have to work (very hard) with coaches to help them understand the benefits of communicating with parents before any issues can arise. Structured approaches to sharing information and offering opportunities for parents to feed back can be useful.

* Evaluating and assessing the needs of parents to identify what specific challenges they are encountering in that club or organisation. Then working with parents individually to identify potential strategies to manage these issues and taking collective feedback to managers or coaches to encourage change, or at the very least reflection.

Cultural demands and expectations

In addition to the challenges encountered as a result of organisational demands, parents also recall stressors relating to their child's development, and particularly the pressures on them to make the 'right' decisions for their child's future (Harwood & Knight, 2009b). Parents want to provide their children with the best possible chances for success in the future and, as such, it is their responsibility to decide such things as how much time children should commit to sport, whether they should leave school and attend sports schools or academies, and how long they should support their children's sporting dreams when they look out of reach. Such decisions are made against broader societal expectations of what it means to be a 'good' parent in today's society (cf. Coakley, 2006).

Unfortunately, certain youth sport cultures might directly oppose what parents feel is best for their children or guide parents' decisions in a direction that might actually make their experience of developmental stressors worse (cf. Clarke & Harwood, 2014; Dorsch, Smith, Wilson, & McDonough, 2015). For instance, most youth football academies in the UK require children to leave school at 16 and limit the level to which they study, while in the tennis environment it has long been common for parents to take their children out of school for some of the day to train. For many parents, their child's education is paramount; however, through exposure and involvement in these sporting environments they can find themselves having to make difficult decisions regarding the balance of sport and school. Further, some sports cultures may endorse such things as unhealthy dieting practices (e.g. McMahon & Penney, 2015), winning over enjoyment (cf. Dorsch, Smith, Wilson, et al., 2015), and early specialisation (Chapter 6). As a result of being part of these cultures, parents can subsequently find themselves reinforcing such messages (Dorsch, Smith, Wilson, et al., 2015).

As with the organisational demands, given the impact that culture can have on parental involvement, we commit to critically appraising the environments in which we are working. Where appropriate and possible, we then seek to engage with coaches and organisations to review the culture they are creating (see Chapter 20 for further details). Unfortunately, however, this is often beyond the scope of our work.

Overall, when seeking to understand the experiences of parents and subsequently help others (e.g. coaches, managers, sometimes parents themselves) to reflect upon the complexity of the parenting role, we find an (oversimplified) figure to be helpful (e.g. Figure 27.1). Although simple, such a figure can play an important role in

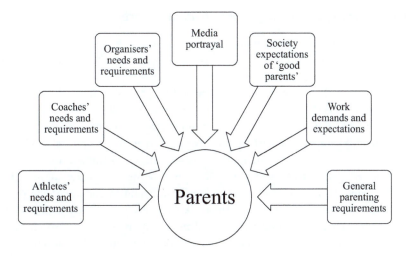

FIGURE 27.1 Influences and demands on parents

helping all parties (ourselves included) to remember that parental involvement in and beyond sport is continually influenced by expectations of, and interactions with, others. Only by examining, critiquing, and appreciating these external influences can we begin to appreciate just what it is like to try and support a young athlete.

Personal experiences of working with parents

Practitioners may work with parents for many reasons and using varying approaches. Below we discuss some challenges we have encountered when working with parents in different situations, along with suggestions to overcome these.

Working with parents to support athletes' sport psychology programmes

When working with individual athletes or teams, practitioners may also work with parents so that they understand and reinforce what their child is learning (see Chapters 22 and 24 for examples). In our experience, if expectations and methods of communication are established early, there are minimal demands on parents, and it is clear to parents why their engagement is valuable, this type of involvement is usually relatively straightforward. However, parents can harbour some reservations about engaging in sport psychology, often due to their lack of understanding of what sport psychology is (Chapter 22; Knight, Love, & Berrow). As such, clearly articulating what sport psychology is and how easily parents can support their children's psychological development is useful. Further, when feasible, we have found that offering informal drop-in sessions for parents to discuss the programme and ask questions confidentially is useful.

Working with parents to address children's concerns

Practitioners may also engage with parents in response to information shared by children in one-to-one or group sessions. For example, when we have been working with young athletes in individual sessions they often describe aspects of their parent(s)' involvement that they dislike or wish would change. Then, having identified these concerns, they often ask us to talk to their parent about it. Depending upon the quality of the relationship that we have developed with both the child and parent(s), these conversations have varied from relatively easy to extremely challenging. When parents have engaged in the consultation process from the outset and asked us to tell them how they can better support their child, a brief, informal conversation is usually sufficient to encourage the parent to reflect on their involvement and then talk to their child (usually with our support) about what they could change, and most importantly, why this change is important. However, other parents have taken our attempts to share insights from their child as criticisms of them as parents or they have dismissed their child's experiences entirely.

We understand that no matter what our intentions are when delivering feedback to parents, it may be hard for them to hear. As such, we prepare for emotional reactions and spend time planning what we are going to say and ensuring that it is positively framed (e.g. what children would like from the parent rather than what they do not like). Further, we select a time and location that is appropriate for a conversation of this nature. Nevertheless, if negative reactions do occur it can be very challenging, especially if we feel we have let the child down. In such situations, we often want to end the conversation quickly and never return to it! However, rather than do this, we make sure that we take more time with these parents and try to help them understand that this information is being shared so that we can all work towards helping their child enjoy their sport involvement and perform to their best. We have found it particularly helpful to draw on stories and examples from other cases (without any identifying information) to help normalise and contextualise the feedback.

Further, we have learnt from our previous experiences that, rather than jumping into conversations with parents about their involvement, we must take time to ensure we have developed a strong and trusting relationship with both the parent and child and have demonstrated a commitment to them as a family. Relatively simple strategies such as texting parents when their child is competing and asking them how their child is performing and if they are enjoying the day, as well as asking the parent how the experience was for them, can go a long way in fostering such a relationship. Further, taking time to learn about the parent's day-to-day demands and experiences helps them understand that you are there to support them as well as their child. Once we have developed these relationships and helped parents to realise that we are always there to help, not judge, we find parents are much more receptive to conversations about their involvement.

Group support programmes

Finally, we also work with groups of parents. In our group sessions, our aim is always to increase parents' feeling of support, so that they can subsequently enhance the support they provide to their children. Group sessions are often delivered at the request of coaches or sports organisations and range from one-off workshops to year-long programmes. In delivering these sessions, we frequently encounter an issue that appears to be common in youth sport parenting work (e.g. Richards & Winters, 2013; Vincent & Christensen, 2015). This problem is parent attendance at sessions, and particularly the attendance of parents who might benefit most from our support. To understand why parents do not always attend sessions, we have recently sought extensive feedback from parents we are working with and identified some strategies to overcome these, which are detailed below.

Marketing and value of the product

When introducing sessions for parents, they (and coaches) are often sceptical about the purpose of the sessions, as well as the potential value or impact of them. When talking with parents, we have learnt that the negative portrayal of parents in the media, the perception that they should be 'dealt with' by coaches, and the idea that an 'outsider' might be trying to teach them how to parent all contribute to their scepticism and subsequent attendance. Given these concerns and through our conversations with parents we have learnt that:

1) Cultural change must accompany the programme. Simply introducing a support programme for parents within an environment that generally dismisses or criticises parents will be ineffective. Working with coaches, managers, and organisers to ensure a coherent message in the environment is necessary to ensure parents see that there is some value to the programme.
2) Spending time in the environment so parents are familiar with us and understand our purpose and philosophy is important. As such, rather than just turning up, delivering a session to parents, and leaving, we build in time to informally chat with parents around training sessions and competitions, and ensure that we provide regular communication to parents who have missed sessions.
3) The marketing of the sessions as supportive and parent-focused is critical. Providing examples of topics to be covered, the underlying rationale for the sessions, and the intended outcomes in advertising/marketing materials is useful. Further, it is important to provide clear expectations for the programme and the sessions so that parents know what they will gain from attending – and then ensure you deliver!

Location of delivery

A practical challenge that we encounter is that parent sessions are usually delivered in classrooms or meeting rooms. When reflecting with parents, some of them have told us that they associate being in a classroom with previous negative experiences of being in school and meeting rooms with work. Consequently, for some, the location creates negative perceptions of sessions before they have even arrived. Unfortunately, we usually do not have access to any other space for delivery, so all we can do is change how we deliver sessions to minimise similarities to work or school. For instance, we design our sessions to incorporate a range of practical scenarios and activities, rather than using powerpoints or lecturing. Further, we encourage parents to bring coffee and snacks to make the sessions seem less formal, and try to keep our delivery informal. Additionally, rather than leading sessions from the front, we often structure sessions around group discussion and encourage parents to take the lead in guiding conversations and topics.

Perception of sessions as adding to demands

Based on our understanding of parents' experiences, we are always conscious that we do not want our sessions or programme to negatively impact upon the already overstretched parents. However, it is not uncommon for parents to refer to workshops as 'another thing we're expected to do'. By appropriately marketing sessions we try and minimise this perception and we also schedule sessions when children are at a training so that we do not add to the time commitments required from parents. Further, based on our engagement with parents we have learnt that the following steps are useful in overcoming this negative perception:

- Provide parents with as much information and notice to plan as possible.
- Avoid making changes to or disrupting the plan to both facilitate parents' scheduling but also demonstrate the importance of the programme.
- Allow parents to bring other children with them to sessions.
- Keep sessions short, interactive, and focused.
- Incorporate group discussions and encourage sharing of experiences.
- Tailor sessions and materials to the specific needs of parents following consultation with them.
- Engage in ongoing dialogue with parents to assess the utility of the programme and make changes based on this ongoing feedback.

Conclusion

Children and parents travel through youth sport together; when children experience highs so too do their parents, and when children experience challenges or setbacks it is their parents who are there to pick up the pieces and help them continue moving forwards. For parents to be able to successfully and effectively support their children's sporting endeavours they too may need support. However, for this support to be welcomed and positively received it needs to be provided in a manner that demonstrates an understanding of the challenges and demands that parents of young athletes are facing. Parents are the linchpins in youth sport and demonstrating an appreciation for everything they do is an important first step in engaging and working with them.

References

Bean, C. N., Fortier, M., Post, C., & Chima, K. (2014). Understanding how organized youth sport may be harming individual players within the family unit: A literature review. *International Journal of Environmental Research and Public Health, 11*, 10226–10268.

Bronfenbrenner, U. (1992). Ecological systems theory. In R. Vasta (Ed.), *Six Theories of Child Development: Revised Formulations and Current Issues* (pp. 187–249). London: Jessica Kingsley.

Burgess, N. S., Knight, C. J., & Mellalieu, S. D. (2016). Parental stress and coping in elite youth gymnastics: An interpretative phenomenological analysis. *Qualitative Research in Sport, Exercise and Health, 8*, 237–256.

Clarke, N. J., & Harwood, C. G. (2014). Parenting experiences in elite youth football: A phenomenological study. *Psychology of Sport and Exercise, 15*, 528–537.

Clarke, N. J., Harwood, C. G., & Cushion, C. J. (2016). A phenomenological interpretation of the parent-child relationship in elite youth football. *Sport, Exercise, and Performance Psychology, 5*, 125–143.

Coakley, J. (2006). The good father: Parental expectations and youth sports. *Leisure Studies, 25*, 153–163.

Dorsch, T. E., Smith, A. L., & McDonough, M. H. (2015). Early socialization of parents through organized youth sport. *Sport, Exercise, and Performance Psychology, 4*, 3–18.

Dorsch, T. E., Smith, A. L., Wilson, S. R., & McDonough, M. H. (2015). Parent goals and verbal sideline behavior in organized youth sport. *Sport, Exercise, and Performance Psychology, 4*, 19–35.

Grolnick, W. S. (2003). *The Psychology of Parental Control: How Well-Meant Parenting Backfires.* Hillsdale, NJ: Lawrence Erlbaum Associates.

Harwood, C., Drew, A., & Knight, C. J. (2010). Parental stressors in professional youth football academies: A qualitative investigation of specialising stage parents. *Qualitative Research in Sport, Exercise and Health, 2*, 39–55.

Harwood, C., & Knight, C. (2009a). Understanding parental stressors: An investigation of British tennis parents. *Journal of Sports Sciences, 27*, 339–351.

Harwood, C., & Knight, C. (2009b). Stress in youth sport: A developmental investigation of tennis parents. *Psychology of Sport and Exercise, 10*, 447–456.

Harwood, C. G., & Knight, C. J. (2015). Parenting in youth sport: A position paper on parenting expertise. *Psychology of Sport and Exercise, 16*, 24–35.

Holt, N. L., & Knight, C. J. (2014). *Parenting in Youth Sport: From Research to Practice.* Abingdon, UK: Routledge.

Holt, N. L., Tamminen, K. A., Black, D. E., Sehn, Z. L., & Wall, M. P. (2008). Parental involvement in competitive youth sport settings. *Psychology of Sport and Exercise, 9*, 663–685.

Kinder, L. (2014). Touchline dad trips up opposition player in teenage rugby match. *The Telegraph.* Retrieved from www.telegraph.co.uk/men/relationships/fatherhood/10800727/Touchline-dad-trips-up-opposition-player-in-teenage-rugby-match.html.

Knight, C. J., & Harwood, C. G. (2009). Parent-initiated coaching stress: A developmental study. *International Journal of Sports Science & Coaching, 4*, 545–565.

Knight, C. J., & Harwood, C. G. (2015). *Strategies for optimising parental involvement in elite youth sport.* Workshop at FEPSAC International Congress, Bern, Switzerland.

Knight, C. J., & Holt, N. L. (2013a). Factors that influence parents' experiences at junior tennis tournaments and suggestions for improvement. *Sport, Exercise, and Performance Psychology, 2*, 173–189.

Knight, C. J., & Holt, N. L. (2013b). Strategies used and assistance required to facilitate children's involvement in tennis: Parents' perspectives. *The Sport Psychologist, 27*, 281–291.

Knight, C. J., Holt, N. L., & Tamminen, K. A. (2009). Stress and coping among youth sport parents. In C. H. Chang (Ed.), *Handbook of Sports Psychology* (pp. 347–359). Hauppauge, NY: Nova Science.

Knight, C. J., Love, T. D., & Berrow, S. R. (2017). *Parents' knowledge and application of sport psychology and nutrition information*. Presentation at the Young Athletes Forum Foundation, Montreux, Switzerland.

Lafferty, M. E., & Triggs, C. (2014). The working with parents in sport model (WWPS-model): A practical guide for practitioners working with parents of elite young performers. *Journal of Sport Psychology in Action, 5*, 117–128.

McConnell, J. V. (1974). *Understanding Human Behavior: An Introduction to Psychology*. Oxford: Holt, Rinehart, & Winston.

McMahon, J. A., & Penney, D. (2015). Sporting parents on the pool deck: Living out a sporting culture? *Qualitative Research in Sport, Exercise and Health, 7*, 153–169.

Paton, G. (2014). Hysterical parents set a bad example on the sports field. *The Telegraph*. Retrieved from www.telegraph.co.uk/education/educationnews/10559447/Hysterical-parents-set-a-bad-example-on-the-sports-field.html.

Philipson, A. (2013). Gary Lineker: Pushy parents need to learn to stay quiet. *The Telegraph*. Retrieved from www.telegraph.co.uk/news/celebritynews/10401108/Gary-Lineker-pushy-parents-need-to-learn-to-stay-quiet.html.

Rafaholics.com (2010). *Rafa Nadal's mother Ana Maria Parera interview*. Retrieved from www.rafaholics.com/2010/12/rafa-nadals-mother-ana-maria-parera.html.

Richards, K., & Winter, S. (2013). Key reflections from 'on the ground': Working with parents to create a task climate. *Journal of Sport Psychology in Action, 4*, 34–44.

Ross, A. J., Mallett, C. J., & Parkes, J. F. (2015). The influence of parent sport behaviours on children's development: Youth coach and administrator perspectives. *International Journal of Sports Science & Coaching, 10*, 605–621.

Thrower, S. N., Harwood, C. G., & Spray, C. M. (2016). Educating and supporting tennis parents: A grounded theory of parents' needs during childhood and early adolescence. *Sport, Exercise, and Performance Psychology, 5*, 107–124.

Vincent, A. P., & Christensen, D. A. (2015). Conversations with parents: A collaborative sport psychology program for parents in youth sport. *Journal of Sport Psychology in Action, 6*, 73–85.

White, J. (2017). You're off! Amateur ref reveals why he is joining a strike following years of vile abuse from players, children and even parents. *The Mail Online*. Retrieved from www.dailymail.co.uk/news/article-4282650/Amateur-ref-reveals-joining-strike.html.

INDEX